AF606751

HENRY DAVID THOREAU

AND

THE NICK OF TIME

This provocative collection probes Thoreau's thoughts about time, helping us rethink our own fleeting brevity—the nick of time held so dear by each of us. Whether illuminating the nature of eternity or deep time, contemplating settler history or this precise, troubled moment, these moving essays demonstrate Thoreau's relevance to science and art, teaching and reading, and learning and living like it counts, deliberately.

— Rochelle L. Johnson, Bernie McCain Chair
in the Humanities & professor of
Environmental Studies, The College
of Idaho; and immediate past
president of The Thoreau Society

Henry Thoreau valued both the preciousness and the elusiveness of Time. The fifteen essays in this volume take up Thoreau's absorption with temporal concerns—from the mythic, the epic, and the historic, to the spiritual, the Indigenous, and the paradoxical. They range widely, focusing not only on *Walden* but on *A Week on the Concord and Merrimack Rivers, Cape Cod*, the Journal, and other writings, discerning his awareness that time relentlessly speeds ahead but also takes us back. For those new to Thoreau as well as specialists, this expansive collection offers productive approaches to Thoreau and the myriad notions of Time.

—Sandra Harbert Petrulionis, distinguished
professor emerita of English and
American Studies, The Pennsylvania
State University

Henry David Thoreau and the Nick of Time is a timely volume in more ways than one: a wide-ranging collection that explores a stunning variety of temporalities that resonate in Thoreau's writings, from the cosmic and geologic to the social, Indigenous, historical, spiritual, and ecological. Based on a 2022 conference held in Reykholt, Iceland, the essays feature an equally stunning range of interdisciplinary and international scholars. In all, a stimulating volume that both specialist and general readers will profit from going "a-fishin" in.

—William Rossi, professor emeritus of American
Literature, University of Oregon

Henry David Thoreau
and
the Nick of Time

TEMPORALITY AND AGENCY IN THOREAU'S ERA AND OURS

Edited by
Kathryn C. Dolan
John J. Kucich
Henrik Otterberg

MERCER UNIVERSITY PRESS
Macon, Georgia

MUP/ H1050

© 2025 by Mercer University Press
Published by Mercer University Press
1501 Mercer University Drive
Macon, Georgia 31207
All rights reserved. This book may not be reproduced in whole or in part, including illustrations, in any form (beyond that copying permitted by Sections 107 and 108 of the U.S. Copyright Law and except by reviewers for the public press), without written permission from the publisher.

Sponsorship of this publication has been received from
Kagaku Analys AB in Gothenburg, Sweden

29 28 27 26 25 5 4 3 2 1

Books published by Mercer University Press are printed on acid-free paper that meets the requirements of the American National Standard for Information Sciences—Permanence of Paper for Printed Library Materials.

Printed and bound in Canada.

This book is set in Adobe Caslon.

Cover/jacket design by Burt&Burt.

ISBN 978-0-88146-073-5 (Print)
978-0-88146-113-8 (eBook)
Cataloging-in-Publication Data is available from the Library of Congress

MERCER UNIVERSITY PRESS

Endowed by

TOM WATSON BROWN

and

THE WATSON-BROWN FOUNDATION, INC.

CONTENTS

PREFACE

For more than two decades, Reykholt, the important medieval center in Borgarfjörður, in West-Iceland, has been a locus of extensive interdisciplinary research, mainly concerning the medieval Icelandic author and historian Snorri Sturluson (1179–1241 CE), both in his own era and through the ages concerning the reception of his works. The present volume, *Thoreau and the Nick of Time*, is one of the fruits of this undertaking.

The influence of Old-Icelandic literature on Henry David Thoreau is quite remarkable, as he found extensive inspiration in Snorri. Old-Icelandic literature held such sway over Thoreau and his contemporaries, like his mentor, Emerson, because it offered captivating accounts from what until recently had been seen as the periphery of the world. More generally, Old-Icelandic literature, and especially the works of Snorri, offered accounts of the virtues of freedom-loving, self-reliant, courageous and roaming characters, in many ways reflecting how Thoreau and his Transcendentalist friends wished to see themselves.

This book delivers papers from the international conference *Thoreau and the Nick of Time,* held in May 2022 at the medieval and cultural institution Snorrastofa, which is located in the tiny village of Reykholt. The gathering was both fruitful and inspiring, and with the joint effort of participants from ten countries we were able to create a landmark event. The program had the necessary depth and variety to foster a rich conversation, and the conference produced much needed fellowship, as everyone was hungry to reconnect after the pandemic. All the way to the barren country just under the Arctic Circle came many established Thoreau scholars, plus some newer ones, with a broad representation not only from America but Europe as well.

It was an honour for us in Snorrastofa to be able to accommodate three pleasant days listening to the interesting and versatile presentations and performances. Hosting a conference dedicated to exploring an American writer from a range of perspectives—historical, philosophical, literary, and environmental—gives us at Snorrastofa a new dimension and a stronger profile. Our institution does not wish to be stuck in conventional medieval studies, and this event, with its fruitful dialogue, will influence the future work and the development of the institution, helping us broaden our mission. The spirit of the conference was an inspiration for the constant striving to find new ways of defining and interpreting literature. Research is the main aim in Snorrastofa, and all new viewpoints and ideas are of course of great help.

I thank everyone who made this event possible. I express my special gratitude to Dr. Henrik Otterberg, who was the heart of the preparations, and without whom the conference would never have taken place. I also thank The Thoreau Society for its partnership and the positive reaction when Henrik and I presented the idea of hosting a conference in Iceland—one that would, we hoped, build on a wonderful prior conference, *Thoreau in an Age of Crisis,* organized by Otterberg amongst others in 2018. Otterberg was responsible for the whole concept of the fruitful spring days in Reykholt and molded the intent of the conference.

I also wish to thank our sponsors: The Thoreau Society, the Cultural Fund in West-Iceland, Otterbergs's company Kagaku Analys AB, and The Ministry of Culture and Commerce in Iceland. I am grateful as well to Mercer University Press for capturing in print the spirit of collaboration and inquiry that filled, for a time, our small village in the Icelandic countryside.

Bergur Thorgeirsson,
Director of Snorrastofa
Reykholt, Iceland

ABBREVIATIONS

CC—Henry David Thoreau. *Cape Cod*. Edited by Joseph J. Moldenhauer. Princeton: Princeton University Press, 1988.

Corr—*The Correspondence of Henry David Thoreau*. Edited by Walter Harding and Carl Bode. New York: New York University Press, 1958.

EEM—*Henry David Thoreau. Early Essays and Miscellanies*. Edited by Joseph J. Moldenhauer and Edwin Moser. Princeton: Princeton University Press, 1975.

Exc—Henry David Thoreau. *Excursions*. Edited by Joseph J. Moldenhauer. Princeton: Princeton University Press, 2007.

FS—Henry David Thoreau. *Faith in a Seed: The Dispersion of Seeds, and Other Late Natural History Writings*. Edited by Bradley P. Dean. Washington, DC: Island Press, 1993.

IN— Indian Notebooks. Extracts Relating to the Indians, MA 596–606, Morgan Library, New York. Citations follow Robert Sayre's numbering in *Thoreau and the American Indians*. Princeton: Princeton University Press, 1977.

OJT—"Online Journal Transcripts," The Writings of Henry D. Thoreau. University of Santa Barbara. https://thoreau.library.ucsb.edu/writings_journals.html.

MW—Henry David Thoreau. *The Maine Woods*. Edited by Joseph J. Moldenhauer. Princeton: Princeton University Press, 1983.

PCorr—Henry David Thoreau. *The Correspondence*. Edited by Robert Hudspeth, Elizabeth Witherell, and Lihong Xie. The Writings of Henry D. Thoreau. 2 volumes to date. Princeton: Princeton University Press, 2013–.

PJ—Henry David Thoreau. *Journal*. The Writings of Henry D. Thoreau. Edited by Elizabeth Hall Witherell et al. 8 vols. to date. Princeton: Princeton University Press, 1981–. Volumes indicated by Arabic numerals.

RP—Henry David Thoreau. *Reform Papers*. Edited by Wendell Glick. Princeton: Princeton University Press, 1973.

W—Henry David Thoreau. *Walden*. Edited by J. Lyndon Shanley. Princeton: Princeton University Press, 1971.

Week—Henry David Thoreau. *A Week on the Concord and Merrimack Rivers*. Edited by Carl F. Hovde. Princeton: Princeton University Press, 1980.

WF—Henry David Thoreau. *Wild Fruits: Thoreau's Rediscovered Last Manuscript*. Edited by Bradley P. Dean. New York: Norton, 2000.

INTRODUCTION: THOREAU TIME

Kathryn C. Dolan, John J. Kucich, Henrik Otterberg

If time is short then you have no time to waste.
Thoreau, Journal, November 16, 1851

Time is having a moment. As the COVID pandemic slowly transforms into recent history, as we slowly come to terms with raising a generation shaped by the relentless rhythms of social media algorithms, as we struggle with the twin horizons of climate change, a crisis of geological scope with tipping points measured in very short years, any sense of "normal" time has evaporated. We are newly reminded of time's elasticity, its constructedness, its power to shape our perspective of the world and its adaptability to different human purposes.

Jenny Odell's two recent books, *How to Do Nothing: Resisting the Attention Economy* (2019) and *Saving Time: Discovering a Life Beyond the Clock* (2023), have captured the centrality of time as a key medium for shaping and reshaping our lives. Doing nothing, for Odell, is at once an act of self-healing, of finding clarity and connection in a world that, by demanding constant attention, makes it impossible to know our selves, and an act of resistance—political and economic—against systems that depend on commanding our attention for profit and power. Saving time, Odell argues, is a process of naming the ways our late capitalist system uses a certain construction of time (tightly measured and precisely valued) to shape us into pliable consumers and producers, and then nurturing alternatives. We need, Odell says, to learn to run our lives according to different clocks. Or no clocks at all.

If this sounds familiar, it is because Henry David Thoreau made similar points more than a hundred and fifty years ago, at a moment when the systems that Odell decries and rallies us against were just taking shape. Thoreau moved to Walden Pond three years before Karl Marx wrote the *Communist Manifesto* and died five years before he published *Das Kapital,* but Thoreau's critique of an emerging industrial capitalist system is organized on very different terms, focused less on the cruel machinery of exploitation and more on the quiet desperation, the soul- and nature-killing disconnection and alienation, he saw settling over New England and America. His focus was not on describing and analyzing this system but on imagining alternatives. The essays in this collection explore the many different aspects of his effort. Some are very much located in a specific time and place—Concord in the mid-nineteenth century. Others are keyed to family dramas of connection and loss that are universal in nature. Yet others draw on cultures and timeframes that reach far beyond Concord—to the sacred stories of the Hindus, Greeks, and Native Americans. All take place in the very nick of time, and all speak to Odell's, and our own, efforts to focus on time in order to reimagine our world.

Thoreau went to Walden Pond for the same reason Odell went to a rose garden in Oakland—to find a place not cut off from the village or the city but slightly removed from it, a place where one could step outside the rhythms and pressures of ordinary life. If the Morcom Amphitheater of Roses was, for Odell, a place where she could turn off her computer and do nothing, Walden Pond, for Thoreau, allowed him to escape the quiet desperation of the village, the pencil factory, the crowded household, and reimagine the foundations of his life. He knew the tyranny of the heavy mortgage and the teeming marketplace, understood the grim tradeoffs of the cotton mills and railroads, of cheap clothing at a terrible cost and railroads that ride on us. He bemoaned the grown men who visited him at his small house on Walden's shore but never really left their shops and offices behind. Children, he was delighted to find, could still fully be in the woods, quickly attuning their minds and bodies to the natural world. Thoreau often gestured fondly towards an earlier era of Yankee self-reliance, when families made or gathered or traded for almost all of what they needed from their farms and their neighbors, but at Walden, he didn't celebrate the relentless work such a world demanded. If Lydia Maria Child, in her chapter "Economy" in the *American Frugal Housewife* (1829), recommended that children use any spare time learning to sew and mend or gather firewood, Thoreau admired children's ability to do nothing. He, too, learned this skill, sitting all morning on his doorstep rather than hoeing his beans, growing, in these seasons, like corn in the night. Instead of minutes and hours measured in the shop or the factory, Thoreau spent his time on long reveries and meditative walks. And instead of working to buy from the increasing flood of goods arriving by rail from all parts of the world, he bought a few simple items and humble foods. Better still, he gathered huckleberries, chestnuts, and groundnuts from the woods and meadows, food that was as much poetry as produce.

As Thoreau recognized the innate ability of children to quickly attune themselves to the rhythms of the woods around Concord, we too can look to our students for fresh ways to engage with *Walden* at this pivotal moment, this nick of time. It can be a challenge to teach the classics of literature to new generations of students, with their changing concerns and desires. This was the theme of the 2017 edition of *The Concord Saunterer*, where it was discovered that Thoreau turns out to be uniquely suited to such a task. Thoreau is a practical person, as well as a philosopher. His bumper-sticker line, "I am a mystic—a transcendentalist—& a natural philosopher to boot" resonates with students and laypeople alike (*PJ* 5: 469). Thoreau meets us all where we currently are. *Walden* continues to resonate with a diverse range of students—farmers, scientists, future eco-warriors, and ranchers alike. Though it may seem a cliché, Thoreau's words are perhaps more vital and necessary now than ever before.

A line from *Walden* that has remained relevant to college students well into the twenty-first century is "Our whole life is startlingly moral" (*W* 218). Students often push back against the weight of this concept, sparking rich discussions. Students might be provided an example from grocery shopping, for example, considering various factors involved in buying produce. They often ask how they can be expected to account for so many elements with every purchase or decision they make. Their objections sometimes resemble the dilemmas from the philosophical comedy program, *The Good Place*. Yet, Thoreau would likely argue that we are still responsible for all our choices—the conscious ones as well as those we make without much forethought. Each choice has consequences. What if we spent more time considering our decisions? Inevitably, something would change—likely for the better. This doesn't mean we will never make careless or thoughtless decisions again, but we would become more thoughtful actors in the world. We would become better critical thinkers and more mindful consumers, which can only be beneficial in today's world and as we look to the future.

The students continue: Are we as culpable as the global elite, the one percent, who buy and sell the lives of entire generations and the more-than-human world? Of course not. Like the pieces of machinery Thoreau describes in "Resistance to Civil Government" (more commonly known as "Civil Disobedience"), we are part of larger systems. But we can also be the counter friction that disrupts the machine. When we consider our daily actions, whether metaphorically or literally looking in the mirror, we confront the consequences of those actions. Have we done our best that day? Can we truthfully say yes? That's the moral life Thoreau challenges us to live. As Maya Angelou famously said, "When you know better, do better." Thoreau echoed this sentiment in his own time: "Be not simply good, be good for something."

Students then argue that we should not let the global elite and big business off the hook that easily. They claim that the focus on individual responsibility places too much blame on those who are, in many ways, victims of these larger actors. And they're absolutely right. This is precisely what Thoreau means about being the counter friction. In the parlance of students of this era, we can turn to Taylor Swift: "I got smarter, I got harder in the nick of time." We must hold those in power accountable and act accordingly. In *Walden* and elsewhere, Thoreau emphasizes being deliberate about our actions. Will one person composting change the world? No. But will we live in a world where consumption patterns will have to change—by choice or by necessity? Absolutely. Thoreau suggests that we start today to live more thoughtfully. Indeed, once we start living with more care and attention, we will enjoy our lives more and "meet with a success unexpected in common hours" (*W* 323).

Walden continues to encourage experiments in living—Chris McCandless's journey in *Into the Wild* (1996), being one of the most famous and tragic examples. It is also being used to demonstrate climate change, as in Richard Primack's *Walden Warming* (2014), and has even been remediated into a video game (www.waldengame.com, University of Southern California). Interest in Thoreau, and in *Walden* in particular, remains high. Largely, this is because *Walden* continues to ask fundamental questions in ways that resonate across the centuries. Readers are still asked to consider the value of our time as well as the essence of a good life. We consider whether or not we own our possessions, or if they own us. "Men have become the tools of their tools," as Thoreau squarely put it (*W* 37).

We also consider consequences as we lose and alter the wild and natural spaces around us and how our technological advances often simultaneously help and hurt us. As long as we live in a world requiring us to confront such dilemmas, Thoreau provides a kind of road map as to how to approach them. A perennially favorite section of *Walden* for students is the ant battle of "Brute Neighbors." The ant serves as a perfect example of Thoreau's timeless relevance—they are everywhere, accessible to anyone, and they invite curiosity. The same lesson applies to Thoreau's discussions of the birds throughout *Walden*—creatures that are as interesting in the twenty-first century as they were in Thoreau's time.

Walden also strikes a chord with anyone who feels deeply connected to a place—or yearns to. Thoreau's intense focus on one specific location over time does more than idealize one single pond among many across the United States. It also encourages us to find our own Walden Pond. He encourages us to discover a place where we can devote our care and attention, and he suggests that this place should be nearby. Traveling to distant lands, he argues, will not necessarily bring the same kind of meaning. Today, this might be seen in contrast to the social media-driven vacation, which prioritizes appearance over authentic experience; having been many places rather than truly learning about one, or a few. Thoreau would urge us to find something close, natural, and beloved. Whether in urban, suburban, or rural settings, beauty is available to us—it's a matter of the quality of our attention. This message remains especially useful in an increasingly uncertain and changing world. Thoreau reminds us to look with love at the human and more-than-human world right in front of us right now.

In his Journal of August 28, 1856, Thoreau gives eloquent voice to unhurried observation and a faith in slow and steady process, in a rumination on a favorite reptile incorporating these traits. He writes:

> June—July—& August—the tortoise shells are hatching—a few inches beneath the surface in sandy fields—You tell of active labors—of works of art—& wars the past summer—Meanwhile the tortoise eggs underlie this turmoil. What events have transpired on the lit & airy surface 3 inches above them! Sumner knocked down—Kansas living an age of suspense. Think what is a summer to them—How many worthy men have died & had their funeral sermons preached—since I saw the mother turtle bury her eggs here. They contained an undeveloped liquid then, they are now turtles.

> June July &August—the live long summer—what are they with their heats and fevers—but sufficient to hatch a tortoise in. Be not in haste; mind your private affairs. Consider the turtle. A whole summer—June July &August—are not too good nor too much to hatch a turtle in. Perchance you have worried yourself—despaired of the world—meditated the end of life—& all things seemed rushing to destruction; but Nature has steadily & serenely advanced with a turtle's pace. (OJT 21: 290–91)

In addition, as Thoreau wrote drafts of *A Week on the Concord and Merrimack Rivers* and the earliest version of *Walden*, he explored different human ways of organizing time. In *A Week*, he countered the nationalist narrative of heroic settlement and divinely-ordained progress that shaped the countless histories of the era with very different clocks—gesturing towards the *longue durée* that reached before European settlement in Native New England and applying the long cycles of geologic time he learned from reading Charles Lyell to a landscape that sprouted canals, railroads, and factories at a dizzying clip. If Thoreau sent "Ktaadn" to the *Sartain's Union Magazine*, a champion of manifest destiny, his work more often captured the skepticism of the nationalist project embodied in Thomas Cole's epic cycle of landscape painting, "The Course of Empire" (1833–36). If Thoreau read Arnold Guyot's *The Earth and Man* (1849) carefully, drawing on its theory of westward movement in "Walking," his argument for sauntering, and his destination, the Spaulding Farm at the western edge of any local pine wood, is a far cry from the teleology of American progress. His attitude toward political reform, too, followed a different clock from those ticking in activist circles, not keyed to anniversaries or elections but to principled resistance that would bring change in its own time. In the meantime, Thoreau focused on learning to see the eternal in the now, the slow churn of seasons in the first robin of spring, the first huckleberry brought to the village, the first sprouting of an oak sapling in a stand of pines.

Indeed, Thoreau's writing offers a long list of ways to change the clocks. He invites us to sit, to join him at the threshold of his house at Walden Pond and watch the morning unfurl into a new day, or lie with him on the newly-formed ice on the pond, watching bubbles form and peering into the leaf litter looking for caddis larvae; he invites us to walk, for four hours a day, if we can manage it (as he does), turning each excursion into a journey towards the Holy Land. We can, like him, read widely and voraciously, especially in books that take us far away in place and time from our desks and devices. Thoreau teaches how to look, and to see—a process that takes time and patience, as we slowly learn the names and habits of our more-than-human neighbors, and, gradually, enter into the world they (and we) make together. Thus at length we may turn turtle in a positive sense, flip vantages and consider a summer from the perspective of a gentle reptilian. Eating, too, changes the clocks—Thoreau was no gourmet cook, but simple meals of rice and Indian meal became, for him, ceremonies of frugality and simplicity, while the taste of a wild huckleberry or wild apple opened up a world of connection.

Perhaps Thoreau's most potent and malleable time machine was his pencil. He gathered notes from his readings that took him far and wide, brought his brother back to life to sail up the Concord River towards home, and, as he gradually learned in his Journal, turned his daily walks in his neighborhood into something at once achingly specific and utterly universal. And Thoreau teaches us, too, how to act when the moment is right. For Thoreau, the act sprang from the moment. He might be prompted, in turn, to build a house, go to jail, help a fugitive to freedom, measure a felled pine tree, plant a forest, or make a speech. He would do what was necessary. But he would do these things in his own time. If we make time to read Thoreau carefully, we can make time our own, even as it appears to us short, and with the stakes everywhere high. While climate change is rapid in the Anthropocene, it still strikes many people as slow, even imperceptible. Would that they had heeded Thoreau's words in *A Week,* which admonishes us not to neglect slow change, and to act quickly when truly needed: "The longer the lever, the less perceptible its motion. It is the slowest pulsation which is the most vital. The hero then will know to wait, as well as to make haste. All good abides with him who waiteth *wisely*; we shall sooner overtake the dawn by remaining here than hurrying over the hills to the west" (*Week* 128).

CHAPTER 1

THOREAU IN THE NICK OF TIME

Laura Dassow Walls

What might it mean for Thoreau to say he had "been born into the most estimable place in all the world— & and in the very nick of time, too" (OJT 22:115)? Dictionaries tell us that the "nick of time" is the last possible moment before something awful happens, as in, "The ambulance arrived in the nick of time." The expression relies on the kind of long-lost word history that Thoreau loved to exploit: in pre-modern English, "nick" meant "the exact critical moment," or that singular point in time when opportunity opens—but look out! It won't stay open for long. One could say that Thoreau wrote radiant with that singular urgency, pressing the critical moment of his too-brief life toward a variety of opportunities: protesting the Mexican War, freeing the slaves, honoring the Indian in his homeland, saving the last green commons from the axe. Thoreau lived with the perpetual sense that, as he mourned in "Wild Apples," the evil days were coming, and we who would be born a century hence would not share in his peculiar good fortune: "Ah, poor man, there are many pleasures which he will not know!" (*Exc* 288). Nevertheless, Thoreau gave us other kinds of good fortune, especially the gift of his words, which gather us together in just the nick of time. Aligned as we were, at the "Thoreau in the Nick of Time" conference in Iceland in May 2022 (some of us, due to COVID, from faraway time zones), we resonated with peculiar force to that ancient temporality warning us that time does not wait on us. Windows close. Opportunities vanish. We too, like Thoreau, must stay alert, ready to seize the moment before we lose it forever.

Our awareness of time's passing at this historical moment, a time of COVID and climate change and desperate political destinies, applies considerable pressure and confers a perhaps unbearable burden of responsibility. Every few weeks another scientific report arrives to tell us that there is no time to wait, that now, *right now*, is the time we must act if we are to save the future of the planet, of humanity itself. For decades we have heard that the window for action, once wide open, is closing by the year. And yet we seem powerless to act—we the collective, at whatever scale, as well as each of us as individuals. How do we link our personal lives, lived in the messy demands of the passing hours, with the great collective life of the planet whose fate we know we are foreclosing?—let alone with the still greater Cosmos of which our Earth is but a small if proud citizen. I'd like to think more closely about this problem, of how Thoreau's "nick of time" confronts us with our current sense of time as simultaneously accelerating, like the steam-driven locomotive he named "a fate, an *Atropos*, that never turns aside" (*W* 118), even as it shrinks to a vanishing point. We feel ourselves impelled toward a dire future unless we act *now*, without delay or prevarication; yet we remain paralyzed by a political economy that bereaves us of agency, and a spiritual economy that points not downwards to an ancient and imperiled Earth but upwards to an escapist heaven. And when we peer ahead, as if blinded by some sorcerer's spell, we confuse futurity with apocalypse, bending the arc of a furious universe to its righteous end. We beg to know what can one person do when time, history itself, rushes towards us, yet no matter how loud we shout or how often we vote or how many meetings we attend, we cannot head off what's coming.

As a "boomer," I resonate with Thoreau's self-satisfied urgency. I was born in 1955, in Alaska, and grew up in Seattle in the nick of time, too (as we all used to say). Back then Seattle was a backwater town, pre-Amazon, pre-Starbucks, pre-Microsoft, off in what they called "the forgotten corner" of the nation. It fancied itself on the cusp of the future, yet few outsiders agreed, which meant we still had plenty of green spaces far and near. Yet I was also born into a post-World-War-II moment riven with social injustice and natural catastrophe and a sense of doom just around the corner. I grew up drinking milk laced with plutonium fallout from a nearby nuclear arms plant (of course at the time neither the dairy farmers nor their customers knew this), while in grade school we played the game of duck and cover under our comically small desks, rehearsing nuclear holocaust. Just recently I came across my old metal dog tags, given to children back then so our burned-out bodies could be readily identified once the radiation cleared. But I must tell you, it was a beautiful world. Old growth forests still stood tall, glaciers still abided, oceans still ran clear, and no one imagined that we were, simply by our ordinary acts of growing and being, precipitating the insect apocalypse and the sixth mass extinction of life on Earth. We thought of ourselves as truly born in the nick of time, at the last saving moment: we demonstrated against The War and marched against The Bomb; our legislators passed laws to end pollution and poverty and extend civil rights; we read Leopold, and Carson, and Thoreau, we founded Earth Day and flew green-striped "Ecology" flags, we read that this was "The Greening of America" and sang that it was "the Dawning of the Age of Aquarius."[1] And we knew for certain that time was on our side. As Martin Luther King, Jr. assured us in 1968—shortly before he was assassinated—"We shall overcome because the arc of the moral universe is long, but it bends toward justice." We could imagine, in our complacency, that whatever setbacks sent us backwards, in time the Cosmos would set things right.

Today, as bombs fall on Kyiv and Tel Aviv and Rafah and now Beirut, and we shiver in anticipation of World War III; as we are told that we must learn to live—even those of us who literally cannot live—with COVID forever; as we recalibrate over and over again just how many more years we can keep burning carbon before it is really, truly, yes we really mean it this time, too late to save life as we know it—we too feel ourselves alive in the nick of time. But this time, unlike the 60s and 70s, we doubt we have sufficient power to bring progress, let alone world revolution. Thoreau sensed, in the future bearing down on his own beautiful and terrible world, not only calamitous possibility but also the potential to head it off. He not only lived, but *wrote*, in the nick of time, too, handing us the tools and modeling the courage to use them. Whatever we have managed to save, whatever we have managed to heal, we have saved and healed partly in thanks to him. His political writings above all deployed this nick-of-time sensibility to inspire moral reflection and political action. "Civil Disobedience" is nothing less than a textbook on how to leverage the exact critical moment of now into a movement for radical, wholesale revolution. Sam Staples happens to confront his friend Henry Thoreau on his way to the shoemaker; Henry seizes the critical moment to offer himself to the Middlesex County jail. Then, upon his release, Henry seizes both pen and lectern to transform a single night in jail into an enduring model for effective political action. How to leverage individual weakness into collective strength. How to seize the nick of time to make progress for eternity.

But there are other kinds of time, too, such as those we feel on our pulse as the present passes into the past. What is the relationship between things that pass us by, and things that endure beyond us? Just as "Thoreauvian" as the fierce urgency of "Civil Disobedience" is the moment in *Walden* when Thoreau, in bending to the Earth, sees time as eternity: "Time is but the stream I go a-fishing in. I drink at it; but while I drink I see the sandy bottom and detect how shallow it is. Its thin current slides away, but eternity remains. I would drink deeper; fish in the sky, whose bottom is pebbly with stars" (*W* 98). In this vision, shallow time falls away to reveal cosmic time. It is the revelation of cosmic time that gives us courage to "fish in the sky" among the eternal stars, even as we bend to Earth to drink of whatever local time we are given as mortal beings—whether that time be, as Thoreau says elsewhere, "good or bad" (*RP* 74).

This is all so persuasive that we forget Thoreau *didn't* reach Walden Pond in the nick of time, not really. By the time he was building his house there, in April 1845, the sylvan drapery of his childhood dreams had been ripped away. By the time of *Walden*'s publication in 1854, Walden Pond was largely deforested; indeed, I've speculated that Thoreau reopened his Walden manuscript for the final push after finding, late in November 1851, the oak that once shaded his house reduced to a stump. "Where is my home?," he wondered (*PJ* 4:200).[2] In winter 1855 he watched as Alex Therien cut down the two great chestnut trees that had once companioned and perfumed his Walden days (OJT 18:203)—a moment now all the more poignant, since our nation's once-great chestnut forests were lost first to blight and now even to memory. There was no saving those trees, not in Thoreau's lifetime. Given the asynchrony between the trees' slow clock and his own too-rapid one, they were gone forever. It was time, instead, to cleave away the diabolical present, in which his house, sold, was rotting away as a corncrib and the trees that had sheltered it were being logged off and sold for timber, and to live instead in cosmic time, the vast temporality opened by the page in which it could all come back to life—a life capable of endlessly reiterated renewal. The nick of time past fell away to reveal cosmic time: and that was the time in which *Walden* became the text we honor in our own time. Thoreau, of course, was the artist of Kouroo, working in time as if it were more truly eternity. In the cosmic time his writing engendered, Walden endures, forever green, forever pure, unchanged, "the same water which my youthful eyes fell on" (*W* 193). Fallen today, it is ever-rising tomorrow, like the morning star.

But this deeper, cosmic time exists only if we *re-member* it, as Thoreau made a point of re-membering Walden. This is the danger: that we won't. Or what truly frightens: that we can't. Ecologists have identified the "shifting baseline" syndrome, by which each new generation assumes the world they grew up in is "the" world, the best world, the real world as it is and can only be. For instance: Once I saw a series of photographs of proud fishermen (yes, all men), taken over a period of perhaps fifty years at the same fishing resort. In the first photo, the fishes are all huge, about as big as the fishermen themselves. Decade by decade the fishes dwindle in size until by the end each fisher is holding a string of little fishes, not one whose tail would overlap the side of a frying pan. But here's the thing: in each photograph the smiles are just as big, the fellowship just as jubilant, the pride just as endearing: Look at me! Isn't this world, in which I can cast a line into these waters and bring up such treasures, isn't this world grand? I got here just in the nick of time! And *here's* the photo to prove it. Yes, it has always been and will always be a grand world. Future generations will find beauty in it, too. Time is generous that way; they literally won't know any better.

And of course, neither do we. At least, neither do we unless we can fall under the spell of a writer who, like Thoreau, does not only read about, but actually becomes, one of the artists of Kouroo, someone for whom and for whose work "the former lapse of time had been an illusion" (*W* 327), who can bring a lost world back to life in our minds and hearts—a world that we can feel to be as real as the one we live in today, a world that we can share with each other and renew with each rereading, passing it down through the generations. This is what I mean by "cosmic time": not some remote world, cold and unchanging and eternal as the stars that reign above all human care and concern, but "Cosmic" in the sense of Alexander von Humboldt's book *Cosmos* (which Thoreau read and admired), in which "Cosmos" refers not only to the ordered physical universe apart from us, but also to the beauty of that ever-changing, dynamic and evolving living universe as shaped and perceived by human minds and hearts. In this sense, cosmic time isn't just "out there," with or without us. It needs us, for only in the dance of world and mind does it come into being.[3]

How, then, does one create the conditions for cosmic time, that transgenerational time that joins our many pasts and our diverse presents toward a future that carries us together, to reveal itself?

Thoreau created his own cosmic time by turning his Walden retreat into a watchtower, from whose fastness he could observe how industrial modernity was dissolving the world of his youth, reshaping it into another world that he struggled to understand and vowed to resist. As a result, Thoreau created not just one, but *three* new entities, a conjoined trinity that is still part of our world today. Confusingly, all three entities share the same name. First there's Walden Pond itself, the glacial kettle lake still with us today, although it was inflected by Thoreau's presence on its shores from a little-known local lake to a world-famous site of pilgrimage and reverence, a popular state park that must be both open to and protected from the tens of thousands drawn to its shores, directly or indirectly, by Thoreau's words. The second is *Walden* the book, in which Thoreau layers his evolving thoughts on what he lived and experienced, both at the Pond and afterward, creating one of the world's great statements of spiritual anguish and rebirth. But many who have never read *Walden* will still know the third entity, "Walden" the concept, as in "going Walden," an icon and measure of the ideal life and an interpretive lens through which to view all the world's natural areas and wild entities—even the world itself, the planetary Cosmos for which Walden is a metonym. Walden Pond, the physical material translated by Thoreau into *Walden* the book, belongs to the world, not to the individual self; but by assimilating his selfhood to the life of Walden Pond, Thoreau, the artist, reissued it in new form, giving the world a new object, a new concept, a new being of the imagination.[4] As he says of the artist of Kouroo, "The material was pure, and his art was pure; how could the result be other than wonderful?" (*W* 327).

All three of these entities—pond, book, concept—rely on what Emerson called "creative reading," a process of invention in which "the page of every book we read becomes luminous with manifold allusion. Every sentence is doubly significant, and the sense of our author is as broad as the world."[5] Thoreau expanded Emerson's words into an ethic of what he called living, and reading, "deliberately," into one of his most elaborate wordplays: into its Latin root *deliberare* or *to weigh* (derived from libra, or scales), he folded the similar-sounding roots for *to read*, from the root of *library*, and *to be free*, from the root of *liberty*. One might sum up all of *Walden* in this word—as Thoreau himself did when he tells us, "I went to the pond because I wished to live deliberately," which is to say, to live with the freedom to read the world in its fullness and weigh the meaning of its every part. To become a reader of *Walden* is not, then, just to read about living deliberately; it is to be instructed—that is, to learn how to instruct oneself—in the art of *living* deliberately. This would mean learning how to live a life in which each object becomes not a mute thing to be passed by but a legible event that gathers past, present, and future, allying the nick of time—whatever passing time we have, however "mean and shabby" it may seem—with the emergence of the time that endures.

Through this alchemy Thoreau transforms "Walden" from an object into an event—that is, from pond-as-thing to pond-as-ongoing-being; or, from a book published in 1854 to an ongoing and collective work of continuous creation, a three-faceted work at once a place, a book, and a concept, which when articulated together becomes an ethic passed from author to reader. To pass "Walden" from reader to reader, from teacher to student, or friend to friend, turns the singular event of Walden into a continuing journey of what Bruno Latour calls *instauration*—that is, of renovation or restoration, a constant taking up of the past in a rebirth of the same in ever-renewed form, as in the successive rebirths, or instaurations, of seventeen-year-locusts.[6] This journey demands of everyone along the way a constant recreation or renewal of oneself, not apart from but entangled amidst one's world or surroundings—one's "environment," in Carlyle's now-familiar coinage. Thoreau was a close reader of Carlyle, yet his own sense of life in its environs is closer to the German word *Umwelt*, meaning the surrounding world that every being creates even as, in creating it, it simultaneously creates itself in relationship to it.[7] That is, what Thoreau discovered at Walden is that we are bonded together, renewed, and instructed by the world we create together—and that we have the agency to make this world as large, or as diminished, as we choose.

Like Walden Pond itself, this continuously renewing act of trivalent creation—pond, book, concept—cannot be bounded by the limits of the human world, but extends across—more, dissolves away—the boundary that we (we who are descended from Descartes) insist on erecting between human and natural; for this continuously renewing act of creation, of rebirth down the generations, demonstrates to all who participate that worlds are created and sustained only in history, across time, by *every one* of their participants, human and other-than-human. Thoreau's innovation thus records the entry into history of a new Earth, what he called in "Walking" "this holy land" (*Exc* 185), "heaven...under our feet" (*W* 283)—not as a stage on which to perform, but as a living entity in which we are immersed,...one that has been constituted by living beings who have given themselves across immeasurable generations to making this world in which we humans are enveloped, who made and are still making it into the habitable world that makes us possible. For Thoreau, the one who initiated "Walden" as a particular series of continuing creations, to "read" is to read not only *in* time, but also to read time *itself*, creating, layering, recreating a manifold texture that weaves us together in the present with the past and future of our co-creation, the Cosmos whose dance depends on us even as our lives depend on it. One can say, then, that *Walden* exists as scripture, designed to lead us through a process of conversion to a new way of life, holding open that place still awaiting its fulfillment, while bent on creating in its audience the reader who might be capable of that future.

This sounds complicated, but the very fact that we are here together, whether at the inceptive conference in Iceland that occasioned this book, or as the readers who comprise this book's audience, speaks to the fact that we intuitively understand this perfectly well. Start with the past, 1845, and with the first Walden, the familiar pond itself, together with the biographical person who answered to the name "Henry Thoreau." Why does this Henry go to this Walden? He doesn't tell us; he reveals very little of his actual past. What he does tell us is a complex stratigraphy of memory and meaning:

> When I was four years old, as I well remember, I was brought from Boston to this my native town, through these very woods and this field, to the pond. It is one of the oldest scenes stamped on my memory. And now to-night my flute has waked the echoes over that very water. The pines still stand here older than I; or, if some have fallen, I have cooked my supper with their stumps, and a new growth is rising all around, preparing another aspect for new infant eyes. Almost the same johnswort springs from the same perennial root in this pasture, and even I have at length helped to clothe that fabulous landscape of my infant dreams, and one of the results of

my presence and influence is seen in these bean leaves, corn blades, and potato vines. (*W* 155-56)

Memories, as John Dewey observes, are organically incorporated into the very structure of the self, becoming organs of perception, ways of seeing, "the nutriment that gives body to what is seen."[8] In this sense, Thoreau's childhood memory of Walden Pond becomes the very organ of perception with which he sees Walden—here, the food, literal as well as figurative, that feeds and gives body to his further observations of the pond's many moods and transformations. The depth of his perception transforms Walden into an organ of vision. As he'll say deeper into the book, the lake becomes "earth's eye; looking into which the beholder measures the depth of his own nature" (*W* 186). Deeper still, and perception has ripened into mutual recognition: "Walden, is it you?" (*W* 193).

This means that "Walden" feels less like a personal memoir than a religious retreat—and indeed, the journal Thoreau opened on his first morning at the pond records the depth of his devotion. His house would be a temple, "pure and undefiled"; eating would be "a sacrament—a method of communion"; every morning he would baptize himself anew in Walden water. He vowed to "meet the facts of life—the vital facts,...the phenomena or actuality the Gods meant to show us,—face to face." As for writing, surely it was time once again "for the written word—the *scripture*—to be heard."[9] These are Christian references, but Thoreau also found in Hindu writings what he called "a manual of private devotion" that showed how the most domestic and intimate was simultaneously the most public and impersonal, "not only true but true for the widest horizon." To him, the Hindu writers had not merely made art, but made life itself an art. But writing such scripture for an industrializing New England posed a difficult problem. What could possibly be the "actuality the Gods meant to show us" in a modernizing capitalist economy? Such a question had seemed impossible to answer while living in the center of town. But out by the pond Henry could discipline himself, control the distractions, and give his life to enacting Walden as a three-fold, experimental work of performance art, one whose journey has continued unbroken until today.

Thoreau's material, utopian experiment at the physical Pond began its mutation into a *narrative* experiment early in 1847, when he walked into town to give his curious and often skeptical neighbors a series of lectures explaining what he was doing. Traces of the give and take of oral delivery still linger in *Walden*, but by the time of its publication, the qualifying past tense of the book's opening phrase—"When I wrote the following pages, or rather the bulk of them"—make clear that even in the writing, the Thoreau of Walden Pond is long gone, as is, as we've seen, the Walden Pond of 1845, let alone of his childhood. Hence the Thoreau who takes up the pen to convey these words to us is different from the Thoreau who once, long ago, took up axe and plow with ink-stained hands. As he unfolds his story, this distance between autobiographical author and fictional narrator grows ever wider: the author chatting away in our ear (who promised, you'll remember, "a simple and sincere account of his own life" [*W* 3]) barely alludes to his actual life, the one in which he walked almost daily to town, dined with friends, and funded his adventure in minimalism with day-labor. Meanwhile, the narrator of the book entitled *Walden* cultivates an impression of hermetic solitude and purity, an intimate, and privileged, experience that tests our relationship with the actual man who wrote it. Take these famous lines from "Solitude":

> I was suddenly sensible of such sweet and beneficent society in Nature, in the very pattering of the drops, and in every sound and sight around my house, an infinite and unaccountable friendliness all at once like an atmosphere sustaining me, as made the fancied advantages of human neighborhood insignificant, and I have never thought of them since. Every little pine needle expanded and swelled with sympathy and befriended me. (*W* 131-32)

What the reader of *Walden* remembers are lines like these, Thoreau's intense poetry of solitude and reflection, an experience as intimate as our dreams. Yet it also seems supremely removed from us. Who can live like this, in "the midst of Nature"—assuming we even believe that "Nature" still exists! At the very least, has not the author used his wealth and privilege to escape from the "real life" the rest of us feel compelled to endure? Good for him, we might be thinking, but useless for us. We can't all move to Walden Pond.

As we read on, it gets worse. The autobiographical Thoreau is having the time of his life, far removed from the realities of *our* trivial lives, living as we are in our shallow time. This sets up the writerly Thoreau's real task: how he can move *his* lived experience, *his* experiential knowledge and discoveries, into *our* lived experience. We must believe in the absolute veracity of his life, and in the absolute material truth of his environment, even as he elaborates that life into a mythic hero's journey and that ordinary backyard lake into the navel of the cosmos. Any break from that factual veracity, the grounded thread that ties us to both Thoreau and to the Pond, will fracture the whole experiment, turn it into a make-believe—just another woven web of words and no more. Worse, if we feel betrayed by "the facts," we may even charge Thoreau with hypocrisy and walk away forever. Only to the extent that we invest ourselves in the *reality* of Thoreau and Walden Pond can we inhabit this world ourselves.[10] As Thoreau, still ringing from reading the Hindu *Laws of Manu*, observed in 1842: "It is not merely a voice floating in space for my own experience is the speaker" (*PJ* 1:424). Exactly: he can't merely instruct us intellectually, another voice floating in space. He must get under our skin, make *our own* experience into the speaker we hear.

How? By needling us until we reach our own most personal, even hidden, feeling of discontent. As John Dewey remarked, "In the kingdom of art as well as of righteousness it is those who hunger and thirst who enter."[11] Thoreau knew from his personal experience of "quiet desperation" how we all get through our days, our weeks and years, by repressing our unease, refusing to admit it to ourselves lest we stoke the panic that leaves us miserable with our powerlessness to change our lives—let alone remake a global economy that destroys the world we love, destroys the very conditions for life on Earth. You disagree? You like your life just fine? You flourish in this collapsing late-stage capitalist economy? Then *Walden* is not for you. As Thoreau warns us repeatedly, his book is addressed to "poor students," not "strong and valiant natures" or those who approve the status quo. If that describes you, he begs you to put his book down before you "stretch the seams" and ruin it for the person whom it fits (*W* 4, 16). However, if you're one of those malcontents, he invites you to try it on for size—try, that is, *re-creating* his experience in *your own* life. Not, of course, please, literally to give up all family responsibilities for good and move to Walden Pond (even Thoreau kept up with the former, and he left the latter after his "experiment" was done), but in some real sense to rethink your conventional assumptions and reorient your life toward some higher meaning. Are you ready to win your subjectivity through *Walden*, to identify yourself as the kind of person who appreciates Thoreau?[12] Then Thoreau will take you to meet the vital facts face-to-face, and see what they have to teach you.

How does *Walden* move us through this bivalent landscape, this marriage of text and experience? The first step is to displace us from our familiar, shallow world. This is the task of that long, essential, and almost universally disliked opening chapter, "Economy." The word, from the Greek *oiko-nomia*, literally means "household management," including the familiar dynamics of production and consumption which, in Thoreau's world, still took place in a capitalist market economy of cash, barter, and direct exchange, or of loan against eventual return plus interest. Only after his death does "ecology" (or *oiko-logia*) break off as a separate word naming the biological study of plants and animals in their habitat. Thus, where we see two things, a human world run by political economy and, embedded within it, a natural world of tools and resources upon which we can draw at will, Thoreau asserts their continuing and constant interplay. True, he knows and reverences a "wild" nature wholly apart from the human, but that terrain is reserved for those other works, *The Maine Woods* and *Cape Cod*. The specific task of *Walden* is to emphasize, instead, interpenetration and reciprocity.

This task begins the instant our hero picks up a borrowed axe to cut down the trees to build his house, and it intensifies when he wakes up in his new home and realizes that all around him are forest birds—wood thrushes, scarlet tanagers—that he never sees in town. Instead of caging them for his pleasure, he has in essence caged himself in their world, where they remain wholly free. This inversion reinforces *Walden*'s opening insight, when Thoreau calls himself "a sojourner in civilized life again": it turns out that while nature can live quite happily without us, we can't live any kind of a life without nature. Thus in civilization we can only be "sojourners," never dwellers. Later he will point out that we are sojourners in nature, too. Hence there can be no border—or rather, border is all there can be; we humans are forever in a state of transit. What this means is that those who erect and defend a border despite this truth have unaccountably made a serious mistake, which our hero must correct by building a home—literally, managing a household—in which both flourish together, in a mutually sustaining relationship.

Of course this reciprocity doesn't exist, not yet. That it still might is *Walden*'s utopian project. That project begins by defining what, then, is "essential," and how it is attained. Thoreau famously strips this question down to four categories, "Food, Shelter, Clothing, and Fuel" (*W* 12), and in this borderline green world of Walden Woods and Pond, it becomes painfully clear that while animals can get their essentials without erecting walls, humans cannot. We must build walls, actual literal walls, which means cutting down trees; we must grow our food, which means inventing husbandry and agriculture. Paradoxically, the more we defend ourselves from a state of nature, the more deeply we are tied to it. Nevertheless, we keep pulling away from it, erecting and elaborating a vast and expanding economic infrastructure—"civilization"—which we believe is essential to our survival. But by a terrible irony civilization has had the opposite effect, not enhancing our humanity but destroying it, making us quietly desperate. We cultivate our bodies, but not our dreams; we cultivate our beans, but not our minds; we build ever grander houses, forgetting to build our lives. Hence Thoreau's master metaphor: the painstaking care he takes with his house means rebuilding his life, hence our collective life, from the ground up.

As Thoreau spars with the economic infrastructure of his era—namely, capitalism—he shows it undermining us in two ways. First, by obscuring our sense of free choice by imposing upon us its own circular structure: earn money, buy stuff, earn more money, buy more stuff—all, ironically, in the name of a "progress" that sacrifices the fullness of the present to secure a speculative future. Second, by distinguishing those who succeed at this rat race from those who are enslaved to it. *You* may be proud of your fine new horse and carriage, but, Thoreau prods, "are we certain that what is one man's gain is not another's loss, and that the stable-boy has equal cause with his master to be satisfied?" (*W* 56). His larger question becomes, How have we, individually and collectively, conceded to an economic infrastructure that, rich or poor, doesn't "progress" at all but undermines our very humanity?

Because, he answers, we are essentially asleep. As his title page declares, "I do not propose to write an ode to dejection, but to brag as lustily as chanticleer in the morning, standing on his roost, if only to wake my neighbors up." *Walden* is a book of the dawn, of religious awakening: Thoreau at his watchtower waits out the night, ready to jar us awake at the first streaks of light so that we too may greet the sunrise. "To be awake is to be alive," he tells us (*W* 90): why, look, his forest birds are all fully alive, alert and engaged in their worlds. Why aren't we? They put us to shame. Sleepers, awake! Because while all natural beings grow and develop, only *human* beings have the capacity to take charge of their growth, to in effect grow *themselves*, or as he puts it, to elevate ourselves "by a conscious endeavor" (*W* 90). But tragically, we don't believe in our freedom. To reach us, off and away in our own time zones, Thoreau must find a way to break through the page and actively engage us—first with his life, and thence with our own.

"Economy" bends to this task with that notorious brash "chanticleer" voice, loud, bold, strutting, braggart. This can work, as when Thoreau launches into the clothing that you—yes, *you*, dear reader!—are wearing *right now*, this moment, even as you read his book, thrusting his hands through the page to finger your threads and demanding to know if the factory workers who made them have equal cause to celebrate your good fortune in buying them. But it entails a risk, to accuse your audience like this. In lectures, the living Thoreau could wink at his audience, spar with their head-shaking skepticism, bring them around with his deadpan New England humor, and he does let a little of this twinkle leak into *Walden*. But today, in print, his edginess often misfires. Many walk away from his narrative in disgust or umbrage. But a few will be intrigued enough to keep reading, just long enough to realize that this risky strategy, engagement via insult, also reveals Thoreau's willingness to "spend himself" wholly on our behalf. He'll literally risk it all just to get our attention.

Thoreau must have known that taking such a risk would cost him many readers. Wouldn't a gentler, less confrontational Thoreau have gained a better hearing? Perhaps, but Thoreau didn't want *more* readers, he wanted *more daring* readers—the select few willing to take on a fight. After all, his target is immense, and very dangerous—nothing less than a whole way of life, capitalism itself. Today many resonate with the remark, often attributed to Fredric Jameson, that it is easier to imagine the end of the world than to imagine the end of capitalism. Thoreau, too, could intuit this dilemma, but in trying to see alternatives he had very little help. He didn't even have a name for capitalism; he knew it only as a historical force, fate or *Atropos*, sweeping inexorably over everything and everyone. His great advantage was that he witnessed that fate emerge in his very lifetime, as he watched the Concord of his childhood, which still bore traces of its 200-year-old colonial subsistence economy of small farms and artisanal manufactures (such as his family's pencil business) transformed into a global industrial consumer capitalist economy, the dawning of our own world. Except that, unlike us, Thoreau can see that world as a wrong turn to be righted rather than as an unstoppable, hydra-headed monster that cannot be turned aside.

As Thoreau watched modernity congeal, like a smog, from a subtle shift in the weather to an all-obscuring climate, he knew that to shake his future audience loose he must unsettle us profoundly, dislocate us from all that we take for granted—for only the ontologically unsettled can be turned around. The relentless probing continues, item by item, as he opens our cupboards, pinches our trousers and dresses, points to our furniture, thrusts his bank account into our guilty faces. He may be a squatter living on next to nothing but at least he owns himself, and his house, free and clear. How about you? Only then, after flaunting his successes and taunting us with our failures, does he switch perspective (in his second chapter, "Where I Lived and What I Lived For") by imagining all possible places as the site of all possible houses, inviting us to imagine ourselves in his place, living our lives in a house of our own, but now living, like him, for higher ends. The hectoring gives way to a mystic lyricism that exhilarates through sheer boldness and beauty, lifting into *Walden*'s famous statement of purpose: "I went to the pond because I wished to live deliberately, to front only the essential facts of life and see if I could not learn what it had to teach, and not, when I came to die, discover that I had not lived." Notice how the "I" of these words opens to the "we" of what follows, looping into the "you" of the reader: "Still we live meanly, like ants.…Our life is frittered away by detail.… Simplicity, Simplicity, Simplicity! I say, let our affairs be as two or three…and keep your accounts on your thumb nail" (*W* 90–91).

Tempting as it is, I cannot continue with a full reading of *Walden*. Suffice it to say that each chapter grows out of the preceding like a series of buds unfolding. The growing twigs ramify into branches, as vague ideas burrow into the physical reality of life at the pond and take to themselves material reality. Watch how "Reading" makes you breathe your literal breath of life, the renewal of now, into the very words Thoreau wrote so long ago; how "Sounds" grows out of "Reading" as the breath of your readerly voice turns into what Thoreau calls "the language which all things and events speak without metaphor" (*W* 111); how the sounds of falling rain invite the next chapter, "Solitude," which in turn invites "Visitors," who engage Thoreau as he works in his "Bean-field," consciously stitching the human and natural worlds together into a half-wild, half-cultivated field that opens to include "The Village," where human activity is defamiliarized and we see ourselves, briefly, as he sees us, trading places once again. Finally, returning from the village to "The Ponds," Thoreau opens to us the rest of his emerging cosmos by taking us fishing—casting a line of communication between our two worlds, catching, he muses, "two fishes as it were with one hook" (*W* 174–75), one wholly now and material and vanishing (better eat that fish before it spoils!), the other wholly cosmic and enduring, flowering indivisibly into our own lives.

In such a living world, every action can potentially link world with self and self with world, drawing each into the other in a bond that enriches both. The outer world signifies, not accidentally, not arbitrarily, not according to humans only, but intrinsically, and constantly, unto the least of its squeaking and squirming inhabitants. As our mutual cosmos expands—even, or especially, after the crisis at Baker Farm, Thoreau's terrible failure to create a common world with John Field and his family, a darkness that follows him into "Higher Laws"—the circle, the cosmogram Thoreau is tracing with both pen and feet around the Pond itself, is finally completed in "Spring," as the frozen soul who opened the book in anger and denunciation sees in Walden's melting the release of his own soul, sweeping us into the cosmic regeneration of all life, surmounting even death and decay and the cruelty of nature in a metaphysical vision as fiercely visceral as the stench of that dead horse's rotting corpse. By the end, the willing reader is ready to accept Thoreau's language of prophecy, to feel it not just on the pages of some book but in the bones of her own life. The once desperate and defeated fellow-traveler who has stayed with Thoreau throughout this great ceremony of exfoliation, death, transgression, and ecstatic rebirth is released into Thoreau's famous final lines, which took over 300 pages to earn: "There is more day to dawn. The sun is but a morning star."

The ceremony Thoreau has made us enact is complete.

Thoreau said he left Walden for as good a reason as he came there, without quite detailing what that reason was, but on some deep level, he must have been ready to leave. His climactic, life-defining experience had lapsed into mere routine. He had completed his Walden work, both the writing (with a full draft of *A Week* completed and *Walden* well underway), and the working out of his philosophy. It was time to bring the results of his lonely experiment back to town and apply them to social life—to transform Walden from something that passes, into something that endures. For all the many instaurations that have renewed Walden again and again, from Thoreau's time to our own, keeping its trajectory in time unbroken, the one immutable condition, the one we must never fail, is this: the understanding, the *enactment* of the understanding, again and again without remission, that our world and all the objects of meaning that compose it will continue only if we give them our constant care and solicitude. Without us as readers, breathing life into it, *Walden* will cease to exist. Of course there will still be a book by that title, but it will sit lifeless on a shelf; there will still be a Walden Pond, but its meaning will fall away, and with the meaning, its protection too; when that happens, the word "Walden" will no longer signify, as it does today, the wider natural commons, the household of Earth, that holds us together exactly to the degree that we hold it—together. For just as *Walden*, the book, isn't a single creation, issued once in 1854 and needing nothing more from us, so the planetary life it embodies and celebrates is, too, a continuous act of creation, a living pathway that needs us if it is to continue its trajectory into the future. This is Thoreau's essential philosophy of life, ratified by his reading of Charles Darwin's *Origin of Species* in 1860, when he declared that Darwin's theory of evolution rings true because it "implies a greater vital force in nature...equivalent to a sort of constant *new* creation" (OJT 32:197).

Thoreau engaged with Darwin rather as we have engaged with Thoreau, reader and text joining to combat the old biblical sense of Creation as a singular act that happened long ago, needing nothing more from us, to insist instead that creation is a constant process, a sublime engendering, continuing all around us all the time—an engendering that has never not been part of us. As Thoreau said in the climax of *Walden*, watching the spring sun melt the frozen soil, "The earth is not a mere fragment of dead history, stratum upon stratum like the leaves of a book, to be studied by geologists and antiquaries chiefly, but living poetry like the leaves of a tree...not a fossil earth, but a living earth." The resurrection was complete; "Walden was dead and is alive again" (*W* 309, 311). Thoreau's gospel, that which transforms the absent into the present and the dead into the risen, is now in our hands.

Through such alchemy does the three-faceted journey of *Walden*—pond, book, concept—become nothing less than the narrative we in our today are co-authoring with the materiality that we are, that same materiality that through us finds its way to speech, writing, culture, to the growth and cultivation of the Cosmos that was, and is, and was to have come. For our world, our Cosmos, that heaven under our feet, is not given to us but, like *Walden*, is anthropogenic. It holds together, and it holds us together, exactly insofar as we take responsibility for its continuing journey of instauration—and no farther. Despite our shame-faced attraction to the bleak comforts of apocalypse, the future of our Cosmos is nowhere written. Thoreau anticipated the evil days not because he believed dystopia was inevitable—the future was as unknowable to him as it is to us—but because as a writer of scripture, he was preparing that place still awaiting its fulfillment, in hopes of converting his reader into someone capable of embracing the future in defiance of the coming darkness. As Thoreau keeps on insisting, the chips are not yet down, the future is still to be negotiated. You have to choose, now,[13] for the moment is now, always now, the risk is real, and the choice is ours, only ours, yours and mine, in the now that is always the nick of time.

Acknowledgment: My thanks to Katja Lehming and De Gruyter Brill for permission to include herein a revised excerpt of my essay, "16. The Continuous Creation of Walden," in *Handbook of American Romanticism*, edited by Philipp Löffler, Clemens Spahr, and Jan Stievermann (Berlin and Boston: De Gruyter, 2021), pp. 355–374.

Works Cited

Dewey, John. *Art as Experience*. New York: G. P. Putnam's Sons, 1958.

Emerson, Ralph Waldo. *Essays and Lectures*. New York: Library of America, 1983.

Latour, Bruno. *An Inquiry into Modes of Existence: An Anthropology of the Moderns*. Cambridge: Harvard University Press, 2013.

———. *Rejoicing, Or the Torments of Religious Speech*. Cambridge: Polity, 2013.

Reich, Charles A. *The Greening of America.* New York: Random House, 1970.

von Uexküll, Jakob. *A Foray into the Worlds of Animals and Humans* (1934). Trans. Joseph D. O'Neil. Minneapolis: University of Minnesota Press, 2010.

Walls, Laura Dassow. *Henry David Thoreau: A Life.* Chicago: University of Chicago Press, 2017.

———. *Passage to Cosmos: Alexander von Humboldt and the Shaping of America.* Chicago: University of Chicago Press, 2009.

CHAPTER 2

TIME ON ICE: THE MELTING SKIN OF WALDEN POND AND OK GLACIER'S SWANSONG

David G. Kristinsson

In a time of climate crisis people meet up in the countryside in mostly treeless Iceland to talk about the nick of time. From a native perspective one might expect a conference on such a theme to be somehow connected to the writer, former presidential candidate, and environmental activist Andri Snær Magnason. Since this was the first thing that came to mind when seeing the congress announcement of the Thoreau Society to be held at the Snorrastofa in Reykholt, Iceland, in May 2022, I resolved to compare Thoreau's *Walden* and Magnason's *On Time and Water* of 2021 (now translated into more than thirty languages).[1]

Magnason spent his early years in New England: "From the age of three until I was nine, I lived in the US, catching frogs and tadpoles in a pond behind our house" (*TW* 249). He is probably not that well-known to Thoreau enthusiasts west of the Atlantic Ocean, although the situation might have changed slightly the following year, when Magnason in June 2023 presented a lecture before the Thoreau Society on "Obedience and the Sixth Mass Extinction," where he thematized the climate crisis in the light of Thoreau's "Civil Disobedience." I will hence introduce Magnason by briefly comparing him with Thoreau.

Magnason and Thoreau are both what Thoreau would call "lovers of Nature" (*W* 238). They combine their writing on nature with quotations from classic literature and poetry, and furthermore write poems themselves. Their romantic view of nature is combined with a trust in the scientific measurements of nature. And their love of nature is accompanied by a critical interest in technical progress symbolized by "the locomotive…sounding like the scream of a hawk" in Thoreau's ears (*W* 115).[2]

They have a pinch of irony and a patriotic undertone, being members of states that had attained their independence (1776/1944) respectively a few decades prior to their birth. Thoreau moving to Walden Pond on the American Independence Day (*W* 84); Magnason establishing (with others) the ecological movement The Futureland (Framtíðarlandið) in 2006 on Iceland's Independence Day (17 June). And they both "loved so well the philosophy of India" (*W* 61), the ancient Hindu philosophy.[3]

Both naturalists are social critics as well. Thoreau is an abolitionist, Magnason a critic of neo-colonialism. They criticize what Magnason calls "overconsumption and waste" (*TW* 200) and tend to the philosophy that small is beautiful,[4] represented by Thoreau's "Simplicity, simplicity, simplicity!" (*W* 91) and him criticizing "our object being to have large farms and large crops merely" (*W* 165).

They like fishing and both connect time to water. Moreover, both have an interest in ice, Thoreau in the frozen pond and the international ice trade, Magnason in frozen water and glaciers. They delight in the observation of water and ice. The core of their thinking is the new, the young. Both see an awakening as their mission, to wake men up from their slumbering, in Thoreau's case so that they can become real men, whereas Magnason encourages them to face the current ecological challenges and prevent the end of the world.

One of the main *differences* between these two lovers of nature is the fact that Magnason is writing one and a half centuries later. Even though he too is a cheerful and optimistic character, today's ecological situation deeply worries Magnason and affects his worldview. In *Walden* we of course do not sense a grain of what Magnason calls "the anxiety that comes with worrying about the Earth's future" (*TW* 256). Social faults like war and slavery certainly did trouble Thoreau. But in the case of nature, there still did not seem to be any reason for *major* worries about its *future*.

Still, when a present-day environmentalist like Magnason examines the writing of Thoreau for sentences that resonate with his own modern worries, he does find such passages (some beyond *Walden*—which will remain our focus here). For his forementioned lecture to the Thoreau Society Magnason chose the following well-known quote from Thoreau's Journal (March 23, 1856):

> [W]hen I consider that the nobler animals have been exterminated here—the cougar—panther—lynx—wolverine wolf—bear—moose, deer, the beaver, the turkey &c &c—I cannot but feel as if I lived in a tamed &, as it were, emasculated country—Would not the motions of those larger & wilder animals have been more significant still—Is it not a maimed & imperfect nature that I am conversant with?... The whole civilized country is to some extent turned into a city, & I am that citizen, whom I pity. (OJT 20: 166–67)

Although we in this slightly self-centered reflection discern an unease concerning animal extinction in a limited geographical area,[5] it seems fair to say that Thoreau's uneasiness regarding the development of nature in Concord doesn't show clear signs of worries about *the future of nature at large*—compared to the naturalist one and a half centuries later, who fears that the earth will burn. Magnason writes: "Previously, people feared that the world's oil wells would run dry; now studies show that if we burn all our oil, the world will burn too" (*TW* 298). The burning of oil causes the Earth to warm and hence, among other things, the melting of the glaciers.

Magnason's worries about nature are primarily directed towards the future. "Scientists have shown us that the foundations of life, of Earth itself, are failing" (*TW* 8). Or to formulate it even more dramatically: "The earth and the sky are dying and so, too, is the sea" (*TW* 203). Early in *On Time and Water* Magnason is more specific.

> Over the next hundred years, there will be foundational changes in the nature of water on our Earth. Glaciers will melt away. Ocean levels will rise. Increasing global temperatures will lead to droughts and floods. The oceans will acidify to a degree not seen for fifty million years. All this will happen during the lifetime of a child who is born today and lives to be my grandmother's age, ninety five. Earth's mightiest forces have forsaken geological time and now change on a human scale. Changes that previously took a hundred thousand years now happen in one hundred. Such speed is mythological; it affects all life on Earth, affects the roots of everything we think, choose, produce and believe. (*TW* 9)

Time is out of joint, moving at an augmented speed, changing the very roots of our thinking. In the following I wish to touch upon the question of how these changes affect the way a modern naturalist, compared to Thoreau one and a half centuries earlier, thinks about time and the nature of water, including its frostier forms known as snow and ice. It goes without saying that the differences between Magnason and Thoreau on these subjects are considerable. Let us demonstrate these with a few examples.

Thoreau wrote at a time when no one was thinking seriously "about the way humanity is changing the atmosphere's composition" since he and his contemporaries still had not experienced big scale "human-made climate disasters" (*TW* 61, 205), to use the words of Magnason. Thoreau occasionally uses words that might sound concerning to modern ears, for instance when he speaks of "us who live in a climate of so great extremes" (*W* 303). But obviously he does not mean what we most often do when using them nowadays.

Before limiting the perspective to water in its different forms, let us raise one example of their common attitude towards nature in general, i.e., their critique of those viewing nature under the sole perspective of its market value. In *Walden* we find a critical remark about the farmer who measures cranberries "by the bushel and the dollar only" (*W* 238). Earlier in the same work we find the critique of a man

> who would carry the landscape, who would carry his God, to market, if he could get any thing for him; who goes to market *for* his god as it is; on whose farm nothing grows free, whose fields bear no crops, whose meadows no flowers, whose trees no fruits, but dollars; who loves not the beauty of his fruits, whose fruits are not ripe for him till they are turned to dollars. (*W* 196)

And speaking of two ponds in his area Thoreau writes: "They are too pure to have a market value" (*W* 199).

> In the documentary version of his prior book *Dreamland*, Magnason asks the following pecuniary question: "how much is a mountain worth? Two billion? Twenty billion?"[6] In his more recent *On Time and Water* he writes: For "the prevailing discourse…nature is merely an untapped *resource*" (*TW* 58). From Magnason's perspective, on the other hand, the Kárahnjúkar area in East Iceland (part of the largest wilderness in Europe)—which was flooded for the building of the country's largest hydroelectric dam that fuels an American

aluminum factory—was "fifty square kilometers of beauty" (*TW* 58). In other words,

> almost everything that was beautiful and sacred in Iceland's highlands was at risk of being dammed, exploded or drowned in order to sell cheap energy to multinational producers. The possibility that nature could be something higher, something more exalted, something beyond definition and even 'holy'—in our time, that isn't considered a valid argument. (*TW* 58)

To Magnason, nature is not holy in the sense that it is the creation of God but rather because it is sacred to the Icelandic nation and part of the "nature-centred nationalism that can be traced back to Iceland's 19th century Romantic movements."[7] In *Dreamland,* Magnason appeals to the holiness of Icelandic nature, a view that he presumes is shared by most other Icelanders: "The beauty of Iceland lies at the heart of our image of the country and the way this nation perceives itself."[8] Still, this did not prevent the building of a hydroelectric dam in the highlands.

Whereas Magnason mostly discusses water in a troubling context, to Thoreau the pond, the lower heaven, symbolically connected to eternity, is "full of hope" (*W* 312). It "rises and falls" (*W* 180), and there are no signs of concern that the future will bring a *permanent* imbalance.

> This same summer the pond has begun to fall again. It is remarkable that this fluctuation, whether periodical or not, appears thus to require many years for its accomplishment. I have observed one rise and a part of two falls, and I expect that a dozen or fifteen years hence the water will again be as low as I have ever known it. (*W* 181)

A pond is indeed a vulnerable ecosystem. "The largest pond is as sensitive to atmospheric changes as the globule of mercury in its tube" (*W* 302). But this sensitivity to atmospheric alteration is nothing to be concerned about. Even a possible flood and the potential loss of animal life is no reason to worry *about the future*. "The life in us is like the water in the river. It may rise this year higher than man has ever known it, and flood the parched uplands; even this may be the eventful year, which will drown out all our muskrats" (*W* 332–333). This would only be an occasional happening in a cyclical time, like the ups and downs of our inner selves.

Thoreau thinks not only about water from the perspective of the present, or in the frame of a few years. He thinks in centuries as well, but it is with water as with most other themes. Thoreau mainly thinks backwards in time rather than into the far future, as when he comments: "It was not always dry land where we dwell. I see far inland the banks which the stream anciently washed, before science began to record its freshets" (*W* 333).

Regarding the pond, Thoreau speculates about whether the conclusions he draws from its measurement could also apply to other forms of water. "Who knows but this hint would conduct to the deepest part of the ocean as well as of a pond or puddle?" (*W* 289). Magnason, on the other hand, lives in a time when the future of the ocean is worrisome.

> Ocean acidification is one of the largest unique geological events that the Earth has undergone in the last fifty million years. And it introduces another concept to which we connect poorly: time itself. Although time is properly called linear, imagining that the ocean will change more in the next hundred years than it has in the last fifty million years is a challenge. (*TW* 241)

In *Walden* Thoreau rarely thinks on such a timescale, mostly in not much more than a millennium: "The water laves the shore as it did a thousand years ago" (*W* 186). He does though think of how the "Concord River…in some other geological period…may have flowed" (*W* 194) and reflects on things that might "become a puzzle to future geologists" (*W* 305). But when Thoreau is thinking drastically in millions this is more likely to happen when he is contrasting the genius to the masses: "The millions are awake enough for physical labor; but only one in a million is awake enough for effective intellectual exertion, only one in a hundred millions to a poetic or divine life" (*W* 90).

Let us now move the focus from water to its frozen form, ice. In *Walden* we read: "Ice is an interesting subject for contemplation" (*W* 297). Describing his observation on a glacier in Iceland Magnason writes:

> I lay down on the cold ice and put my ear to a narrow crevasse that seemed a whole eternity deep, though only a few inches wide. The ice in the wound was as clear as crystal. I looked at the veins and bubbles in the body of the glacier, which created a strange three-dimensional feeling. I heard how the water gushed far down in the quivering space like a dark bass, water dancing somewhere deep

> down at the bottom, like a giant xylophone, a rock harp, an ice harp. The glacier's swansong. (*TW* 186)

Like Thoreau, Magnason is interested in Hindu culture and the river "known as Ganges, India's mother herself. Here, for the first time, I encounter the holy water that springs from the frozen teats of Audhumla in the Heaven Mountains" (*TW* 284). According to the "Nordic mythology, the world begins with the cow Audhumla, a cow created from hoarfrost. From her teats come four milk rivers which feed the world" (*TW* 98). Magnason is telling this cosmogonical story to the Dalai Lama, whom he visited in his exile in Dharamshala, India, after having interviewed him the year before in his own hometown, Reykjavik.[9] In Thoreau's case the circulation between Walden Pond and Himalayan India differs somewhat from Magnason, who takes the Nordic cosmogonical philosophy with him to visit the spiritual leader in India. Still, like Magnason, Thoreau relates ice to spiritual India.

> Thus it appears that the sweltering inhabitants of Charleston and New Orleans, of Madras and Bombay and Calcutta, drink at my well. In the morning I bathe my intellect in the stupendous and cosmogonal philosophy of the Bhagvat Geeta....The pure Walden water is mingled with the sacred water of the Ganges. (*W* 297–298)

The circulation Thoreau is referring to here is the export route of the New England ice trade, using among other sources Walden Pond. Here Thoreau has an unusually global perspective on a natural phenomenon. But the significant difference versus Magnason is that Thoreau's global aspect here is less linked to global nature issues than to global trade. Thoreau is quite fascinated by the frozen water trade. He relates the story when "the ice-men were at work here in '46–7" (*W* 292). They enrich Thoreau with their speculations on the waterflow in the pond while their work on "the skin...of Walden Pond" (*W* 294) does not permanently alter it.[10]

> Though the woodchoppers have laid bare first this shore and then that, and the Irish have built their sties by it, and the railroad has infringed on its border, and the ice-men have skimmed it once, it is itself unchanged, the same water which my youthful eyes fell on; all the change is in me." (*W* 192–193)

The formation of ice enables Thoreau to conduct new studies of the pond. Like Magnason on the more "thick-skinned" (*W* 302) glacier, Thoreau is on the ice, looking down at the bottom: "The first ice is especially interesting and perfect, being hard, dark, and transparent, and affords the best opportunity that ever offers for examining the bottom where it is shallow" (*W* 246). Furthermore, ice gives Thoreau a new perspective on the surrounding landscape. "When the ponds were firmly frozen, they afforded not only new and shorter routes to many points, but new views from their surfaces of the familiar landscape around them" (*W* 271). Regarding ice itself, Thoreau compares its different colors, the Walden ice being blue, the Cambridge ice white (*W* 325). To the environmentally troubled Magnason the water running at the bottom of the fading glacier sounded like an ice harp; at night Thoreau listens to the ice booming: "I also heard the whooping of the ice in the pond, my great bed-fellow in that part of Concord, as if it were restless in its bed and would fain turn over, were troubled with flatulency and bad dreams" (*W* 272).

Ice does not trouble Thoreau. He measures and examines it for the enjoyment of it, having no reason to expect that the measured numbers could in any way be troublesome. A century and a half later Magnason, on the other hand, probably seldom reads a study on frozen water where the numbers are not worrying. In *Walden* we do find sentences which might be concerning if they came from Magnason's pen, like: "We go on dating from Cold Fridays and Great Snows; but a little colder Friday, or greater snow, would put a period to man's existence on the globe" (*W* 254). This speculation of Thoreau's is not really meant as an apocalyptic scenario, and accordingly did not scare his contemporaries as plausible or imminent.

By way of contrast, Magnason's relation to ice, as his connection to water, is predominantly troubled. Thoreau is interested in ice, the ice trade, transportation of ice. Magnason likewise pays attention to the movement of ice, its melting, caused mainly by industry. Thoreau is fascinated by this amazing movement, whereas Magnason is alarmed. The latter is less interested in the first ice of the season than in the end of ice, the consequence of global warming that could put a period to man's existence on the globe. Magnason's concern with ice comes primarily through his interest in glaciers. And he is not only associated with glaciers as a common Icelander, his connection runs in the family, through time. In his climate change book with a personal touch, Magnason tells us that his grandparents were associates in the Icelandic glaciological society and took their honeymoon on a glacier. To Magnason "[g]laciers are frozen manuscripts that tell stories just like tree circles" (*TW* 179). These scripts are melting away, and Magnason has already started his work as an undertaker.

Although Magnason seldom blurs the difference between man and nature, the way Thoreau poetically does (as e.g. when the ice becomes his bedfellow), he describes his emotion following the flooding of a large wilderness area through the Kárahnjúkar dam in Iceland's eastern highlands as "the death of a friend" (*TW* 60). A decade later Magnason once again finds himself mourning nature.

> In the summer of 2019, I was given the strange task of writing a memorial for the Okjökull glacier.... I wondered who I was addressing with the words on the plaque; I wondered at the absurdity of the task. How do you say goodbye to a glacier? In the end I came up with this: Ok is the first Icelandic glacier to lose its status as a glacier. In the next 200 years, all our glaciers are expected to follow the same path. This monument acknowledges that we know what is happening and what needs to be done. Only you know if we did it. (*TW* 176)

Whereas Thoreau wakes up every morning, ready to experience nature from a new angle, Magnason is more in the mode of saying farewell to vanishing nature. He sees nature to a lesser extent from the perspective of the following day, than from the standpoint of the next century. Magnason tries to stay active and optimistic, even though the melting of glaciers is alarming. "According to scientists' predictions about global temperature increases, ocean levels will rise by between thirty centimeters and one meter this century due to the melting of glaciers and the swelling of the seas" (*TW* 60–61). Whereas this is worrisome to a lover of nature, from an economic standpoint it seems to some like a positive development. Magnason is frustrated when former United States Secretary of State Mike Pompeo talks "about the melting of the Arctic ice as 'a new business opportunity'" (*TW* 209).

Let us now move the focus away from the combination of time and water (ice) and concentrate more on time as such. From Thoreau's perspective the future is mainly tomorrow. The day after tomorrow and the other days to follow are, from today's standpoint, secondary since tomorrow is a clean sheet for a fresh start, a never-ending second chance.

> A single gentle rain makes the grass many shades greener. So our prospects brighten on the influx of better thoughts. We should be blessed if we lived in the present always, and took advantage of every accident that befell us, like the grass which confesses the influence of the slightest dew that falls on it; and did not spend our time in atoning for the neglect of past opportunities, which we call doing our duty. We loiter in winter while it is already spring. In a pleasant spring morning all men's sins are forgiven. (*W* 314)

Thoreau does not mourn the past, he lives in the present and mostly looks optimistically into the near future, as redemption is always possible the following morning. For Magnason and the climate-crisis generation, the possibility of forgiving our climate sins, and those of our forefathers, does not exist. What Thoreau calls the "pardon which he [God] freely offers to all" (*W* 315) is not there for the modern environmentalist. God might forgive us our sins, but He will not repair manmade destruction of nature through forgiveness. He does not offer us a fresh start; there is no new beginning through a new day or a new spring. The consequences of our environmental misdeeds cannot be undone, but at best slowed down.

Thoreau does not only contemplate the following morning or next spring on Walden Pond. Occasionally he also ponders the morning on a bigger timescale, mostly going back in time. "Perhaps on that spring morning when Adam and Eve were driven out of Eden Walden Pond was already in existence" (*W* 179). Thoreau does not seem to consider much about the people who will be using the land in the far future, but he repeatedly reflects on former inhabitants of the land, different generations, nations, races, native people. So

> the first who came to this well have left some trace of their footsteps. I have been surprised to detect encircling the pond...a narrow shelf-like path in the steep hill-side,...as old probably as the race of man here, worn by the feet of aboriginal hunters, and still from time to time unwittingly trodden by the present occupants of the land. (*W* 179–180)

And although here, as elsewhere, his attention is set on former than future inhabitants, we find in *Walden* a few sentences like the one where he speaks about the "ornamented grounds of villas which will one day be built here" (*W* 180). Even though there have been some changes in the landscape around Walden Pond through the years and Thoreau expects changes in the future, his attitude towards the pond to some degree symbolizes his thoughts about nature and its relation to mankind in time. The pond has "[s]ky water. It needs no fence. Nations come and go without defiling it" (*W* 188).

Whereas Thoreau might think more about the past than the far future, he has higher hopes for the future generations than the past ones. While he is skeptical about us learning from the older generation and encourages us to go our own way, Thoreau has a positive attitude towards the new, including future generations. Speaking of the bean-field and his own youth he writes: "a new growth is rising all around, preparing another aspect for new infant eyes" (*W* 156). A few pages later, Thoreau adds: "Why concern ourselves so much about our beans for seed, and not be concerned at all about a new generation of men?" (*W* 164)

Compared to Thoreau, Magnason has a rather positive attitude towards the elder generations, including when he is seeking solutions to problems of the future generations. "The solutions partly involve what our grandmas always told us: eat everything on our plates, hand down siblings' clothes, darn socks, practise frugality" (*TW* 306). A way of thinking not only echoing Magnason's grandmother's but also Thoreau's advocacy "sometimes to be content with less" (*W* 36). On the whole though, Magnason's thoughts circulate more around the grandchildren than the grandmother, rather around the future and the future generations, than the past and past generations. The problem with the future is not merely the climate crisis but also that we, and the democratic capitalism we live in, have difficulties thinking about the time after our time.

> We expect functioning governments to restrict an individual's freedom to cause others harm; it is a fallacy of democracy if the system does not allow us to think decades into the future in this respect. Business interests and human comfort have been seen as more important than the ocean, the atmosphere and all the world's grandchildren—for all time. (*TW* 247–248)

Thoreau visualized a "new generation of men" (*W* 164), new individuals who would realize themselves, become real men. From Magnason's perspective, because of the climate crisis, the generation of today must put self-realization on hold while they try to save the world.

> Because of climate chaos, an entire generation is being asked not what they want to become but what they need to become. That situation is actually not entirely negative: a whole generation will feel it has a role, a higher purpose. Those who want to try to "find themselves" might need to postpone their soul-searching for thirty years while the world is saved. (*TW* 300)

Since from Magnason's perspective the focus is mainly on the endangered future and less on the here and now, tomorrow, or next spring, Thoreau's immediate experiences of nature mostly recede into the background for Magnason, with a few exceptions. "We are further from nature than ever before, if nature can be measured in the amount of time a child spends playing out in the open air" (*TW* 297). Nature must be saved for the grandchildren of the future, and at the same time the child of the here and now, that exists today and not sometime in the future, needs its experiences in nature and the opportunity to realize itself. It deserves the chance to experience the sky-water of today, even though the water in the sea might die tomorrow.

Since Iceland is a barren country, there is no life in the woods for Thoreau's modern counterpart. Still, Magnason's Iceland is where Nordic mythology was written down, including the description of Ragnarök: "The Sun goes dark, the lands sink, the shining stars disappear from the skies, the great ash will burn and fierce heat will lick the skies....A shiver ran down my spine: this was Ragnarök itself, the end of the world as described in the original prophecy in the poem 'Völuspá'" (*TW* 14), the best known poem of "the Poetic Edda,... the greatest treasure in all of Iceland, perhaps even the whole of Northern Europe" (*TW* 13).[11] The Poetic Edda also includes the description of Yggdrasil, the sacred tree that holds the world together and survives Ragnarök to become the foundation of a new beginning. It seems appropriate to close this comparison of Magnason's *On Time and Water* and Thoreau's *Walden* by tying this old Norse pagan myth loosely to an alleged North European protestant reference. The sentence attributed to Martin Luther seems to us to unify Thoreau's high regard for the present, and his optimism for tomorrow, with Magnason's future worries and his awareness of what needs to be done: "If I knew the world ended tomorrow, I would plant an apple tree today."[12]

Works Cited

Hennig, Reinhard, "Postcolonial Ecology: An Ecocritical Reading of Andri Snær Magnason's Dreamland." In *The Postcolonial North Atlantic*, edited by Lill-Ann Körber and Ebbe Volquardsen, 105–126. Berlin: Nordeuropa-Institut der Humboldt Universität, 2014.

Jónsson, Marteinn Sindri and David G. Kristinsson, "'How Much is a Mountain Worth?' Artistic Critique of the Icelandic State's Sellout of the 'Shitlandic Highlands' to a Foreign Multinational." In *Plurale Verschränkungen. Zur Entdifferenzierung von Kunst, Politik, Wissenschaft und Wirtschaft,* edited by Marie Rosenkranz and Nina Tessa Zahner. Berlin: Springer Verlag (forthcoming).

Magnason, Andri Snær. *Dreamland: A Self-help Manual for a Frightened Nation.* Translated by Nicholas Jones. London: Citizen Press, 2008.

———. *On Time and Water.* Translated by Lytton Smith. London: Serpent's Tail, 2021.

Schneider, Richard J. *Thoreau's Sense of Place: Essays in American Environmental Writing.* Iowa City: University of Iowa Press, 2000.

CHAPTER 3

"THE TIME IS ALWAYS NOW": ON VIKTOR IV'S LIFELONG DIALOGUE WITH THOREAU

Henrik Otterberg

On Friday, April 27, 1951, a tall, able-bodied young man with close-set eyes and intense gaze walked the perimeter path of Walden Pond. Crew-cut, blond and with powerful hands, he had been a champion swimmer in his high-school days in his native New York City. He had served as a lifeguard during a few summers, alternating with working in a liquor shop and ice cream factory. The afternoon was sunny and balmy, with mere sprinkles of cloud achingly high up. Carrying a small frameless backpack, the man could easily be mistaken for a swimmer seeking a more secluded spot from which to wade in than offered by the main beach. But as it happened, he was not there for exercise or relaxation. His strapped bag contained a wax-cloth wrap of sandwiches, a thermos, a blanket, and a box of matches. It also held a well-thumbed anthology of Thoreau's writings.[1] The book's original binding was fortified by a home-styled, navy-blue, textured vinyl wrapping, the spine smeared with a stripe of bold white paint. Upon this, in coarse, capital letters, was written: **H.D.T.** The text-block edges were grimy from frequent handling, and several signatures leaned out to varying degrees, apparently on account of its owner's ambitious grangerizing. Inside were glued a fold-out, full-color tourist map of Cape Cod facing the title-page of Thoreau's eponymous book; a nineteenth-century railroad engraving; and various *Thoreau Society Bulletin* snippets. Also added were a hand-written Thoreau bibliography as well as detailed notes toward further reading in Thoreau's favored classical authors. Among several loose inserts were reviews of Thoreau's works, while a back flap housed personal letters and photographs. Furthermore, a free front endpaper held a full transcription in tidy hand of Robert Frost's "The Road Not Taken," while ample running commentary to Thoreau's texts was added in the margins. The latter were frequently underlined in ink and pencil, as well as quote- and section-marked with red crayon arrows. Clearly this was not a random visit. It was a pilgrimage.

The man reclined in the shade, resting his back against a broad pine tree up the steep slope toward Emerson's Cliff, careful to choose a dry bunch of yesteryear's leaves as his pillow. The sandwiches tasted good, the coffee welcome. As the shadows gradually lengthened toward evening and the air became crisp, the man watched the remaining swimmers and fishermen exit the water by turns, while the main beach steadily emptied of visitors. Eventually he rose and made his way down toward the perimeter path again, continuing the long way round toward Thoreau's house site. When he reached it, Walden's surface was placid and silent. He placed a small red stone from his pocket on the nearby cairn, then left his sandals behind and made his way down to Thoreau's cove, anthology in hand, to savor the cool clayey sand under his feet. On a whim, he opened the book, bent down and pressed it distinctly like a stamp against the moist surface. Then he added a note in ink beside the mottled portions of the page-spread: "Mud + Water of Walden Pond," along with the hallowed day's date.[2] Wrapping his blanket around his shoulders, he made his way back to the house site, gathered twigs and a few dry branches from the nearby ground, and kindled a small fire abutting the cairn.

The next morning he rose early, and went down to the cove to quench his thirst. He felt a gentle breeze ruffling the water and saw a pair of geese crash-land in their typical brash fashion, disturbing a group of mallards scouring the shallows among the waterfront reeds. A gull up in the firmament momentarily gyred toward the commotion, but changed course once it spied him and sailed on. Then he returned to smother the lingering embers with sprinkles of soil before dousing them with water from his thermos. In his other hand, he had saved two blackened twigs, and next sat down once more with his Thoreau anthology, accompanied by the fading hiss from the dying embers. Flipping the book's pages to the *Walden* chapter "House-Warming," he stopped at the spread containing Thoreau's famous poem "Smoke." There he drew undulating grey bands with his makeshift, blunt charcoal pencils, akin to rising smoke, to visually accompany Thoreau's words. Turning to the next spread, he sketched Thoreau's house and its wooded environs as he remembered them from the iconography, again with bold strokes, adding curls of smoke ascending from Thoreau's chimney.[3]

Two days later, on April 29 and back in New York City, the same man returned to his anthology to summarize his experience. Under the heading "Walden visited 104 years later," he wrote that "the pond no longer enjoys the solitude it afforded Henry. A superhighway to Boston roars only 300 yds from the hut site. A public bathhouse sprawls along the entire east shore. The place is quite littered with picknickers' and fishermen's trash. Otherwise I am certain the pond is still the same in every respect as the 1847 Walden. It is a very lovely pond & must be seen before the book can be best appreciated."[4]

Over the next several years, and likely throughout his life, the Thoreau anthology and especially *Walden* remained a lodestone to him. Its pages eventually came to resemble palimpsests, with their mass of notes, underlined passages, and arrows made with different pens. Its owner would in time mark its lower title page "Copy III / Personal Copy / not to be loaned out" in black ink, while its penciled superscript read "ORA NON OLIT / BUT FREEDOM IS SWEETEST"—the latter a combination of Spanish and Latin to the effect that "Gold does not smell." This while his own focus would remain on shaping a life as he saw fit, unencumbered by conventional expectation or ambition. He was born in 1929, the son of immigrants to the USA, his father German, rising to become a senior manager at the Eastman KODAK company, his mother Greek, a dedicated housewife and homemaker. His full name, as he carefully noted and dated it beside on the front endpaper of his Thoreau anthology, was Walter Karl Glück, February 2, 1951. His surname was German for "happiness" or "good fortune," to compare with the English "lucky." And so he was, whether by nominative determinism or not, as he was endowed with supportive parents with the means to accommodate an idiosyncratic youth well into adulthood. He would also embrace a positive, life-affirming philosophy throughout his life and career.

As his early private-school report cards attest, Glück, who early on went by Walter, later and at his own preference by Karl, was a highly intelligent but non-conformist child, immersed in his own projects rather than the curriculum, an outsider from the outset. Athletically gifted, he eventually enrolled at the College of Journalism & Communication in

[Figure 3.1]

228 THE WRITINGS OF THOREAU

ment, and warms that, instead of robbing himself, makes that his bed, in which he can move about divested of more cumbrous clothing, maintain a kind of summer in the midst of winter, and by means of windows even admit the light, and with a lamp lengthen out the day. Thus he goes a step or two beyond instinct, and saves a little time for the fine arts. Though, when I had been exposed to the rudest blasts a long time, my whole body began to grow torpid, when I reached the genial atmosphere of my house I soon recovered my faculties and prolonged my life. But the most luxuriously housed has little to boast of in this respect, nor need we trouble ourselves to speculate how the human race may be at last destroyed. It would be easy to cut their threads any time with a little sharper blast from the north. We go on dating from Cold Fridays and Great Snows; but a little colder Friday, or greater snow would put a period to man's existence on the globe.

The next winter I used a small cooking-stove for economy, since I did not own the forest; but it did not keep fire so well as the open fireplace. Cooking was then, for the most part, no longer a poetic, but [illegible]. It will soon be forgotten, in these days of stoves, that we used to roast potatoes in the ashes, after the Indian fashion. The stove not only took up room and scented the house, but it concealed the fire, and I felt as if I had lost a companion. You can always see a face in the fire. The laborer, looking into it at evening, purifies his thoughts of the dross and earthiness which they have accumulated during the day. But I could no longer sit and look into the fire, and the pertinent words of a poet recurred to me with new force.—

"Never, bright flame, may be denied to me
Thy dear, life imaging, close sympathy.
What but my hopes shot upward e'er so bright?
What but my fortunes sunk so low in night?
Why art thou banished from our hearth and hall,

WALDEN 229

Thou who art welcomed and beloved by all?
Was thy existence then too fanciful
For our life's common light, who are so dull?
Did thy bright gleam mysterious converse hold
With our congenial souls? secrets too bold?

Well, we are safe and strong, for now we sit
Beside a hearth where no dim shadows flit,
Where nothing cheers nor saddens, but a fire
Warms feet and hands—nor does to more aspire;
By whose compact utilitarian heap
The present may sit down and go to sleep,
Nor fear the ghosts who from the dim past walked,
And with us by the unequal light of the old wood fire talked."

[Figure 3.2]

Gainesville, Florida. Upon graduation in 1954, his college yearbook described him as follows: "He was everywhere. Doing things nobody else would do. /---/ He was a non-conformist if ever there was one. /---/ Karl Gluck was Karl Gluck."[5] With his studies completed, he felt a keen urge to expand his horizons, and for five years became a globetrotting itinerant. He obtained his seaman's papers in New Orleans and worked on a freight ship to Europe. On his maiden voyage he noted in his Thoreau anthology, below the *Walden* juncture where Thoreau plays with the concept of supernumerary sleepers, that "I travel as a supernumerary on the S.S. Liberty Flag / means—free passage but to possible damage claims."[6] The book evidently never left him, even as he returned to bicycle across Mexico, Peru, and Ecuador, sending photos and letters home to family and friends. Continually marking, commenting, and dating his readings of Thoreau passages, Glück eventually signed on to a freighter bound for Asia across the Pacific. The tentative idea was to become a freelance journalist and photographer, with photography clearly taking the upper hand. Once having reached Shanghai, Glück signed off and traveled for months by bicycle in China and Japan, also working for a time for the CARE organization in South Korea. He became skilled as a portrait photographer of people in everyday settings, his appearance an odd combination of imposing frame and steady eye, his manner ever softspoken and affably curious.

In the spring of 1961, having returned to the USA during the preceding winter, Glück set his sights on Europe. In France he bought a small Renault Estafette truck that became his mobile home, and with this he traversed the continent's patched quilt of countries, venturing as far as Scandinavia and the Soviet Union. For a stint he also tried to make a living as a photographer in Hamburg, where parts of his father's family still lived. Yet by the same autumn, after an extended period of perambulation, he fell hard for Amsterdam. As his old friend Fred Ward put it, "the wanderlust was suddenly over. /---/ He had found, for what I felt the first time in his life, a home. Amsterdam was it and he settled in like into an old shoe. The city, the people, the atmosphere and the encompassing art history all embraced Karl like a comfortable suit. There was little doubt that he would remain in Holland for the rest of his days."[7]

Glück got by renting various simple apartments and set up shop as a plein-air portrait photographer, adding humorous slogans ["Used Photographer," "Fijne Fotos 2.95 p. kilo" ("Fine Photos at 2.95 per kilogram")[8]] while also kindling a passion for customized rubber stamps, which he commissioned from local artisan Vernier in his shop on Oude Spiegel Straat. Suddenly, however, late in 1963, with the assassination of U.S. president Kennedy, Walter decided to give up photography outright. Not being there for the event and recognizing that his craft likely demanded constant travel if he were to press on, he realized he wished for something else. A calmer, more deliberate pace of artistic work, with a firm anchor in a specific place. Hence he decided, in early 1964, with funds squirreled away from photographs sold over the years to a gallery in New York City, to purchase a *tjalke,* or barge, and to make this vessel his new floating home. The *tjalke* was decommissioned from commercial shipping and berthed in central Amsterdam, near the bustling old flea market on Waterlooplein. To restrict access for curious passersby and tourists, Glück deliberately made the gangplank very narrow—less than three inches wide. This in effect made his craft an island, giving him a modicum of isolation amidst the urban din while allowing him to venture out at will. Recognizing the event as a watershed, Glück renamed his vessel the *Kamakura Buddha*, in honor of the thirteenth-century bronze statue of the Buddha in the Kanagawa Prefecture of eastern coastal Japan, and also himself: he now went by the new moniker of Viktor IV. He considered April 4, 1964, his nativity as an artist, and perhaps the tripling of (6)4/4/4—hence a compound IV—was found suitable to mark his victorious emergence.[9]

Intrigued by their weathered contours, textures and shades, as well as their sheer heft, Viktor had since about a year back begun to salvage anything from 20- to 200-pound *luiken* from the Amstel River. These ranged from one to two inches thick, and he hoisted them ashore with a pike pole. Then he loaded them onto his self-fashioned cargo bicycle—which he advertised as part of what he called his SECOND QUALITY CONSTRUCTION COMPANY. He went on to dry them above deck and in the hold of the *Kamakura Buddha*, which also held driftwood and assorted wooden discards from the Amsterdam harbor. Here is how Viktor describes the *luiken* in his first vernissage catalogue, issued in February 1965. The catalogue is composed entirely in lower-case letters and employs merely rudimentary punctuation:

> 'luik' is the dutch word for a wooden ships hatch. it is my material and the direct cause of all the preceding work [as pictured in the catalogue]. before i began this work i had often wandered along the Amsterdam harbor waterfront and admired these extraordinary large pieces of driftwood. i learned that often they are from fifty to a hundred years old. they are used to cover the decks of the long, black, iron cargo boats that ply the inland waterways of northern europe. a hundred, two hundred, three hundred seasons of weather and rough useage renders the once sturdy hatch to a battered condition till the time when the captain finally decides it is worthless—and throws it overboard. the luik is thus released, finished, drifting from one corner of the harbor to another ahead of shifting winds. the luik is now 'havens vuil' or harbor dirt and if found is hauled out by a city maintenance flatboat and burned. if it escapes the flatboat it eventually waterlogs – and sinks. and so it has been for a long time, but early in 1964 i began to collect some of these luiken and in april i began painting upon them. some of the results were startling right from the very beginning. startling but not really surprising for the luik, the thing-in-itself, has a personality, a history, is beautiful—and the artist tries to build from this already-existent beginning to give it a more meaningful expression. the resulting finished works seem to almost defy classification, are almost a new art form often combining techniques common to painting, sculpture, and etching. /---/ what an intense and sustained experience working with this remarkable material has been. spared from the city incinerator or an eventual sinking the luiken as finished paintings seem almost grateful for their new life. if i speak as if these pieces of wood are alive i only repeat myself, they are alive and always have been. my work is only an attempt to give them greater meaning as vehicles of a new form of artistic expression. in this i think, i, we, have been successful.[10]

Viktor called these works his Ikons, and he produced a staggering 170 of them by his own count during his first eleven months of newfound artistic activity. They strike many viewers, then as now, as sizeable or even massive palimpsests. Their rough and often worn-down, scraped and pockmarked surfaces may furthermore recall the weathered sails on the cargo wagons of the locomotive thundering past Thoreau at Walden Pond, as described in the "Sounds" chapter of *Walden*. That is, they indicate their own natural and nautical history, while also—with Viktor's later contributions—a new incarnation as sacred artworks. They are properly named Ikons—Greek for "images" in general, while in Christian iconography connoting religious import—in the sense that most reveal a storied past intertwined with a textured present, while some also gesture toward mythological, ageless truths. Viktor's commentary on the *luiken* that formed his Ikons is also tangential to Thoreau's following gambit in "Sounds":

> When my floor was dirty, I rose early, and, setting all my furniture out of doors on the grass, bed and bedstead making but one budget, dashed water on the floor, and sprinkled white sand from the pond on it, and then with a broom scrubbed it clean and white.... It was pleasing to see my whole household effects out on the grass, making a little pile like a gypsy's pack, and my three-legged table, from which I did not remove the books and pen and ink, standing amid the pines and hickories. They seemed glad to get out themselves, and as if unwilling to be brought in. I was sometimes tempted to stretch an awning over them and take my seat there. It was worth the while to see the sun shine on these things, and hear the free wind blow on them; so much more interesting most familiar objects look out of doors than in the house. A bird sits on the next bough, life-everlasting grows under the table, and blackberry vines run round its legs; pine cones, chestnut burs, and strawberry leaves are strewn about. It looked as if this was the way these forms came to be transferred to our furniture, to tables, chairs, and bedsteads,– because they once stood in their midst. (*W* 112–13).

This seemingly ludic measure had a serious undertone, however, forming part of a larger quest by Thoreau to convey his cherished Nature as faithfully as possible, perhaps even toward an absolute language he could not hope—in the final analysis—to attain.[11] Viktor for his part also ventures that his salvaged and transformed *luiken* are grateful for their change of context. Their life is sustained, kindled even, and they emerge akin to butterflies unfurling out of their chrysalis pods from a prior larva state. The artist working with them acts at most as a midwife, inspiring a maieutic rebirth toward clearer, fuller expression of what was innate all along.

Viktor proceeded to paint his Ikons with naively stylized human figures, animals, or objects, often reduced to their most basic, geometric forms. The Ikons' varnished surfaces simultaneously gave them a playful, billboard-like, even circus-ad allure and gleam. The underlying tar and oil affected the colors Viktor employed, his lead paints blending congenially with the rough shades of the ship: whites becoming ivory, yellows the vanillas and browns of withered leaves; all given an instantaneous patina by the wizened wood of the old *luiken*. One Ikon, recalling an enormous ticket stub, read: "PLEASE ADMIT ONE ELEPHANT"; another, captioned "OLIFANT & RAJAH," showed a star-studded elephant ridden by an Indian lord against a glimmering night sky, explained as part of "THE NEW COSMOLOGICAL CONSTELLATION CHARTS." As in this instance, Viktor's Ikons were often supplemented by stenciled, curious mottoes or humorous descriptions of the scenes involved. An example portraying our own star's luminous rings was captioned: "I WOULD MEET YOUR EYE TO THANK YOU SUN, BUT YOUR COMPLETE GENEROSITY DOES NOT ALLOW THAT"; another, depicting the Queen of Spades in full splendor, "GOD IS MUCH TOO GOOD"; yet another, again of our gracious granter of light, "WHO CAN BETRAY THE SUN/OR FRAME HIS FLIGHT…." Yet others, more granular, rendered bird's-eye views of particular Amsterdam streets; of chessboards at play; of a New York City subway line with stations "WHICH I RODE HUNDREDS OF TIMES 1933–1959." Furthermore, a rounded Ikon formed a half-dollar with the ironic motto "IN GOD WE TRUST * SOMETIMES," with the telling addition "PECUNIA NON OLET."[12]

From Viktor's catalogue description of his Ikons and related works in wood, one also gathers that his beachcombing was not for found objects *sensu stricto*, but for ones in which he sensed at once a compressed history and potential transformation into new life through his agency. Summing up his practical philosophy of recycling a decade later, Viktor described his habitual process as "one of becoming and leaving behind and not wanting and working with what is about and freely available namely the waste materials of the normal society and doing with what is possible and then maintaining it and building and maintaining becoming and enduring."[13] Over the next twenty years and more in Amsterdam, he would carefully map and navigate his urban and riparian environment akin to an intricate ecosystem, paying particular attention to possibilities of repurposing its flotsam and jetsam; its leftovers; its flea-market offerings and discarded scraps. Living for many years without running water or electricity, a daily

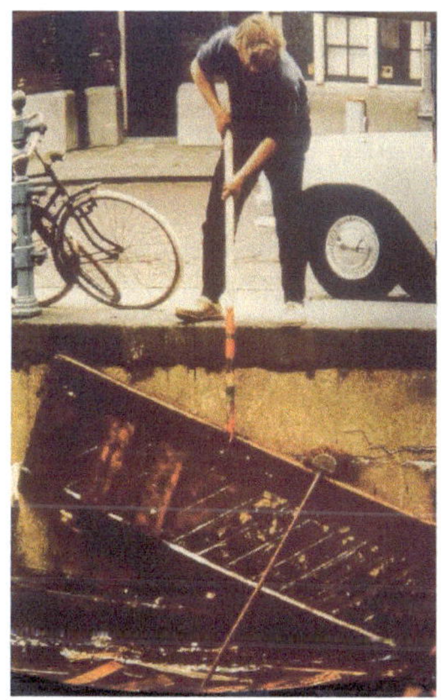

[Figure 3.3]

[Figure 3.4]

chore for Viktor involved carrying pails of water from a public tap onboard his *tjalke*, supplemented during winters by forays on behalf of the ship's stove, seeking wooden planks at city trash stations and branches to dry from the Amstel. Containers were considered gifts, and backyards at the time were seldom cordoned off, offering more opportunities. Befriending local restauranteurs, café- and bar-owners, Viktor was often enough offered unsold meals and snacks during his habitual early-morning forays. As for clothing, Viktor relied on cheap Waterlooplein offerings, which he tended to seek at closing time most days, mending his clothes as wear and tear took their toll. He also saved on grooming by letting his hair and beard flow free.

Viktor was 36 years old when he held his first Amsterdam exhibition of his Ikons in 1965. It was a resounding success. "I feel like a tiger riding an elephant!" he exclaimed. He was less concerned with the proceeds than with the new creative energy he felt coursing through him. Viktor also penned a telling comment to the inside cover-leaf of his exhibition catalog. It read: "this first catalogue is dedicated to henry david thoreau, who some how brought me to amsterdam. the rest of the trip i will make on my own." As we shall see, this would prove a truth with qualification. While Viktor's life in many external ways differed significantly from Thoreau's, there were many internal correspondences which remained resonant with him. With the favorable reception of his Amsterdam exhibit Viktor felt emboldened to seek representation back home. A well-received exhibition followed in early 1966 at the Lefebvre Gallery in New York City. Viktor used the proceeds from the combined sales to invest in a larger vessel: an 80-foot, 110-tonne, iron-hulled Amstel barge called the *Berendina Fennegina*. This had more space in the hold to house his raw materials, workshop and studio, as well as kitchen and living quarters (a chamber pot had to suffice by way of toilet). One of the first things Viktor did once the move was accomplished, was to fashion a proud new name-plaque for his ship, in white-washed wood and vivid, black-stenciled letters. He called it the *Henry David Thoreau*. Up on deck he had an axe similarly named and marked, with which to hew larger branches and planks to size before hauling them down below, for art or fuel or yet again material for furniture. By way of insulation against the ship's damp cool, he spread ample straw on all flooring, and over time arranged passable wooden insulation against the worst of the winter cold.

Viktor's further artistic career rather indicates that he never dropped his dialogue with-, or appreciation of, Thoreau. Importantly, it was a relationship and indebtedness freely acknowledged, again and again, across a range of artistic media. There seem to be no instances of anxiety of influence, in Harold Bloom's sense: in other words, no quest to self-consciously denigrate and reject the mentor, once the learning-cum-imitative period was deemed over. An example is seen with the Ikon entitled "THE WHITE CIRCLE," which shows a nondescript quadruped in its circled center. At the Ikon's lower end Viktor has stenciled the following: "AN ORIGINAL ARTIST IS NEVER HESITANT TO CREDIT A TEACHER. RECENTLY ANTON HEYBOER TAUGHT V4 TO DRAW AN ANIMAL. SO I PUT HIM IN MY WHITE CIRCLE AND THANK HIM."[14] We may compare this to Thoreau's rollercoaster friendship with Emerson. This included at least one period of severe crisis, as Thoreau came into his own furthering Emersonian ideas, but also practices and interests very much his own. In Viktor's case, his long acquaintance with Anton Heyboer, who was a few years older and already established by the time Viktor arrived on the scene, also did include several documented periods of falling out. But importantly the conflicts never spilled over to the artistic level: Viktor kept on openly and generously crediting Heyboer in his work, throughout his career.

Regarding his family life, Viktor formally remained a bachelor, although a long succession of girlfriends joined him on his barges, often for shorter stints. He had a serious relationship with a young Dutch woman, Ans IJpelaar, in the early to mid-1960s, although she opted to have an abortion once pregnant with their child, and they broke up soon afterwards. The experience traumatized Viktor to the extent that he claimed to have become celibate in its wake, although he continued to court female company on his vessels. In 1967 his mother Mary died, and he returned briefly to the USA and New York City. After the funeral, he invited his father Ferdinand to join him in Amsterdam, and even bought an old *klipper* ship for him to live on, which he baptized *The Angel of the Amstel.* Despite the brave gesture, the ensuing damp and often bitingly cold winter on the water proved too much for Glück senior. He returned to America, while keeping in contact with his adventurous son, supporting him financially when need arose. Viktor also kept in touch with his beloved maternal aunt Fani, who was enamored of Viktor and appreciated his keen sense of humor and many idiosyncrasies. She once invited him to the USA at her own expense, and also saw to some of his finances there. She regularly gifted him an expatriate subscription to *The New Yorker* and, as the 1960s turned toward a new decade, also a membership to the Thoreau Society, including then as now a subscription to the *Thoreau Society Bulletin*.

In the later 1960s, Viktor gradually abandoned the rather cumbersome Ikons in favor of what he came to call his Logbooks. These were initiated by a bulk purchase of matte, tight-fibred, cream-colored paper (slightly larger than the standard A3 format) commissioned from a local stationery shop. Upon these bespoke sheets Viktor would subsequently stamp, daub, draw, apply watercolors, print and glue, to illustrate a vast range of topics and concerns as they spontaneously occurred to him. While not a daily production, the Logbooks were precisely serialized, Viktor employing rubber stamps to designate the place (inevitably the *Henry David Thoreau*), the month number since his birth as an artist (4/64) and daily date, in addition to a wide variety of postal stamps from across the world to signal variants. Viktor would stencil out several "original copies," as he tended to designate his Logbooks, adding flourishes of different colors to the leaves, or slightly dulling or brightening their tone. While often humorous, with homespun philosophical undertones supplementing anything from quotidian happenstances to spins on well-known fables, many Logbooks also showcased Viktor's innate creativity as an industrial designer and quality controller at a remove: he would comment in detail on anything from improving the performance of water pistols to faucets over ship's tackle to electrical cord connections. One example, from March 26, 1970, is prominently stamped as forming part of "The Logbook of the Ship 'Henry David Thoreau.'" While recalling stylized tulips or poppies when viewed at a distance, it proves actually to concern a spread of matches spilled from their box, their ends blackened, arranged in neat rows, each a little different from the other in its degree of charring and withering. Viktor's printed text comments the mise-en-scène as follows: "CONSUMER REPORT: TESTED ONE BOX OF TORDENSKJOLD WOOD MATCHES. ALL FIRED AND BURNED. PERFECT PERFORMANCE. RECOMMENDED." Then, a little further down, he ruminates: "A BOX OF (48) WOOD MATCHES IS SYMBOL FOR A SMALL FOREST WHICH MAY BE CARRIED IN A PANTS POCKET." A regular smoker, Viktor was partial to this Danish brand of matches, sporting a dashing portrait of their Dano-Norwegian naval hero Peter Tordenskjold (1690–1720).

The Danish connection in 1970 is important to note, for this year marked Viktor's momentous meeting with Elizabeth Munck from Copenhagen. Married with two young daughters, while long troubled by bipolar depression and doubting her capabilities as a mother, her chance meeting with Viktor in the context of a vernissage sparked a correspondence that quickly flamed beyond friendship. Elizabeth, who would soon go by Ina, abruptly took the radical step of leaving her family in Copenhagen, to live instead with Viktor the same winter. Her husband Flemming Johansen, who was the director of the Ny Carlsberg Glyptotek Art Museum in Copenhagen and who had brought Ina and Viktor together, came to support the move. They retained a close friendship, although it was admittedly a challenge for Ina's young daughters, Julia and Sara, to be raised solely by their father. Viktor and Ina's life together would last until Viktor's accidental death in 1986, while his passing did not, as Ina later and memorably put it, end their relationship. Her arrival brought Viktor a steady companion, tending both to household chores and providing artistic support. Together they built rafts from drifting logs to accompany the *Henry David Thoreau*, which Viktor swam out to gather. Some of the rafts Viktor adorned with objects found at the nearby flea market, others he made into new workspaces—one labeled the "BRANCH OFFICE." Ina chose some to flower into floating green islets. In the end the combined area of the rafts—some fourteen in all—grew to twice the size of the *Henry David Thoreau*. Ina also arranged for swans, geese, rabbits, chickens and cats to live on the little man-made archipelago, as well as a dovecote for a pair of white pigeons they called Goodminton and Badminton. In the summer of 1976, Viktor and Ina were invited to build a raft on a pond on the grounds of the famed Louisiana Museum of Art in Humlebæk, Denmark, in the context of an exhibit on alternative architecture.

Viktor created his Logbooks in a cockpit studio in the hold of the *Henry David Thoreau*, lit by skylights during the day, and passably by a kerosene lamp at night. He sequestered himself in this private space, which he affectionately called his *organ*, where he was not to be disturbed. It was in effect a cramped studio, holding his typewriter, office and Logbook

[Figure 3.5]

[Figure 3.6]

papers, inks, glues, scissors, paints, pens, a bristling crown of brushes, a multi-tiered carousel rack of stamps (resembling a festively adorned, tapering Christmas tree)—all within his ready grasp. Furthermore a trove cutouts of magazines, cartons, and posters for collages, as well as various works-in-progress both sculptural and paper-based. Viktor also surrounded himself with labels and mottoes printed on wooden plaques and sundry implements: his typewriter had "WORDS" stenciled on its front frame, while a wide wooden cabinet opposite his seat was marked "PAPER." A little to the side was lengthier statement capped by the familiar adage "THERE IS NOTHING NEW UNDER THE SUN."

What is more, a sheet of postal stamps was thumbtacked onto the frame of the rectangular storage compartment behind the typewriter. These stamps, of a U.S. 5-cent denomination, showcased Leonard Baskin's controversial portrait of Thoreau, marking the sesquicentennial of the writer's birth in 1967. Viktor likely appreciated Baskin's decidedly scruffy-looking Thoreau, as he had himself for some time sported a bushy beard and flowing locks. As a portable companion, Viktor kept beside him a beloved, battery-powered radio, where he would regularly tune in to the BBC World Service and its classical music channel. Brahms, Haydn, Beethoven and Mozart were his particular favorites, and he would play them while seated at his *organ*, as well as up on deck when the weather allowed. He did not appreciate popular music, whether jazz, rock, or standards, and bristled at any suggestion that he was "a lazy hippie." He had hewn and fashioned nearly six hundred Ikons, and his Logbook pages would in the end number in the thousands, ballooning to even more if one counted the 'original copies.' He remained restless, productive, and creative to the last. Once asked what he would like to do in his next life, he replied: "I would like to be Mozart!"[15]

Several Logbook pages from the early 1970s evince Viktor's ongoing engagement with Thoreau. One, featured at left below, numbered #86 and dated May 7, 1971, consists of Viktor's handwritten, verbatim reproduction of Thoreau's early *Walden* passage on the common burden of arrears among his contemporaries. "It is evident to me what mean and sneaking lives many of you live…always on the limits, trying to get into business and trying to get out of debt, a very ancient slough, called by the Latins, *aes alienum*, another's brass." On the right-hand side, by way of contrast, is a Logbook page numbered #72 of March 6, 1970, consisting of a glued-in, typewritten stencil copy of a letter to prominent Thoreau scholar Walter Harding. At the top Viktor has drawn and colored a favorite motif, a personalized sun, appended by the following handwritten text as copied from Thoreau's Journal: "Sunday, 18 February 1838, rightly named Sunday, or day of the sun...," followed by "Thank you Henry David Thoreau." Below this, in the middle of the typed letter—which forms a response to Harding's prior reaching out to learn more of Viktor's work and life—is a passage that reads as follows, echoing and fleshing out the artist's catalogue declaration of several years earlier:

> Thoreau did somehow bring me to Amsterdam in that he was my first teacher, a man impossible to set barriers against, and so when I read his opening words of the first chapter of *Walden* in April 1950 in central Colorado, I had found my first true friend, and it was the only voice to set against the many voices about me which urged my following some normal work enterprise. Thoreau's example was the single real confirming voice against traveling an established direction, and it was that single voice that aided my detachment and brought me to Amsterdam, where my real work began. It is as simple as that, and naming the ship is only my thank you. You ask for a sketch of my own former personal life, but that for me is only foundation and lies below the ground, and my writing is always NOW and Thoreau is NOW for me.

Harding reciprocated by profiling Viktor as follows in the *Thoreau Society Bulletin #112* (Summer, 1970):

> Quite regularly we hear from visitors to Amsterdam, Netherlands that they have seen a ship named "Henry D. Thoreau" anchored in the Amstel River. We investigated and discovered it was the home of an American artist who uses the name Viktor IV and who salvages pieces of wood floating about the Amsterdam harbor, converting them into what he calls 'secular ikons.' He extends a welcome to any Thoreau Society member visiting Amsterdam to drop in and visit his [onboard] gallery. The address is opposite 4-9 Amstel, Amsterdam, Holland.[16]

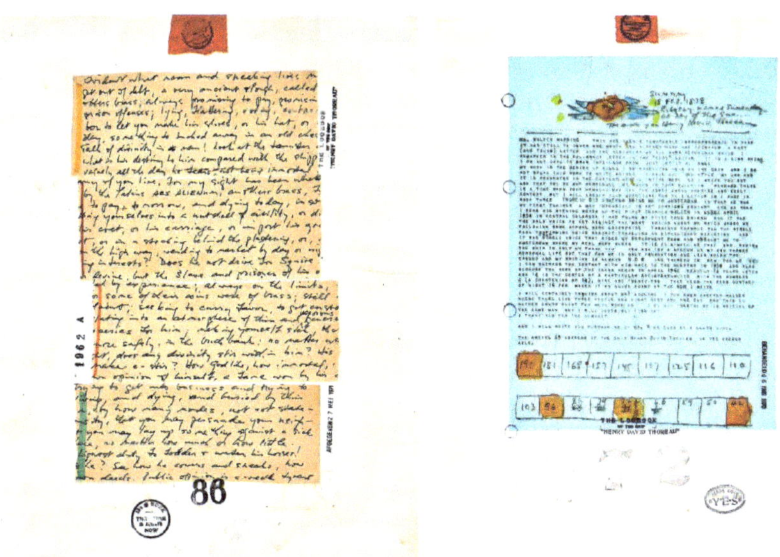

[Figure 3.7]

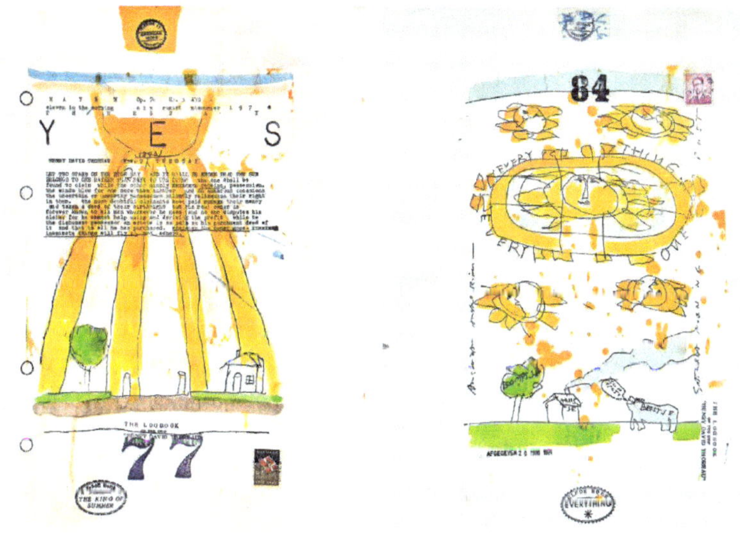

[Figure 3.8]

To showcase a couple of more visually oriented Logbook pages, the one at above left, numbered #77 and dated August 6, 1970, depicts Thoreau's Walden house radiant in buttery sunlight, illustrating a passage from his November, 1843 Journal: "Let two stand on the high way and it shall be known that the sun belongs to one rather than the other. The one shall be found to claim, while the other simply retains possession." To the right in turn is a Logbook page #84 from March 20, 1971, forming a visual verso of the former, with Viktor's appreciative illustrations of the sun and its generative, inspiring, lifegiving light once more the underlying theme. It is known that Viktor became a member of the Thoreau Society around 1970, and for several years received the *Thoreau Society Bulletin* to his barge, as well as letters and personal visits from avid Thoreauvians of the time, Mary Sherwood and Leonard Kleinfeld among them. He also carried on an intermittent correspondence with Walter Harding and adorned many Logbooks with scraps and cutouts from the *Thoreau Society Bulletin*, especially ones rendering Thoreau's house at Walden.[17]

Back from a rare autumn journey to New York City in 1977, having unsuccessfully pitched a remaining selection of Ikons, Viktor reflected, in his Logbook #168, dated Nov. 22, on how divergent he had long felt from his birth nation and its vaunted mores and traditions. This while he singled out Thoreau as a valued fellow protester, a champion of enthusiasm and individualism over duty and conventionality:

> The lesson of this visit [to the USA] is how very far apart are our values and the ones I was born into and accepted uncritically when very young and the slow travel away from those values beginning perhaps even long before reading Henry Thoreau /…./ Enthusiasm when it is not met by ~~counter~~ responsive enthusiasm simply sighs sadly and flies somewhere else for it is not a donkey to pick up ancient arguments to hash and rehash them over and over and endlessly over as a Sissyphus [*sic*].

As the 1970s waned, Viktor's plan was to release his Logbooks as a series of vast tomes, held together by wooden covers, sturdy leather strings and iron clasps. While this hope was never to be realized, he channeled his artistic energy into new outlets, among them elaborate envelopes sent to friends and acquaintances. Notwithstanding that the addresses were at times difficult to make out, the local postmen enjoyed handling them, to the extent that they eventually arranged an exhibit of Viktor's envelopes at the Danish Post and Tele Museum (Viktor's correspondents having retained the vast majority, making them available for display). Viktor also became interested in the Futhark alphabet of the Viking Age, and began making modern Runes of his own, on smaller, sturdy pieces of wood. The messages were often humorous mottoes of his own twist. His return to wood was also evinced by the manufacture of colorful Measuring Sticks, where he left out the number "six" (as he felt it deserved a vacation), as well as thick, rectangular black blocks, upon which he stenciled maxims in white. Many of these offered a Buddhist-cum-Stoic-cum-Thoreauvian piquancy: "TO WANT IS TO LOSE WHAT YOU ALREADY HAVE"; "BE WORTHY OF THE GIFT LIFE IS"; "THESE ARE THE GOOD OLD DAYS." Furthermore the distinctly Thoreau-flavored: "YOU CANNOT KNOW WHERE YOU ARE UNLESS YOU HAVE BEEN SOMEWHERE ELSE," and "THE NOW IS ALWAYS NEW."[18] Compare Thoreau's "Not till we are lost, in other words not till we have lost the world, do we begin to find ourselves, and realize where we are and the infinite extent of our relations" (*W* 171), and "Time hides no treasures; we want not its *then*, but its *now*" in the Journal of August 9, 1841.

While annually represented at galleries and art shows in Denmark and Holland, Viktor and Ina rarely had the steadier income Viktor had enjoyed during his photographer and ikon-maker days.[19] Instead they relied on savings, and to some extent on family support, while living frugally and occasionally taking on commissions for carpentry work. Above all, they valued the time freed for artistic pursuits by having few fixed costs and obligations. Viktor at some point returned to his Thoreau anthology—since complemented by two paperbacks, reinforced by stiff paper covers, one a combo of *Walden* and "Civil Disobedience," the other a selection from Thoreau's Journal—to comment on Thoreau's summation regarding necessary upkeep work. Where Thoreau tallied this to six weeks in his time and place, Viktor opined in the margins of his Thoreau omnibus that "this is indeed possible / personally extend it / to 10–12 weeks."

To turn finally to Viktor's last major artistic reincarnation, begun with a rapidly burgeoning amount of sketches in 1978, and running into the mid-1980s, when he became a designer of clocks and wristwatches of unique aspect. This mature phase, which also saw Viktor change his name to Bulgar Finn (while I will retain Viktor here, for clarity's sake), was precipitated by long ruminations on the nature of time, how we spend it, and how we frequently ignore its NOW while dwelling on past and future events. To *toe the line of the present*, in distinctly Thoreauvian fashion, was evidently what Viktor had striven for during his life, and also wished to promote. His peculiar way of conveying this was to construct timepieces under the banner of Bulgartime, which unsettled the normal pace and direction of conventional ones. Hence he devised watches and clocks primed to show the precise time, yet revolving (as we say) counterclockwise, or yet again at double or triple speed with dials and faces modified to match the unexpected action. These complications forced the glancing observer of the timepiece faces to pause and work out what the time actually was, and thereby—or so Viktor reasoned—becoming better grounded and present to the pertaining NOW. Investing his remaining savings in the project, Viktor contacted a Swiss watchmaker, and convinced them to take on his challenging designs. Over the course of several years Bulgartime then offered a series of unconventional Swiss quartz wristwatches, as sold directly by Viktor himself. While never a resounding commercial success (not least due to marketing being limited to word-of-mouth endorsements from pleased customers), neither was the initiative a failure. Eventually, in early 1986, an innovative firm called Art Expo in Odense, Denmark, agreed to promote and sell the four wristwatch models Viktor had come to see as definitive. These were presented in a black felt folder titled "THE TIME IS ALWAYS NOW," containing a neatly depressed bed for the numbered watches, and furthermore a slender hardcover book with many of the sketches and proposals underlying the project.[20]

On Thursday, June 26, 1986, a towering, solid, white-bearded man in his mid-50s stood by the gunwale of a barge in central Amsterdam in his swimming trunks. His gaze wandered knowingly over the water, spying for eddies or surfaces disturbed by gusts of wind. In his hands he held a cluster of discarded, empty plastic 20-liter cans, with long cords attached to the handles. He was recognized and appreciated, even loved, as an anarchic but sympathetic figure by the local townspeople, having lived on the same wharf for over twenty years. Though he hardly bothered to learn a word of Dutch, he came to embody a mentality congenial to the city. He was never a disturbance to anyone, save occasionally to the Amsterdam Harbor Authority, which at times saw fit to gently chastise him for select aspects of

[Figure 3.9]

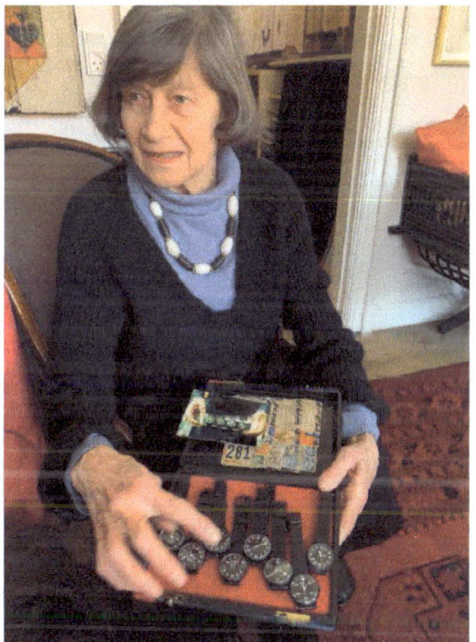

[Figure 3.10]

his floating menagerie. Yet he gave back freely, and had signs on his vessel as well as prints boldly declaring "THANK YOU AMSTERDAM." He also had stamps with which he alternately called himself "THE BIG FOOL," "THE CLEVER IDIOT" and "THE TOLERANT FANATIC." Once a child, encountering him lost in thought, had asked its mother, "Does it speak?"[21] The late June afternoon was balmy, and the slow-flowing Amstel showed no signs of concern. He dipped his toes into the water and found it pleasantly cool. As he had countless times before, the man next lowered himself nimbly into the river.

A week later, on a sunny July 3rd afternoon, thousands of Amsterdam residents lined up along the bridges and wharves of the Amstel to watch a river funeral procession pass by. They tenderly tossed flowers and wreaths after the boat serving as hearse, slowly chugging down with the current. The coffin was placed on a bed of straw, adorned with a large American flag. On one of its sides, a stenciled wooden sign read: "THIS SIDE UP." Only a week before, Viktor had dived down to underprop a sizeable new raft he had built with Ina to house a painting studio. Once he had attempted using empty oil barrels for the purpose of improved flotation, but he found these quickly rusted away. Instead he had taken to locking smaller, emptied liquid containers from restaurants under the rafts, marking some of them "PLASTIC POSSIBILITY." This time, however, the dive did not go as expected. Whether having gotten entangled in his cords, or simply having lost his breath and orientation, Viktor failed to surface. He was found a day later, submerged under the raft. To the end, he was engaged in putting the foundations under his expanding castle in the air above.

Amidst her grief, Ina found that Viktor had written a note to his Swiss colleagues that carried his watch designs, still fastened to the roller of his typewriter on the day he died. The letter speaks of a favorable watch design, to be sure, but also of Viktor's wider ambition as an artist: namely to become as one with his material, much like Thoreau strove to lose himself in his natural surroundings. Their environments and external circumstances may have been very different, but their yearning to be free whilst drawing deeply on their chosen ground was something fundamental they shared. Thoreau wrote in *Walden* that he wished for none to copy his example outright, but to seek their own roots of freedom. He wished, as he also put it, that there be as many different persons in the world as possible. In these senses, Viktor proved himself the quintessential Thoreauvian.

It seems fitting here to allow Viktor's longtime companion Ina Munck the final words: "Contrary to the image that many people have of Viktor, he was [...] a man who lived his life consciously, who was cultivated, interested and well-spoken. As to his extreme individuality and his mentality and lifestyle that were inspired by Thoreau's ideas, I do not think that he experienced them as being unavoidably on the edge of our society, but rather that he very consciously wanted to set an example, to show a possibility."[22]

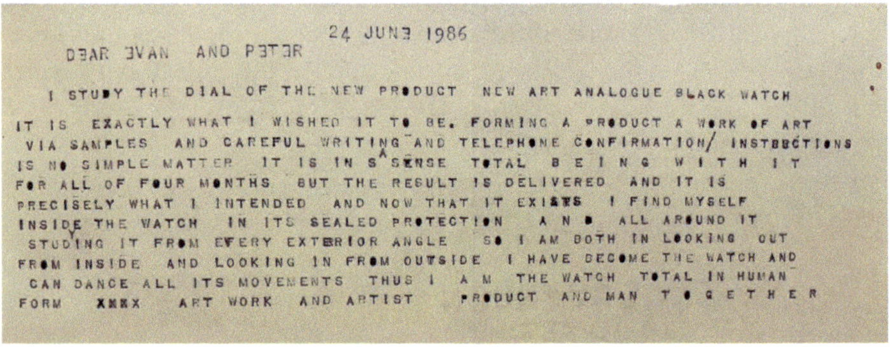

24 JUNE 1986

DEAR EVAN AND PETER

I STUDY THE DIAL OF THE NEW PRODUCT NEW ART ANALOGUE BLACK WATCH
IT IS EXACTLY WHAT I WISHED IT TO BE. FORMING A PRODUCT A WORK OF ART
VIA SAMPLES AND CAREFUL WRITING AND TELEPHONE CONFIRMATION/ INSTRUCTIONS
IS NO SIMPLE MATTER IT IS IN A SENSE TOTAL B E I N G W I T H I T
FOR ALL OF FOUR MONTHS BUT THE RESULT IS DELIVERED AND IT IS
PRECISELY WHAT I INTENDED AND NOW THAT IT EXISTS I FIND MYSELF
INSIDE THE WATCH IN ITS SEALED PROTECTION A N D ALL AROUND IT
STUDYING IT FROM EVERY EXTERIOR ANGLE SO I AM BOTH IN LOOKING OUT
FROM INSIDE AND LOOKING IN FROM OUTSIDE I HAVE BECOME THE WATCH AND
CAN DANCE ALL ITS MOVEMENTS THUS I A M THE WATCH TOTAL IN HUMAN
FORM XXXX ART WORK AND ARTIST PRODUCT AND MAN T O G E T H E R

[Figure 3.11]

Works Cited

Johansen, Sara and Møller, Heidi. Viktor IV website: "www.bulgartime.com"

Koslow, Francine Amy. *Henry David Thoreau as a Source for Artistic Inspiration. Exhibition Catalogue June 6 – September 9, 1984.* Lincoln, Mass: The DeCordova and Dana Museum and Park, 1984. (Viktor IV not treated.)

Munck, Ina. Personal interviews with the author, 2022–2024.

———. *Viktor IV: An American in Paris.* Odder, Denmark: Narayana Press, 2013.

Otterberg, Henrik. "Liber Resartus: On Thoreau & the Book of Nature" in *The Oxford Handbook of Henry David Thoreau.* Edited by Kristen Case and James Finley. Cambridge, MA: Oxford University Press, forthcoming.

Petersen, Ad & Munck, Ina. *Viktor IV.* Amsterdam: Meulenhoff/Landshoff & The Second Quality Construction Company, 1988.

Thoreau, Henry David. *Selected Journals of Henry David Thoreau*, ed. With a foreword by Carl Bode. New York & Toronto: Signet Books, 1967. [Marked "SUNA" in bold orange marker above Thoreau portrait on lower front cover, similarly in orange by publishers. Stated as "From Els" (Elisabeth/Ina Munck) 16 II 1970).]

———. *Walden and Other Writings.* Edited and introduction by Brooks Atkinson. New York: The Modern Library, 1937. [Viktor IV's extensively grangerized copy, marked "Copy III / Personal Copy / Not to be loaned out."]

———. *Walden and Other Writings*, ed. & with introduction by Joseph Wood Krutch. New York, Toronto, London: Bantam Books, 1962. [Viktor IV's second "Studio copy," original paperback covers supplemented by brown wrappers, dated "21 VI 1968" and marked on back "FIRE-place – reserve." Sparsely read, few annotations.]

———. *Walden; or, Life in the Woods and On the Duty of Civil Disobedience* (1942; New York: Mentor Books, 1957). [Tenth edition paperback. Supplemented by brown wrappers and stamped "Karl Glück." Some underlining & with several cutouts from the *New Yorker* at rear. Viktor IV's first copy on his boats.]

Victor IV. "Catalogue One: '4' Paintings" (Amsterdam: self-published, 1965).

———. Logbooks (various, as cited in the text).

———. Logbook sketch, unstamped, dated June 16, 1974.

CHAPTER 4

PARADIGMS OF EXTINCTION IN *A WEEK ON THE CONCORD AND MERRIMACK RIVERS*: FROM THE SAXON CHAIN TO JUSTICE FOR THE SHAD

Robert Sattelmeyer

When Henry Thoreau began to compose his first book, he faced a practical dilemma. The details of his summer boating and hiking vacation with his brother John in 1839 were unremarkable, lacking any of the drama, conflict, or exotic settings that characterized such successful narratives of the 1840s as *Typee*, *The Oregon Trail*, or *Two Years Before the Mast.* Even with the inclusion of many of his often-unrelated early efforts in poetry and prose in the text, the story itself was, in Emerson's phrase, "a very slender thread for such big beads and ingots as are strung on it."[1] Thoreau addressed this problem primarily by deepening and expanding his portrayals of both the human and the natural history of the Concord and Merrimack River valleys. In doing so, he began to explore the richness of two subjects that would become foci of his study and work for the rest of his life: the flora and fauna of his native region, and the Native American and early European history of New England and adjacent areas of Canada.

In many ways, these subjects are fused, for even at the outset of his career Thoreau saw natural and human history as deeply connected, long before it became fashionable to talk about anthropogenic change or the effects of the Columbian Exchange. Both figuratively and literally the Concord and Merrimack Rivers constitute the stream of time, carrying Thoreau not forward but back into the past. Turning north up the Merrimack River brings him physically to sites important to his region's colonial past, and floating the rivers exposes him to the region's biological past as well, and the environmental changes wrought by European settlement. Both Native peoples and native flora and fauna have been replaced. In *A*

Week on the Concord and Merrimack Rivers (1849), through the specter of real and imagined extinctions, Thoreau both echoes and begins to question some of the received wisdom and cultural assumptions of his age about the history of human and non-human life in North America. In depicting Native Americans in *A Week*, Thoreau for the most part drew upon local accounts of the wars of early colonial history, retelling well-known incidents that took place at various sites along the route of the brothers' travels. He used this material to build out and add human interest, conflict, and a mythic dimension to the slim narrative of his 1839 excursion.[2] Although the Transcendentalists were prone to denigrate history ("the *past* cannot be *presented*" Thoreau proclaimed in his mini-essay on the topic in *A Week*), it could be useful when it leads back to mythology and fable, in which truth may be embedded and grasped imaginatively (*Week* 155). So Thoreau typically emphasizes the remoteness of that era, which actually ended less than a century earlier, calling it "the dark age of New England" in another early essay, "A Walk to Wachusett" (*Exc* 44). And these incidents also suggest to Thoreau a heroic age (on the models of the Greek epics) in contrast to his prosaic industrializing present. But his endorsement of colonial heroes is not unconditional, for he also registers a nascent awareness of the distorted representations of Native Americans contained in such episodes as the accounts of the sachems Wannalancet and Tahatawan of the "praying Indians," Lovewell's Fight, and, climactically, Hannah Dustan's slaughter of and escape from her captors in King William's War, the most widely retold of the colonial captivity narratives.[3]

While Thoreau mined these well-known episodes from the frontier wars to add quasi-epic and legendary dimensions to his narrative, he had scarcely begun to encounter the complexities of the pre- and post-contact history of Indigenous people in North America. He relied primarily on biased local histories, and he fell back for the most part on the prevailing imagined order of his time, which saw early New England's history as the point of the spear in the inevitable spread of Euro-American civilization into a virgin wilderness, made possible by the preordained extinction of its original inhabitants. Even the epigraph he chose for the first chapter, from Emerson's poem "Musketaquid," emphasizes the buried past of Indigenous New England and describes the current farmers as "supplanters of the tribe." And in the first paragraph of the text itself the native inhabitants are referred to as "an extinct race."

Thoreau expands this prevailing view further in the "Sunday" chapter, in passages attributing this arc of history to racial characteristics originating with the Anglo-Saxons. In the same meditation, he links the disappearance of the Native Americans to the simultaneous displacement of native American flora by more "civil" European plants, putting a positive spin on the New England version of the cascading environmental and cultural disruptions that we now label the Columbian Exchange[4]—a global phenomenon whose consequences are still playing out today. As opposed to the later periods of nearly perpetual conflict, Thoreau imagines the settlement phase of his native region's history—especially along the Concord River—as a spontaneous and naturally-occurring sequence best represented by the apple tree: "Some spring the white man came, built him a house, and made a clearing here, letting in the sun, dried up a farm, piled up the old gray stones in fences, planted orchard seeds brought from the old country, and persuaded the civil apple tree to blossom next to the wild pine and the juniper..." (*Week* 52). This vision omits to mention that early English settlements—Concord included—were sited in places where Native Americans had built houses and towns, cleared land, managed forests, and planted a variety of crops for many hundreds of years. Thoreau treats the arrival of agriculture as though it were a European invention. And, while the white man seems to appear out of nowhere ("Some spring the white man came"), he arrives with a specific set of inherited traits that will guarantee his predominance:

> The white man comes, pale as the dawn, with a load of thought, with a slumbering intelligence as a fire raked up, knowing well what he knows, not guessing, but calculating; strong in community, yielding obedience to authority; of wonderful, wonderful common sense; dull but capable, slow but persevering, severe but just, of little humor but genuine; a laboring man, despising game and sport, building a house that endures, a framed house....And this is New Angle-land, and these are the new West Saxons, whom the Red Men call, not Angle-ish or English, but Yengeese, and so at last they are known for Yankees. (*Week* 53)

The arrival of the white man, "pale as the dawn," his skin a literal enlightenment, signals the coming of intelligence, community, and steadfast purpose to the heretofore dark wilderness of the Red Man. Thoreau's linking of these traits to "New Angle-land" and the "new West Saxons" is more than etymological play. It reflects a widespread belief in the nineteenth century that the roots of United States civilization and democracy lay in Anglo-Saxon England and, ultimately, in the northern European homelands of these tribes. It was not just white people, in other words, who were responsible for the development and progress of the United States, but a racialized subset of white people. Nineteenth-century writers took great pains to subdivide various gradations of cultural whiteness and assign them hereditary traits.[5]

Thoreau would later encounter other contemporary racial theorists, especially the so-called "American School" of ethnology led by Samuel G. Morton, who argued on the basis of skull measurements that races were separately created and that—no surprise—Caucasians were the most intelligent, for his Indian project in the 1850s.[6] At this early stage in his career, however, Thoreau was mostly reflecting ideas that were current in New England and endorsed by Emerson, whose lecture "The Anglo-American," for example, was first titled "The Anglo-Saxon," as though the terms were interchangeable. Emerson would ultimately relax his notion of fixed racial identities and characteristics as he became more committed to abolitionism, but he was still comfortable as late as *English Traits* (1855) in summarizing the putative Anglo-Saxon race in terms very similar to Thoreau's:

> Whatever 'circumstance that mixed for them the golden mean of temperament,' the Saxons are 'the best stock in the world, broad-fronted, broad-bottomed, best for depth, range and equability; men of aplomb and reserve, great range and many moods, strong instincts, yet apt for culture'; they comprise 'a race to which their fortunes flow, as if they alone had the elastic organization at once fine and robust enough for dominions.'[7]

The corollary of this racial anatomizing was to disqualify other varieties of whiteness, especially the "Celt" (i.e., the Irish) and the "Norman" (i.e., the French)—not to mention the Slavs, southern Europeans, and especially the "colored races"—from a seat at the table of American greatness. There was an amplification in power and accomplishment at each progressive link in this "Saxon chain," from the northern tribes to the

British Empire to the unlimited potential for expansion and manifest destiny of the United States.

The notion that English government, the idea of personal freedom, and the spread of English power flowed not just from Anglo-Saxon institutions but primarily from hereditary racial characteristics operated powerfully in New England, where men believed themselves to be the inheritors of this historical advance in the 1840s, and Thoreau saw little reason to question this theory. Probably at Emerson's urging, he read and took notes on Sharon Turner's *History of the Anglo-Saxons*, the work that did the most to promote this view, and some of his earliest journal passages in 1837 transcribe unflattering contrasts between Saxons and Franks from Turner's work (*PJ* 1: 21).[8]

What is problematic, of course, is that since Thoreau had significant French ancestry, he presumably did not possess all these fine qualities. And for Emerson, in fact, Thoreau's mixed-race ancestry was a key to his contradictions and his failings. After Thoreau's death in 1862, Emerson began his profoundly ambivalent eulogy, soon printed in the *Atlantic Monthly* and later reprinted as an introduction to Thoreau's works, by citing the unfortunate facts of this mixed heritage: "Henry David Thoreau was the last male descendant of a French ancestor who came to this country from the Isle of Guernsey. His character exhibited occasional traits drawn from this blood, in singular combination with a very strong Saxon genius."[9] All posthumous criticism of Thoreau thus begins with this commonplace racial stereotyping.

In later years, while working on the final "Provincetown" chapter of *Cape Cod,* Thoreau would substantially revise his conception of early European American history, elevating the French and other nationalities among early explorers, and severely demoting the English. But during the 1840s, despite his own ancestry, he remained under the sway of the trope of the "Saxon tide," so much so that when he made his excursion to French Canada in 1849 (just after *A Week* was published), he described the population as appearing "very inferior, intellectually and even physically, to that of New England." This inferiority was so pronounced that the French-speaking inhabitants of North America could be lumped with Indigenous people as doomed to inevitable extinction: "The impression made on me was, that the French Canadians were even sharing the fate of the Indians, or at least gradually disappearing in what is called the Saxon current" (*Exc* 132, 134).

In *A Week,* Thoreau sings the praises of "the rude Saxon pioneer" (54), the first civilizing influence upon the wild landscape, who transforms it from primeval forest into an English countryside that literally leaves no room for the native inhabitants:

> He rudely bridged the stream, and drove his team afield into the river meadows, cut the wild grass, and laid bare the homes of beaver, otter, muskrat, and with the whetting of his scythe scared off the deer and bear. He set up a mill, and fields of English grain sprang in the virgin soil. And with his grain he scattered the seeds of the dandelion and the wild trefoil over the meadows, mingling his English flowers with the wild native ones. The bristling burdock, the sweet-scented catnip, and the humble yarrow, planted themselves along his woodland road, they too seeking "freedom to worship God" in their way. And thus he plants a town. The white man's mullein soon reigned in Indian cornfields, and sweet-scented English grasses clothed the new soil. Where, then, could the Red Man set his foot? The honey-bee hummed through the Massachusetts' woods, and sipped the wild flowers round the Indian's wigwam, perchance unnoticed, when, with prophetic warning, it stung the Red child's hand, forerunner of that industrious tribe that was to come and pluck the wild flower of his race up by the root. (*Week* 52–53)

In contrast to the opening paragraph of the book, where he had described the changes brought to the Musketaquid watershed by agriculture and industry, Thoreau imagines here a benevolent transformation of native flora by both purposeful and accidental introduction of invasive English plants. Eventually this subject, along with plant dispersion and succession more generally, would become one of his major fields of study, leading to the carefully researched manuscripts on the "The Dispersion of Seeds" and "Wild Fruits" that were only published more than a century after his death.[10] But here his interest is not yet scientific, although his powers of observation and extrapolation are already evident. Here the introduced plants are useful, pleasing, and benign. They even share the desire for religious freedom that is part of the Pilgrim origin myth of the founding of the United States, "they, too, seeking 'freedom to worship God' in their way." For Thoreau in *A Week,* American history and environmental change may be said to begin at this moment, sharing a common providential cause.

Like the native plants, the native race is powerless to resist this colonization. His habitat transformed, "where, then, could the Red Man set his foot?" The seemingly innocuous European honeybee, which ranged ahead of settlement like the introduced diseases that ravaged native populations, becomes for Thoreau the precursor of those "industrious" Anglo-Saxon tribes that doomed the Native Americans, pictured here under the paradigm of their fated extinction as a plant violently plucked up by the root. Thoreau reveres the "wildness" that the Indian represents, but it is a kind of literary wildness that he wishes to infuse into modern culture: "If we could but listen to the chaunt of the Indian muse, we should understand why he will not exchange his savageness for civilization" (*Week* 56). Even while praising this wildness Thoreau repeats the stereotype of the Native Americans' supposed obduracy in refusing civilization.

Introduced plants do spread themselves, of course, but the missing part of the picture here is human agency: the deforestation of New England and rapid depopulation of its native fauna did not occur spontaneously but under the remorseless pressure of expanding settlement, demand for fuel, and extractive commerce in lumber and furs. Despite their apocalyptic decline, Native Americans' growing dependence on European goods meant that they also played a significant role in this transformation as the primary suppliers of furs to global markets.[11] But Thoreau's purpose, of course, is not yet environmental history but a kind of natural history fable that harmonizes with the underlying myth of a progressive and benevolent civilization springing naturally from the virgin soil and made possible by the providential disappearance of the Indigenous population.

Despite his unconscious repetition of many of these unexamined assumptions of his age—the "pristine myth" of North American emptiness, the inevitability of "Saxon" domination, and the typing of Native Americans as unchangeable savages fated for extinction—Thoreau also demonstrates in his first book a nascent awareness of anthropogenic change that includes Native Americans. And, what is even more unusual in his era, he begins to articulate an environmental ethos from a sense of affiliation with the natural world, without which an understanding of its complexity could not progress. Fittingly, it was in looking closely at his immediate environment along and in the Concord River that this new, proto-ecological awareness began to manifest itself—with a contemplation of its fish.

The book opens with a description of the Concord River watershed, in which Thoreau highlights environmental changes brought on by agriculture and industry, especially due to the dams erected downstream. He picks up this thread in the next chapter, "Saturday," with an essay on the Concord River and its fishes, based on a lecture he gave at the Concord Lyceum in early 1845, just before he moved to Walden Pond.[12] It gives us a preview of the rich and multi-layered natural history essays Thoreau would write later in his career. The common fish of the river are not simply to be described and enumerated. They embody, rather, "forms and phases of the life in nature universally dispersed," so universally that there may be said to be a "fish principle in nature" that proclaims the fecundity and ubiquity of life: "The seeds of the life of fishes are everywhere disseminated, whether the winds waft them, or the waters float them, or the deep earth holds them; wherever a pond is dug straightway it is stocked with this vivacious race. They have a lease of nature, and it is not yet out." Emphasizing the "seeds of the life of fishes" and their means of dispersal again prefigures Thoreau's later project on the dispersal of the seeds of plants. But here, his interest still veers toward the literary, as he concludes by alluding to Izaak Walton's well-known description of fishing: "the fruit of the naturalist's observations is not in new genera or species, but in new contemplations still, and science is only a more contemplative man's recreation" (*Week* 25).

But one can see the scientist beginning to emerge. The second year Thoreau lived at Walden Pond, while he was working on *A Week,* he became acquainted with and began collecting specimens for Louis Agassiz, the leading natural scientist in the United States, who had recently accepted a professorship at Harvard.[13] Thoreau's descriptions now include proper Latin taxonomic names and a kind of humble brag allusion to his new connection to the distinguished scientist: "There is also another species of bream found in our river, without the red spot on the operculum, which, according to M. Agassiz, is undescribed" (*Week* 28). Thoreau would later reject Agassiz in favor of Darwin, but at this stage of his scientific career, Agassiz was an influential if secondhand mentor in the nuances of taxonomy and classification.

Because he had also begun to look at early accounts of the region's flora and fauna, such as John Josselyn's *New England's Rarities* (1672), Thoreau's catalogue of fishes includes species no longer present, raising the possibility of extinction in the natural world, a phenomenon relatively new to natural science, which had long held that species were neither created nor destroyed. Tracing the river's piscatory history also lays out a chain of events that links pre-contact environmental changes to large-scale industrial activity: "Salmon, Shad, and Alewives, were formerly abundant here, and taken in weirs by the Indians, who taught this method to the whites, by whom they were used as food and manure, until the dam, and afterwards the canal at Billerica, and the factories at Lowell, put an end to their migrations hitherward" (*Week* 33). Here—in contrast to his account of the beginnings of agriculture—he acknowledges that the process of settlement involved a complex cultural exchange rather than a simple replacement of a weak race by a strong. Just as the Native Americans taught the English how to grow corn, beans, and squash together they also taught them how and where to harvest fish efficiently. These weirs—which redirect the river's current—also provide a brief glimpse into the larger issue of Native Americans' impact on the environment, which was obscured in Thoreau's day (and to some extent still in ours) by the pristine myth.[14]

The principal cause of habitat alteration, though, was the dam at Billerica, constructed in 1711, and gradually raised and modified over the next century and a half to power mills.[15] Upstream, the economic impact of the dam was chiefly on the farmers along the river's banks. The higher water levels compromised their ability to exploit the meadow grasses for hay. This eventually led to a series of lawsuits in the late 1850s, in which Thoreau served as a consultant for the farmers, undertaking a careful survey of the entire watershed.[16] In *A Week,* Thoreau voices concern about the negative impacts of the dam on the floodplain primarily from this economic standpoint, still operating largely under the rubric of the "civilizing" influence of English domesticated plants. Urging the removal of the dam, he argues, "Innumerable acres of meadow are waiting to be made dry land, wild native grass to give place to English" (38).

But, significantly, his main concern is not for the farmers but for the shad and the restoration of its habitat. Like the other anadromous fish Thoreau mentions, the salmon and the alewife, the American shad must return from the ocean to a freshwater stream to spawn, and the dam caused its disappearance in the Concord River watershed.[17] The shad, though, was more than just a fish. Its incredible seasonal abundance annually in the rivers of the east coast from Florida to Maine had an enormous cultural and economic impact on the lives of Native Americans, European colonists, and United States residents well into the nineteenth century. Like the American bison and the passenger pigeon, it was once so abundant that extinction was unthinkable. It was central to the survival of the Pilgrims in 1621. Legend (if not historical fact) credits the arrival of the shad run in the Schuylkill River with saving Washington's army at Valley Forge from starvation in the spring of 1778. Near-wars were fought over favored seining locations.[18] And Thoreau understood, generalizing from its fate in the relatively minor Concord River, that the shad, like the passenger pigeon or the American bison later, illustrated how seemingly inexhaustible abundance could quickly turn to near-extinction.

Thoreau directs a lengthy speech to the departed fish that begins, "Poor shad! where is thy redress?" The somewhat comic artificiality of this passage, using the archaic "thy" and "thee," ought not to obscure either its seriousness or its importance. This mask allows Thoreau to suggest the actual removal the dam or even an act of what we might today call eco-terrorism: "I for one am with thee, and who knows what may avail a crowbar against that Billerica dam?" His threat stems not so much from a disgust at the economic system that put the dam in place as from a sense of what E. O. Wilson in his 1984 book by this title would call "biophilia," which he defines as "the innate tendency to focus on life and lifelike processes."[19]

> Away with the superficial and selfish phil-*anthropy* of men,—who knows what admirable virtue of fishes may be below low-water mark, bearing up against a hard destiny, not admired by that fellow creature who alone can appreciate it! Who hears the fishes when they cry? It will not be forgotten by some memory that we were contemporaries. Thou shalt ere long have thy way up the rivers, up all the rivers of the globe, if I am not mistaken. Yea, even thy dull watery dream shall be more than realized. If it were not so, but thou wert to be overlooked at first and at last, then would not I take their heaven. Yes, I say so, who think I know better than thou canst. Keep a stiff fin then, and stem all the tides thou mayest meet. (*Week* 37–38)

Thoreau's address to the shad expresses more than a glimmer of a radical environmental ethos. He urges his readers to abandon their anthropocentric view of the natural world (the "selfish phil-*anthropy* of men") and to use their purported higher abilities to respond to the distress of other creatures: "Who hears the fishes when they cry?" Like the findings of modern research in the biological sciences that began with Darwin and continue today,[20] he posits higher abilities in the supposedly lower forms of creation: "Who knows what admirable virtue of fishes may be below low-water mark?" He rejects the Judeo-Christian notion that humans were given dominion over the earth and that the natural world was made to serve us: if the rights of other beings are not respected, "then would not I take their heaven. Yes, I say so." He even imagines a post-human landscape in which the cycles of migration to "all the rivers of the globe" are restored and the "dull, watery dream" of the shad is realized.

Perhaps because of Thoreau's archaic shaping of this passage as an apostrophe to the shad, its strikingly prophetic nature has generally been unrecognized. The environmental costs (and disruption of Native rights) of dam-building in the United States went largely unchallenged for more than a hundred years, until opposition began to crystallize around the construction of the Glen Canyon Dam on the Colorado River in the 1950s.[21] Since then momentum has shifted, and dam removal has become an important weapon in the arsenal of the rewilding movements around the world. At the time of the writing of this article (May, 2024) hundreds of dams in the United States have been dismantled and the largest dam removal project in the country's history is under way on the Klamath River in Oregon. Even the shad's "dull, watery dream" may be realized in the Concord River: funding for the removal of the dam at Billerica (formally known as the Talbot Mills Dam) has been authorized by the U.S. Fish and Wildlife Service.[22]

Like *Walden, A Week* went through a long and complex process of composition that saw Thoreau adding material based on his reading in various kinds of history to the relatively short first draft. Not surprisingly, then, it reflects his own process of growth during these years and expresses sometimes conflicting attitudes toward its subjects. Even though the book, weighed down with so many digressive essays, was a commercial failure, Thoreau found the genre of travel narrative itself appealing, for it offered opportunities for more remunerative magazine publications. Most important, his new practice of researching the history of the places he traveled would lead to larger and more ambitious projects on a much larger canvas of early American history, both human and natural. Thoreau's interest in Native American history and cultures would continue throughout the 1850s, although it was hampered by his own lack of direct experience, the embryonic nature of such disciplines as archaeology and anthropology, and the persistence of racist theories in the authorities he read. But his fascination with how landscapes and habitats change, and how human actions affect and drive these changes, would grow stronger and more focused through the last decade of his life. He would not live to see the decimation of the American bison and the extinction of the passenger pigeon, but he saw enough in the disappearance of the shad and the loss of so much of the native fauna of the eastern U.S. to know that radical measures—including crowbars against dams—might be necessary.

Works Cited

Cronon, William. *Changes in the Land: Indians, Colonists, and the Ecology of New England.* New York: Hill and Wang, 1983.

Denevan, William M. "The Pristine Myth: The Landscape of the Americas in 1492." *Annals of the Association of American Geographers*, Vol. 82, No. 3, (Fall 1992): 369–85.

Ellard, Donna Beth. "Ella's bloody eagle: Sharon Turner's History of the Anglo-Saxons and Anglo-Saxon history." *Postmedieval: A Journal of Medieval Cultural Studies*, 5 (2014): 215–34.

Flores, Dan. *Wild New World.* New York: W. W. Norton, 2022.

Hanlon, Christopher, "The Old Races Are All Gone": Transatlantic Bloodlines and "English Traits." *American Literary History*, 19, No. 4 (Winter, 2007): pp. 800–823.

Johnson, Linck. *Thoreau's Complex Weave: The Writing of* A Week on the Concord and Merrimack Rivers *With the Text of the First Draft.* Charlottesville: University Press of Virginia, 1986.

Mann, Charles C. *1493: Exploring the New World Columbus Created.* New York: Alfred A. Knopf, 2011.

McPhee, John. *Encounters with the Archdruid.* New York: Farrar, Straus and Giroux, 1971.

———. *The Founding Fish.* New York: Farrar, Straus, and Giroux, 2002.

Painter, Nell Irvin. *The History of White People.* New York: W. W. Norton, 2010.

Thorson, Robert M. *The Boatman: Henry David Thoreau's River Years.* Cambridge, MA: Harvard University Press, 2017.

Wilson, E. O. *Biophilia.* Cambridge: Harvard University Press, 1984.

Yong, Ed. *An Immense World.* New York: Random House, 2023.

CHAPTER 5

FOOLISH PREACHERS, POETICAL FARMERS, AND VICIOUS MEN IN THE WOODS: EMERSON'S AND THOREAU'S REPRESENTATIVE MEN

Robert A. Gross

The Transcendentalists lived in changing times, and they knew it. The movement originated in a bid to revitalize religion in Massachusetts, just as the Bay State was ending its 200-year-old system of support for public worship. No longer would churches enjoy official recognition and compulsory taxes. Religious bodies would have to compete for followers on their own. Could Congregationalists—and especially, the liberal Unitarian wing, from which the Transcendentalists emerged—meet the challenge? The clerical reformer George Ripley signaled the alarm. "Great changes [are] taking place on every side; old ideas, old institutions, old habits of thought" are giving way. "Will the progress of society...leave religion in the background, and reject it as an outworn and useless thing?"[1]

Three years later, in his Phi Beta Kappa address at Harvard College, Ralph Waldo Emerson broadened the message of social change. As he surveyed the audience, the erstwhile minister sensed a profound uneasiness among the young men before him, graduating into a world that threatened to narrow their minds and crush their spirits. "They find themselves not in the state of mind of their fathers, and regret the coming state as untried." The youth were not alone. Americans were caught up in a time of transition affecting every area of life, religion included. To those made anxious by uncertainty, Emerson held out the stimulus of starting over.

> If there is any period one would desire to be born in,— is it not the age of Revolution; when the old and the new stand side by side, and admit of being compared; when the energies of all men are searched by fear and by hope; when the historic glories of the old can be

compensated by the rich possibilities of the new era? That time, like all times, is a very good one, if we but know what to do with it.[2]

Henry Thoreau, twenty-year-old graduate in the Class of 1837, was not present for Emerson's address, but the day before, at his commencement ceremony, he offered his own take on "the Commercial Spirit of Modern Times" and its "influence" on the "Political, Moral, and Literary Character of a Nation." The topic was not his choice, but he made it his own. It was assigned by the Harvard authorities in recognition of his academic merit. Ranking in the top half of the class, the graduate from Concord and two classmates were directed to give short talks on the appointed theme. Fittingly, Thoreau discoursed on morals. But rather than point out the personal sins and social evils of the day, he took a wider view of a society in change. The dominant feature of the epoch, he pronounced, was a "perfect freedom— freedom of thought and action," which expressed itself, first and foremost, in pursuit of economic gain. To this end, "man thinks faster and freer than ever before," remaking the world to serve his will. If only the goals of that mental excitement were as worthy as the means! But no, Thoreau noted ruefully, the American mind aimed too low; its "ruling principle" was a "blind and unmanly love of wealth." Selfishness infected "our patriotism," "our domestic relations," even "our religion." Were "buying and selling, money-changing and speech-making" the best uses of our "entire and universal freedom" (*EEM* 115–18)?

The young man identified what would become a central theme of his writing. From the very first version of *Walden*, he celebrated the intellectual ferment of the age. "No way of thinking or doing, however ancient," was fixed. Longstanding customs were losing hold. "Men have left off rum safely and imprisoning for debt." Chattel slavery was under attack. These advances hinted at the untold possibilities of human nature. "Man's capacities have never been measured; nor are we to judge of what he can do by any precedents, so little has been tried" (*W* 8. 10; Shanley 109). Was it not time to seize upon the spirit of the age and put this prospect to the test?[3]

Emerson and Thoreau got it right. From the 1820s to the 1840s, New England underwent a profound social transformation remaking city and country alike. Although Concord numbered little more than two thousand souls, the small town was as subject to the upheavals of the age as the booming metropolis. It was a community in ferment, whose small, ordered society, founded by Puritans and defended by Minutemen, was dramatically unsettled by the advance of capitalism and democracy. During the several decades around Thoreau's childhood, youth, and coming into maturity (1815–1847), his hometown was economically expansive, religiously diverse, racially heterogeneous, politically divided, and receptive to social and political reforms. It stood in the mainstream of Jacksonian America with an excellent vantage on a society in rapid change.

While the most visible signs of the transformation were the material changes on the local landscape—the factories along the Assabet River; the remaking of the town center into a fashionable "White Village," thriving with stores, offices, and banks; the expanded array of crops on the farms to feed and fuel consumers in the burgeoning cities; and the new highways and bridges carrying passengers and freight to and from urban markets, culminating in 1844 with the arrival of the Fitchburg Railroad—the fundamental shift was in the minds and manners of the inhabitants. In colonial Concord, people joined together in a common way of life; a few institutions—household and family, town and church, militia and schools, along with the village tavern—sufficed to organize everyday affairs. The yeomen farmed the land as their fathers and grandfathers had, raising much the same livestock and crops and assisting one another in need. The families worshiped together on the Sabbath, in keeping with the shared ideal of "one town, one church." The children attended common schools. The citizens—more precisely, the white male property-owners—governed the community through town meeting, usually deferring to the well-born and rich. To be sure, Concord was often beset by conflict; the inhabitants feuded with one another, treated strangers with suspicion, enslaved men and women of color, and pulled away from older communal practice. But they aspired to perpetuate the world as they had known and preserved it in the Revolution.[4]

Three decades after the dawn of the American republic, a new mentality was in evidence, as the townspeople abandoned old practices, pulled apart from one another, and innovated in every realm of life. The established church could no longer bind together the community; dissenters, led by Henry Thoreau's aunts, split off to form a congregation more in line with their Calvinist beliefs. Political parties, tied to state and national coalitions and controlled by professional politicians, turned town meetings into battles for power and gain. The public schools competed with private academies, where ambitious parents enrolled their children for improved education in an exclusive setting. The village taverns, once centers of sociability that could cut across class lines, came under attack by an aggressive crusade against "ardent spirits." New voluntary associations—especially, the agricultural society, the debating club, the social library, the lyceum, the female charitable society, the temperance campaign, and the anti-slavery organizations—mounted a sustained assault on traditional ways. The heart of their message was emphatic. Jettison the antiquated customs and constraints of the past. Adopt the latest knowledge of science in pursuit of progress. Encourage individuals to make their own choices. Inherited institutions and involuntary associations lost support; the premium was on personal autonomy and voluntary choice.

A "new consciousness" was awake in the land, to which Emerson gave voice. In 1837, as Concord quickened with change, the resident philosopher took to the lecture platform and announced that New England was at a turning point in human history. "The former men [i.e. previous generations] acted and spoke under the thought that a shining social prosperity was the aim of men," proclaimed Emerson, "and compromised ever the individuals to the nation. The modern mind teaches (in extremes) that the nation exists for the individual, for the guardianship and education of every man." In that "new consciousness" lay the revolution the Transcendentalists hoped to usher in.[5]

Emerson was savvy about the world around him, so much so that it is tempting to celebrate his prescience as a social observer. At the very moment the French thinker Alexis de Tocqueville was popularizing the term individualism in the Western world, the Concord Sage put the individual at the center of his own vision of democracy in America. But that is only part of the story. His outlook was as much aspirational as actual. To decipher the "tendencies" of the age and the "signs of the times," as Emerson did in imitation of his Scottish friend Thomas Carlyle, was to claim influence in the here and now, so as to shape the unfolding future. Moreover, the study of revolution was still novel; to naturalists like Thoreau, the term connoted cyclical movements—the annual circuit of the earth around the sun and the succession of the seasons. These were tangible phenomena following regular natural laws. But how to distinguish an "age of Revolution"? If the key to change lay in the hearts and minds of men, as Emerson suggested, then it was imperative to divine popular sentiments.[6]

How to identify the "historic glories" of a waning age and the "rich possibilities" of its emerging successor? It would take a Bob Richardson to answer this question by carefully scrutinizing Emerson's reading.[7] But there is another route into the Transcendentalist's thinking. Emerson sought out "representative men" to stand for historical epochs, and no one was more salient than Ezra Ripley, Concord's minister from 1778 to 1841. The parson embodied for his grandson Waldo the heroic age of the New England clergy, and in his career the younger man traced the fate of the Puritan tradition through good times and bad. Ripley was at once informant and specimen of New England religion and society. Together with Waldo's aunt Mary Moody Emerson, Ripley proved a crucial contributor to the Transcendentalist's oral history of a past on which he was eager to close the door. By contrast, Thoreau longed to connect with a time and place gone by, when alternative routes to the future were still open, and in this quest, he found his own representative men on the margins of the community: the hardscrabble farmers, the landless laborers, the fishermen and hunters, all of whom scraped a living from the rivers and woods of the town and provided the inquisitive Harvard graduate with information about the flora and fauna of the environs and with reminiscences of a world where "wildness" was in easy reach. His conversations with these men, before and after *Walden*, constitute an oral history of Concord unlike the version Emerson discerned in his grandsire's career. These divergent approaches to the past also illuminate the contrasts between the two Transcendentalists. Emerson was a cheerleader for the modern age of individualism taking shape under America's version of free markets and popular democracy. Thoreau was always on the lookout for other pathways to the present. He struggled to reclaim a past fast disappearing from view.[8]

To live in an "age of Revolution" was an exhilarating opportunity, as Emerson saw it. Normally, the past weighed so heavily on the present that change came about slowly and undetected. But once in a while the march of time paused for a changing of the guard, and an alert observer could survey the field and gauge the competing claims for the old and the new. The Transcendentalist relished that moment. Born in 1803, he grew up in Boston at a time when the struggle for independence was still a living memory and a new republican order was being created out of the Puritan legacy and Enlightenment ideals. In the city, following the death of his father in 1811, the boy lacked a paternal figure to pass on that tradition. In

Concord, where he made periodic visits to "the Old Manse," he encountered its most stalwart representative in his grandfather, Ezra Ripley, the last man in town to wear the fashionable garb of the eighteenth-century, with his grey wig under broad-brimmed hat, knee breeches, high stockings, and silver-buckled shoes.

No one did more to uphold the faith of New England's fathers than the long-serving pastor of Concord's established church. Like an English country vicar, he presided over the community with boundless energy and a relentless will. "In this town," he once declared, "I am placed a watchman and a monitor." True to that trust, he treated the character and conduct of every person in the parish as his personal responsibility. Few inhabitants escaped his scrutiny. "My people," he called them with proprietary pride. The minister participated in the vital events of their lives. He married the couples, baptized their babies, prayed at the funerals of young and old. He composed epitaphs for the gravestones and obituaries for the press. He was sure to pay an annual call on every household, and twice a year he catechized the children. As they grew up, he counseled the young on their choice of a calling and penned countless letters of recommendation on their behalf. Like a modern college professor, he was forever endorsing applications to schools, for jobs, even for pardons from the state prison.

The parson expounded his social ethic from the pulpit for over six decades. In some 2,500 sermons he discoursed on the duty of his parishioners to one another, to the Commonwealth, and to God. In the gospel according to Ripley, the fundamental value was community. "Who could live alone and independent?" he once asked the congregation. "Who but some disgusted hermit or half-crazy enthusiast will say to society, I have no need of thee; I am under no obligation to my fellow men?" Just the opposite was the case: "Every member of the community is obliged to seek and promote the public good." When Mary Moody Emerson resisted his plea to give up residence in the backwoods of Maine and settle in civilized Concord, "the place of your nativity and the land of your ancestors," he could not fathom her choice:

> Why then fly into the wilderness, or bury yourself in the desert? Surely, it cannot add to your happiness or improvement to hear the screaming of loons, the hooting of owls, and the howling of wolves. The wildness and simplicity of nature you may see and enjoy

without being surrounded by that in her which is savage, terrible, and unsocial.

In language dating back to the Puritan founders of New England, Ripley sought to bind the townspeople together through an ideology of interdependence. In a letter of 1831, he reminded Edward Bliss Emerson, younger brother of Waldo, that "No man lives to himself or dies to himself. He is necessarily connected with others, with society, and is obliged to contribute of his powers and worldly goods for the benefit of his fellow creatures; —and it is thus doing good to others that we find the richest comfort to ourselves."[9]

It was just this boundless commitment to community that alienated the "venerable" clergyman from his younger Transcendentalist kinsman. As a boy, Waldo acquired a prejudice against the parson from his Aunt Mary, who could not abide the rationalist sermons and lukewarm preaching of the man she dubbed "Dr. Reason." In later years, as the ex-minister of Boston's Second Church settled into Concord, he observed his grandsire on pastoral rounds, praying at sickbeds and funerals, offering counsel and comfort with natural eloquence and grace—the very skills in which Emerson himself was deficient. With intimate knowledge of his people, the parson never hesitated to dispense unwelcome advice. The younger man watched with admiration as Ripley called on a grieving family following the death of the male head and warned the eldest surviving son, a notorious drunkard, that "the name and respectability of your family rests on you." Three generations in a row had led useful lives on this farm. Would the latest heir betray that legacy? "Sir if you fail—Ichabod—the glory is departed. And I hope you will not." Maintaining continuity between generations was central to the minister's calling.[10]

Ripley's virtues were abundant, and Emerson was quick to praise the old man for his simple manners and blunt speech, his native dignity and integrity. His horizons were bounded by the parish; his language smacked of the fields and woods. In his grandson's eyes, the parson derived his notions of life not from books and reading but from "things within his experience." That was at once a strength and limitation. Thanks to his closeness to nature and his familiarity with the parish, he possessed "the most robust common sense." But Ripley was no Romantic. He derived no spiritual inspiration from the countryside. He "idealizes nothing"; he never goes beyond "literal facts." Though the preacher spent long hours at his desk reading and writing, he was akin to "an Indian Sagamore," in Emerson's judgment, "a sage within the limits of his own observation, a child beyond." And with so mundane a mentality, he had little but platitudes to deliver from the pulpit. One Sabbath in July 1838 Emerson listened to the "foolishest preaching" that "bayed at the moon." "Go, hush, old man, whom years have taught no truth," he fumed privately. A few weeks later the fury spilled over into the Divinity School Address, where it joined with his disgust at the preaching of Ripley's assistant minister, Barzillai Frost.[11]

Here was "the old" not in its historic glory but in its senescence. When Ripley died in September 1841, the grandson gathered up the observations in his journal and composed an obituary for the local newspaper. Aiming to define the significance of Ripley's long ministry, Emerson stressed that the minister's virtues, for all their worthiness, had come at a heavy cost. While the parson was in tune with the ordinary range of human life, "the common temptations, the common ambitions," he had no sympathy "with extraordinary states of mind, with "enthusiasm" or "enlarged speculation." Repeating outworn formulas and routines year after year, he had brought the ancient heritage of New England into a dead end. With his passing, "the rear-guard of the of the great camp and army of the Puritans" was leaving the scene, and the way was clear for a more open, uncertain, and individualistic future.[12]

As in the "American Scholar" address, so in the obituary. Emerson bid to pre-empt the future with his take on the past. Ripley and the tradition he represented belonged in the dustbin of history. That verdict proved controversial. Presented as a neutral statement of the late minister's historical significance, it was actually a salvo in the war of words within the Unitarian fold, as the official organ of the denomination, the *Christian Register*, was quick to discern. The periodical reluctantly reprinted the notice, which it deemed inadequate, and it deliberately omitted the judgment that the world view of the Concord minister was no longer relevant. In the last years of his life, Ripley had felt despondent over the Transcendentalist heresy in his family. Now, he lashed back through his soul-mates in the clergy. The obituary "falls far short of giving such a view of Dr. Ripley's character and services as the Christian part of the community ought to desire," the editors pronounced. Emerson's was not the final word.[13]

While Emerson could glimpse the twilight of the eighteenth century during his boyhood in Boston, Thoreau, fourteen years junior, grew up with the new age. His parents welcomed the spirit of improvement, worked tirelessly to rebuild the family fortunes, sacrificed for their children's education, campaigned against social injustice, and fostered a love of nature and an openness to innovation. Henry was a native of this new world in the making. Yet, as Concord farmers cleared every available acre for commercial crops, as the forests were decimated and the landscape tamed, with bear, moose, and wildcats a distant memory, the observant writer set about preserving a record of the natural and social worlds vanishing before his eyes. Having signed off a respectable life of economic striving and status seeking, and spending his days amid the fields, rivers, and woods, he was in a unique position to do so. "I have never got over my surprise that I should have been born into the most estimable place in all the world—," he congratulated himself in December 1856, "& in the very nick of time too" (OJT 22: 115).[14]

Thoreau was actually dubious of the historical enterprise. Could the passing moments caught in his journals ever come together and tell a larger tale? "The *past* cannot be *presented*," he quipped in *A Week on the Concord and Merrimack Rivers* (1849); "we cannot know what we are not.... It is the province of the historian to find out, not what was, but what is." For this reason, "ancient history...should be more modern." "Biography...should be autobiography." When history consists of a litany of facts, it is devoid of interest. We require a living connection to the inhabitants of distant times and places. And that can come about only through the power of the writer to engage us. Let us think the thoughts and feel the emotions of the ancients, and they become our contemporaries. Our relationship is *now*, not then. And we notch that connection in the nick of time (*Week* 155–56).

Perhaps for this reason, Thoreau was averse to the sweeping statements about the course of history that were Emerson's stock in trade on the lecture platform. "Most revolutions in society have not power to interest," he observed in *A Week*, "still the less alarm us" (*Week* 129). His abiding interest was the "revolution of the seasons" (*PJ* 1: 87).[15] In this spirit, though *Walden* is set in a specific place—in the woods by the shores of a pond a mile from the center of Concord—it is largely adrift in time. The author evokes "Indian fables" and repopulates his neighborhood with "former inhabitants," but, as John Hildebidle points out, "of historical facts of the more commonly valued sort, Walden Pond is blessedly innocent." The local histories of New England that proliferated in Thoreau's lifetime were just such dry compendia. Lemuel Shattuck's *History of Concord* (1835) became a model of the genre. The book cast a wide net; it teems with extracts from original sources, tables and lists, genealogies of founding families, biographies of college graduates. Shattuck collected and preserved as much information as possible in print. But the details were chiefly of institutions, rather than individuals—the reverse of Thoreau's priorities. "I love mankind," he remarked. "I hate the institutions of their forefathers" (*PJ* 2: 262). While Thoreau was familiar with Shattuck's work and drew on its details—"I love to quote so good authority," he said with mock humor on the opening page of *A Week* (5)—his imagination would never be seized by a history that traced in impersonal prose the steady increase and improvement of the town, one generation after another. "The researcher," according to Thoreau, should be "more memorable than the researched" (*Week* 154). In Shattuck, it is the other way around.[16]

Nor was Thoreau particularly engaged by his own family history. The American Revolution had raised one branch to sudden but short-lived success and dispatched the other into exile and ruin. Colonel Elisha Jones, his maternal great-grandfather, was "a man of standing and influence" in the nearby town of Weston, who took the side of King and Parliament, as did several of his sons (*PJ* 3: 15–16). The family estate was confiscated by the Patriots; the Loyalist sons took refuge in Canada. By contrast, the French immigrant sailor Jean Thoreau built a mercantile house in Boston on the profits of wartime privateering, only to die at age 47, not long after moving to Concord; his substantial estate, drawn down by the widow and orphans, gradually dissipated over the years. If Thoreau wanted lessons in the impermanence of wealth and the insecurity of social station, he need only consult his genealogy. He was well-aware of these facts, including Col. Jones's slaveholding, but said little about them. In his journals he recorded tidbits about eccentric relatives and unusual events. The anecdotes were detached from context, ill-remembered pieces of family lore. At his father's death in 1859, the writer paid tribute to John Thoreau's wealth of local knowledge. "He belonged in a peculiar sense to the village street...he remembered more about the worthies (and unworthies) of Concord village 40 years ago—both from dealing as a trader and from familiar intercourse with them—than any one else" (OJT 28: 172). If only his son had detailed these stories in his journal or made explicit use of them in his books! Then again, why bother about such minutia? At the end of 1855, with his father's help, he laboriously compiled a list of all the houses and towns in which he had lived with his family and on his own, only to dismiss their significance of such facts "in a true history or biography." In his journals "the most important events in my life—if recorded at all, are not [even] dated—" (OJT 19: 234-35). Intent on speaking in the first-person singular—an individual in his own right—Thoreau would come before the public free from family claims.[17]

Skeptical of the written record, Thoreau sought out his own sources about Concord life. As he explored the natural surroundings, he ran into men from all walks of life with whom he exchanged information about the flora and fauna of the area. While he would talk with anyone, his favorite informants were farmers, laborers, fishermen, and hunters—workingmen with an intimate knowledge of the environment and an ability to wrest a living from its resources. Thoreau peppered them with questions, took mental notes, and recorded the responses in his journals. It would be too much to say that he was doing oral history. He had no formal agenda; his conversations were impromptu. The man of letters was keen to hear whatever the men of the rivers and woods had to say. Even so, Thoreau took the measure of their character and gauged the significance of their ways of life. Philip Gura once proposed that Alex Therien, the French-Canadian wood-chopper, and Joe Polis, the Penobscot guide to the Maine woods, were Thoreau's "representative men." They were not the only ones. A variety of such figures attracted the writer's scrutiny, each offering an implicit answer to the Transcendentalist's urgent query. Was it possible to resist conventional existence and live simply and independently in nature? *Walden*'s agenda was uppermost in his mind.[18]

Nobody made a deeper impression than George Minott, whom Thoreau idealized as "perhaps the most poetical farmer" in Concord (*PJ* 4: 116). The man was a few years older than the writer's own father. That age gap made no difference. Henry trudged up the hill to Minott's house above Lexington Road some eighty times over the 1840s and 1850s and recorded their conversations more than with anyone else except his poet-friend Ellery Channing. Born in 1783, Minott came from a family even more illustrious in the colonial era than were Thoreau's Jones forebears; by the time the Harvard graduate got to know him, the inherited estate was reduced to a mere six acres in the town center, from which the lifelong bachelor and his spinster sister, a tailoress by trade, derived a subsistence. Though the acreage was small, the yeoman treated the land as tenderly and received its bounty as reverently as did Thoreau his bean field. Nothing was wasted; in contrast to "speculating, money-making farmers," he harvested the entire corn crop—ears, husks, and stalks—without leaving any unsightly stubble. Such intensive cultivation struck many observers as uneconomical. Minott didn't care. In Thoreau's telling, he performed his labors for their own sake and *not* for the money his crops and livestock yielded. In fact, he boasted of never having taken goods to market.

Minott was a nonconformist in all his affairs. He didn't attend town meeting; he skipped Sabbath worship; he never joined a voluntary association. Without a family of his own, he withdrew into himself and made no demands on anyone. His solitary example showed that a man could be a hermit in the village just as easily as in the woods.

Actually, Minott preferred to spend his time in the wild, rather than labor on the land. From early on he delighted in hunting the abundant game around Concord, and he took equal pleasure in recounting his exploits to Thoreau. Rabbits and squirrels; pigeons, partridges, ducks, and geese: all were easy prey to his keen eye and steady finger on the fowling pieces he treasured as affectionately as his hunting dogs. "Minott has a story for every woodland path," commented his scribe.

The anecdotes evoked a wilder, rougher, less domesticated era. In Minott's memory, winters were colder and longer, summers shorter, fish and game more profuse, and crops bigger in the "holy days" of his boyhood. The men were as outsized as the creatures: they flocked to impromptu turkey-shoots in the woods, where the rum flowed as freely as the shots; they gambled over dice on Concord common during Court Week; and they took every opportunity to challenge one another to wrestling matches. Their masculine world was free from the restrictive rules of respectability that constrained the educated, middle-class young men and women of Thoreau's generation. For this reason, the writer appreciated Minott's adamant resistance to change. Better to hold his ground in the name of principle than to try something new and expand the "capacities" of human nature. Thoreau was untroubled by the contradiction. As Emerson said, "a foolish consistency is the hobgoblin of little minds."[19]

The hinterland remained a refuge from the village well into the 1850s. As Thoreau traipsed about the countryside on his naturalist's errand, he encountered such men as John Goodwin and George Melvin with fishing rods, fowling pieces, and hunting dogs. Rain or shine, winter and summer, these workingmen were out not for sport but for survival. Melvin, "our Concord Trapper" (*PJ* 2: 126), was unrelenting in the quest for minks and muskrats, whose skins he sold to Boston traders. He shot duck and other waterfowl for food, fished for pickerel and perch, and did occasional labor for farmers. "He follows hunting, praises be to him—as regularly in our tame fields as the farmers follow farming." Thoreau saluted Melvin, three years older than he, for his nonconformity. "How good in him to follow his own bent—& not continue at the Sabbath school all his days!—What a wealth he thus becomes in the neighborhood!" (OJT 22: 99) He was a fount of knowledge about wildflowers, where and when they were in bloom. Usually, he generously shared his discoveries with Thoreau, but on one occasion, he was reluctant to divulge the site of an azalea bush he had found. The college graduate forced it out of him. "Well I told him[,] he had better tell me where it was—I was a botanist & ought to know.…I told him he'd better tell me & have the glory of it" (*PJ* 6: 163–64). As for Goodwin, a fisherman who had moved to Concord from New Hampshire sometime after 1850, he won the writer's admiration for his skill in providing for his needs. One late October evening, Thoreau saw the "one-eyed Ajax" (OJT 27: 302) on the river's shore, taking the piles of driftwood he had collected on his boat and loading them onto a handcart to carry home. It was a simple, virtuous action—the man needed his "winter's wood" and went out and found it—prompting the writer to celebrate this poetry in motion. How superior was Goodwin, generally considered to be "a vicious character," to the proper villagers, like the brokers who commuted by train into Boston for unsatisfying jobs buying and selling stock in order to earn the money to heat their homes (*PJ* 7:107–09)! Goodwin did not postpone life; he gathered his woodpile at no cost and profited from the experience. His life was testimony to the wisdom of *Walden*, which would appear in print nine months later. Thoreau overflowed with joy at the sight. "I am not only grateful because Veias, and Homer, and Christ, and Shakespeare have lived, but I am grateful for Minot [sic]—&…Melvin--& Goodwin…I see Melvin all alone, filling his sphere—in russet suit—which no other could fill or suggest. He takes up as much room in nature as the most famous" (OJT 22:103).

Lost in this tribute to Concord's ne'er-do-wells was any coming to terms with their marginal status. The Harvard graduate spurned the inequality and class consciousness that typically came with his diploma. Educated to be a gentleman and scholar, he astonished the neighbors with his preference for the company of disreputable woodsmen, common farmers, and Irish laborers. Why would he deny the requests of polite peers to guide excursions into nature but spend endless hours with "the quaint people of the town, those who were racy in speech and personal in character"?[20] The question answered itself. Thoreau admired the fund of natural lore these outcasts accumulated as they tracked prey across the landscape. He was fascinated by Melvin's account of muskrats gnawing their legs off to escape from traps. "Even the water rats lead sleepless nights—and live Achillean lives.... The hunter regards with awe his game" (*PJ* 2:127). With their keen eyes and inquisitive minds, the denizens of Concord's backwoods may have never attended the lyceum. But for Thoreau, they formed an *ad hoc* natural history society, sharing their discoveries and trophies. Let the simple and sincere observers of the world around them, such as Minott, occupy the lecture platform, instead of the usual mediocre "hirelings" from out of town. "I would rather hear [Minott]...decline" than the paid speakers hold forth. (*PJ* 4:196–97).

Where Emerson found his representative men at the center of society, Thoreau located them on the fringes. Ezra Ripley had embodied the ethos of the village, with its meetinghouse and courthouse, its appreciation for ornamental trees and well-cultivated farms. He had no sympathy with wilderness. That outlook had altered, with the demise of the old order he represented, but only up to a point. To spend your days in the woods, apart from the neighbors, still aroused suspicion a decade after Thoreau had settled into Main Street and his house at Walden had been removed. Thoreau liked to think that "Goodwin cannot be a very bad man-- he is so cheery" (OJT 28:63), and he pretended that his motley crew had chosen life in the outdoors for the independence it allowed. He should have known better. Minott's cramped circumstances—occupying an old house on a few acres with his unmarried sister—were increasingly common on the eve of the Civil War. His once-eminent family had descended even farther down the social scale than the Thoreaus and, like them, was going to seed. George

Minott had sacrificed his prospects and stuck in Concord out of loyalty to his widowed mother, with little to speak of as a reward. George Melvin, the first-born in his family, inherited nothing from his landless father. Never marrying, he resided with his mother and, as Thoreau conceded, was a "trial" (OJT 22:99) to her because of his heavy drinking. The writer looked past that defect and did not live to see the family tragedy play out, as the widow Melvin died of insanity in 1864 and George drowned in the Concord River at age fifty-four.[21]

Similar stories inform the biographies of the other isolates Thoreau met in the woods—most of them unwed and childless, whose family lines would expire with them. They survived on the edges of the local economy, selling the hides of minks and muskrats or, like the Black "man of wild habits," Elisha Dugan, whom Thoreau memorialized in the poem "Old Marlborough Road" (*Exc* 193–94), cutting down the alder trees around town to supply charcoal for the gunpowder works in nearby Acton (*PJ* 6:35, 52–53). It was still possible to scrape together a meager subsistence on the bounty of the ponds, rivers, and woods in a town where nobody had to pay for a fishing or hunting license. In the cities modern capitalism made room for junk dealers, rag pickers, and pawn shops; the still-rural suburbs offered healthier options. And, as Thoreau recognized, it took resourcefulness and resilience to employ them. It was a harsh existence, about which Goodwin had no illusions. In the "severe" winter of 1857, he shot a partridge and took it for sale to John Cheney, the cashier of the Concord Bank. The tender-hearted official, a Harvard classmate of Emerson, expressed a pang of regret. "It was a pity to kill it," he averred. "It must find it hard to get a living." The 55-year-old hunter was unmoved by such sentiment. "I guess she didn't find it any harder than I do" (OJT 22:259). The way of life of Goodwin and Melvin, with its transient freedom, was as doomed as Ezra Ripley's, with its impermanent constraints.

Toward the end of his essay "Walking," Thoreau recalls climbing a tall white pine atop a hill and gazing on a new sight, "a few minute and delicate red conelike blossoms, the fertile flower of the white pine looking heavenward." He took "the topmost spire" for a specimen and, once back on solid ground, hastened into the village to show off the "minute blossoms" to the admiring eyes of the neighbors. The naturalist trusted correctly that "farmers and lumber-dealers and woodchoppers and hunters" would stop in their tracks to behold this example of nature's beauty. For Thoreau, the incident confirmed his conviction that "we cannot afford not to live in the present. He is blessed over all mortals who loses no moment of the passing life in remembering the past" (*Exc* 220). But I like to imagine Goodwin and Melvin as well as Minott enjoying a moment of camaraderie with Thoreau and the respectable folk in a spontaneous community that Ezra Ripley himself would have approved. For a brief moment in an age of revolution, Transcendentalism would unite them all.

Works Cited

Emerson, Ralph Waldo. "The American Scholar" (1837). In *Ralph Waldo Emerson: The Major Prose*, edited by Ronald A. Bosco and Joel Myerson, 91–109. Cambridge: Harvard University Press, 2015.

———. "Historic Notes on Life and Letters in New England." *Atlantic Monthly* 52 (October 1883): 529–43.

———. "Introductory" lecture to series on "Human Culture." In *The Early Lectures of Ralph Waldo Emerson,* edited by Stephen E. Whicher, Robert E. Spiller, and Wallace E. Williams. Volume II: 1836–1838, Harvard University Press: 1964.

———. *The Journals and Miscellaneous Notebooks of Ralph Waldo Emerson*, edited by William H. Gilman et al. 16 vols.; Cambridge, Mass.: Harvard University Press: 1960–82.

Gross, Robert A. "'The Nick of Time': Coming of Age in Thoreau's Concord." In *Thoreau at 200: Essays and Reassessments*, edited by Kristen Case and K. P. Van Anglen. New York: Cambridge University Press, 2016.

———. *The Transcendentalists and Their World.* New York: Farrar, Straus and Giroux: 2021.

Gura, Philip F. "Thoreau's Maine Woods Indians: More Representative Men." *American Literature* 49, no. 3 (Nov. 1977): 366–84.

Harding, Walter. *Thoreau as Seen by His Contemporaries*. New York: Dover, 1989: 82–83.

Hildebidle, John. *Thoreau: A Naturalist's Liberty*. Cambridge: Harvard University Press, 1983.

Kaag, John. *American Bloods: The Untamed Dynasty That Shaped a Nation.* New York: Farrar, Straus and Giroux, 2024.

Richardson, Robert D. *Henry Thoreau: A Life of the Mind.* Berkeley: University of California Press: 1986.

Ripley, George. "Jesus Christ, the Same Yesterday, Today, and Tomorrow." In *The Transcendentalists,* edited by Perry Miller. Cambridge: Harvard University Press, 1950.

Shanley, J. Lyndon. *The Making of Walden with the Text of the First Edition.* Chicago University Press, 1957.

CHAPTER 6

"NO TIME TO BE ANYTHING BUT A MACHINE": *WALDEN* AND THE CONDITION-OF-(NEW) ENGLAND QUESTION

Ben Schacht

Walden is a work of social criticism whose targets are famously close to home. "I would fain say something, not so much concerning the Chinese and Sandwich Islanders as you who read these pages, who are said to live in New England, Thoreau writes—"something about your condition, especially your outward condition or circumstances in this world, in this town, what it is, whether it is necessary that it be as bad as it is, whether it cannot be improved as well as not."

What was it about the "condition" of his fellow New Englanders that Thoreau found so objectionable? Simply put, they worked too much:

> The twelve labors of Hercules were trifling in comparison with those which my neighbors have undertaken; for they were only twelve, and had an end; but I could never see that these men slew or captured any monster or finished any labor. They have no friend Iolas to burn with a hot iron the root of the hydra's head, but as soon as one head is crushed, two spring up. (*W* 4–5)

Although Thoreau takes aim at the behaviors of his neighbors in New England and emphatically eschews any interest in far-flung places, his use of the word "condition" and his concern with excessive labor in the book's opening pages signal his participation in a broader transatlantic discourse known as the "Condition-of-England Question." Coined in 1839 by Thomas Carlyle—a writer whose influence on Thoreau is hard to overstate—the phrase "Condition of England" has come to stand for a British literary tradition that began in the 1830s, flourished in the 1840s, and continued into the 1850s. Synonymous with the novels and social criticism of such authors as Benjamin Disraeli, Charles Dickens, Elizabeth Gaskell,

Charlotte Brontë, and Charles Kingsley—and identified with subsequent writers such as John Ruskin and William Morris—Condition-of-England literature highlighted the social and technological changes associated with industrialization, especially their consequences for the poor and working classes.[1]

Placing *Walden* in dialogue with this literary tradition, I argue, helps to illuminate the nature of its social critique. Some 170 years removed from *Walden*'s publication in 1854, twenty-first-century readers are liable to overlook the book's social, historical, and intellectual context.[2] On the one hand, such lack of context threatens to turn *Walden* into a trite collection of inspirational quotations—feel-good exhortations to "be ourselves" and "seize the day." On the other, Thoreau's unabashed individualism and contempt for social niceties can make him appear as a proto-libertarian[3] thinker and have even elicited comparisons with the arch-capitalist philosopher Ayn Rand.[4] Reading *Walden* as part of the Condition-of-England tradition, however, helps to establish Thoreau's credentials as a sharp critic of industrial capitalism who was acutely aware of its effects on labor, leisure, and time itself.

Like all social criticism, Thoreau's was a product of its age. In the first half of the 19th century, Western European and North American society was embarking on a period of profound and rapid change. The rise of political democracy, capitalism, and industrial technology lent the era a self-consciously "progressive" character. It was the age of "steamboats, viaducts, and railways,"[5] in the words of romantic poet William Wordsworth, developments which he thought should inspire hope in humanity's power to overcome the limitations of space and time; but it was also the era of workhouses and factories, which another poet, William Blake, famously described as "dark Satanic Mills."[6] Though it may have been an "age of improvement" in historical terms, in the everyday and biographical terms of lived experience, it was marked by strong contrasts—rich and poor, master and slave, capitalist and proletarian—the analysis of which helped to define Condition-of-England writing.[7]

The 1840s—the decade most classically associated with Condition-of-England literature and the period when Thoreau lived at Walden Pond—were particularly marked by such contrasts. In Britain, these years became known as the "Hungry Forties" due to the hardship and privation that many people experienced amidst the transition to an industrial capitalist economy and the precipitous ups and downs of the recently entrenched trade cycle. Such experiences fueled the rise of Chartism, whose working-class constituency demanded universal male suffrage; inspired concerted campaigns for the legal limitation of the working day; provoked labor unrest and strikes; and forced the mass emigration of the Irish, who fled conditions of famine.[8]

While the situation in the U.S. differed from that of England by virtue of a somewhat wider franchise and a large western frontier, the society was riven by similar contrasts and was undergoing a broadly similar process of industrial development. In the words of historian David Montgomery, the 1840s witnessed a "paradoxical rise of a proletariat in the Age of Equality." While on the one hand, the widespread introduction of machinery heightened productivity, on the other, the wages and living standards of the workers failed to keep pace. The early years of the decade thus presented, in Montgomery's terms, "a classical counterpoint of progress and poverty."[9]

As I shall argue in the chapter that follows, Thoreau was highly attuned to the era's social and historical changes. He was not only conversant with Condition-of-England literature; his commentary was part of a wider Condition-of-(New) England discourse in which a new transatlantic awareness of time and labor played a central role. At the most general level, Condition-of-(New) England literature attempted to comprehend and critique the broad reorganization of social time engendered by the rise of industrial capitalism. Through employing many of the classic tropes and motifs of this discourse, Thoreau registered his own peculiar brand of skepticism toward the age, which he expressed in a sweeping critique of industrial capitalist temporality that sought to expose its pathologies and mythologies.

Thoreau, Carlyle, and the Condition-of-England Question

Before turning to *Walden* itself, it is necessary to briefly discuss Thoreau's relationship to Carlyle, who is generally considered the initiator of the "Condition-of-England" tradition. Thoreau engaged deeply with Carlyle's writings, and anyone familiar with them will immediately recognize numerous allusions to Carlyle throughout *Walden*. As Robert Sattelmeyer observes, Thoreau drew heavily on Carlyle's 1836 novel *Sartor Resartus* ("The Tailor Re-Tailored") in *Walden*'s multiple passages on clothing.[10]

Thoreau was conscious of his debts. In 1846 while residing at Walden Pond, he penned "Thomas Carlyle and His Works," a wide-ranging and warmly appreciative essay on the Scottish writer and his oeuvre.[11] Offering a panoramic overview of Carlyle's life and career, Thoreau's essay shows how strongly the Condition-of-England question helped to define Carlyle's literary identity in Thoreau's eyes. It also reveals some of the ways that Thoreau sought to adapt, extend, and deepen core Condition-of-England themes around labor and leisure in his own life and writings, prefiguring later writers in the Condition-of-England tradition.

Thoreau's discussion is largely concerned with Carlyle as a literary stylist, a focus which accords with Sattelmeyer's claim that Carlyle exerted a strong stylistic influence on Thoreau as he was writing his first draft of *Walden* in the mid-1840s.[12] As an aspiring writer who aimed to accomplish something "in the literary way" (*Corr* 1: 224) himself, it would only make sense for Thoreau to analyze the style of a renowned contemporary. But even confining himself to the literary realm, Thoreau cannot avoid confronting the urgent social issues which motivate Carlyle to write in the first place. "This man has something to communicate," Thoreau observes. Yet far from undermining his literary stature by entangling the immortal realm of art with the transient world of politics and current events, Carlyle's urge to communicate social realities starkly is integral to what makes him a consummate prose stylist in Thoreau's view. He is the "Hero as Man of Letters," as Thoreau remarks (borrowing one of Carlyle's own phrases), a writer for whom—to paraphrase a popular slogan—the pen is not just a paintbrush with which to depict reality but a tool with which to shape it. "Carlyle's are not, in the common sense, works of art in their origin and aim," Thoreau writes, "and yet, perhaps, no living English writer evinces an equal literary talent. They are such works of art only as the plough, and corn-mill, and steam-engine" (*EEM* 234).

When Thoreau addresses the Condition-of-England question explicitly, it is to connect it with precisely this "practical" respect in which Carlyle distinguishes himself as a writer: "The condition-of-England question is a practical one. The condition of England demands a hero, not a poet" (*EEM* 246).

Accordingly, *Past and Present*—one of Carlyle's main Condition-of-England works—becomes, in Thoreau's metaphor, a sword, "a cutting cimiter...going through heaps of silken stuff, and glibly through the necks of men, too" (*EEM* 235)—a kind of literary guillotine for executing social complacency. The purpose of such writing is to awaken the reader and prompt action, not stoke reflection merely. Carlyle's works "contain not the highest, but a very practicable wisdom, which startles and provokes, rather than informs us," Thoreau writes. "Carlyle does not oblige us to think...he compels us to act" (*EEM* 253).

A related way that Carlyle distinguishes himself as a writer, according to Thoreau, is his validation of labor as something heroic and ennobling. "Literature has come to mean, to the ears of laboring men, something idle, something cunning and pretty merely," Thoreau laments. Carlyle's embrace of the worker differs refreshingly from those writers who ply their trade merely "for fame and amusement" (*EEM* 244). As evidence of Carlyle's distinctness on this front, Thoreau cites a long passage from *Sartor Resartus* in which Carlyle's fictional narrator, the eccentric German philosopher Diogenes Teufelsdrokh, praises the laborer and the artist alike, celebrating both "the toil-worn craftsman" and the "inspired thinker." He reserves his most emphatic praise, however, for the figure who combines the earthly and spiritual qualities of both, so that "he that must toil outwardly for the lowest of man's wants, is also toiling inwardly for the highest" (*EEM* 245).

In this ode to the synthesis of manual and intellectual labor, Thoreau sees a model for his own project, which he seeks to take yet further by putting into practice the ideal which Carlyle expresses in *Sartor*. As welcome as he finds Carlyle's literary celebration of labor, Thoreau argues that both Carlyle and his contemporary Emerson fail to address the worker on equal terms. With respect to "the Man of the Age, come to be called working-man, it is obvious that none yet speaks to his condition, for the speaker is not yet in his condition," according to Thoreau. "There is poetry and prophecy to cheer him, and advice of the head and heart to the hands; but no very memorable cooperation" (*EEM* 251).

As David Herreshoff suggests, Thoreau's experiment at Walden Pond—and his subsequent recounting of it in *Walden*—can be read as an attempt to initiate such cooperation. "Thoreau's ostensibly stoical, ascetic experiments in doing without some culturally defined 'necessities' as well as his study of the historically changing scope of human needs were efforts to discover a standard of living that would permit him, and not only him, to maximize leisure time without violating the principle that work is a human need," Herreshoff writes.[13] On this interpretation, Thoreau is less like

Ayn Rand than Karl Marx. He seeks to overcome the alienation that afflicts working and owning classes alike and prevents them from realizing their full human potential. By forsaking luxury and relying on the labor of his own hands, he offers an example of the type of synthesis between work and thought that he finds suggested but ultimately lacking in Carlyle.[14] In so doing, Thoreau anticipates the ideas of another prominent inheritor of the Condition-of-England tradition, the British artist and designer William Morris, who looked forward to a time when there would be "neither idle nor overworked, neither brain-sick brain workers, nor heart-sick hand workers."[15] In Thoreau's day, however, such a time remained a distant prospect.

Thoreau, the Factory, and the Condition-of-New England Question

The Condition-of-England question did not concern England alone but also New England, where the first American factories took root. In Rhode Island, Samuel Slater partnered with the merchant Moses Brown to open the country's first modern textile factory in 1790. Slater was born in England and had overseen a northern English textile factory owned by Jedediah Strutt before emigrating to the United States, the legally protected secrets of machine spinning hidden safely inside his own head.[16] Cotton mills soon began to proliferate in the region, giving rise to conflicts over water resources—which the mills relied on to power their machines—and introducing new social relationships between employers and workers, new methods of industrial discipline, and new experiences of time.[17]

The new relations engendered by the rise of the factory came to a head in May of 1824 in the first strike of factory wage workers in the United States.[18] In Pawtucket, Rhode Island, a group of women workers organized a work stoppage in response to their employers' decision to implement longer hours and lower wages.[19] The strike, which attracted roughly 500 participants, lasted for a week. Tensions mounted as protesting workers and their allies in the surrounding community threatened the factories and property of their wealthy employers. While the strike's exact outcome is unknown, it ended in what contemporary sources referred to as a "compromise," suggesting that the strikers won at least some concessions.[20]

The class tensions manifested in the strike elicited comparisons to the situation in England, providing a clear example of Condition-of-(New) England discourse in action. One local newspaper stated that the "excitement and disorder…reminds us of the accounts we frequently read of the tumults of the manufacturing places in England." About a decade earlier, the Luddites had smashed machines and burned factories in the north of England to protest industrialization's effects on the working population. According to the newspaper report, the situation in New England was not quite so dire. The Pawtucket action was "unattended with the destruction and damage usually accompanying" such English protests.[21]

Even so, it did have significant effects. Among the strike's longer-term outcomes was the erection, in 1828, of a public clock whereby the workers of Pawtucket might have an objective standard by which to judge the claims of their employers, who were wont to use their control of timekeeping to extract more work from their operatives. The clock, like the strike itself, represented an act of self-assertion on the part of the workers; but as the 1824 strike's foremost historian, Gary Kulik, observes, it was also a tacit admission that the basic temporal framework of the factory was there to stay.[22]

The spread of industrialization brought with it the spread of workers' agitation for various reforms, including a shorter working day and stricter regulation of factory labor. England continued to loom large in this discourse, providing advocates of reform an example of what New England might become if the factory system was allowed to grow unchecked. For advocates of the United States' burgeoning manufacturing sector, however, England—then "the workshop of the world," a phrase popularized by Benjamin Disraeli and invoked by Thoreau in *Walden*—was a lodestar showing the way toward economic progress and national prosperity.

A dramatic illustration of the conflict between these views of England can be seen in a sharply polemical pamphlet by Seth Luther: *An address to the working men of New England, on the state of education, and on the condition of the producing classes in Europe and America*. Born in Rhode Island the son of a Revolutionary War veteran, Luther was a carpenter, factory worker, and articulate advocate of social and economic reform whose writings were influential and widely read, contributing, for example, to a successful 1835 strike in Philadelphia on behalf of the ten-hour day.[23] In *An Address*—which first appeared in 1832 and went through several editions[24]— Luther decried long hours of labor as a drain on the intellectual powers of the workers, whose enervated state left no time for the cultivation of democratic faculties required to question their leaders and govern themselves. How could workers become the informed citizens that democracy requires if they were shut up in factories all day? He declared himself an "enemy to all systems the tendency of which is to prevent the diffusion of intelligence,"[25] and he began and ended his pamphlet by invoking the Declaration of Independence, quoting in bold capital letters its proclamation that "all men are created equal." Although Thoreau dismissed the fact that he moved into his house at Walden Pond on Independence Day as a mere "accident"—which he nevertheless saw fit to note—clearly the date and its egalitarian associations already had currency in the working-class radical discourse of the times.[26]

At the heart of Luther's polemic was a rejection of the idea—propounded by contemporary businessmen and politicians—that New England should follow the "splendid example of England," a phrase which he quoted from a report by the diplomat Alexander Hill Everett on the state of American manufacturing. The phrase appeared as one of several epigraphs on the pamphlet's title page, along with a quotation from Senator Henry Clay that underscores the connections between the factory and the changing experience of time: "Who has not been delighted with the clockwork movements of a large cotton manufactory."

Luther argued that England's "splendid example" was belied by the impoverished state of its populace, nearly half of whom, he claimed, had "been humbled to the condition of *paupers*."[27] If New England's factories were permitted to continue unchecked in their "avarice" for profits, manufacturing towns like Lowell would soon resemble Manchester in England, Luther warned, citing the dire reports of Dr. James Phillips Kay. (Kay, who had documented industrial pathologies in his 1832 book *The Moral and Physical Condition of the Working Class Employed in the Cotton Manufacture in Manchester*, was also a key source, along with Carlyle, for Friedrich Engels in his own 1845 work *The Condition of the Working Class in England.*) In one excerpt quoted by Luther, Kay describes the long hours and inhuman pace of work under industrial conditions, using language that closely resembles Thoreau's remark in *Walden* that "the laboring man…has no time to be anything but a machine." According to Kay, the factory system turned workers into "drudges, who watch the movements, and assist the operations, of a mighty material force, which toils, ever unconscious of fatigue. The labor of the operative must rival the mathematical precision, the incessant motion, and exhaustless power of the machine."[28]

Whether Thoreau read Luther's pamphlet is unclear. None of his works appear in Thoreau's library as documented by Sattelmeyer. Luther was a notorious figure, however, even more so after participating in Dorr's Rebellion—an armed attempt to build an alternative state government in Rhode Island that took place in 1841–2 as part of the popular struggle to win manhood suffrage in the state, one of the last to insist on property requirements for voting.[29] It thus seems likely that Thoreau would have at least been aware of him. But even if Thoreau did not consciously draw on Luther's ideas, he clearly shared his concerns about the effects of the factory system and expressed them in similar terms.

Like Luther, Thoreau compared what he witnessed in New England's burgeoning manufacturing sector to reports from across the Atlantic. "I cannot believe that our factory system is the best mode by which men may get clothing," he writes in *Walden*, part of his extended riff on the clothing theme that he borrowed from Carlyle. "The condition of the operatives is becoming every day more like that of the English; and it cannot be wondered at, since, as far as I have heard or observed, the principal object is, not that mankind may be well and honestly clad, but, unquestionably, that corporations may be enriched." In tracing the workers' downtrodden state to corporations' desire to make money, Thoreau's language verges on Marxist. It would hardly be a stretch to say that he blames the workers' poor condition on the subordination of clothing's use-value—cladding people—to its exchange-value—selling it for money. Such similarities are unsurprising considering the philosophers' shared historical and social context and the fact that both were strongly influenced by Carlyle in style and substance.[30]

Besides being a prominent part of the ambient discourse surrounding social and technological change in industrializing New England, especially that of workers agitating for reform, the Condition-of-(New) England question occupied the pages of Transcendentalist and Transcendentalist-adjacent publications. One key figure in this regard was Orestes Brownson.[31] Brownson was a founder of the New York Workingmen's Party in the 1820s and a leading exponent of Transcendentalist philosophy whose journal, *The Boston Quarterly Review*, Thoreau read.[32] As Sattelmeyer observes, he exerted a strong philosophical influence on the young Thoreau and was a "catalyst" for his interest in Transcendental ideas. Thoreau boarded with Brownson during his junior year at Harvard in 1836. Among the subjects they studied together were German literature and philosophy—the same intellectual terrain that proved so fertile for Carlyle.[33]

Brownson's engagement with Condition-of-England discourse can been seen in his 1840 essay "The Laboring Classes," a critical review of Carlyle's pamphlet *Chartism*, the text in which the Scottish man of letters had first explicitly posed his "Condition-of-England Question." In Brownson's estimation, though "Carlyle unquestionably ranks among the ablest writers of the day" and "his works are characterized by freshness and power,"[34] his acute diagnosis of the era's social ills—the poverty, indignity, and discontent that made up the "wrong condition" of the English worker in Carlyle's view—lacked a correspondingly cogent prescription for positive change. Brownson criticized Carlyle's recommendations of "universal education" and "emigration" as means by which the condition of the English worker might be ameliorated.[35] For Brownson, such solutions were unworkable because they failed to strike at the root of the poverty and alienation that fueled worker discontent. These were endemic to the factory system of wage labor, which, by exploiting the worker, was laying the groundwork for cataclysmic class conflict. Emigration could only delay the reckoning, "for the colony will soon become an empire and reproduce all the injustice and wretchedness of the mother country," he wrote. Anyway, it wasn't needed because the real cause of the workers' poverty had nothing to do with the "overpopulation" to which emigration was the supposed solution—the problem, Brownson argued, was that workers "produce not for themselves but for their employers."[36]

As for education, Brownson readily acknowledged its desirability, but he wondered how it would occur when the laboring classes must work all day: "We have little faith in the power of education to elevate a people compelled to labor from twelve to sixteen hours a day, and to experience for no mean portion of the time a paucity of even the necessaries of life, let alone its comforts," he observed soberly. For education to be meaningful, it required a basis of leisure and material security: "Give your starving boy a breakfast before you send him to school, and your tattered beggar a cloak before you attempt his moral and intellectual elevation," he pleaded.[37]

Although Thoreau may not have championed the workers' cause quite as militantly as Brownson, he did borrow from Brownson's rhetoric in *Walden*, suggesting that he sympathized with his views. This is evident from the larger passage in which Thoreau's comparison of the laborer to a machine, quoted above, occurs. While Thoreau initially blames "mere ignorance and mistake" for the fact that "most men" devote their time to the "superfluously coarse labors of life" when they could be sampling "its finer fruits," he quickly acknowledges that many people have no other choice:

> Actually, the laboring man has not leisure for a true integrity day by day; he cannot afford to sustain the manliest relations to men; his labor would be depreciated in the market. He has no time to be anything but a machine. How can he remember well his ignorance—which his growth requires—who has so often to use his knowledge? We should feed and clothe him gratuitously sometimes, and recruit him with our cordials, before we judge of him. The finest qualities of our nature, like the bloom on fruits, can be preserved only by the most delicate handling. Yet we do not treat ourselves nor one another thus tenderly. (*W* 6)

Like Brownson, Thoreau locates the source of "the laboring man's" plight in his circumstances—especially his lack of leisure—which must change before he can be expected to cultivate his mind and morals. In true Socratic fashion, Thoreau sees ignorance as the ground of wisdom but argues that workers' minds are too overstimulated by the pressure to keep pace with the machine to engage in any genuine search for truth. Thoreau also alludes to the workers' exploitation when he says that the market "depreciates" their labor. Finally, in a clear echo of Brownson's appeal to "give your starving boy a breakfast…and your tattered beggar a cloak," Thoreau proposes the same material solution—the bestowal of free food and clothing (admittedly qualified by the adverb "sometimes")—to the problem of the worker's intellectual and spiritual degradation. His faith in the justice and utility of unconditional aid would be surprising—as would his subsequent lament that we do not treat ourselves or each other "tenderly" enough—if Thoreau adhered to an austere Randian philosophy that denigrated altruism and praised selfishness. By contrast, this passage's appeal to feelings of mutuality has distinctly welfarist implications that point in an altogether different, social democratic, direction.

Thoreau, the Railroad, and the Ideology of Modern Progress

Thoreau's critical attitude toward his industrial capitalist surroundings is also evident in his discussion of commerce and the railroad, which are closely linked. Although he questioned the era's obsession with commerce, Thoreau could not help but be impressed by its bold spirit, which he found invigorating. He admires commerce's "heroic" side, in which nature yields to human will and humanity asserts itself as the master of its own fate. "What recommends commerce to me is its enterprise and bravery," he writes in "Sounds." "It does not clasp its hands and pray to Jupiter" (*W* 118). He also celebrates commerce's cosmopolitan qualities, which he connects with modern modes of transport, especially the railroad. "I am refreshed and expanded when the freight train rattles past me, and I smell the stores which go dispensing their odors all the way from Long Wharf to Lake Champlain, reminding me of foreign parts, of coral reefs, and Indian oceans, and tropical climes, and the extent of the globe," he enthuses. "I feel more like a citizen of the world" (*W* 119). Thoreau's attitude here resembles not only Carlyle's, who marveled at the increase of humanity's productive forces, but also that of Marx and Engels, whose rhetorical debts to Carlyle are evident throughout the *Communist Manifesto*. Writing in 1848 at the climax of a decade marked by revolutionary upheavals, the young German radicals rhapsodized the era's technological progress and cosmopolitan commercial spirit—before calling for the supersession of the bourgeoisie by the organized proletariat, who, they argued, would put the productive forces unleashed by industrialization to more rational and humane uses.

Thoreau was similarly concerned with how the industrial era's new powers would be used. But while the young Marx and Engels appeared to put their faith in inexorable technological development as the road to an eventual social revolution, predicting that the forces of production would burst the fetters of outmoded social relations to usher in a new form of cooperative society, Thoreau evinced a more cautious skepticism toward the ideology of progress associated with commerce and industrialization. With respect to so-called "modern improvements," he warned, "there is not always a positive advance...Our inventions are wont to be pretty toys, which distract our attention from serious things. They are but improved means to an unimproved end" (*W* 52). The railroad was a case in point.

While the factory preceded the railroad—its outline was already distinct by the latter half of the eighteenth century—it was the railroad, whose spread began in earnest during the 1830s and 40s, that had some of the most obviously dramatic effects on temporal attitudes and institutions. Besides a producing a new sense of speed, the railroad promoted an unprecedented regularity and coordination in the measurement of time. "The startings and arrivals of the cars are now the epochs in the village day," Thoreau observed in *Walden*. "They go and come with such regularity and precision, and their whistle can be heard so far, that the farmers set their clocks by them, and thus one well conducted institution regulates a whole country." This regulation reached deep into people's psyches: "Have not men improved somewhat in punctuality since the railroad was invented?" (*W* 117). Indeed, the need for a high degree of temporal coordination created by the railroad reshaped time the world over. The division of the globe into time zones and the establishment of "World Time" toward the end of the nineteenth century can be traced directly to the advent of railroad timetables several decades earlier.[38]

Like his view of commerce, Thoreau's view of the railroad is conflicted. On the one hand, it is a marvel of human inventiveness. The "new people" of the industrial age "put a little dry wood under a pot, and are whirled round the globe with the speed of birds" (*W* 8). But its speed and relentlessness also suggest something more portentous: "When the smoke is blown away and the vapor condensed, it will be perceived that a few are riding, but the rest are run over,—and it will be called, and will be, 'A melancholy accident'" (*W* 53). Thoreau would thus appear to share what cultural historian Wolfgang Schivelbusch calls the era's "curious ambivalence" toward the railroad. While witnesses to its advent expressed awe at the railroad's ability to transport people and goods swiftly across vast distances, as if by flight, they also experienced "a sensation of violence and potential destruction." According to Schivelbusch (who somewhat surprisingly does not mention Thoreau), "this sensation became concretized in the metaphor of the railroad train as a projectile shot through space and time."[39] Or as Thoreau put it in *Walden:* "The air is full of invisible bolts" (*W* 118).

Here too, Thoreau is on well-trod Condition-of-England territory. In Condition-of-England literature, the metaphor of the steam engine as a dangerous "projectile" served to express the double-edged nature of the era's technological progress. It symbolized humanity's power and its heedlessness, its exuberance but also its soullessness. In *Sartor Resartus*, it swells to cosmic proportions, representing an increasingly mechanized world, devoid of spirituality: "To me the Universe was all void of Life, of Purpose, of Volition, even of Hostility: it was one huge, dead, immeasurable Steam-engine, rolling on, in its dead indifference, to grind me limb from limb."[40] Charles Dickens, who, like Thoreau, was strongly influenced by Carlyle,[41] used the railroad as an ambiguous symbol of change[42] in his 1848 novel *Dombey and Son*, linking it explicitly with industrialization and death: "The power that forced itself upon its iron way—its own—defiant of all paths and roads, piercing through the heart of every obstacle, and dragging living creatures of all classes, ages, and degrees behind it, was a type of the triumphant monster, Death."[43] Likewise, in *Walden*, the railroad appears as an unstoppable force, barreling through New England snowstorms to carry goods to market, possessing an inevitability that Thoreau finds admirable but which he also associates with mortality: "We have constructed a fate, an Atropos, that never turns aside. (Let that be the name of your engine)" (*W* 118).

For Thoreau, however, the railroad's darker side symbolizes something more historically specific than modernity's existential dread. Rather, it exposes the class basis of industrial progress, with its lopsided distribution of work and wealth, of labor and leisure—and ultimately of life. As he observes in "Where I Lived and What I Lived For," access to the advantages of the railroad is not shared equally, "so that, if some have the pleasure of riding on a rail, others have the misfortune to be ridden upon." It is not only that, as he waggishly suggests, the time required to earn the railroad's fare may exceed the time it takes to reach one's destination by foot, so that viewed in terms of how much life it costs—the ultimate measure of value for Thoreau—riding the railroad represents a bad deal for all but the wealthiest passengers. It is also that the workers who build the railroad must pay the price of its construction, a sacrifice that Thoreau depicts with his metaphor of the "sleepers"— the human railroad ties upon which the train runs. "Did you ever think what those sleepers are that underlie the railroad?" he asks. "Each one is a man, an Irish-man, or a Yankee man" (*W* 92).

According to Thoreau, the human cost of constructing the railroad represents a visceral challenge to its status as the ultimate symbol of modern progress.[44] It also throws into relief larger existential questions about how the burgeoning industrial capitalist economy allocates time. These he raises in a passage that combines his overarching concern in *Walden* to "get my living honestly, with freedom left for my proper pursuits" (*W* 29) with the specific case of the workers whose lives are devoted to constructing the railroad:

> This spending of the best part of one's life earning money in order to enjoy a questionable liberty during the least valuable part of it, reminds me of the Englishman who went to India to make a fortune first, in order that he might return to England and live the life of a poet. He should have gone up garret at once. "What!" exclaim a million Irishmen starting up from all the shanties in the land, "is not this railroad which we have built a good thing?" Yes, I answer, *comparatively* good, that is, you might have done worse; but I wish, as you are brothers of mine, that you could have spent your time better than digging in this dirt. (*W* 54)

It is worth pausing to note that Thoreau's reference to the Irish workers in this passage and elsewhere in *Walden* represents another typical feature of Condition-of-England discourse. Carlyle wrote of the desperate state of the Irish workers in *Past and Present*, as did James Phillips Kay in his work on the condition of the Manchester working class. In his book *The Condition of the Working Class in England*, Friedrich Engels devoted a chapter to "Irish Immigration" in which he quoted Carlyle at length and cited Kay. While the depiction of Irish people in these works—replete with lurid descriptions of dissipation and filthy living conditions—was far from flattering and often employed ugly stereotypes, Condition-of-England writers tended to blame the impoverished and intemperate lifestyles they observed on the social environment. Engels, who rooted his analysis in the fact that the "numerous and impoverished population of Ireland" served as an industrial reserve army for the expansion of English capitalism, noted the Irish workers' physical strength, remarking that they were often employed in unskilled trades that required muscular exertion.[45] As builders of the railroad, Thoreau saw them similarly, while also deploring the poverty they endured as an indictment of modern society: "Their condition only proves what squalidness may consist with civilization," he wrote (*W* 35). In the passage quoted above, there is an unmistakable note of condescension in Thoreau's tone, but it is also clear from his fraternal form of address that he speaks with sympathy and solidarity, and perhaps even a hint of admiration for what their work and sacrifice have accomplished.

Indeed, Thoreau understood that society's wealth depends on labor, which historically has rarely been well compensated. "It certainly is fair to look at that class by whose labor the works which distinguish this generation are accomplished," he insists. "The luxury of one class is counterbalanced by the indigence of another. On the one side is the palace, on the other are the almshouse and 'silent poor'. The myriads who built the pyramids to be the tombs of the Pharaohs were fed on garlic.... The mason who finishes the cornice of the palace returns at night perchance to a hut not so good as a wigwam" (*W* 34). Thoreau strikes a similar note in his discussion of monumental architecture, invoking the pyramids again to argue that the only "wonder" they ought to provoke is "that so many men could be found degraded enough to spend their lives constructing a tomb for some ambitious booby, whom it would have been wiser and manlier to have drowned in the Nile, and then given his body to the dogs" (*W* 58).

Much like the English poet Percy Shelley, who similarly used the romantic trope of the ruin as a historical foil for the social and political relations of the industrial age in his poems *Queen Mab* and "Ozymandias"—works with which Thoreau was certainly familiar[46]—the author of *Walden* adopts a rhetoric that was popular among nineteenth-century working class radicals, especially the Chartists.[47] Such rhetoric persisted in radical social criticism well into the twentieth century, where it was picked up by writers such as Bertolt Brecht and Walter Benjamin. In his poem "Fragen eines lesenden Arbeiters" (A Worker Reads History), Brecht enumerates a series of great monuments and historical feats while posing the question of who made them possible: "Who built seven-gated Thebes? / The names of kings are printed in books. / Did the kings drag the slabs of rock themselves?"[48] Benjamin—who likened revolution to the pulling of an emergency brake on a runaway train[49]—memorably summed up the idea in his "Theses on the Philosophy of History": "There is no document of culture which is not at the same time a document of barbarism."[50] Great works—even the technological marvels of the modern age—are not in themselves good indicators of the health or happiness of a society. They do not reflect the experience of the anonymous masses whose labor makes them possible. "It is a mistake to suppose that, in a country where the usual evidences of civilization exist, the condition of a very large body of the inhabitants may not be as degraded as that of savages," Thoreau writes. To see the truth of this proposition,

> I should not need to look farther than to the shanties which every where border our railroads, that last improvement in civilization; where I see in my daily walks human beings living in sties, and all winter with an open door, for the sake of light, without any visible, often imaginable, wood pile, and the forms of both old and young are permanently contracted by the long habit of shrinking from cold and misery, and the development of all their limbs and faculties is checked. (*W* 35)

Thoreau's depiction of the glaring contrast between the technological progress represented by the railroad and the abject poverty of the (mainly Irish) working classes surrounding it in this paragraph employs multiple Condition-of-England motifs. Appropriately, it also contains his densest use of the term "condition" in all of *Walden*. "Such too, to a greater or less extent, is the condition of the operatives of every denomination in England, which is the great workhouse of the world," he adds, echoing once more the anti-factory rhetoric that Luther had helped popularize in the 1830s and paraphrasing Disraeli's turn of phrase cited above. (Thoreau, with perhaps deliberate irony, transforms "workshop" into "workhouse") (*W* 35).

Yet this litany of poverty and misery is to say nothing of the conditions endured by "the laborers in our Southern States who produce the staple exports of this country, and are themselves a staple production of the South." By invoking slavery in this context, Thoreau not only qualifies his remark that it is harder to have a northern than a southern overseer,[51] but also shows a keen awareness of the interrelated, transatlantic oppressions of the industrial capitalist economy of the mid-nineteenth century, in which the cotton exports of the U.S. South fed the textile mills of England. He might well have agreed with Karl Marx, who wrote in Horace Greeley's *New York Tribune* in 1861: "As long as the English cotton manufactures depended on slave-grown cotton, it could be truthfully asserted that they rested on a twofold slavery, the indirect slavery of the white man in

England and the direct slavery of the black men on the other side of the Atlantic."[52] Indeed, during the first half of the nineteenth century, wage laborer and enslaved laborer alike were in the process of being "mastered by the clock" as a new awareness of time as a force for work discipline came to dominate both factory and field.[53]

Conclusion

Later, in his posthumously published essay "Life Without Principle," Thoreau depicts the railroad devoid of the admirable qualities he attributed to it in *Walden*. It becomes more purely the grim symbol of a world so obsessed with round-the-clock commerce that even sleep becomes an elusive respite from the daily grind: "The world is a place of business. What an infinite bustle! I am awaked almost every night by the panting of the locomotive. It interrupts my dreams. There is no sabbath. It would be glorious to see mankind at leisure for once. It is nothing but work, work, work" (*RP* 156). As Thoreau noted in a letter to a friend, the passage's final sentence derives from Thomas Hood's poem, "The Song of the Shirt,"[54] the lyrical lament of an imagined seamstress whose life is utterly consumed by the work of sewing— "a kind of work which you may call endless," Thoreau remarked in *Walden*. Published in the British periodical *Punch* in 1843—the same year that Carlyle's *Past and Present* appeared—Hood's poem epitomized what Charles Dickens, in his 1854 novel *Hard Times*, called the age's 'severely workful' attitude.[55] Besides underscoring Thoreau's opposition to excessive labor and desire for increased leisure—sentiments more often associated with the social democratic left than advocates of unfettered capitalist markets—the allusion is yet another example of the enduring influence that Condition-of-England literature had on his writing and social criticism.

Works Cited

Adam, Barbara. *Time.* Cambridge: Polity Press, 2004.

Beckert, Sven. *Empire of Cotton: A Global History*. New York: Vintage Books, 2014.

Benjamin, Walter. "On the Concept of History." In *Selected Writings Vol. 4*. Cambridge: Harvard University Press, 2003.

Brownson, Orestes. *The Laboring Classes.* Boston: Benjamin H. Greene, 1840.

Carlyle, Thomas. *Sartor Resartus.* Oxford: Oxford University Press, 1987.

Diniejko, Andrzej. "Thomas Carlyle and the Origin of the 'Condition of England Question,'" https://www.victorianweb.org/authors/carlyle/diniejko1.html, accessed September 13, 2012.

Engels, Friedrich. *The Condition of the Working Class in England.* Oxford: Oxford University Press, 1993.

Hartz, Louis. "Seth Luther: The Story of a Working-Class Rebel." In *Peaceably If We Can, Forcibly If We Must: Writings by and about Seth Luther*, edited by Scott Molloy, Carl Gersuny, and Robert Macieski. Providence: Rhode Island Labor History Society, 1998.

Herreshoff, David. *Labor into Art: The Theme of Work in Nineteenth-Century American Literature.* Detroit: Wayne State University Press, 1991.

———. *The Origins of American Marxism: From the Transcendentalists to DeLeon.* Detroit: Wayne State University Press, 1967.

Hobsbawm, Eric. *Industry and Empire: The Birth of the Industrial Revolution.* New York: The New Press, 1999.

Kulik, Gary. "Pawtucket Village and the Strike of 1824: The Origins of Class Conflict in Rhode Island." In *Material Life in America, 1600-1860*, edited by Robert Blair St. George. Boston: Northeastern University Press, 1988.

Marcus, Stephen. *Dickens: From Pickwick to Dombey.* New York: Basic Books, 1965.

———. *Engels, Manchester, and the Working Class.* New York: Norton, 1974.

Marx, Karl. *Dispatches from the New York Tribune: Selected Journalism of Karl Marx.* Edited by James Ledbetter. New York: Penguin, 2007.

Montgomery, David. "Social Attitudes of American Workers in the 1840s." In *A David Montgomery Reader: Essays on Capitalism and Worker Resistance*, edited by Shelton Stromquist and James R. Barrett. Chicago: University of Illinois Press, 2024.

Morgan, Jen. "The Reception of P. B. Shelley in Owenite and Chartist Newspapers and Periodicals." PhD Thesis, University of Salford, UK, 2014.

Morris, William. "How I Became a Socialist." In *How I Became a Socialist*, edited by Owen Holland, with an introduction by Owen Hatherley. New York: Verso, 2020.

Prude, Jonathan. *The Coming of Industrial Order: Town and Factory Life in Rural Massachusetts, 1810-1860.* Amherst: Massachusetts University Press, 1999.

Purdy, Jebediah. "A Radical for All Seasons." *The Nation*, June 2017.

Rosa, Hartmut. *Social Acceleration: A New Theory of Modernity*. Translated by Jonathan Trejo-Mathys. New York: Columbia University Press, 2013.

Sattelmeyer, Robert. *Thoreau's Reading: A Study in Intellectual History*. Princeton University Press, 1988.

Schivelbusch, Wolfgang. *Railway Journey: The Industrialization of Time and Space in the Nineteenth Century*. Oakland: University of California Press, 1977.

Schulz, Kathryn. "The Moral Judgements of Henry David Thoreau." *The New Yorker*, October 2015.

Smith, Mark M. *Mastered by the Clock: Time, Slavery, and Freedom in the American South.* Chapel Hill: University of North Carolina Press, 1997.

CHAPTER 7

THOREAU'S INDIAN NOTEBOOKS, SETTLER HISTORY, AND INDIGENOUS TIME

John J. Kucich

The Shad Moon. The Sugar-Making Month. The Month of Roasting Ears. The Month the Sun Returns to the Them. The Strawberry Moon. Moon of the Drying Earth. Moon of the Deer's Horn Dripping. Thoreau was fascinated by Indigenous time, and in his Indian Notebooks—eleven commonplace books he wrote between 1847 and 1861—he recorded a dozen versions of Native calendars, lingering in particular over the names of months that captured both the grand annual cycle of the seasons and a fine-grained understanding of local ecology. In the thousands of pages of the Indian Notebooks, an Indigenous world emerges that is defined not by the teleology of Western history but by timeless patterns of renewal and change rooted in the rhythms of the natural world and propelled by the intricate patterns of subsistence and ceremony. And yet Thoreau saw this world as one that was vanishing, or vanished—indeed, he gathered the notebooks in part to reconstruct the world of the Native people who had been driven out of Concord centuries before. One of the paradoxes of the Indian Notebooks is that it was a settler historical project that took Thoreau to a world that existed outside of that history.

Thoreau's Indian Notebooks remain one of the great critical puzzles of his career. They might be termed the dark matter of Thoreau studies, a vast mass of words whose impact on the more visible universe of Thoreau's writing is hard to measure but impossible to ignore. Robert Sayre, in his *Thoreau and the American Indian* (1977), makes the case that Thoreau did not so much abandon his proposed Indian Book—the presumed goal of all these notes as reimagine it. In Sayre's words, if the Indian Notebooks didn't lead to a distinct Indian Book, "then the thousands of pages of notes on Indians must be construed more broadly as self-education and preparation for what he *did* write."[1] This essay will take up that question, and I will argue that the best way to understand the Indian Notebooks is to see them as Thoreau's effort to learn from the people who had lived in North America from time immemorial how best to live in the Concord of the mid-nineteenth century. If that project sounds at once deeply hopeful and profoundly problematic, it is both. Both the problems and promise of Thoreau's Indian Notebooks bring the whole of Thoreau's work into sharper focus, and they have much to say about Thoreau's time, and ours.

The Indian Notebooks

The texts at the heart of this essay have written on their covers "Extracts Relating to the Indians" (whether by Thoreau or a later owner is unclear); they are numbered from 2–12.[2] They are not widely available.[3] The notebooks themselves are commonplace books of material Thoreau copied from books and articles he gathered from a number of libraries, especially Harvard's. There are a few scattered passages of Thoreau's original writing—a short, rough essay on Indians in Notebook 7, written in 1852, and briefer comments on some of the notes he copied, often made when he returned to earlier passages in light of new reading. They comprise something of a personal library culled from a huge range of material, hundreds of sources from the earliest European explorations of North America to the most recent government reports and memoirs, with a focus on Native peoples from the northeastern United States and southeastern Canada but also including material from across the continent and around the world, including texts on early and pre-historic Europeans. Additionally, some items in Thoreau's personal library, namely George Copway's *History of the Ojibway* (1850), which Thoreau heavily annotated, might best be seen as part of the Indian Notebooks.[4]

Thoreau began gradually, filling the first volume we have, 82 manuscript pages, between 1847 and 1850; the pace picked up from 1850 (63 pages) to 1852 (when he filled two notebooks of more than 300 pages), peaking in the mid-1850s. Thoreau filled a 500-page notebook between 1852 and 1855, then filled a 437-page notebook in 1855. His pace then settled, with roughly 200 pages per year between 1856 and the final entry in 1861. Thoreau never turned these notes into a finished book, as Franklin Sanborn suggested he had planned to do, but he did assemble a comprehensive personal library of material on Native Americans.[5]

What's in them? Well, just about everything, which makes them at once hard to summarize and easy to cherry pick. Do they contain a stirring defense of the humanity and dignity of Native peoples? Yes. Are they a detailed record of the savagism and virulent racism that shaped the rise of ethnology and anthropology in the U.S.? Yes. Do they portray Native people as sophisticated and admirable, undercutting notions of European cultural supremacy? Offer vivid images of savage squalor? Yes and yes. If one approaches them looking for an archive of powerful Native American myths, or a sustained exploration of how language shapes our perception of reality, or a deep meditation on rituals of grief and mourning, you will find them. And more. Detailed instructions on how to build canoes from birchbark, tree-trunks, or buffalo hides. Recipes galore, especially for the myriad ways Native peoples prepared corn. A surprising range of sexual norms. Descriptions of stone tools and earthworks. Brutally intimate descriptions of torture. Military tactics. Ceremonies, prayers, and shamans. Clothing to beat the heat and keep out the bitter arctic wind. Hunting and fishing techniques for every North American ecosystem, and for some in South America and Australia. Fun and games and funerary rites. Lots and lots of plants. These topics come in no particular order but are scattered throughout the Indian Notebooks as they appear in the various texts Thoreau took in hand. Any conclusions about Thoreau's attitudes towards these texts can only be tentative. The Indian Notebooks are not a product that represents Thoreau's settled views on Native people, but an inclusive and evolving process of understanding that continued to the end of his short life. In their unfolding, accumulative, recursive, and unfinished nature, they follow a very different structure than the narratives, histories, and scientific accounts that went into them. Time, in the Indian Notebooks, is anything but linear. Sixteenth-century accounts of explorers are interspersed with just-published reports from military expeditions, and accounts of Native culture weave together contemporary depictions of hunts, harvests, and ceremonies with the oldest stories and traditions that survive on the continent. We don't know why, exactly, Thoreau never turned this unruly and wide ranging assemblage of information into a coherent book, but we do know that what he left is anything but an orderly history.

Savagist Time

The disordered nature of the Indian Notebooks is noteworthy in part because Thoreau gathered them in an era that was increasingly obsessed with history. In the antebellum era, the new nation was full of efforts to turn the complex and messy origins of this rapidly evolving society into a coherent story of the birth a new nation, replete with a pantheon of founding fathers and a carefully constructed teleology that pointed to the inevitable rise of this particularly vigorous scion of Anglo-Saxon stock. Joshua Bellin and Richard Schneider have laid out a clear case that Thoreau fully absorbed the ideology of Indian vanishing that permeated just about every account of Native peoples in Thoreau's era.[6] The nineteenth-century sources that Thoreau carefully read and copied into his Indian Notebooks hewed closely to a narrative that began with an essential racial difference between the European and the Indian, quickly moved to the innate inferiority of the latter (often with a nod to some noble but primitive traits), and ended with the inevitable Indian decline when the two races came into contact. Such accounts framed this encounter not as what it was, that is, one of brute conquest, but as a natural process couched in the dispassionate language of history and science.

A certain view of time was foundational in these accounts. In the many histories of this era—the most influential of which was George Bancroft's magisterial, multi-volume *History of the United States* (1834–74)—Native peoples serve as savage counterpoints to the main story of English, and then American, progress. They were an obstacle that sharpened the cohesion and tested the vigor of the often disorderly and sometimes feckless colonists. These national histories were joined by a host of local histories, particularly in New England, as town after town marked, in the early nineteenth century, the bicentennial of its founding, eager to claim cultural and social status in a world marked by uncertain economic fortunes and a tide of immigration. Jean O'Brien, in her survey of hundreds of these histories, has traced the process of "firsting and lasting" that shaped the narratives of early settlement, as historians celebrated the first English settlers of a new town and a new era and memorialized the last of the Indians, even while noting a Native elder's living descendants.[7] Thoreau read many of these histories, mining them for accounts of the Native world the settlers displaced; he, too, famously memorialized the "last" of the

Musketaquid tribe, Tahattawan, in an early entry in his Journal, and *A Week on the Concord and Merrimack Rivers* is, among many other things, a long engagement with New England's Native American past. Thoreau takes part in what Kevin Bruyneel terms "settler memory"—focusing on a colonial past as a way of disavowing accountability to Native peoples in the present.[8]

The other narrative force taking shape during this era was a more "scientific" approach to Native peoples, an effort that would take more formal shape after Thoreau's death as the disciplines of ethnology, anthropology, and cultural geography. When Thoreau consulted more sources written in the mid-nineteenth century, he found descriptions of Native Americans that shifted from missionary records and explorers' reports, to more systematic efforts to encompass Native history and culture by Ephraim Squier, Henry Rowe Schoolcraft, and Lewis Henry Morgan, to broader accounts of human development by Alnold Guyot, and to confident assessments of the capacities of different races by Samuel Morton and Josiah Nott. Thoreau read works by all of these men carefully. Notes on the two topics at the heart of these works—Native origins and racial categorization—are scattered throughout the Indian Notebooks, and they are at the heart of the savagist ideology that was the softer cultural wing of the brutal politics of nineteenth-century American colonization. Most frequent are speculations about Native American origins and history. The Notebooks capture a vigorous contemporary debate. Did Native Americans originate in the New World as a separate creation, as a number of Native traditions (and the racist theories of leading scientists like Louis Agassiz) claimed? Did they migrate from central Asia, as their physical characteristics and cultural practices seemed to suggest? Or were they offshoots of an early European migration, one of several rounds that toppled the civilizations that left behind the mounds and relics scattered across the land? Most striking about Thoreau's notes on Native origins is his general attitude of detached curiosity. Thoreau copied contemporary theories at modest length and without emendation. And yet in settler colonial ideology, these questions had high stakes.

Thoreau's own views have been a matter of long debate among readers of the Indian Notebooks. Early accounts, from Franklin Sanborn to Henry Salt to Albert Keiser, saw Thoreau as a "friend of the Native" in what was essentially the primitivist mode of savagism.[9] Richard Fleck and, to some degree, Suzanne Rose, argue that the Notebooks offer, on the whole, a strong case against the darkest elements of savagism, gathering evidence from their pages that highlights the injustice of colonization and captures the richness of the Native world. Far from limning the scientific inevitability of racial succession, the Notebooks capture a culture that was anything but primitive, and that has much to offer European Americans, particularly, for Fleck and Rose, a rich heritage of myth that Thoreau draws on in his own effort to remake American culture. Such a view, that sees Thoreau mining vanished Indian communities for cultural treasures that would benefit a settler society, offers a clear example of primitivism, and to the extent that it ignores the on-going political struggles of Native communities, it partakes of the savagism that is at the core of settler colonialism. Robert Sayre recognizes how thoroughly embedded the Indian Notebooks are within the larger project of savagism, even as the sheer wealth and range of information they contain belie the savagist stereotype of Native people as a primitive, static, hunter race. Joshua Bellin is not so sure. In his reading of the Indian Notebooks, Bellin sees Thoreau as settling increasingly into the orbit of savagism, falling into Morgan's stance on the essential sameness of Native cultures, seeing the many notes on Indian origins as a sign of racial distinction, and noting the pull of the vast compendiums of Schoolcraft, "the dean of racial difference," on the later Indian Notebooks. "Taken as a whole," Bellin argues, "the Indian Books prove Thoreau to be far more the antiquarian than the advocate."[10] Time here has real stakes. Thoreau's impulse to focus on a Native past, to preserve the traditions of Native people as relics, a resource to benefit the settler colonial society that drove them off their land, makes it difficult for him to even see Native people living and adapting to the present, much less to aid their struggle for cultural and political sovereignty. By turning Native culture into what Paul Giles has termed "medieval American literature," writers like Henry Wadsworth Longfellow, in *Hiawatha*, turned living Indigenous people into ghosts.[11]

Yet while Thoreau read widely and deeply among these architects of savagism, he did not fully share their goals. Schoolcraft and the many Indian agents, leaders of military expeditions, and compilers of scientific surveys were writing in the service of the U.S. government, actively feeding the many-headed hydra of colonization. Morton and Nott worked tirelessly to establish a scientific basis for the racism at the heart of white nationalism. Ephraim Squier and Lewis Henry Morgan are better suited to Bellin's category of antiquarianism, preserving the pre-contact heritage of the United States in the amber of folio pages and museum exhibits and thereby consigning surviving members of the Native communities they described to the status of anomalous relics, soon to vanish. Thoreau did none of these things. That he seriously considered writing a book about Indians seems likely; what is certain is that he didn't, even though, in the aftermath of *Walden*, he had plenty of time to move forward with such a project.

Against History

History and science, of course, are never as orderly and conclusive as their tidy narratives imply, and Thoreau's Indian Notebooks, never systematized into a scientific treatise nor gathered into a tight narrative, are a good reminder of how much work—both intellectual and ideological—goes into telling a story. They show us how unruly the raw material of these stories can be, even if, as with Thoreau's Notebooks, the material is itself assembled from other stories. The Indian Notebooks certainly are largely drawn from settler history, the building blocks of savagism. But they are also full of sources that work against this kind of history. For one, the Indian Notebooks gather rich evidence of the complex, flourishing world that settler colonialism destroyed. These typically came from people who worked to move that destruction forward: European explorers eager to plant colonies, missionaries looking to win over converts, settlers setting the scene for their own succession. But Thoreau's notes, plucked from theses narratives and gathered in pieces throughout the Notebooks, show not an empty space before settler history begins but a sophisticated, largely peaceable, and teeming world. This was not a story featured in national or local histories.

A second theme running throughout the Indian Notebooks was a corollary of the first—the toll of colonization on Native peoples. As Thoreau pieced together the world of Native New England and beyond, he watched that world dissolve, often through the actions of the very writers he copied. Thoreau was keenly aware that they had not, as some of his sources phrased it, simply melted away. He recorded time and again the impact of the diseases that ripped through Native populations as Europeans arrived, first in Virginia and New England and Quebec, and then across the West, including the epidemics of smallpox and other diseases that tore through the Plains and West Coast communities in his own era. Many of his sources—early explorers, colonists, and missionaries—were stunned by the devastation caused by these diseases, and many noted as well the toll taken on Native communities by alcohol and the allure of the marketplace, which led to overhunting and famine. Thoreau often included the voices of Native peoples themselves. One Huron assessment was recorded by a Jesuit missionary, Julien Perrault, in 1635: "It is not these drinks that take away our life, but your writings, for since you have described our country, our rivers and our land & woods, we all die, which did not happen before you came" (IN 7:84). The Jesuits themselves had a sense of their role in this devastation. Charles Lalemont noted with grim resignation in 1640 that, "where we were most welcome, where we baptized the most people, it was there in fact that they most died" (IN 8:136). And yet missionaries and settlers kept coming—and, as Thoreau's own Notebooks show, they kept writing.

Other colonists were not content to let disease work unaided. Thoreau was certainly familiar with the cycle of wars that wrested control of the American landscape from Native peoples. Episodes in this struggle played a major role in *A Week on the Concord and Merrimack Rivers* (1849), and references to King Philip occur throughout the Indian Notebooks, including a letter from Philip to colonial authorities that Thoreau examined in Plymouth. Notebook 8 closes with a string of speeches by Native leaders protesting various acts of colonization. Thoreau copied a speech by the Onondaga chief Canassatego in 1742: "We know our lands are now become more valuable; the white people think we do not know their value; but we are sensible that the land is everlasting, and the few goods we receive for it are soon worn out and gone" (IN 8:490). As Thoreau clearly notes, Native peoples did not "vanish" quietly or without resistance. They were both eloquent and blunt in naming the acts of treachery and violence that drove them from their lands.

Thoreau, in writing these notes, complicated the narrative of quiet vanishing and the natural succession of races. The Indian Notebooks are full of examples that were neither. Yet as the Huron comment to Perrault suggests, his writings enacted a colonial violence of their own. He may have recorded the end of an Indian world with unusual attention and sympathy, but in focusing so squarely on this pre-colonial world, he helped to relegate it to the past—not an everlasting world, as Canassatego asserted, but one that was now bound to history and, like the goods exchanged for land, doomed to vanish. As Thoreau wrote to the American Association for the Advancement of Science in 1853, his main interest was the "Manners & Customs of the Indians of the Algonquin Group previous to contact with the Civilized Man"—a field that put him neatly into the category of "antiquarian" Bellin mentions above, confining his subject to a dead past rather than a living present. Many of the sources in the Indian Notebooks carried the story of Native communities beyond the event horizon of colonization; some advocated fiercely for Native peoples in the present. Thoreau, however, left that part of the story out.

Yet if the Indian Notebooks tend to relegate Native cultures to a vanished American past, other elements of the Notebooks complicate settler history. One was his use of sources written by Native writers, including Henry Aupaumut's "History of the Muh-he-con-nuk Indians" (c. 1790) and Samson Occom's "Account of the Montauk Indians" (1761) in Indian Notebook 2, both from the Collections of the Massachusetts Historical Society.[12] It is worth noting that Thoreau completely ignored a long account of the Mohegan tribe in the late eighteenth century that precedes Aupaumut's history; he instead copied from Aupaumut a detailed account of how Mahican farmers (mainly women) cleared fields by girdling and then burning trees, and how the men managed the wild game of the region by hunting sparingly in different seasons. "They were not to kill more than necessary, for there was none to barter with them that would have tempted them to waste animals ------ consequently game was never diminished" (IN 2:47). Aupaumut's brief description of how to organize a society that thrived by nurturing its environment rather than exploiting it—a history of the green world settlers eradicated—sets up a theme that would increasingly occupy Thoreau's later work. From Occom's more ethnographic survey, Thoreau copied different ways of arranging marriages, as well as their many gods: "They had gods etc. as S. west—north and south—there was a god of corn, another over their beans, another over their pumpkins and squashes, etc.... But there was also one great good God and one great evil one" (IN 2:49). Occom wrote as a Christian minister working with a neighboring tribe, a complicated stance that gave him greater sympathy with, and access to, Montauk traditions than a white minister would have had, even as he worked to transform traditional Montauk culture. Thoreau picked up on the rich spiritual heritage that Occom sketches, one that may have been more aligned with Thoreau's Transcendentalism than it was with Occom's Calvinism. He would return to this theme, too, in his later work.

Thoreau was more dismissive of the work of the Tuscarora writer David Cusick, whose *Sketches of the Ancient History of the Six Nations* he read about in Ephraim Squiers' work in 1850 and then read in full in 1857. Thoreau's reaction may have reflected his hope that Cusick's history would align more neatly with the settler histories and ethnographies that make up the bulk of material in the Indian Notebooks. His initial response was one of disappointed condescension: "Almost entirely fabulous and puerile," he wrote, "only valuable in showing [in imperfect English] how an Indian writes history [and perhaps for some dim and on the whole interesting suggestions and traditions]" (IN 10:109). The bracketed comments (later emendations), however, suggest that Thoreau may have turned to Cusick for a Native perspective on origins and migrations and found instead sacred traditions that had a very different value than he had initially sought. Thoreau may have begun to recognize in Cusick what he had learned from Emerson. Branka Arsič argues that a "radically anti-teleological understanding of life" was shared by both Thoreau and Emerson, and in coming across a similar view in Cusick's ante/anti-settler history of the Haudenosaunee, he begins a long education in how Indigenous stories, in Mark Rifkin's phrase, "push against the imperatives of settler sovereignty," building a discursive world of "temporal multiplicity" that opens a chronospace beyond settler time.[13] What Thoreau read in Cusick in 1857 he saw firsthand that same year in the Maine Woods, as Joe Polis guided Thoreau through a Penobscot world that ran according to very different clocks than the ones structuring life in the United States.

If Thoreau was not quite sure what to do with the rich Haudenosaunee heritage that Cusick so carefully assembled, he was more comfortable with another Native account of tribal history, George Copway's *Traditional History and Characteristic Sketches of the Ojibway Nation*, which he decided to purchase rather than copy into the Indian Notebooks. Copway doesn't offer an account of the original peopling of the Americas, beginning instead with the more recent cultural memory of a migration from the east to the tribe's then-current home in the vicinity of Lake Huron; most of his book instead describes the flora and fauna of the region and the tribe's many techniques for making a good living among its bounty. This was right up Thoreau's alley, and he marked up the book heavily. In addition to his heavy annotations of Ojibwe history and ecological knowledge, Thoreau's annotations highlight his interest in birchbark writing and oral traditions. He omitted material about missionary efforts among the community and Copway's strong pleas for more just political treatment.

Thoreau's notes on Copway are one more example of his growing interest in Native traditions, gathered in his earliest sources and from the expanding corpus assembled by Henry Rowe Schoolcraft. These stories fed into Thoreau's interest in Algonquian religion, from sacred origin myths (including a half dozen earth-diver stories) to ceremonies of welcome, initiation, thanksgiving, and mourning to beliefs about gods and spirits and the nature of the soul. The Huron Feast of the Dead, in which villages gathered together at intervals of a decade or so to ritually mourn and sanctify the carefully preserved remains of those who died in the intervening years, serves as a good example of Algonquin ceremony. In Indian Notebooks 6 and 7, Thoreau devotes some twenty pages to copying an account from the Jesuit Relations in 1636, clearly fascinated by the way in which death is refashioned from a fixed endpoint into a broad tribal network of renewal. Thoreau copied the skeptical accounts of the tribal shamans or powwows who managed the ceremonial life of tribal communities—they were, after all, the key points of resistance to Jesuit, Puritan, and Moravian missionaries—but he included enough details about their ceremonies and beliefs to give a sense of their role in the spiritual world of Native peoples. From these many sources, Thoreau grew increasingly attuned to the cycles of ceremonial time that structured the Indigenous world.

What emerges from Thoreau's immersion in largely savagist accounts of Native America, then, does not fit easily within settler history: a portrait of Native peoples deeply rooted in place, their communities woven together in a web of ceremony, language, and belief that yields a society that was not a blank space of pre-history but a rich world existing outside of settler time.

Ceremonial Time and Remaking the World

The complex and ambivalent view of Native America that emerges from the Indian Notebooks doesn't explain what Thoreau hoped to do with this vast body of material. Why did he keep filling the Notebooks as he revised and re-revised *Walden*, and then as he pursued other writing projects in its wake? Sayre suggests that Thoreau himself may not have been sure of the answer. The Indian Notebooks may have begun as source material for *A Week* and *Walden*, and then as the possible source for a separate work. But such an idea seems to have remained very much on the back burner. It may be, as Sayre argues, that the Indian Notebooks evolved into more of a practice than a product, that the discipline of gathering, reading, copying, and reviewing material about Native Americans became, to some degree, its own end.[14] They may have played a role that was less like the natural history notebooks and more like the Journal, which in the early 1850s shifted from serving mainly as source material for lectures and essays to became instead a meditative discipline for honing Thoreau's ability to see the world around him, a way of stepping outside the currents of an American history that seemed less and less hopeful in the mid- to late-1850s.

The Indian Notebooks, then, served as another means for Thoreau to leave behind the village. Thoreau immersed himself in the Jesuit Relations for the same reason he immersed himself in Beck Stow's swamp: to see the world from a different perspective and to allow himself to be jolted out of village complacencies and national ideologies alike. To see the world from the perspective of a birchbark canoe threading the upper reaches of the St. Lawrence in the 1630s, to settle in with people who farmed, fished, hunted and gathered different foods than were served at Concord tables, in houses built from saplings and bark, whose stories told of a woman who fell from the sky or warned of the depredations of a neighboring tribe, was to see Concord through different eyes, and to open up new insights. The Indian Notebooks, then, served as a kind of time travel, a way of visiting, briefly, the green world before European settlement that had all but vanished from New England.

And in the many accounts of Native American spiritual beliefs—the presence of what Schoolcraft called the "diurgis" (IN 6:54) and what many others described as a pantheism that saw the whole of Nature drenched in spirit, with every feature of the landscape endowed with personhood, animate, and woven into a world thick with story and ritual—Thoreau saw a version of his own Transcendental ontology, in which time was an endlessly renewing cycle and Nature a living process, where he could gaze into the Earth's eye in the form of a humble pond he sanctified in his own ceremony and myth. Thoreau must have felt a shudder of recognition as he read Heckewelder: "All animate nature, in whatever degree, is in their eyes a great whole from which they have not yet ventured to separate themselves" (IN 9:267). John Hunter may have been writing about the Osage when he wrote, "Every Indian of any standing has his sacred place, such as a tree, rock, fountain, etc. to which he resorts for devotional exercises....None is compelled to do this, but those who omit it are thought less of, and their conduct is ascribed to an indifference to holy things, and a want of solicitude for the general welfare" (IN 8:417). But as Thoreau copied this into his Notebook, he surely thought of himself, of his own sacred places on the edge of the village, and of his own evolving effort to imagine a different future for New England.

This is not to say that the Indian Notebooks were not integral to Thoreau's own turn to science in the years following *Walden*. Indeed, they are crucial to understanding the on-going and evolving studies of the ecology in and around Concord that increasingly occupied his later years. His response to the American Association for the Advancement of Science in 1853 captures something of his own difficulty in articulating what exactly this project was. If Thoreau's interest was the "manners and customs of the Algonquian tribes prior to contact with civilized man," this was not an effort to categorize these people and parcel them out to museums. He was, after all, still "a mystic, a philosopher, and a Transcendentalist to boot" (*Corr* 2:151–53; *PJ* 5:469–70). What he sought in the Indian Notebooks was the Native understanding of the immensely complicated web of relations that made up a world, an understanding embodied not in charts, tomes, and exhibits, but in a more intuitive understanding of what Thoreau calls, after mystical night of walking through Walden Woods, "the infinite extent of our relations" (*W* 171).

This web of relations reaches in all directions: out among the many beings that share this moment of time and space, reaching into the distant past and towards the far future. In his *Walden* reveries, Thoreau hears his hoe tinkle against ancient stone artifacts in the bean-field or imagines the distant geological ages that produced this quiet pond and feels these times bleed into the present. This layering of timescapes, interweaving historical chronology with a timeless present, is one of the defining characteristics of myth—what Mircea Eliade calls "sacred time" and identifies as the primary goal of religious ceremony. Myths in any culture bring the sacred, the eternal present, into the profane world of ordinary life. This is what drew

Thoreau again and again to the well of classical Greek literature, and what drove him to read widely and deeply in Eastern spiritual traditions. By the early 1850s, he was increasingly familiar as well with Native American mythology. From early accounts of English and French missionaries he got his first glimpses of Algonquin cosmologies, and from Squier and Schoolcraft he gained a growing understanding of the scope and nature of traditional Native stories.

Oddly, this body of sacred Native literature plays hardly any role in Thoreau's published works.[15] And yet the broader elements of Native American sacred stories infuse his work, particularly "Walking" and *Walden*. "Walking" is framed as a quest towards Holy Land, a ceremonial vision quest enacted in Thoreau's daily walks that are closer to shamanic ritual than to regular exercise.[16] The beings he glimpses at Spaulding Farm at the end of "Walking" are as close to the totems and spirit animals found across Native American cultures as they are to any similar beings in the Western tradition. And *Walden* might be read as a winter story, the long accounts of the earth's creation and how the natural order of things came to be that were told night after night in tribal communities as a way of both reminding the people gathered in the circle of the Original Instructions and as a ceremonial remaking of the universe in a process of continuous creation.[17] They were also, unlike the stories that European settlers brought with them from the Mediterranean world, firmly rooted in place. Native American storytelling, as Lisa Brooks and Keith Basso have suggested, was essential in creating a place-world, a specific landscape saturated with story that provided practical, ethical, and ontological guidance to those who traveled the land and knew the stories. The key feature of such stories is their rootedness. For the Western Apache who shared their stories with Basso, and for the Southern Algonquian world that Brooks recovers, stories live not in the minds of their tellers but in the interplay of person and place.[18] The stories exist not in some archive of unwritten human memory but are keyed into the elements of landscape. Time, Thoreau learns to see, occurs, and recurs, in place.

The decade-plus project of gathering the Indian Notebooks, then, was a way of helping him see his own world through the deeply experienced eyes of Concord's former inhabitants and their widespread kin. This long practice also made him keenly aware of what he could not see—what had been lost in driving out the land's Indigenous people. Thoreau's work is, from beginning to end, shaped by the empty space once occupied by the Musketaquid people. Thoreau circles this void in ever-widening loops, hoping to fill in their knowledge of this place by turning to the Jesuit Relations, Schoolcraft's endless compilations, and other accounts of Native people near and far, current and ancient, as he chased down notes about plants, hunting techniques, traditional stories, recipes, and ceremonies that helped him re-imagine, and re-weave, the web that bonded Concord's original people with their place. He was aware, to the end, of what he did not know. His broken task, his effort to write a new Book of Musketaquid that would restore the web of relationships among its human and more-than-human inhabitants, one tied not to the teleology of settler colonialism but woven from the strands of Indigenous time, might be seen as a response to this absence.

All this is not to say that Thoreau ever fully renounced savagism, or ever escaped the settler colonial dynamic that shaped his world. Even as he copied account after account of Native communities and immersed himself in their traditions and practices, Thoreau remained a settler using traditional ecological knowledge to better root himself in stolen land, part of what Jace Weaver calls the "uneasy illusion of indigeneity" on the part of a settler culture.[19] He may have done so admiringly, but he did so without devoting much attention to the political aftermath of this long theft. In gathering his Indian Notebooks, Thoreau ignored passages or sources that spoke to the brutal policies of conquest and removal in his own day, he bypassed accounts of how Native communities adapted and survived in the wake of colonization, and he made no effort to connect with the Nipmuck, Massachusetts and Wampanoag communities that remained in Massachusetts. This absence is both striking and typically colonial. In noting the difference between Thoreau's fierce opposition to slavery and his relative silence on Native dispossession and genocide, Sayre suggests that African Americans called on Thoreau's sense of duty, while Native peoples instead gripped his very being. Thoreau thus failed to see that this was part of colonialism—in Patrick Wolfe's terms, the structure that followed the event.[20]

The Native people Thoreau wrote about in these pages, of course, were well aware of the complications of settler colonialism, and many imagined very different futures than the ones crafted by settler pens. Thoreau concludes his long extract from John Heckewelder's account of the

Delaware/Lenape with a widely shared prophecy: "That when the whites shall have ceased killing the red man, and got all their lands from them, the great tortoise which bears the island upon his back, shall dive down into the deep and drown them all, as he once did before, a great many years ago; and that when he rises again, the Indians shall once more be put in possession of the whole country" (IN 9:303). One Indigenous response to the pressure of colonialism, then, was to subsume it within the broader mythic cycles of Indigenous time, and to look past colonial history to an Indigenous future.

While Thoreau was never able to come to terms with his position in a settler colonial world, he, too, was trying to use Indigenous time and Indigenous wisdom to help live more ethically in the world, and to save an emerging capitalist United States from the disaster he could see coming before almost anyone else. It is important to note that the Indian Notebooks were not the final word on Indians for Thoreau—indeed, they only barely count as Thoreau's words at all. He travelled to Maine, learning from Joseph Attean and Joe Polis in particular that Native communities were addressing some of the same issues that he was struggling with in Concord. This may have been the final nail in the coffin of any imagined "Indian Book" drawn from the Notebooks' pages. Instead of writing a book about Indians, then, he started writing a book of Concord, where the seeds planted in his long gleanings might, in time, bear a different fruit.

Works Cited

Basso, Keith. *Wisdom Sits in Places: Landscape and Language among the Western Apache*. Albuquerque: University of New Mexico Press, 1996.

Bellin, Joshua. "In the Company of Savagists: Thoreau's Indian Books and Antebellum Ethnology." *The Concord Saunterer* 16 (January 2008): 1–32.

Bringhurst, Robert. *A Story as Sharp as a Knife: The Classic Haida Mythtellers and Their World.* Vancouver: Douglas and MacIntyre, 1999.

Brooks, Lisa. *The Common Pot: The Recovery of Native Space in the Northeast.* Minneapolis: University of Minnesota Press, 2008.

Bruyneel, Kevin. *Settler Memory: The Disavowal of Indigeneity and the Politics of Race in the United States*. Chapel Hill: University of North Carolina Press, 2021.

Fleck, Richard F. *The Indians of Thoreau: Selections from the Indian Notebooks*. Albuquerque: Hummingbird Press, 1974.

Giles, Paul. *The Global Remapping of American Literature*. Princeton: Princeton University Press, 2011.

Keiser, Albert. *The Indian in American Literature*. New York: Oxford University Press, 1932.

O'Brien, Jean. *Firsting and Lasting: Writing Indians Out of Existence in New England*. Minneapolis: University of Minnesota Press, 2010.

Rose, Suzanne. "Following the Trail of Footsteps: From the Indian Notebooks to Walden." *New England Quarterly* 67:1 (March 1994) 77–91.

———. "Tracking the Moccasin Print: A Descriptive Index to Thoreau's Indian Notebooks and a Study of the Relationships of the Indian Notebooks to Walden." Ph.D. diss, University of Oklahoma, 1994.

Sanborn, Franklin. *Henry D. Thoreau*. Boston: Houghton Mifflin, 1882.

Salt, Henry. *Life of Henry Thoreau*. London: Richard Brentley and Son, 1890.

Sayre, Robert F. *Thoreau and the American Indian*. Princeton: Princeton University Press, 1977.

Schneider, Richard J. *Civilizing Thoreau: Human Ecology and the Social Sciences in the Major Works*. Rochester, NY: Camden House, 2016.

Weaver, Jace. "Indigenousness and Indigeneity." *Companion to Postcolonialism*, edited by Henry Schwartz and Sangeeta Ray. Hoboken: Wiley, 2003.

Wolfe, Patrick. "Settler Colonialism and the Elimination of the Native." *Journal of Genocide Research* 8:4 (December 2006), 384–409.

CHAPTER 8

HENRY THOREAU'S SPIRITUAL TIME

Kathy Fedorko

As a young adult Henry Thoreau made the radical choice to compose his life while living it. His calling would be to live with the most joy, integrity, and meaning. While creating a fulfilling life, Thoreau developed practices that provided him with spiritual time, a richer, fuller, more personal relationship with time than he saw those in his society experiencing. In the "Economy" section of *Walden* (1854) he describes his belief that his fellow Concordians were ruled by work they often did not enjoy in order to gain and maintain conventional wealth, rather than their relishing the "finer fruits" of life, such as living with "a true integrity day by day" and sustaining relationships with others (*W* 6). Some are "crushed and smothered" by the load of their inherited farms. Others are employed, they assume by "necessity," in order to become wealthy. "It is a fool's life, as they will find when they get to the end of it, if not before," Thoreau observes, bringing them only "incessant anxiety and strain," in good part because they have "no time to be any thing but a machine" (*W* 5, 11, 6).

He will find confirmation for this belief about the futility of working only for reward in his reading of the *Bhagavad Gita*.[1] A quote from it that he includes in *A Week on the Concord and Merrimack Rivers* (1849) makes clear that he is on strong spiritual ground: "Be not one whose motive for action is the hope of reward." The *Bhagavad Gita* makes clear that inactivity is not the solution, but rather acting according to one's principles. The wise person understands that there may be "inaction in action, and action in inaction," depending on one's intentions to act without need for or expectation of reward (*Week* 139).

Thus, instead of entering a profession his society might have expected of a Harvard graduate, Thoreau resolved to live consciously and fully in time rather than spending it in a job he didn't enjoy. He chose to treasure his time by wandering the Concord woods and fields, boating and swimming the streams and rivers; by reading and writing essays, poems, and journal entries; by being with friends. Concordian Mary Hosmer Brown remembers, "That a young man, just out of college, should not choose a profession but prefer to spend his Sabbaths in a boat on the river seemed to the good villagers quite sacrilegious."[2] Thoreau made only as much money as he required for his basic needs, first as a teacher and then as a surveyor. He did odd jobs for farmers and friends. He worked with his father in the "John Thoreau & Co." pencil business and made money for the family by inventing a process for milling high quality graphite.[3] As Hosmer Brown puts it, "The family being provided for, Thoreau was free to carry on his true business, that of 'Living.'"[4] Refuting his need for a "real job," he writes in an 1840 journal entry that, although the farmer, the craftsman, and the trader are busy at work, he will "have nothing to do—." He chooses to opt out of the game of "fortune," both the money and the luck. Instead, he counters, fortune "may reach me in my Asia of serenity and indolence if she can" (*PJ* 1:144).

Thoreau felt secure in his decision to disregard social expectations about how time is correctly used: "When my friends reprove me for not devoting myself to some trade or profession, and acquiring property I feel not the reproach—I am guiltless & safe comparatively on that score—" (*PJ* 2:248). In a cheeky dismissal of planning one's time and being concerned about using it productively, he explains in an 1841 journal entry that he "religiously" postpones "all action" other than resolving to relax and breathe. Rather than accomplishing a "thrilling purpose," he intends to "saunter with prepared mind," because "Sometimes a day serves only to hold time together" (*PJ* 1:332). His reading of the *Bhagavad Gita* supported his idea of spiritual time spent contemplatively sauntering, which he notes in an 1846 journal entry: "The oriental unlike the western mind discerned action in the inactive contemplative mind. And everywhere they affirm that he who is actually & truly inactive is the best employed—" (*PJ* 2:254). As the *Gita* explains, the person who is "self-delighted and self-satisfied," who is "happy in his own soul," has "no interest either in that which is done, or that which is not done."[5] Eleven years later, in an 1857 journal entry, Thoreau draws a direct distinction between work time and spiritual time in nature, between wading "in the very shallowest streams of time" while surveying and returning to "the serenity of nature" where, he writes, "I would now bathe my temples in eternity" and "devote myself to the infinite again"

(OJT 22:173–4). Thoreau's ability to ignore his society's disapproval and immerse himself in his spiritual practices and the spiritual time they provided was influenced and enabled in part by his special "difference," which led to misunderstanding about and harsh judgment of him by some, both in his own day and afterward. Recognizing his "difference" no doubt led to his stubborn insistence on being himself and to developing spiritual practices that gave him spiritual time in nature to nourish that self.

This "difference" took several forms. Biographical essays and books written not long after Thoreau's death, often by those who had known him or with the help of those who had, refer to his intensity, reserve, abruptness, and acute senses. Early biographers often refer to Thoreau as some form of "odd." His friend Ralph Waldo Emerson tells us that Thoreau's fellow townsmen knew him only as an oddity until he grew to be "revered and admired."[6] Descriptors like "peculiar" and "strange" come up often. John Weiss remarks on his "peculiar genius."[7] Annie Russell Marble, who used the memories of friends and acquaintances for her biography of Thoreau, refers to his "peculiar temperament," his "strange, complex nature," and his "peculiar philosophy of life," noting also how misunderstood he was in his own time, as well as after his death.[8] Thoreau's friend Joseph Hosmer comments that, "He possessed a character and lived a life peculiar to himself" and that, "Thoreau was an enigma to all of us. No one could place him. His reticence and shyness, together with his rambling over the fields, waters and woodlands, by night and day, was uncommon and mysterious to his townspeople, to say the least."[9]

Thoreau realized his peculiarity, that he had the "spines" of a thistle, and that his well-being depended on his ability to find a way to nourish his individuality. He writes in an entry in 1841, with some defensiveness yet also declarative strength, that he accepts who he is. He also has no intention of explaining or defending himself: "What I am I am—and say not." As he states, "In the attempt to explain shall I plane away all the spines, till it is no thistle but a cornstalk" (*PJ* 1: 273). Later, in *A Week*, he quotes the *Bhagavad Gita* about honoring one's individuality: "A man's own calling with all its faults, ought not to be forsaken" (*Week* 135).

To Thoreau's credit, self-acceptance almost always trumped the opinion of others. He asserts in his Journal, "Public opinion is a weak tyrant compared with private opinion—What I think of myself—that determines my fate" (*PJ* 2:220). He realized that, in choosing to live as he did, his is a "peculiar calling" that involved cherishing his time. His "slight labors" gave him pleasure and provided his livelihood. Were his "wants" to increase, so would his labor. Losing his personal time would result in nothing "worth living for" (*PJ* 3:176–7). To maintain this self-acceptance and self-confidence to live in time as he chose, Thoreau had spiritual practices to help ground him and provide solace and energy when the pressures of society closed in. Though imbued with Western Christianity in his boyhood, Thoreau's journal entries show how attuned he was to Eastern spiritual ideas that were reflected in his practices, even before reading the Eastern literature he discovered in Emerson's library.

The early entries provide us with the backbone of those ideas. In his twenties Thoreau understood one of the basic premises of Eastern spirituality, that change is constant, that all life is transient, and that he will die, as all living things die. In an 1843 journal entry he notes that after death, human beings return as new growth: "So the human life but dies down to the surface, but puts forth a green blade to eternity" (*PJ* 1:470). Understanding this basic truth, that after death he would be put in the earth and become new growth rather than continue to live in heaven, propelled Thoreau to live each day fully aware of the preciousness of each moment of life, lived consciously and conscientiously, deliberately rather than automatically. In a letter to Daniel Ricketson after Thoreau's death, his sister Sophia recalls his "perfect contentment" while he was dying and his revealing comment to a friend visiting his deathbed, "When I was a very little boy I learned that I must die, and I set that down, so of course I am not disappointed now. Death is as near to you as it is to me."[10]

Given life's transitoriness, what could be more important, Thoreau insisted, than to observe how one is living, to decide if that is the life one wants to live, and then to live it fully? As he exclaims in his Journal, "How to live— How to get the most life!... Can a youth—a man—do more wisely—than to go where his life is to [be] found?" (*PJ* 4:53, 54). This belief becomes refined and embedded within *Walden*. There he emphasizes the "glorious" privilege to choose where and how to focus our attention, to "carve and paint the very atmosphere and medium through which we look." By so doing we "affect the quality of the day." This is both "the highest of arts" and a necessity, for, "Every man is tasked to make his life, even in its details, worthy of the contemplation of his most elevated and critical hour" (*W* 90). Affecting the quality of one's day, however, involves practicing the art of choosing "where and how to focus our attention."

As a young man Thoreau developed the inward and outward activities—life-giving practices—that would provide him with what I call "spiritual time" in which to focus his attention. The practices Thoreau relished that I will discuss are: 1) immersing himself in silence and using all his senses while in nature, especially deep listening; 2) being awake in the present moment, through awareness and meditation; 3) walking as a meditative activity; and 4) experiencing immersion in the divine, beyond consciousness.[11] Thoreau's spiritual activities took place in nature—walking in it, sitting in it, living in it, being *of* it, "as much a pensioner in nature as mole and tit-mice" (*PJ* 1: 387). These activities became essential to creating a life free from constraint, a spiritual life that gave him the freedom to find, listen to, and support his essential self. In nature he could lose himself in time.

Silence and Deep Listening

Being immersed in silence was essential to Thoreau's well-being—as a source of insight, of comfort, of renewal, of timelessness. Experiencing silence usually meant solitude. Among Transcendentalists, as Barry Andrews writes, "Solitude was not sought to exclude society but to enable the self to become more individualized and authentic, and thus less conforming and compliant."[12] This was surely the case with Thoreau, who used his time in solitude to figure out who he was and what mattered to him when among others. In a Journal entry entitled "Some scraps from an essay on 'Sound and Silence'" he notes the elemental quality of silence, that it "*was*—say we—before even the world was, as if creation had displaced her—. . . ." and that it allows us to drop into ourselves: "Silence is the communing of a conscious soul with itself. – – If the soul attend for a moment to its own infinity, then and there is silence" (*PJ* 1:60).

Silence provided an escape from social time, as well as comfort and even protection. Sometimes, Thoreau admits in a Journal entry, "I almost shrink from the arduousness of meeting men erectly day by day – –" (*PJ* 1:230). His observation that "Silence is the universal refuge—the sequel of all dry discourses and all foolish acts—as balm to our every chagrin—" suggests that it soothes regrets and provides solace after social humiliation and disappointment (*PJ* 1:62). As Thoreau writes, silence "remains ever our inviolable asylum" (*PJ* 1:63). One who is silent can be strong, centered, and fully present: "With what equanimity does the silent consider how his world goes— He is one with Truth—Goodness—Beauty.— no indignity can assail him—no personality disturb him. – –" (*PJ* 1:63).

Immersing oneself in silence fosters wisdom when one listens for it. "By reverently listening to the inner voice," Thoreau writes in his journal, "we may reinstate ourselves on the pinnacle of humanity" (*PJ* 1:233). "Reinstate," of course, suggests that we become aware again of the transcendent, peak experiences available to us, in this case by honoring our "inner voice," our truth about who and how to be in our lives. Alan Hodder observes that Thoreau "recognized that the depths of his own consciousness offered the most direct access to the divine life," to one's inner divinity.[13] Thoreau also suggests this when he writes that "Heaven is the inmost place" (*PJ* 1:349).

Thoreau finds silence most compelling in "the recesses of nature," which, he believes, one should enter and enjoy silently, serenely, and reverently: "The beauty there is in mosses will have to be considered from the holiest—quietest nook" (*PJ* 1:230). From earliest boyhood he realized that his "spirit" *required* the kind of silence and "sweet solitude" found at Walden Pond, where his imagination and inner life could flourish:

> [W]hen I was 5 years old, I was brought from Boston to this pond [Walden], away in the country which was then but another name for the extended world for me....That woodland vision for a long time made the drapery of my dreams. That sweet solitude my spirit seemed so early to require that I might have room to entertain my thronging guests, and that speaking silence that my ears might distinguish the significant sounds. Some how or other it at once gave the preference to this recess among the pines where almost sunshine & shadow were the only inhabitants that varied the scene, over that tumultuous and varied city—as if it had found its proper nursery. (*PJ* 2:173 4)

Thereafter Thoreau recognized nature as his place of worship and spiritual insight, that nature contains "a reality and health" not "found in any religion....I suppose that what in other men is religion is in me love of nature" (*PJ* 2:55). His spiritual life, he realized, requires such a "recess among the pines" where he can listen to the "speaking silence" of birds, and animals, and insects, and water rather than the noise of "tumultuous" Boston.

It takes deliberate effort to immerse oneself in silence and attentive listening. It involves staying aware in the moment and bringing one's own "serenity & health of mind" to nature, no matter where one is. Thoreau reminds us that we must be aware of our distracted mind, our busy lives, and our over-scheduled commitments. We need to be calm and centered enough to "hear the sound of crickets" whenever and wherever they sing (*PJ* 3:291).

Thoreau experienced all his senses intensely, but hearing was perhaps his most acute and most spiritual. Alan Hodder even alludes to Thoreau's moments of "acoustic rapture" and "acoustically triggered ecstasy."[14] Solitude and silence enabled Thoreau to "distinguish the significant sounds" (*PJ* 2:174). Silence is thus not the absence of sound, but rather the absence of societal noise and the presence of natural sound. Upon seeing "the beauty and full meaning of that word sound," Thoreau notes playfully in an 1841 entry that the "sound state" of nature is indicated by "a certain sonorousness" coming from "the hum of insects—the booming of ice—the crowing of cocks in the morning and the barking of dogs in the night—" These natural sounds filled Thoreau with calm and balance and suggested physical, emotional, and spiritual health, "sound health" in other words: "God's voice is but a clear bell sound. I drink in a wonderful health—a cordial—in sound. The effect of the slightest tinkling in the horizon measures my own soundness" (*PJ* 1:277). He writes that he recovers "my spirits—my spirituality" from "the sound of the wind in the woods." Fear and despair are dispelled by "the rippling of the rivers" (*PJ* 3:368, *PJ* 1:342).

Natural sounds enveloped Thoreau in a sense of the divine and its connection to one's body and mortality. In August 1838 he writes in an entry titled "The Time of the Universe" that God touches our souls in a way to bring us into harmony with all of life. As a result, "Every pulse beat is in exact time with the crickets [sic] chant," as well as with our sense of mortality, "the tickings of the deathwatch" on the wall (*PJ* 1:50). In the experience of sensory delight, Thoreau realizes that he inhabits social human time but also spiritual time: "All sights and sounds are seen and heard both in time and eternity," that is, seen and heard at a particular moment but carrying with them a sense of divinity, of life beyond time (*PJ* 1:400).

Deep listening becomes a way into the holy for Thoreau: "Any melodious sound apprises me of the infinite wealth of God" (*PJ* 1:164). In one powerful Journal entry he conflates sound, sight, smell, touch, and the divine life in nature and in oneself while standing outside among rocks. We hear "divine sounds" within us, in our "inward ear" not just our physical ear. In a conflation of senses, we also breathe them in with the wind, see them reflected on the lake, and feel their physical and spiritual impact within us, "noiselessly bathing the temples of the soul" (*PJ* 1:61).

Awareness of the Present Moment, Meditation, Awakening

Understanding at a young age the transitoriness of life, especially after the death in his arms of his brother John at the age of 27 and the death of five-year-old Waldo Emerson, Thoreau acutely understood the importance of staying awake to life when it is happening. As he explains pragmatically in an 1841 entry, "The present seems never to get its due—it is the least obvious—neither before, nor behind, but within us. All the past plays into this moment, and we are what we are" (*PJ* 1:244). That the present is "within us" is significant, for the present moment is ours to experience and act in, the way the past and future are not. In a long entry about history, Thoreau observes, "Time hides no treasures–we want not its then—but its now" (*PJ* 1:318). Since it is only in the present that we can act, paying attention to our moments gives us the power to create our lives as we live them, to choose how to live.

Keeping sight of the present moment takes conscious effort. It means noticing when our restricting stories of reality, our "petty fears and petty pleasures," overshadow our actual life in the moment. When Thoreau practices this, when he is "calm & wise and unhurried," he recognizes what is real, "that only great and worthy things have any permanent & absolute existence—" When we don't stay awake to this tendency of mistaking our "petty fears and petty pleasures" for our reality, we live a life of "routine and habit" that is "built on imaginary foundations" (*PJ* 2:246). Keeping hold of the present moment means being aware that we *aren't* actively present. Thoreau relates feeling "a little alarmed when it happens that I have walked a mile into the woods bodily, without getting there in spirit." Like most meditators, he realizes he "cannot easily shake off the village," which in our meditation might be a work problem, our plans for dinner, or our to-do list. For Thoreau, "some surveying will run in my head and I am not where my body is—I am out of my senses." Admonishing himself, he asks rhetorically, "What business have I in the woods if I am thinking of something out of the woods" (*PJ* 3:150). In *A Week* he includes a long quote from Warren Hastings' letter urging the translation of the *Bhagavad Gita* in which Hastings discusses the "spiritual discipline" of meditation. He notes that "even the most studious of men of our hemisphere will find it difficult so to restrain their attention, but that it will wander to some object of present sense or recollection." He adds, however, that with practice, the mind, like the body, gets stronger (*Week* 138).

When Thoreau is fully present, his moments might extend into hours. Describing such a day of presence at Walden Pond, he explains his choice not to "sacrifice the bloom of the present moment to any work, whether of head or hands" and instead immerse himself in spiritual time:

> I love a broad margin to my life. Sometimes, in a summer morning, having taken my accustomed bath, I sat in my sunny doorway from sunrise till noon, rapt in a revery, amidst the pines and hickories and sumachs, in undisturbed solitude and stillness, while the birds sang around or flitted noiseless through the house, until by the sun falling in at my west window, or the noise of some traveller's wagon on the distant highway, I was reminded of the lapse of time. I grew in those seasons like corn in the night, and they were far better than any work of the hands would have been....I realized what the Orientals mean by contemplation and the forsaking of works. (*W* 111–12)

Thoreau's experience of being "rapt in a revery" of timelessness, in the "seasons" of a day, illustrates the concept of "aimlessness" described by the Buddhist monk Thich Nhat Hanh: "There is nothing to do, nothing to realize, no program, no agenda....Your purpose is to be yourself....Just be. Just being in the moment in this place is the deepest practice of meditation."[15] Thoreau describes such aimlessness when he says "I know not how the hours go" and "It was morning & lo! it is now evening—" He realizes that he is "not living that heroic life I had dreams of—," and that "nothing memorable is accomplished," the kind of life and accomplishments his society expects of him, "yet all my veins are full of life—and nature whispers no reproach—" (*PJ* 2:242).

Thoreau understood that when we are mindful, we pay attention to our thoughts and feelings without judgment. Then we experience and accept life with "wonder" as it unfolds, rather than through a filter of assumptions and theories, "an invisible network of speculations—" This way of experiencing life through "speculation" rather than attentiveness to what we are actually thinking and feeling becomes habitual, and "only at rare intervals do we perceive that it is no progress." He pleads, as much to himself as to others, I suspect, "Could we for a moment drop this by-play—and simply wonder—without reference or inference!" (*PJ* 1:58).

The present is not necessarily joyful. Part of meditative awareness involves paying attention to *all* conditions of one's life, including suffering. One day in January 1843 Thoreau laments about his life, "What am I at present? A diseased bundle of nerves standing between time and eternity like a withered leaf that still hangs shivering on its stem." Unusually downhearted, he continues, "A more miserable object one could not well imagine—but still very dull very insipid to think of. I suppose I may live on not a few years—trailing this carcass after me—or perhaps trailing after it—" (*PJ* 1:447). His Journal contains such entries of sadness, self-doubt, and self-criticism. He knew, however, that being fully alive involves acknowledging whatever one feels in the present moment, and he does this fully and honestly.

With that said, Thoreau realized what experienced meditators do, namely that we are caught in a limited self until we understand that thoughts are *not us* but rather events, fleeting bits of consciousness floating by. In the "Solitude" section of *Walden* he describes the meditation experience, the "conscious effort of the mind," of watching "the scene" of one's thoughts and feelings. As he wittily observes, this effort involves being "beside ourselves in a sane sense." We "stand aloof from actions and their consequences; and all things, good and bad, go by us like a torrent." Repeating this idea of observing "our thoughts and affections," he describes "a certain doubleness by which I can stand as remote from myself as from another" and being a "spectator, sharing no experience, but taking note of it" (*W* 134–5). As the Hastings letter Thoreau quotes in *A Week* indicates, the "spiritual discipline" of "abstracted contemplation" takes practice. This *Walden* passage shows he has been practicing (*Week* 138).

For Thoreau, staying mindful in the present was a matter of staying awake to life, literally and figuratively. A Journal entry written while he was living at Walden Pond describes his ritual of getting up early and bathing in the pond as "one of the best things I do" (*PJ* 2:235). He then makes time spiritual, expanding morning to "the most memorable season of the day" and the "awakening hour," when "some part of us seems to awake which slumbers all the rest of the day and night—" Every morning we can experience a kind of rebirth, a new opportunity to, "by a conscious endeavor," resolve to live the best life we can (*PJ* 2:236). Deliberately distinguishing human time from spiritual time, he writes, "It matters not what the clocks say or the attitudes & labors of men—morning is when I am awake & there is a dawn in me." Taking this awakening metaphor further, he asserts that, "Moral reform & improvement is the effort to throw off sleep & somnolency—" and that "only one in the million is awake enough for mental exertion—only one in a hundred million—spiritually—(more than intellectually) awake. To be awake is to be alive" (*PJ* 2:237).[16] Building on this Journal entry, awakening resonates in the *Walden* chapter "Where I Lived, and What I Lived For," where various forms of the word awake appear repeatedly. He refers to waking in the morning as his "most sacred and memorable life," and his morning bathing in Walden Pond becomes a religious act of renewal, an integral part of his spiritual practice.

Walking

Like contemplatives before him, Thoreau considered walking, particularly in nature, to be a spiritual practice, immersing him in spiritual time.[17] As his Journal entries show, he walked outside at all hours of the day and night and in all weather. He relished this practice of "walking and meditating… as if man & his customs & institutions" didn't exist (*PJ* 4:24). Walking, especially in the evening, revived his inmost authentic, centered self. Bluntly, he reflects that, "With the coolness & the mild silvery light I recover some sanity—" Daytime often brings wandering, trivial thoughts that make meditation difficult; "my life is too diffuse & dissipated—routine succeeds & prevails over us—" he writes regretfully. The moonlight, however, is sobering and centering, "like a cup of cold water to a thirsty man" (*PJ* 3:353–4).

The how of walking, in addition to the where and when of it, served as an act of meditation for Thoreau. He notes that the wise person, because he is not "restless or impatient," while walking, "each moment abides there where he is, as some walkers actually rest the whole body at each step," while those not as attentive "never relax the muscles of the leg till the accumulated fatigue obliges them to stop short" (*PJ* 1:81). This meditative walking provided Thoreau with the salutary effects of immersing himself in his surroundings, letting thoughts and worries pass by.

Thoreau links walking with several values. Although he insists in the essay "Walking" that the kind of ambulation he is writing about "has nothing in it akin to taking exercise as it is called," he does link it to both physical and emotional health. For instance, he notes that, "I think that I cannot preserve my health and spirits unless I spend four hours a day at least...sauntering through the woods and over the hills and fields absolutely free from all worldly engagements" (*Exc* 189, 187). He also connects the health of walking with the virtue of being "aimless" and mindful in the present moment, as well of his being "of" nature not just "in" it. He recognizes that "Health requires this relaxation this aimless life. This life in the present" (*PJ* 5:392). In another entry he makes a connection between movement and creativity: "How vain it is to sit down to write when you have not stood up to live! Methinks that the moment my legs begin to move my thoughts begin to flow—" (*PJ* 3:378).

Walking time is spiritual time for Thoreau. In an early Journal entry, he makes explicit the connection between the soul and the body that walks: "The body is the first proselyte the Soul makes. Our life is but the Soul made known by its fruits—the body" (*PJ* 1:138). Walking thus encourages soul searching. In one entry about his "path." He muses that perhaps he could "live a more substantial life," that he could walk further and harder. Then he quickly realizes that no change is necessary and tells himself, "Go not so far out of your way for a truer life—keep strictly onward in that path alone which your genius points out. Do the things which lie nearest to you but which are difficult to do." Notably, Thoreau's path toward "a purer a more thoughtful and laborious life" involves not just the self but others as well, being "more true to your friends & neighbors, more noble and magnanimous—and that will be better than a wild walk" (*PJ* 4:249). Despite his emphasis on walking by himself, this entry reminds us about the importance of relationships to Thoreau, that, however difficult, being his best self with "friends & neighbors" means more than one of his favorite practices, "a wild walk."

With that said, the therapeutic power of Thoreau's solitary, spiritual time in nature cannot be underestimated. His long, revealing description of a "sanative" walk into the woods during the intense cold of the 1856–1857 winter reveals how acutely he experienced prolonged encounters with society and how much he needed the restoration of nature to help keep him "sane." In this walk, with no one else about, he reflects that in society he feels "cheap and dissipated– –my life is unspeakably mean– –" and that "I wish to be made better." In the woods and fields, he realizes, "I come to myself" and "cold & solitude are friends of mine– –. . . I come to my solitary wood-land walk as the homesick go home– –" He needs to escape all remnants of civilization, the "superfluous," and "see things as they are, grand & beautiful– –" In nature he connects with, as it were, a supportive personal divinity and feels at peace: "It is as if I always met in those places some grand, serene, immortal– –infinitely encouraging, though invisible companion– –& walked with him. <u>There</u> at last– –my nerves are steadied—my senses & my mind do their office." In nature he feels "in my element again, as when a fish is put back into the water. I wash off all my chagrins– –," perhaps humiliation felt while in society. He then recounts that as a young boy he had a dream "night after night over & over again– –which might have been named Rough & Smooth." He is tossed between two extremes, "a horrible– –a fatal– –rough surface – –which must soon indeed put an end to my existence—" or, conversely, "lying on a delicious smooth surface– –as of a summer sea– – –as of gossamer or down– –or softest plush – –& life was such a luxury to live– –" Poignantly and revealingly, he concludes that, "My waking experience <u>always</u> has been and is– –such an alternate Rough & Smooth– – In other words it is Insanity & Sanity." In his description of a solitary, "sanative" walk on an intensely cold day, the contrast between where life felt threatening and where it felt safe could not be more stark.[18]

Immersion in the Divine

When he was nineteen years old, Thoreau described having a mystical, out-of-body experience. In a striking August 1838 journal entry titled "Consciousness," he begins a description of the occurrence with the curious phrase, "If with closed ears and eyes I consult consciousness for a moment—." That is, if I choose to deliberately ignore sensory information from seeing and hearing and instead only pay attention to my inner self, I tumble into a state of being beyond the body and the self:

> immediately are all walls and barriers dissipated—earth rolls from under me, and I float, by the impetus derived from the earth and the system—a subjective—heavily laden thought, in the midst of an unknown & infinite sea, or else heave and swell like a vast ocean of thought—without rock or headland....I am from the beginning—knowing no end, no aim. No sun illumines me,—for I dissolve all lesser lights in my own intenser and steadier light— I am a restful kernel in the magazine of the universe. (*PJ* 1:50–1)

This vignette describes being absorbed into an oceanic present beyond self, "in the midst of an unknown & infinite sea." Thoreau approaches a realization in this magnificent passage that his reading of Hindu scriptures, such as the *Bhagavad Gita*, later confirms and accentuates, that meditative experiences can take one beyond place and time into an infinite space, beyond self, beyond earthly substance.[19]

Thoreau recounts a similar but less dramatic experience the next year, of being dissolved in the eternal sublime, beyond "self," just deliciously "being." In this entry, entitled "Drifting," he writes about lying stretched out in his boat on Walden Pond "in a sultry day on the sluggish waters," when he drifts into spiritual time: "I cease to live—and begin to be." His view of himself, "[a] boat-man stretched on the deck of his craft, and dallying with the noon," becomes "as apt an emblem of eternity for me" when "I am dissolved in the haze" without an identifiable self (*PJ* 1:69–70). The lovely phrase "dallying with the noon" reveals how he treats time not as something to be purposefully noted, but rather as something to play with and in.

Thoreau's spirituality and the contemplative practices it entailed were key, not only to being at peace with his life choices, but also to his peaceful acceptance of death that his sister Sophia and his friends observed. An early Journal entry from October 24th, 1837, when Thoreau was twenty years old, titled "The Mould our Deeds Leave," reveals both his intention to live deliberately in time <u>and</u> his acceptance of death, beyond human time. He accepts that "the passing away of one life is the making room for another" and that this process in nature provides sustenance for the growth that comes after it. Each dead tree, just as each dead human, leaves behind a different kind of "soil" that subsequent living beings can use to grow in (*PJ* 1:5). Thoreau recognizes spiritual time in his notion of "transcience." While living involves continuance, death is "not a state of continuance but of transientness," an evanescent change from one state of being to another: "There is no continuance of death—it is a transient phenomenon—Nature presents nothing in a state of death" (*PJ* 1:372). As these passages suggest, Thoreau understood that one day his physical body would nourish nature as part of its cyclical process of death and new life.

Knowing that he had lived the full life he had created, Thoreau could peacefully accept the end of his physical life. This peacefulness also no doubt derived from his belief that ill health was part of the flow of life. In a February 1841 journal entry, he writes about being "confined to the house by bronchitis." Rather than fuming that he can't be walking in the woods, he faces this time of illness gracefully and fully, enjoying "that quiet and serene life there is in warm corner by the fireside" and looking at the sky "through the chimney top." He transforms this time of illness into spiritual time, an opportunity to do what he advises when he states that, "Sickness should not be allowed to extend further than the body—" Instead of letting it consume our attention, "We need only to retreat further within us, to preserve uninterrupted the continuity of serene hours to the end of our lives" (*PJ* 1:265–6). Accepting suffering as part of life pervades Eastern religion, as does understanding the way out of suffering through spiritual practices. Thoreau realized that acceptance, rather than resistant denial, allows human beings to live with and experience suffering as a gift to learn from. We must not deny illness but rather "make the most of it, for the fruit of disease may be as good as that of health" (*PJ* 1:272).

Thoreau's spiritual practices and the spiritual time they created enabled him, in the end, to defy the ultimate human fear of time, "the ticking of the deathwatch" on the wall. Courageously moving, thoughout his life, beyond his limited, temporal self toward a timeless, boundless self, Thoreau expanded his belief that death is "not a state of continuance but of transientness" to the idea that, just as "Nature presents nothing in a state of death," so we too can live in each moment without fearing or dwelling on death (*PJ* 1:372). Boldly he ignores the limitation of human time and onfirms the joy of spiritual time: "What sort of fruit comes of living as if you were a going to die? Live rather as if you were coming to life. How can the end of living be death? The end of living is life. Living is an active transitive state to life—Life in the green state" (*PJ* 3:30).

Works Cited

Andrews, Barry M. *Transcendentalism and the Cultivation of the Soul.* Amherst: University of Massachusetts Press, 2017.

Brown, Mary Hosmer. *Memories of Concord.* Boston: The Four Seas Company, 1926.

Channing, William Ellery. *Thoreau The Poet-Naturalist.* Boston: Charles E. Goodspeed, 1902.

Emerson, Ralph Waldo. "Thoreau," *Atlantic Monthly* (August 1862): 239–49.

Hanh, Thich Nhat. *The Heart of the Buddha's Teaching.* New York: Harmony Book, 2015.

Harding, Walter. *The Days of Henry Thoreau: A Biography.* New York: Dover Publications, Inc., 1982.

Hodder, Alan D. *Thoreau's Ecstatic Witness.* New Haven: Yale University Press, 2001.

Hosmer, Joseph. "[Reminiscences of Thoreau] (1878, 1881, and 1882)," in *Thoreau in His Own Time.* Edited by Sandra Harbert Petrulionis. Iowa City: University of Iowa Press, 2012.

Lunt, Sarah Hosmer, "Memories of Concord." MS, Evald B. Lawson.

Marble, Annie Russell. *Thoreau: His Home, Friends and Books.* New York: Thomas Y. Crowell & Co., 1902.

Ricketson, Anna and Walton, eds. *Daniel Ricketson and His Friends: Letters, Poems, Sketches, Etc.* Boston: Houghton, Mifflin and Company, 1902; rpt. 2009.

Richardson, Robert D. *Henry Thoreau: A Life of the Mind.* Berkeley: University of California Press, 1986.

Salt, Henry S. *Life of Henry David Thoreau.* Edited by George Hendrick, Willene Hendrick, and Fritz Oehlschlaeger. Urbana: University of Illinois Press, 1890; rpt. 1993.

The Bhagvat-Geeta or Dialogues of Keeshna and Arjoon; in Eighteen Lectures; with Notes. Translated by Sir Charles Wilkins. London: C. Nourse, 1785. Digital Library of India Item 2015.217244. http://archive.org/details/in.ernet.dli.2015.

Walls, Laura Dassow. *Henry David Thoreau: A Life*. Chicago: The University of Chicago Press, 2017.

Weiss, John. "Thoreau," *Christian Examiner* 79 (July 1865): 96–117.

CHAPTER 9

THOREAU'S ETERNAL RETURN

Richard Higgins

Thoreau performed the ultimate act of sustainability by recycling time. He did not think the past was dead. He didn't even think it was past. It ran into the present for him like the springs and rills that flow into that stream of time Thoreau paddled with his brother, the Merrimack River.

The mythic past was present for Thoreau in the crickets' ancient and immortal chant, in the strain of the sparrow, which he called a "voice of eternal wisdom" (OJT, May 12, 1857), and in the song of the wood thrush, which "changes all hours to an eternal morning" (*PJ* 6: 236).

William Blake did it in verse, but Thoreau found eternity in a real grain of sand—in the grains flowing down the Deep Cut or in an Assabet River sandbank. The latter, he said, "revealed an antiquity beside which Nineveh is young" (*PJ* 3: 286).

In such moments, Thoreau entered an island in time not counted on the town clock, an endless moment of fable and possibility. It was a realm of time that mystics have called the Eternal Now, that the historian of religion Mircea Eliade has described as the Eternal Return and that Native Americans have known as Ceremonial Time, in which past, present, and future can be fused in a single moment during a sacred dance or ritual.[1] I think Eliade's concept of the Eternal Return most applies to Thoreau because it entails an imaginative immersion in the past through ritual acts, sacred texts or objects, or contact with the natural world, whereas the Eternal Now of the mystic is more of a pure state of consciousness, independent of the external world. Ceremonial Time, while similar, is more communal and tribal in nature than one could expect from Thoreau.

The Eternal Return, as conceived by historians of religion, is a behavior or mindset that allows one to re-enter the "mythical age" of meaning. It was proposed by Romanian scholar Eliade in his book *The Myth of the Eternal Return* (1949). Building on the work of Émile Durkheim and others, he proposed that religion, at its core, involves the experience of the sacred. He held that *homo religiosus*, the religious person, sees the world in terms of sacred and profane space as well as sacred and profane time. "In imitating the exemplary acts of a god or of a mythic hero, or simply by recounting their adventures," Eliade wrote, "the man of archaic society detaches himself from profane time and magically re-enters the Great Time, the sacred time."[2]

Thoreau saw life through such a lens. He sought to live within that stratum of deep or sacred time that is beyond temporal considerations. Ordinary life, by contrast, is profane, according to Eliade, *not* in any bad sense, as we use the word today, but simply as the opposite of sacred time. It is why the Catholic Church calls the sacramentally uneventful period from Pentecost to Advent "Ordinary Time."

Sacred time would seem to have little to do with the "nick of time," but in Thoreau's mind, they were connected. The "nick of time" goes back to the medieval use of sticks cut with precise notch marks, or nicks, to measure or count things, track time, or tally sales—bushels of barley sold, damsels deflowered, martyrs murdered, that sort of thing. Small and exact, a nick conveyed precision. In the early to mid-1500s, to do something at the last possible moment was not to do it in the nick of time, however, but to do it "in pudding time," the pudding being a meat pie or slurry of sheep's heart, liver, and lungs served at the start of medieval meals. So, if you got there just in time for that dish you arrived in pudding time—a fact that may account for the high rate of tardiness at medieval feasts. But by around 1600, the "pudding" had become a sweet dish moved to the *end* of the meal, like our dessert today, rendering the idiom meaningless. Therefore "in the nick of time" replaced it to mean doing something at the exact last moment.[3]

Thoreau puns on this history to convey the idea that *every* moment is the nick of time. He famously said that he was born in Concord in 1817 "in the nick of time," because, for the attentive person, all time is fused into every second. "In any weather, at any hour of the day or night," he writes in *Walden*, "I have been anxious to improve the nick of time, and notch it on my stick too; to stand on the meeting of two eternities, the past and future, which is precisely the present moment; to toe that line" (*W* 17). To stand on the meeting of two eternities—that was what Thoreau meant when he wrote in his journal in January 1853 that, during rest of the year, he dreamed of "those summery hours when time is tinged with eternity, runs into it and becomes of one stuff with it." It is also why he urges us, "Observe the hours of the universe, not of the cars" (*PJ* 5: 438, 412).

This idea draws on one of Thoreau's core beliefs, which is that we live in the same original moment, with the same heroic possibilities, as anyone who walked in primordial dawn of poetry and myth. "When I go into a museum and see the mummies wrapped in their linen bandages," he wrote in *A Week on the Concord and Merrimack Rivers*, "I see that the lives of men began to need reform as long ago as when they walked the earth. I come out into the streets, and meet men who declare that the time is near at hand for the redemption of the race. But as men lived in Thebes, so do they live in Dunstable to-day" (*Week* 124).

Thoreau seems to have developed this belief while studying the classics at Harvard. "How thrilling a noble sentiment in the oldest books—in Homer...or Confucius," he wrote in 1838, a year after graduating. "It is a strain of music wafted down to us on the breeze of time, through the aisles of innumerable ages" (*PJ* 1: 52).

In his imagination, Thoreau strode the same world that Plato traipsed. The shores of Walden Pond were his Ithaca, and the natural world was "in as rude health as when Homer sang." In Thoreau's day, the Mississippi River was the American frontier and conveyed newness. Yet when Thoreau went to see a panorama of the river, he did not come away thinking it was new. "I saw that this was a Rhine stream of a different kind;...and I felt that *this was the Heroic Age itself though we know it not*" (emphasis his) (*Exc* 202).

Time, in essence, was plastic for Thoreau. He did not accept clock time as fixed or final. He imaginatively embraced abundant time, time that was more than itself. It was porous and liminal, expanding or contracting according to his thoughts and feelings. There was for Thoreau but a blurred boundary between what the Greeks called *kairos* and *chronos*—propitious, qualitative time, time full of promise, which has an eternal or divine quality, and the time that is measured by the hourglass or ticking timepiece.

Thoreau was not interested, however, in capturing the past or venerating its skeletons, as the museum curator is. "It is the province of the historian to find out, not what was, but what is," he wrote in *A Week*. "Strictly speaking, the historical societies have not recovered one fact from oblivion, but are themselves, instead of the fact, what is lost" (*Week* 154). When we live fully and truly, there is only the present moment. "In eternity there is indeed something true and sublime," he famously wrote in *Walden*. "But all these times and places and occasions are now and here. God himself culminates in the present moment and will never be more divine in the lapse of all the ages" (*W* 97).

Thoreau's belief in the unity of time is evident in his early poems, especially "Inspiration," which he wrote around 1841 and wove into *A Week*. The poet says that if he takes pride in his literary genius, his verse will fail. But if he bows "with bended neck" to the flame in his soul, he will hear beyond the range of sound and see beyond the verge of sight. The poet then enters a moment that fuses past, present, and future. "Now chiefly is my natal hour / And only now my prime of life." Thoreau revered not only sacred spaces, such as Walden Pond or a nameless swamp, but also sacred time, his "natal hour."[4]

Thoreau often spoke of the eternal in the present moment, but he also sometimes made a distinction between "eternity" and "time," with the latter representing the trivial time of the railroad schedule. The sound of crickets, he wrote one May, "suggests lateness, but only as we come to a knowledge of eternity after some acquaintance with time. It is only late for all trivial and hurried pursuits. It suggests a wisdom mature, never late, beyond all temporal considerations" (*PJ* 8: 148). And in *Walden*, just before his famous declaration that most people live lives of quiet desperation, he quipped, "As if you could kill time without injuring eternity" (*W* 8). To kill time is to waste it, to get it over with, which is to waste the connection to eternity that the present moment contains.

According to Eliade, traditional societies believed the mythical age was sacred because it was when the gods gave form and meaning to the world. Myths, rituals, liturgies, poetry, an ancient tree or sacred objects (rosary beads, for example, or Queequeg's wooden idol in *Moby-Dick*) can carry one back to the mythic or sacred age. In the modern period, church, temple, or mosque services, for example, mark a break in profane time as participants "return" to the sacred time of their faith. The worshippers no longer experience the time marked on the adjacent sidewalks and streets—what Thoreau called railroad time—but rather sanctified time, be it the Exodus of the Jews, the passion and death of Jesus, or the revelation to Muhammad.

Classical philosophers had their own notion of the Eternal Return, but it was different from Eliade's. First proposed by the Stoics, the Eternal Return of ancient philosophy was the belief that time repeats itself in an infinite loop, with the same events occurring in the same way again and again. Zeno, the founder of Stoicism, believed the world goes through cycles of transformation in which it is periodically destroyed and reborn.[5] This idea fell out of fashion in the West with the rise of Christianity, which emphasizes historical time, which, according to the New Testament, will culminate at the end of the world with the reestablishment of the Kingdom of God. But the notion of cyclic time was revived by Friedrich Nietzsche, who believed that it is our fate as humans to relive every detail of our lives—every pain, frustration, and moment of boredom, as well as every joy, over and over again, like Groundhog Day. In *The Gay Science*, Nietzsche dubbed this the Eternal Recurrence, and he viewed it as an existential challenge: we must choose whether to embrace this fate or give up in despair.[6]

A related notion of time, that all temporality is an illusion, has a long philosophical heritage can be traced back at least to Augustine, who argued that there is no such division of time as past, present, and future. In his *Confessions*, he wrote "neither future nor past exists, and it is inexact language to speak of three times—past, present, and future." The past, he reasoned, is recalled only in the present, as something we remember, and the future is likewise a mental construct, an anticipation that also occurs in the present. Rather than being an external, observable phenomenon, time, according to Augustine, exists within our own consciousness and is indivisible.[7]

Thoreau would seem to agree. In *A Week* he tells us that "one veil hangs over past, present, and future" (*Week* 155). In 1842 he wondered why old things, like rusty nails, betray their age by their appearance. "Why," he wrote, "does God not make some mistake to show us time is a delusion?" He also asked that same year, "What, then can I do to hasten that other time, or that space where there shall be not time," when "there will be no discords in my life?" (*PJ* 1: 392, 362). In *Walden*, time has no linear beginning and no linear end because Thoreau has turned it into a cycle. "For the first time," he wrote in 1852 as he worked on his final revisions of *Walden*, "I perceive this spring that the year is a circle—I distinctly see the spring arc thus far" (*PJ* 4: 468).

There is a paradox in Thoreau's sense of time. On the one hand, he was devoted to the present. "The present seems never to get its due—it is the least obvious—neither before, nor behind, but within us. All the past plays into this moment, and we are what we are" (*PJ* 1: 244). Only by being awake to the present can we act deliberately and create our lives. At the same time, he recognized that the present is to some degree an illusion. It slides away as quickly as it is perceived. "Already the aspens are trembling again—and a new summer is offered me," he wrote (OJT, 23:118). "I feel a little fluttered in my thoughts as if I might be too late. Each season is but an infinitesimal point. It no sooner comes than it is gone. It has no duration. It simply gives a tone & hue to my thought." The present moment, the very nick of time, is for Thoreau as slippery as it is real. It fades as soon as it is felt.

One of my favorite passages in Thoreau's Journal is about cracking the nut of time. As he stood along the Mill Brook in Concord one October, a profusion of red oak acorns fell like hail, sounding like muskrats plunging as they hit the water. Although Thoreau couldn't eat the acorns raw, he vowed to feed his soul on their remembered beauty. He dreamed of a winter evening when these "untasted" "nuts of the gods" would finally be cracked in his memory and their flavors released—at which moment time would suddenly be no more (OJT 27:272–73).

> How munificent is Nature to create this profusion of wild fruit, as it were merely to gratify our eyes! Though inedible they are more wholesome to my immortal part, and stand by me longer, than the fruits which I eat. If they had been plums or chestnuts I should have eaten them on the spot and probably forgotten them. They would have afforded only a momentary gratification, but being acorns, I remember, and as it were feed on, them still. They are untasted fruits forever in store for me. I know not of their flavor as yet. That is postponed to some still unimagined winter evening. These which we admire but do not eat are nuts of the gods. When time is no more we shall crack them.

This "wild fruit" of the oak tree answers to Thoreau's "immortal" part because its sweetest meat, its beauty, is savored by the soul, not the tongue. Thoreau drew the link between the eternity he saw in nature and his own immortality more directly in 1856. That March, he returned to the Deep

Cut, the site of the gestating sandbank he famously wrote about in *Walden*, looking for any new life that the spring sun had called forth from the warm sandy soil. He saw none that day but was still reassured of nature's immortality—and of his own share of it. "I am reassured & reminded that I am the heir of eternal inheritances--which are inalienable--when I feel the warmth reflected from this sunny bank....The eternity which I detect in Nature I predicate of myself also. How many springs I have had this same experience! I am encouraged, for I recognize this steady persistency & recovery of Nature as a quality of myself" (OJT, 20:167).

Thoreau's perception of time does not yield easily to a strict empiricism. It relied upon a felt perception of a longer and deeper strand of time beyond and through the present, a timescale that was fundamentally mystical and sacred. Similarly, the twentieth-century philosopher and process theologian Alfred North Whitehead saw an awareness of the unity of time as the basis of the religious sentiment. "The foundation of reverence," he wrote, "is this perception, that the present holds within itself the complete sum of existence, backwards and forwards, that whole amplitude of time, which is eternity." And in 1941, the Quaker mystic Thomas Kelly wrote: "Eternity is at our hearts, pressing upon our time-torn lives, warming us with intimations of an astounding destiny, calling us home unto itself."[8]

I think Thoreau felt this way. His vision of time was not an abstract philosophical issue as it was for the Stoics but a spiritual discipline and form of contemplation, a foundation of reverence. In *A Week*, he calls the locusts and crickets of a summer day "a continuation of the sacred code" (*Week* 150). And writing about music in his *Journal*, Thoreau asked, "of what manner of stuff is the web of time wove, when these consecutive sounds called a strain of music can be wafted down through the centuries from Homer to me, and Homer have been conversant with that same unfathomable mystery and charm which so newly tingles my ears? These single strains, these melodious cadences which plainly proceed out of a very deep meaning...are the interjections of God" (*PJ* 1: 361–362).

Thoreau's mentor, Emerson, also spoke of the fusion of time. "In the presence of nature, a man of feeling is not suffered to lose sight of the instant of creation," he wrote in an 1837 lecture on human culture. "The world was not made a long time ago. Nature is an Eternal Now."[9]

And in his 1838 essay, "Literary Ethics," Emerson tells of a romantic boy who has just read the life story of Charles the Fifth of the Holy Roman

Empire. As the boy roams his native woods, he wonders what stern decisions, court intrigue, foreign dispatches, or heroic acts filled the emperor's days. Emerson says the boy's soul answers: "Behold his day here! In the sighing of these woods, in the quiet of these gray fields, in the cool breeze that sings out of these northern mountains; in the workmen, the boys, the maidens, you meet—in the hopes of the morning, the ennui of noon and sauntering of the afternoon; in the regrets at want of vigor; in the great idea and the puny execution—behold Charles the Fifth's day....The difference of circumstance is merely costume. I am tasting the self-same life—its sweetness, its greatness, its pain, which I admire in other men. Do not foolishly ask of the inscrutable, obliterated past, what it cannot tell...but ask it of the enveloping now."[10]

One reason I compare Thoreau's sense of time to Eliade's Eternal Return is that each involves a kind of reenactment. In Eliade's view, ritual and commemorative acts, such as marking saints days, fasting, meditating on sacred writings, and dancing are ways to re-enter sacred time. The whirling dervishes of the Sufis are but one example. Native Americans would dance themselves into an altered state of consciousness in which they would commune with their ancestors. John Hanson Mitchell explored this Native American belief in his wonderful book *Ceremonial Time* about 15,000 years in the life of his backyard in a town near Concord.[11]

Thoreau re-entered the past through his reading, his sensory experiences in nature, and his imaginative re-immersion of them through his writing. Emerson, William James wrote, showed that writing can be a sacred act. The "head-spring" of Emerson's outpourings, according to James, was his belief that "the point of any pen can be an epitome of reality; the commonest person's act, if genuinely actuated, can lay hold of eternity."[12]

Another form of reenactment for Thoreau came through his contact with sacred objects, which could be almost anything in nature. Seeing lichens on the trees, he remembered that the ancient Greeks hung the shields of their defeated foes in the Persian War in the Temple of Athena, the circular marks of which, Thoreau was careful to note, are still visible today. In the same way, he sees lichens as the "wrinkled trophies" that nature hangs on the trunks of trees (*Week* 250).

Perhaps the clearest example is his beautiful extended reflection on arrowheads, which, he wrote, would outlast the works of famous painters and sculptors. "They are not fossil bones, but as it were fossil thoughts--

forever reminding me of the mind that shaped them....When I see [them] I know that the subtle spirits that made them are not far off, into whatever form transmuted....the larger pestles & axes may, perchance, grow scarce & be broken, but the arrowhead shall perhaps never cease to wing its way through the ages to eternity." When the British Museum is razed to the earth, he wrote, the arrowheads it contains will lay in its dust "to be picked up for the thousandth time by the shepherd or savage that may be wandering there & once more suggest their story to him" (OJT, 28:314–16). Held in our hands in the present, the arrowhead links us to humans before us and a realm of time gone by.

Even more than natural objects, however, music and nature's sounds were especially the medium that enabled Thoreau to experience the Eternal Return. "I have just heard the flicker among the oaks on the hillside ushering in a new dynasty," he wrote Sunday, April 3, 1842. "It is the age and youth of time....The summer's eternity is reestablished by this note. All sights and sounds are heard both in time and eternity. And when the eternity of any sight or sound strikes the eye or ear—they are intoxicated with delight" (*PJ* 1: 359–360).

In *A Week*, he writes of sitting on the stump of tree whose rings number centuries of growth and reflects that the very ground is composed of ancient remains. "If I listen, I hear the peep of frogs older than the slime of Egypt, and the distant drumming of a partridge on a log, as if it were the pulse-beat of the summer air. I raise my fairest and freshest flowers in the old mould....The newest is but the oldest made visible to our senses" (*Week* 153–154).

The song of crickets in spring stirred a similar thought. "They sit aside from the revolution of the seasons. Their strain is unvaried as Truth. Only in their saner moments do men hear crickets. It is a balm to the philosopher. It tempers his thoughts. They dwell forever in a temperate latitude.... They are not concerned about the news. A quire has begun which pauses not for any news--for it knows only the eternal" (*PJ* 8: 144).

Earlier in his career as a writer, Thoreau's reflections on time were geared, as we have seen, to the mythic past within the present moment. By the time of his natural history essays about a decade later, in particular "Autumnal Tints," and *The Dispersion of Seeds*, his focus shifts slightly to the seeds of the future that exist within the present. "Autumnal Tints," for example, as excellent a guide to fall colors as it is, and as funny as it is, is primarily a meditation on death and resurrection in nature, on the new forests that will spring years hence from the fallen leaves and trees. The seed becomes the perfect metaphor for this sense of promise or future fruition in which he had faith. Watching the seeds of a milkweed pod float over a field in a breeze, he writes:

> I am interested in the fate or success of every such venture which the autumn sends forth. And for this end these silken streamers have been perfecting themselves all summer, snugly packed in this light chest, a perfect adaptation to this end—a prophecy not only of the fall, but of future springs. Who could believe in prophecies of Daniel or of Miller that the world would end this summer, while one milkweed with faith matured its seeds?" (*FS* 93).

I think Thoreau's vision of time was a comfort to him. At some point he realized that he would not have to submit his *Journal* to the approval of Ticknor & Fields. He was not writing it for them. He carved his words with no less devotion to his art than the Artist of Kouroo shaped his staff. And his journal, in fact, did publish itself, by the sheer force of its own beauty, after he died. But Thoreau knew it all along. "Time & Co.," he wrote in 1848, "are after all the only quite honest & trustworthy publishers that we know" (*PCorr* 1: 350).

Works Cited

Allen, Paula Gunn. "The Ceremonial Motion of Indian Time: Long Ago, So Far." In *The Sacred Hoop*. Boston: Beacon Press, 1986.

Eliade, Mircea. *Myths, Dreams and Mysteries*. New York: Harper Bros., 1961.

Emerson, Ralph Waldo. *The Early Lectures of Ralph Waldo Emerson*. Edited by Stephen Whicher, Robert Spiller, and Wallace Williams. Cambridge: Harvard University Press, 1966–72.

———. *Nature, Addresses and Lectures*. Honolulu: University Press of the Pacific, 2001.

James, William. "Address." In *The Centenary of the Birth of Ralph Waldo Emerson: As Observed in Concord, May 25, 1903*. Cambridge: Riverside Press, 1903.

Kelly, Thomas. *A Testament of Devotion*. New York: Harper & Row, 1941.

Mitchell, John Hanson. *Ceremonial Time: Fifteen Thousand Years in One Square Mile*. Hanover: University Press of New England, 1984 and 2013.

Nietzsche, Friedrich. *The Gay Science*. Translated by Josefine Nauckhoff and Adrian Del Caro. New York: Cambridge University Press, 2001.

Whitehead, Alfred North. *The Aims of Education*. New York: Simon & Schuster, 1967.

CHAPTER 10

WALDEN'S CORE IDEA: EARTHLY BIRTH AND RENEWAL

Robert M. Thorson

Early in *Walden's* opening chapter, "Economy," Thoreau wrote: "In any weather, at any hour of the day or night, I have been anxious to improve the nick of time, and notch it on my stick too; to stand on the meeting of two eternities, the past and future, which is precisely the present moment; to toe that line" (*W* 17).

Quoting Merriam-Webster, the nick of time is "just before the last moment when something can be changed." Thus, to improve the "nick of time" is to anticipate that game-changing moment. To "toe the line" comes from foot racing, the positioning of the toes of runners precisely on the starting line while waiting for the starting gun. It also refers to closely following the rules, in this case that of the race.

Unpacking and interpreting Thoreau's quotation, he wants us to be ready and waiting for the next new adventure of our lives at "precisely the present moment." His anxiety is about making the right, or improved, choice before it is too late. Finally, he wants us to notch those moments on the memory stick of our lives.

In this moment, you are at a critical nick of time. Will you improve it by continuing to read this chapter? Or, will you improve it by setting it aside? Your life will be changed either way. To read, or not to read—that is the question. Regardless, don't forget to notch your stick before moving on.

Though your choice might seem like small potatoes in the grand scheme of things, your notch will become part of Earth's high-fidelity archive, which records a continuous stream of divergent, dichotomous paths tracing backwards in time to the moment when time began.[1]

Nicks & Notches

There's a place in Concord, Massachusetts, just south of the railroad station known as the Deep Cut. This is the deepest excavation into the loamy, sandy, and gravelly hills made for the Fitchburg Railroad in 1843. And, except for *Walden's* namesake pond, it's the most important place for the book. There, Thoreau observed and described the behavior of miniature mudflows that formed whenever the frozen embankments began to thaw. Robert Sattelmeyer, along with most Thoreau scholars, agrees that Thoreau's use of this phenomenon as metaphor is the "triumphant climax" of the penultimate chapter that climaxes the book.[2] Each of these tiny rivulets branched again and again in a series of nicks of time to produce the distributary pattern that Thoreau called the "sand foliage" (*W* 306).[3] Each of these beautiful fern-like patterns results from a fractal series of anabranching left-right decisions, or nicks, marked on the stick of time at the scale of seconds to minutes. He suspected that this pattern, if fossilized, would become "a puzzle for future geologists" (*W* 305).

Seeing this continuous creation taking place as he watched inspired Thoreau to conclude: "There is nothing inorganic" (*W* 308). This is my candidate for *Walden*'s most important line.

Scientists have since shown that life emerged from non-life at the first nick below evolutionary time. That's when planet Earth took the road less traveled to create carbon-based life as we know it, the only one of its sibling planets to have done so.[4] At that nick, organic molecules of different kinds came together to create the original microbial cell. For the first time on Earth, something had the ability to draw energy from the environment, replicate, and evolve. The resulting notch is called LUCA, short for the Last Universal Common Ancestor, the great-great-great-great-great-great-great...grandparent of every living thing in Thoreau's world. The first bluebird of spring, the fox barking at night, the beans growing in his field, the mother who nursed an infant boy born in a Concord farmhouse in 1817, and the microbe *Mycobacterium tuberculosis* that killed him forty-three years later. All came from LUCA's notch recorded in the archive of deep time, in this case, a biomarker of carbon isotopes.

From our human perspective, the second critical nick of time is when LUCA took another road less traveled to become a eukaryote, a complex nucleated cell. Nicks 3, 4, 5, 6, and so forth involved that single eukaryote cell teaming up with others to became an animal, that animal attaining a vertebral column, that vertebrate becoming a mammal, that mammal becoming a primate, and so forth through ape, hominoid, hominin, and human. One member of that human species, *Homo sapiens*, is you, a remarkably late notch on the stick of life. The choices you make will—statistically—determine the fate of our planet because we're all in this together.

Thoreau's masterpiece was a notch on the world's stick of literature, a threshold-defining work written during what Thoreau called "This restless, nervous, bustling, trivial Nineteenth Century" (*W* 329). To improve this nick, Thoreau eagerly and loudly prophesized a more joyful human community in which people lived their lives deliberately and sustainably within the full embrace of Nature. For the rest of his life, Thoreau took that path less traveled, as have most of his followers. Alas, most of the world took the much more traveled path, moving ever more thoughtlessly and hurriedly in the direction of industrialization, urbanization, and alienation from Nature to create the Anthropocene makeover. Modern humans are so numerous and so driven by a craving for energy and material goods that—for better or worse—we have become the dominant geo-bio-chem-physical agency operating on Earth's surface, and a highly disruptive one at that.

My candidate for *Walden's* most overlooked line opens his final paragraph:

> I do not say that John or Jonathan will realize all this; but such is the character of that morrow which mere lapse of time can never make to dawn. The light which puts out our eyes is darkness to us. Only that day dawns to which we are awake. The sun is but a morning star. (*W* 333)

This passage makes it clear that *Walden's* fundamental theme is rebirth, and that to see it, we must be awake to it. A rebirth not only each morning, each spring, and each human life, but also each of the many successive worlds that Earth has experienced throughout its seemingly eternal history.

What does he mean by "the character of that morrow which mere lapse of time can never make to dawn?" It's a rebirth of some sort. One clue comes from the trio of earthly allegorical fables that precede this final paragraph: the *Artist of Kouroo* for its message about the depth of time and Earth's many re-creations; the story about the *horse sunk into the swamp* to remind us that the Earth's crust is our "solid bottom everywhere" (*W* 330); and the emergence of the *strong and beautiful bug* reminding us that epochs of life emerge from beneath the pellicle of Earth's surface.

What does Thoreau mean by, "Only that day dawns to which we are awake"? He is returning to a bracketing idea from his first chapter—that he was "anxious to improve the nick of time" (*W* 17). Without being expectant and fully awake, we will not be able to see each new day, year, life, dynasty, or epoch for what it is: a whole new world of possibilities.

There are many kinds of mornings. The most common come from Earth's spinning away from the shadow of night toward the light of the sun, bringing astronomical dawn. The cycle of the year is another kind of morning, one caused by our tilted planet moving around its sun to give us more or less light each day. On a longer timeframe, some mornings arise from deep within the earth as the great biodiversification events in earth history, all of which follow the requisite mass extinctions, most of which arose with colossal plumes of volcanic gas. And on the longest time scale of all, the morning of the birth of Earth in volcanic fury 4.5 billion years ago.

This Hadean scene was "a morning which carries us back beyond the Mosaic creation where crystallizations are fresh & unmelted. It is the poet's hour" (*PJ* 5:454). This passage was perhaps inspired by the charcoal red glow of burning stumps at night, which he described as a Promethean scene of "phosphorescence…a strange, Titanic thing this Fire—this Vulcan, here at work in the night" (*PJ* 5:30). The "era of this creation" was the first in a series in the "order of creation" was that first "spring of the world" (*PJ* 5:454, 7:280, 4:497), "that early age of the world—following hard on the reign of water & the barren rocks" (*PJ* 6:182), when early plants like "lichens and algae" colonized the land (*PJ* 6:162). Then came "alder & the Willow… [which] impress me as a vegetation which belongs to the earliest & most innocent dawn of nature" (*PJ* 7:280).[5]

My candidate for Thoreau's favorite place on Earth is the bedrock Cliff overlooking Fair Haven Pond and the Sudbury Valley. There, he could see the transient modernity of the present moment anchored on the ancient reality of the solid granite beneath his boots. "Let us settle ourselves, and work and wedge our feet downward," he wrote in *Walden,* "till we come to a hard bottom and rocks in place, which we can call reality" (*W* 97). This rock reality was the solid foundation on which he could build the "castles in the air" of his thoughts and dreams (*W* 324).

In Thoreau's nineteenth-century Concord, the Puritan Bible held that there was no such thing as a past eternity.[6] Rather, it held that Earth was created from scratch in 4004 BCE. Thoreau didn't buy it. He knew from geology that time was infinitely deep in both directions, the past and future separated by the present nick of time. Heaven above couldn't possibly be frozen in time but must be experiencing continuous change. Hell below could not be a bad place because its heat was responsible for giving Earth life and keeping it alive.

Thoreau's first book, *A Week on the Concord and Merrimack Rivers,* was composed when Thoreau lived at Walden Pond (1845–1847). Published in May of 1849, it was a commercial disaster, in part because Thoreau's flaunting of deep time enraged his Christian culture. *A Week* is soaked with uncredited paraphrasing of Charles Lyell's *Principles of Geology*, which Thoreau read in 1840 as his first substantial work of science.[7] Robert Richardson noted that Thoreau was "deeply, repeatedly, and lastingly moved by the book" as a "great revelation."[8]

Here and there in *A Week,* Thoreau recapitulated Lyell's key points: That Earth is inconceivably old. That, for all practical purposes, the planet can be considered eternal. That nothing under the sun is really new. That everything everywhere is always being recycled from a previous state of existence. That there is no such thing as progress. That the whole Earth manifests a steady-state equilibrium through an endless series of creations and destructions via the rock cycle. Consider these few quotations:

"In reality, history fluctuates as the face of the landscape from morning to evening" (*Week* 154). This is a foreshadowing of *Walden's* final lines: "The eyes of the oldest fossil remains, they tell us, indicate that the same laws of light prevailed then as now.... The gods are partial to no era, but steadily shines their light in the heavens, while the eye of the beholder is turned to stone" (*Week* 157). Here, he refers to the ancient worlds that succeed one another in the fossil record of a continuously creating planet. "We will not be confined by historical, even geological periods.... we shall expect that this morning of the race... will be succeeded by a day of equally progressive splendor; that, in the lapse of the divine periods, other divine agents and godlike men will assist to elevate the race as much above its present condition" (*Week* 158). This is a foreshadowing of the fable of the Artist of Kouroo in *Walden's* concluding chapter. Lambasting what today we call young-earth creationism, he writes: "Without borrowing any years from the geologist...the lives of but sixty old women,...say of a century each, strung together, are sufficient to...span the interval from Eve to my own mother A respectable tea party merely,—whose gossip would be Universal History" (*Week* 324–325).[9] And in the ultimate questioning of biblical authority, he trumpeted: "Father, Son, and Holy Ghost, and the like...in all my wanderings, I never came across the least vestige of authority for these things. They have not left so distinct a trace as the delicate flower of a remote geological period on the coal in my grate" (*Week* 70).[10] Here he alludes to the objective, tangible, and material geological evidence refuting the ghost stories of world religions.

Thoreau's Geology

Thoreau's thoughts about the deep time of geology and the relentless operations of the whole Earth system were far more important to him than many Thoreau experts realize.[11] His *Journal* is so loaded with such self-taught expertise that I devoted an entire book to the subject: *Walden's Shore: Henry David Thoreau and Nineteenth-Century Science*.[12] Tellingly, Thoreau gathered a fairly substantial rock and mineral collection that he kept in his attic garret, but which went unnoticed by the state geologist when publishing "Minerals of Concord" for the peer-reviewed *The Concord Saunterer*. It is likely that Thoreau was more informed about the rising importance of geology than anyone in greater Concord during his era.

Thoreau returned to reading geology with fervor in early 1851, beginning with Arnold Henry Guyot's *The Earth and Man*.[13] By June 1851, Thoreau's *Journal* begins to overflow with his reading and re-reading of Charles's Darwin's *Journal of Researches into the Natural History and Geology of the Countries Visited During the Voyage of the H.M.S. Beagle Round the World, Under the Command of Capt. Fitz Roy, R. N. 2 volumes.*[14] This book was dedicated to the same Charles Lyell who had so profoundly influenced Thoreau's thinking a decade earlier. Darwin rebuts the strict gradualism of Lyell to envision an Earth experiencing intermittent catastrophes and extinctions. "Certainly, no fact in the long history of the world," he wrote, "is so startling as the wide and repeated exterminations of its inhabitants." He was writing about the big five mass extinctions and the many smaller ones that punctuate the stratigraphic record. These extinction events separate "long intervals" of relative stasis where gradualism is the norm. Darwin also shared his "deepest astonishment" that America "formerly...swarmed with great monsters," yet "now we find mere pigmies, compared with the antecedent, allied races."[15]

What, asked Darwin, "exterminated so many species and whole genera" during the postglacial (Holocene) epoch? "Did man...destroy, as has been suggested," the Pleistocene megafauna? Or was there "some great catastrophe" able to "shake the entire framework of the globe?" Darwin even speculates on the human extinction to come. The "remarkable law so often insisted upon by Mr. Lyell, namely, the 'longevity of the species of the mammalia'" is brief relative to those of other groups of animals.[16]

Continuing his research, on August 11, Thoreau checked out the new edition of Louis Agassiz and Augustus Gould's *Principles of Zoology*. This was an 1848 synthesis of Agassiz's 1846 well-attended Plan of Creation lectures arguing in favor of an evolutionary theory called progressivism. The overall conclusions, captured in the book's elaborate frontispiece, were impossible for Thoreau to accept. First, that God would periodically and catastrophically erase every living thing on Earth and reboot it from scratch, with no continuity through time. And second, that Man is the "crown of creation" the last notch on the stick of time. By this stage, Thoreau had already become very familiar with Rev. Edward Hitchcock's version of the same progressivism, as captured in his 1841 *Final Report on the Geology of Massachusetts*.[17]

By September 9, Thoreau had re-read geologist Robert Chambers' *Vestiges of the Natural History of Creation*, which had been creating a storm of controversy since its publication in 1845 for its radical views that life began as a "chemico-electric operation" with no help from any divine spark, and that the subsequent story was one of natural and continuous evolution. His first "nucleated vesicle," what we now call LUCA, was the "meeting point between the inorganic and the organic—the end of the mineral and beginning of the vegetable and animal kingdoms." Chambers concluded that this process was "as universal or as liable to take place everywhere as are the laws of gravitation and centrifugal force." Additionally, "If there is anything more than another impressed on our minds by the course of the geological history, it is, that the same laws and conditions of nature now apparent to us have existed throughout the whole time, though the operation of some of these laws may now be less conspicuous than in the early ages."[18]

Chambers also added three refinements. First, the importance of and stability of Earth's "central heat" through deep time, which he concluded had cooled from the inferno of the Hadean Eon to a nearly steady state condition. Second, that "geology tells us of the succession of species appears natural and intelligible" and that the "progress of organic creation…seems not long antecedent to the appearance of man." Third, that though organic creation is continuous and ongoing, it is pulsed by spasms of great change.[19]

Seeking support for his affinity with Darwin and Chambers, Thoreau skeptically read by September 28 *Footprints of the Creator*, a polemical refutation these radical ideas by Scottish geologist Hugh Miller. Miller revisited these ideas more scientifically in *The Old Red Sandstone*. The former, writes Robert Sattelmeyer, carried a "laudatory memoir of Miller by the progressivist Louis Agassiz—which, in the climate of the day, amounted to a kind of semi-official imprimatur."[20] Reading this may have sent Thoreau back to Agassiz and Gould's *Principles of Zoology*. By October 14, 1851, Thoreau was working on his own oppositional theory against "antiquaries and geologists" (*W* 309).

Climaxing *Walden*

The Deep Cut was excavated in 1843. *Walden's* first description, in version A, was short and simple: "As I go back and forth over the rail-road through the deep cut I have seen where the clayey sand like lava had flowed down when it thawed and as it streamed it assumed for the forms of vegetation…unaccountably interesting and beautiful."[21] This remained unchanged in versions B and C, dating to 1849. After that, and due to the failure of *A Week*, his Walden manuscript, then titled *A History of Himself*,[22] entered a dormant stage. The simultaneous Journal records dozens of additional observations of the Deep Cut, including bee nests, colors, badlands, stalactites, delicate strata, and micro-metrology, but the *Walden* text about the sand foliage unchanged.[23] The upgraded descriptions in *Walden* would await four years until version F, which dates to 1853–1854.

On November 7, 1851, after all his geology reading, Thoreau had a pair of experiences that allowed him to connect the sand foliage at the Deep Cut with his own life. Walking south toward Long Pond in Natick with his companion Ellery Channing, he journaled: "Chased by an ox whom we escaped over a fence while he gored the trees in stead of us.—the first time I was ever chased by his kind" (*PJ* 4:166). With his own mortality in mind, he saw at the lake "a great body of water—with singularly sandy shelving caving undermined banks" (*PJ* 4:166). As with the Deep Cut, the cause of these earthly exposures was human disturbance, in this case the raising of the water level by a dam to create a water supply for Boston. After sleeping on these experiences, he journaled the next day: "When I see her sands exposed thrown up from beneath the surface—it touches me inwardly—it reminds me of my origin—for I am such a plant—so native to N.E [New England], methinks as springs from the sand cast up from below" (*PJ* 4:169).[24]

With his interest piqued, Thoreau became obsessed with the Deep Cut when it came back with a vengeance on the three final days of the year, December 29, 30, and 31, 1851. Each day has a detailed Journal entry. These collective entries, notes Robert Richardson, became the turning point for the resuscitation of his dormant *Walden* manuscript.[25] They literally gave it new life when Thoreau finally made the connection that "Nature has some bowels" meaning that "Even the solid globe is permeated by the living law" (*PJ* 4:231). He also described the "artist" of creation at work in his laboratory, the word "artist" foreshadowing Thoreau's culminating allegory of the Artist of Kouroo (*PJ* 4:230).

After the deep freeze of January 1852 set in, Thoreau got immediately to work, beginning the frenzied expansion of *Walden* and its shift toward natural science that was to come with versions D and E. Six days later, on February 8, he linked the autonomous and emergent sand foliage to the rebirth of spring in general and the world in particular, the nick of time on the bank with the nick of time on the calendar. Thoreau returned to the Deep Cut in March, 1852 to write exacting physical descriptions of the sand foliage and to expand its scope to the dendritic pattern of all the rivers of the world.

The Deep Cut may not have revealed itself in the winter of 1853. But on February 2, 1854, during the final crunch to complete the *Walden* manuscript, he journaled new details (*PJ* 7:276) and On February 5 rewrote the sand foliage passage, adding, "That sand foliage! It convinces me that Nature is still in her youth,—That florid fact about which mythology merely mutters,—that the very soil can fabulate as well as you or I" (*PJ* 7:268). Here, in yet another foreshadowing of Kouroo, he invokes perennial youth and signals that fact trumps mythology, that science trumps fable. Importantly, he adds that "there is nothing inorganic," that the planet is alive going "full blast within," and, most importantly, that history is not dead but is experiencing continuous creation from below.

One week later, on Feb 8, 1854, he returned to link the sand flowage to the rebirth of spring. On that day's journal entry, Thoreau reached a key insight: the spontaneous emergence of order from disorder, cosmos from chaos, life from non-life, and every new day dawning from the previous one.[26] "How rapidly and perfectly it organizes itself!" (*W* 307), he writes of the sand foliage with an exclamation point. "The atoms have already learned the law" (*W* 306). Earth's crust, Thoreau now plainly saw, was not the residue of something that *has* happened. It was the ultimate raw material for everything that *is* happening in the present moment.

Finally, on March 2, 1854, only eleven days before delivering his manuscript to the printer, Thoreau returned to the Deep Cut and his manuscript for a final tweaking before submission. In this final form, this huge idea became the climax of *Walden*, his poetic alternative to the geological squabbling taking place during his moment in history:

> There is nothing inorganic. These foliaceous heaps lie along the bank like the slag of a furnace, showing that Nature is "in full blast" within. The earth is not a mere fragment of dead history, stratum upon stratum, like the leaves of a book, to be studied by geologists and antiquaries chiefly, but living poetry like the leaves of a tree, which precede flowers and fruit,—not a fossil earth, but a living earth; compared with whose great central life all animal and vegetable life is merely parasitic. (*W* 308–309)

In this passage Thoreau creates life from non-life from the furnace of Earth's geothermal heat, its "great central life." His core idea is that nature is "'in full blast' within," giving rise to everything alive today, an ongoing and continuous re creation. *Walden's* core idea of constant renewal extends to the Earth's multiple past and future worlds—or epochs—arising from below. Iceland, the location of the conference that would lead to this book, was the perfect place for contemplating all this. It is located at a volcanic hot spot directly above one of Earth's mantle plumes, which is rising up from its swirling iron core where the temperature may exceed that of the sun.[27]

In short, without Thoreau's understandings of deep time and earthly processes, *Walden* would not be *Walden*.

Three Allegories

The allegorical "artist in the city of Kouroo" recapitulates *Walden's* climactic passage of the sand foliage. Wanting to "make a staff" (*W* 326), the artist "searched for and rejected stick after stick.... His friends gradually deserted him, for they grew old in their works and died, but he grew not older by a moment" (*W* 326). Being blessed with "perennial youth," the artist "made no compromise with Time," which "kept out of his way, and only sighed at a distance" (*W* 326). While carving his staff, the artist saw that "Brahma had awoke and slumbered many times" (*W* 327). The artist, in making a new staff also "made a new system...a world with full and fair proportions; in which, though the old cities and dynasties had passed away, fairer and more glorious ones had taken their places" (*W* 327). At this scale, the "former lapse of time had been an illusion" (*W* 327).

This whole allegory is about seeing the world through the lens of deep time, one of geology's two signal contributions to intellectual culture, the other being how Earth works as a coherent system.

Today we understand that Earth is a single holistic system, a mechanistic Gaia,[28] run from the inside by geothermal heat and from the outside by solar heat. Its many former worlds are the many sticks of time the Artist tossed aside as "old cities and dynasties had passed away" and "fairer and more glorious ones had taken their places" (*W* 327). These sticks symbolize the former passage of discrete increments of geological time, regardless of scale, whether Eons, Eras, Periods, Epochs, or Ages. Brahma's intervals of wakefulness and slumber are direct analogs for pulsed pace of most earthly processes such as climate change. His replacements of older dynasties with more glorious new ones are a direct analog for the punctuated evolution of life, with its many mass extinctions and biodiversification events, all of which are associated with one of Thoreau's favorite gods, Vulcan, who operates the forge that is "in full blast within." Each of these was a forked branch in the history of life on Earth. Immediately before each was an expectant nick of time, a planet poised for new possibilities that mere lapses of time could not have predicted.

Thoreau used the fossils of paleontology and the co-adaptation of organisms to "suggest a history to Nature, a Natural *history* in a new sense" (*PJ* 4:6), one that included extinctions and renewals, including that of the human species. He writes: "The geologist has discovered that the figures of serpents, griffins, flying dragons, and other fanciful embellishments of heraldry, have their protoypes in the forms of fossil species which were extinct before man was created, and hence 'indicate a faint and shadowy knowledge of a previous state of organic existence'" (*Exc* 210).[29]

In his allegory of the Artist of Kouroo, Thoreau's comment that "the former lapse of time had been an illusion" mirrors Hutton's famous statement that deep time has "no vestige of a beginning,—no prospect of an end."[30] It was Hutton's word "vestige" that was borrowed by Robert Chambers for the title of his *Vestiges,* which inspired Thoreau before his writing the climax of *Walden.*

Thoreau's second of three allegories reinforces the earthly origin and solidity of our very existence as humans.

> We read that the traveller asked the boy if the swamp before him had a hard bottom. The boy replied that it had. But presently the traveler's horse sank in up to the girths, and he observed to the boy, "I thought you said that this bog had a hard bottom." "So it has," answered the latter, "but you have not got half way to it yet." (*W* 330)

Indeed, there is a hard bottom everywhere. That bedrock surface, that *point d'appui* of actual reality, is the actual reality that is earthly reality. To reach its stability, we must descend, not transcend.

This brings us to *Walden's* final allegory of the beautiful bug, crawling up through the many layers of tree rings to reach the surface and start life anew. To set this up, Thoreau writes: "We are acquainted with a mere pellicle of the globe on which we live. Most have not delved six feet beneath the surface, nor leaped as many above it. We know not where we are" (*W* 332). Indeed, we have yet to see—via our deepest drill holes—more than one thousandth of the way down into the three-dimensional globe beneath our feet.

Setting this up further, he watches an insect crawl across the forest floor, prompting him to write: "I am reminded of the greater Benefactor and Intelligence that stands over me the human insect." At this point he narrates the story of the beautiful bug gnawing its way up from beneath the tree-rings of a wooden table: "Who knows what beautiful and winged life, whose egg has been buried for ages under many concentric layers of woodenness in the dead dry life of society…may unexpectedly come forth from amidst society's most trivial and handselled furniture, to enjoy its perfect summer life at last!" (*W* 333).

The direction is important. This is no alien coming to earth's surface from outer space. It is nature rising up from below to take its rightful place in the endless stream of time, a stream with many side branches, each notched on its proverbial stick.

This anecdote brings us to the final paragraph of *Walden*, which I have previously interpreted in this work. The human species stands at the nick of time between present and future. The "morrow which mere lapse of time can never make to dawn" is coming (*W* 333). I refer to the next geological epoch in a seemingly infinite series.

Conclusion

Thoreau's synthetic conclusion in *Walden* was written near the very end of the nine-year writing process. It begins by brilliantly melding the first part of his book—his experiment in deliberate living from 1845–1847—to its second part, the largely scientific nature writing written mainly from 1852–1854. Consider this sequence of quotes beginning with a backward reflection.

"Yet we think that if rail fences are pulled down, and stone-walls piled up on our farms, bounds are henceforth set to our lives and our fates decided" (*W* 320). Indeed, our lives need not be set in stone by the walls of our farms nor like the fossil forms of our predecessors.

"I left the woods for as good a reason as I went there. Perhaps it seemed to me that I had several more lives to live, and could not spare any more time for that one" (*W* 323). Here is a literary bridge between the multiple "lives" within Thoreau's own life, and the many epochs of geological past. At this point, he transitions to *Walden's* main takeaway:

"I learned this, at least, by my experiment; that if one...endeavors to live the life which he has imagined, he will...put some things behind, will pass an invisible boundary; new, universal, and more liberal laws will begin to establish themselves around and within him; or the old laws be expanded, and interpreted in his favor in a more liberal sense, and he will live with the license of a higher order of beings" (*W* 323–324). The invisible boundary he refers to may be the final nick on the time-line of his mortal individuality. Beyond that will be a new life in which the old laws are expanded and the beings are of a higher order. And beyond that will be the next geological epoch to come, the last in a series defined by a paleontology that includes successive human civilizations.

Works Cited

Agassiz, Louis and A. A. Gould. *Principles of Zoology*. Boston: Gould, Kendall and Lincoln, 1848.

Chambers, Robert. *Vestiges of the Natural History of Creation with a Sequel.* New York: Harper & Brothers, 1857. University of Michigan Library Digital Collections, Accessed July 28, 2024. https://name.umdl.umich.edu/AJP4463.0001.001.

Darwin, Charles R. *Journal of Researches into the Natural History and Geology of the Countries Visited During the Voyage of the H.M.S. Beage Round the World, Under the Command of Capt. Fitz Roy, R. N. 2 volumes.* New York: Harper & Brothers, 1846.

Gross, Robert. *The Transcendentalists and their World.* New York: Farrar, Strauss, and Giroux, 2021.

Guyot, Arnold Henry. *The Earth and Man.* 3rd edition. Translated by Cornelius. C. Felton. Boston: Gould & Lincoln, 1851.

Hitchcock, Edward. *Final Report on the Geology of Massachusetts*, 2 volumes and foldout map. Massachusetts Geological Survey. Northampton: J. H. Butler, 1841.

Hutton, James. *Theory of the Earth with Proofs and Illustrations: In Four Parts Volume 1.* Edinburg: Royal Society of Edinburg, 1795. http://www.gutenberg.org/files/12861/12861-h/12861-h.htm.

Lyell, Charles. *Principles of Geology, First Edition, Volume 1*. Edited by Martin J. S. Rudwick. Chicago: University of Chicago Press, 1960.

Miller, Hugh. *The foot-prints of the Creator: or, the Asterolepis of Stromness.* Boston: Gould and Lincoln, 1850.

———. *The Old Red Sandstone.* Boston: Lincoln and Gould, 1852.

Richardson Jr., Robert D. *Henry Thoreau: A Life of the Mind.* Berkeley: University of California Press, 1986.

Rossi, William. "Making *Walden* and its Sandbank," *The Concord Saunterer N.S.* 30 (2022), 10–58.

———. "Thoreau's Transcendental Ecocentrism." *Thoreau's Sense of Place: Essays in American Environmental Writing*. Edited by Richard J. Schneider. pp. 28–43. Iowa City: University of Iowa Press, 2000.

Sattelmeyer, Robert. *Thoreau's Reading*. Princeton: Princeton University Press, 1988.

Thoreau, Henry David. *Walden: A Fluid-Text Edition*. Digital Thoreau. https://digitalthoreau.org/fluid-tet-toc.

Thorson, Robert. *Walden's Shore: Henry David Thoreau and Nineteenth Century Science*. Cambridge: Harvard University Press, 2014.

Tyrrell, Toby. *On Gaia: A Critical Investigation of the Relationship between Life and Earth.* Princeton: Princeton University Press, 2013.

Walls, Laura Dassow. *Henry D. Thoreau: A Life*. Chicago: University of Chicago Press, 2017.

———. *Seeing New Worlds: Henry David Thoreau and Nineteenth-Century Science*. Madison: Univ. Wisconsin Press, 1995.

Walker, Eugene H. "Minerals of Concord,"The Concord Saunterer 9:3 (Spring, 1974), 1–6.

CHAPTER 11

ON BEING NATIVE IN THE WORLD: THOREAU ON THE VALUE OF MOUNTAINS

Ólafur Páll Jónsson

After a walk on May 10, 1853, Henry David Thoreau wrote a long entry in his Journal ending with an extended reflection on mountains, describing them as moral structures which "make it easier to die & easier to live," and then adding "[t]hey let us off" (*PJ* 6:110). When I first read those pages, I saw in them little more than a romanticization of the mountains in the horizon, framing the horizon while fading away in the dusk. After reading more of Thoreau's writings on mountains, and rereading those pages from the Journal, I see in these remarks on mountains an important truth we desperately need for our own survival in this tragic era we have created for ourselves. Mountains are moral structures that help us to live and die.

In the following pages, I will try to explain this important truth I see in Thoreau's journal entry. I begin with a short account of his hike up Mount Katahdin in 1846, where some of the same themes emerge—even if that experience was much more confrontational, even hostile, compared to the mild and gentle tone of the journal entry he wrote six years later. After a brief detour into "Ktaadn," I return to the journal entry and other writings of Thoreau's to explore further aspects of his encounters with mountains and why he might consider them moral structures. I end my discussion by relating Thoreau's writings to the literature of Thórbergur Thórdarson (Þórbergur Þórðarson, 1888–1974), an Icelandic writer, poet, and social critic who believed that the stones could speak when he was growing up in the rural Southeast of Iceland, under steep hills and high cliffs. Thoreau and Thórbergur[1] share more than a name, both being versatile writers whose works do not fit into narrow academic categories. They were also both sentenced to prison, Thoreau for not wanting to contribute the cause of war and slavery, Thórbergur for criticizing Hitler and the Nazis in a series of articles in 1934. But the reason for including Thórbergur here is not his political writings but his intimate reflections on nature, on the cliffs and rocks where he grew up. In those writings I see similarities with Thoreau's thoughts about mountains as moral structures.

A Mountain as a Measure for a Human Life

I will begin by reading through and reflecting on several passages from Thoreau's journal after his walk in May 1853. The entry written that day is ten pages long, but I will focus on a few excerpts that I have separated into small sections which I number for ease of reference. Thoreau describes how he sees the mountains in the distance as terrene temples, imagining them as stepping-stones for leaving Earth for heaven:

> [1] You see, not the domes only, but the body, the façade, of these terrene temples—You see that the foundation answers to the superstructure. Moral structures. (*PJ* 6:109)
>
> [2] They are stepping-stones to heaven,—as the rider has a horse-block at his gate—by which to mount when we would commence our pilgrimage to heaven. By which we gradually take our departure from earth from the time when our youthful eyes first rested on them, from this bare actual earth. Which has so little of the hue of heaven. (*PJ* 6:110)
>
> [3] They make it easier to die and easier to live. They let us off. (*PJ* 6:110)

A reader not familiar with Thoreau might see these remarks about the mountains in the distance as careless ramblings induced by the fading light after a long walk. That is, however, not how Thoreau saw them. In between excerpts [1] and [2], he remarks:

> [4] The value of the mts in the horizon—would not that be a good theme for a lecture? The text for a discourse on real values—& permanent. A sermon on the mount. (*PJ* 6:110)

Thoreau describes the value of the mountains on the horizon as both real and permanent, and puns on the New Testament's portrayal of Jesus speaking to his congregation from up high, while Thoreau proposes to focus on the mountains themselves. We can imagine at least four reasons for this evaluation. Given that he describes them as terrene temples [1], the sheer enormity of the mountains could be seen as a source of value.

> (i) Relating to scale: The mountains put human life into perspective by being so huge; anything personal becomes small and trivial compared to these terrene domes.

The enormity of the mountains certainly contributes to Thoreau's seeing them as having aesthetic value, as sublime in the sense of Edmund Burke.[2]

Another reason for mountains having real and permanent value relates to mountains being structures that maintain their integrity even when viewed from far away. They give us a different sense of place and they show how spatial locations extend far and wide.

> (ii) Relating to spatial location: The mountains in the distance show that the local is but a small part of a larger world, a tiny spot on a land that extends far and wide.

In the paragraphs before describing the mountains on the horizon as having real and permanent value, Thoreau is describing the vegetation and the birds that he can hear around him. One gets the feeling that he is "in" the land, almost as if he was lost and could not see or hear anything but what is right next to him. But then the scenery changes drastically. Instead of being in the midst of the forest, Thoreau suddenly finds himself above it. "From the hill, I look westward over the landscape" he remarks, and then continues:

> From this more eastern hill—with the whole breadth of the river valley on the west—the mts appear higher still—the width of the blue border is greater—not mere peaks, or a short and shallow sierra—but a high blue table-land with broad foundations—a deep & solid base or table land in proportion to the peaks that rest on it. (*PJ* 6:109)

Thoreau is no longer eye-to-eye with his surroundings but is witness to something that extends wide and far, similar to the experience of the vastness of world when hiking in the Maine woods as expressed in the "Ktaadn" text. His experience on Mount Katahdin of being in the midst of an untouched vastness, however, gave him the feeling of being an intruder in a holy land which is very different from the tranquility that he felt while looking at the mountains in the distance, at the horizon, at the end of the day in early May 1853.

The third reason why the mountains might have real and permanent value is more directly related to spiritual awakening. The mountains' sublime beauty also help us lift our spirits.

> (iii) Relating to the spiritual aspect of life: As the mountains rise to the sky, so we might lift our spirits to get a break from the life-sustaining labor that consumes most of our time and energy. In that way, the mountains are stepping-stones to heaven, letting us off as he says, and enabling us to live better.

Thoreau elaborates further on this spiritual aspect of the mountains saying:

> They are valuable to mankind as is the iris of the eye to a man. They are the path of the translated. The undisputed territory between earth & heaven. In our travels rising higher & higher, we at length got to where the earth was blue. Suggesting that this earth–unless our conduct curse it, is as celestial as that sky. (*PJ* 6:110)

On Mount Katahdin, Thoreau too experienced nature as sublime, as Ronald Wesley Hoag argues:

> In essence, the experience that overwhelms Thoreau on Mount Katahdin (though largely retrospectively) is a breathtaking apprehension of the sublime. His journal entry of 1846 concludes with the elliptical comment, "Thus Nature primitive titanic but so beautiful as awful and sublime," culminating with this very word.[3]

When Thoreau says that the mountains are moral structures, he says this as a reflection on the fact that the "foundation answers to the superstructure." This suggests a fourth way in which the values of the mountains in the distance are real and permanent.

> (iv) Relating to moral integrity: The way the foundation answers to a superstructure could be seen as a metaphorical depiction of moral integrity.

Relating mountains to moral integrity brings us right to that striking statement of Thoreau in the "Ktaadn" episode where he says that on the mountain "one could no longer accuse institutions and society, but must front the true source of evil" (*MW* 16). Incidentally, in the entry on May

10th, 1853 he also mentions institutions, including in brackets right after [3] the following: "With Alcott almost alone is it possible to put all institutions behind us–every other man owns some stock in this or that one & will not forget it" (*PJ* 6:110).

Reading *The Maine Woods*, we can see Thoreau describing the mountains, and the wilderness in general, as having real value relating to scale, spatial location, spiritual awakening, and moral integrity. And yet those passages describe encounters with nature very differently from the long and tranquil walk on May 10, 1853.

These four reasons certainly give substance to Thoreau's remark that mountains have "real and permanent value." I think, however, that they do not exhaust Thoreau's ideas about the values of mountains, and there are further reasons which I will explore under four distinct themes: (i) "a mountain is alive," contrasting Thoreau's ideas with that of Immanuel Kant's, or rather using a remark of Kant to help focus on an aspect of Thoreau's writings on mountains; (ii) "thinking like a mountain," comparing Thoreau with Aldo Leopold; (iii) "particular and idealized images," a theme I reflect on with the help of Antonio Casado da Rocha; and (iv) "mountains as narrative viewpoints." After reflecting on these four themes, I turn to a comparison of the ideas I find in Thoreau with ideas from Thórbergur which, I believe, will help us appreciate better some of Throeau's ideas but also expand them, bringing in a temporal aspect that is more evident in the text of Thórbergur.

A Mountain Is Alive

The mountains frame the horizon, almost solidify it, unlike where the horizon forms a thin ephemeral line between ocean and sky. Thoreau captures this materiality with a striking image of the dense skyline above the mountains, "which almost melts them [the mountains] into the atmosphere, like the contact of molten metal with that which is infused" (*PJ* 6:110). The horizon, even far away and out of reach, bears witness to material reality.

In a passage of his *Critique of Pure Reason*, Immanuel Kant reflects on the actual and possible limits of knowledge and says:

> If I represent the earth as it appears to my senses, as a flat surface, with a circular horizon, I cannot know how far it extends. But experience teaches me that wherever I may go, I always see a space

> around me in which I could proceed further; and thus I know the limits of my actual knowledge of the earth at any given time but not the limits of all possible geography. (Kant 1998, B787)

The image Kant offers the reader is very different from the view that Thoreau experienced and described in his journal of 1853, where the horizon is not described as circular, nor as representing the Earth as a flat surface, but rather as a material reality with distinct features. Although we should be careful not to read too much into this quote from Kant, we see a clear difference between his representation of the Earth in abstract terms and the descriptions of a concrete reality we get from Thoreau as situated in a specific and textured place. From the distance, the mountains connect Earth and heaven, matter and spirit; for this connection to be possible, the materiality of the mountains is essential. Such truthfulness to the materiality of our existence is a distinctive feature of Thoreau's thinking—even when he is talking about abstract or spiritual matters.

After remarking that the mountains are moral structures, Thoreau continues to describe the landscape appearing before his eyes on this fading day.

> [5] The successive lines of haze which divide the western landscape—deeper and more misty over each intervening valley–are not yet very dense—Yet there is a light atmospheric line along the base of the mts for their whole length—formed by this denser & grosser atmosphere through which we look next the earth, which almost melts them into the atmosphere—like the contact of molten metal with that which is infused—but their pure, sublimed tops & mainbody rise palpable skyland above it. Like the waving signal of the departing who have already left these shores. (*PJ* 6:109–10)

In the quote from Kant the horizon is a mere limit indicating at every given moment how far the space of actual knowledge extends; with each step, in whichever direction one might go, the horizon moves and represents a new limit. In that sense, the horizon is an abstraction, a concept representing the dynamic limits of human knowledge. Kant was searching for the general, trying to understand the limits of all possible knowledge. And within Western philosophy and science, the general and the abstract have always had their lure. This is very different from the way Thoreau looks at the mountainous horizon, whose sublime peaks are like waving signals of those who have "already left these shores."

The scene that Thoreau describes here reminds me of Caspar David Friedrich's painting, *Wanderer above the Sea of Fog*, from 1818. The painting shows a man overlooking cloud-wrapped landscapes towards distant mountains and has been described as one of the masterpieces of the Romantic era. When philosophers began to talk about the sublime beauty of nature in the twentieth century, they often used this picture to make their point.

The man in Friedrich's painting is overlooking actual mountains that form a concrete, material reality, unlike the abstract concept of a horizon in Kant's image. We can, further, imagine the man in Friedrich's painting experiencing emotions similar to those of Thoreau in 1853, relating life as a journey into a future mapped out by mountains extending into the distance. But even so, the painting does not do justice to Thoreau's perception, for it shows no details of the surroundings. Apart from a few vaguely formed trees, there are no distinguishable plants in the painting, nor does one get the feeling of an animal nearby, whether a wolf, a deer, or a mouse. Even the birds are absent. In that sense, the painting is still too abstract; it merely represents a general idea of a journey into the unknown—not a particular, organic locality.

When I say that the painting lacks organic locality, I am not denying that the view represented may be of mountains which have names and can be found on a map—it is actually painted from sketches of real mountains although the view is not actual. And the man in the painting, too, might actually have a name. But my point is different, namely, that if we look closer, we see nothing. And that is not how Thoreau thought of and wrote about nature. After remarking that the mountains are moral structures and before the description in [5], Thoreau inserts in parentheses the remark: "The sweet-fern leaves among odors now." He is reminding the reader that despite the nature in the distance, which is at the same time both sublime and picturesque, he is situated in a concrete, material, organic place at a specific time, or rather, in a specific season. Not only the sense of sight is active, there are also odors in the air.

When I first read this passage, the remark about the odors of the sweet-fern struck me as out of place. I found it strange that Thoreau would break up the passage about mountains, moral structures, and stepping-stones to heaven by remarking about what he could smell in that particular place at that very moment. But after reading more of Thoreau's Journal, and in particular his descriptions of hikes up various mountains, I find this remark not only typical of him but important to him. In the journals, we often see a person eager to get above the lowlands, get out of the woods for a view of the landscape as a vast and continuous whole; but at the same time he wanted to know what world he inhabited and that world was also a complex, organic locality.

Thoreau is not just harvesting beautiful views; for him, it is important to be on the mountain itself; we read not only about the hikes and the views from the tops, we also read about what he came across on the mountains—what the mountains felt like, smelled like, looked like, sounded like, and what tastes they offered. For instance, when hiking to the top of Mount Wachusett in July 1842, Thoreau writes:

> The summit consists of a few acres, destitute of trees, covered with bare rocks, interspersed with blueberry bushes, raspberries, gooseberries, strawberries, moss, and fine, wiry grass. The common yellow lily, and dwarf cornel, grow abundantly in the crevices of the rocks. This clear space, which is gently rounded, is bounded a few feet lower by a thick shrubbery of oaks, with maples, aspens, beeches, cherries, and occasionally a mountain-ash intermingled, among which we found the bright blue berries of the Solomon's seal, and the fruit of the pyrola. (*Exc* 38)

Later he adds:

> The blueberries which the mountain afforded, added to the milk we had brought, made our frugal supper, while for entertainment the even-song of the wood thrush rang along the ridge. Our eyes rested on no painted ceiling nor carpeted hall, but on skies of Nature's painting, and hills and forests of her embroidery. Before sunset, we rambled along the ridge to the north, while a hawk soared still above us. (*Exc* 39)

And then he remarks:

> It was a place where gods might wander, so solemn and solitary, and removed from all contagion with the plain. (*Exc* 39)

What we see here is a description of a mountain as a *condition* for life. A mountain is a living place with plants, animals, stones, and, if the season is right, with blueberries to add to milk or with the smell of sweet-fern leaves. And it is exactly this earthly, organic reality that makes it a suitable place for gods to wander.

For Thoreau, the spiritual and the material, the abstract and the concrete, are bound together. This holism was a stance that Thoreau developed throughout his lifetime, as Laura Dassow Walls notes in her introduction to *Material Faith: Thoreau on Science*.

> Thoreau's positive idea emerged early, to become a lifelong tenet of his faith: the poet would unite earth and sky, science and philosophy, generalizing "their widest deductions" and so crossing the "chasm between knowledge and ignorance" through his own practical experiences and action in the world. The poet would turn science into "con-science," a moral knowledge.[4]

Unlike the scientist who seeks to abstract from the concrete world to general principles—who sees the horizon as an abstract limit to actual knowledge and all possible horizons as limits to all possible knowledge as in Kant's search for the foundations of philosophy and science—the poet is grounded in the subjective reality of experience. When Thoreau watches the mountains melt into the sky, bringing back waving images of those who have already left while smelling the sweet-fern leaves, he is living the role of a poet. A poet, in this sense, is not someone lost in their first-person experience, but one who sees in the first person experience also something common, something general, and is therefore at the same time a creator of meaning and the one who anchors knowledge in the moral realm.

Thinking like a Mountain

A century after Thoreau had described the mountains in the horizon as moral structures, another American natural scientist and philosopher, Aldo Leopold, encouraged people to think like a mountain in *A Sand County Almanac*.[5] Leopold told the reader that proper thinking about nature must include very many intimately interwoven aspects which might, at first, seem disconnected. A mountain is a world of its own, and thinking like a mountain requires that we are open to this world, accept its complexity, and respect its integrity while also understanding that we are, ourselves, part of the mountain. In the introduction to *A Sand County Almanac*, Leopold writes, "That land is a community is the basic concept of ecology, but that land is to be loved and respected is an extension of ethics."[6] Thinking like a mountain in the sense of Leopold aligns with Thoreau's conception of nature and science as Walls describes it:

> In Thoreau's world, we can hardly afford to separate ourselves from nature and study it as if we bore no part in it; on the contrary, we are hip deep in our subject, busy altering the nature we pretend only to study and knowing ourselves only through the actions by which we pretend to know only the world.[7]

From Thoreau's journals we can also derive two additional senses of "thinking like a mountain" which we do not find in Aldo Leopold's writing. The first has to do with moral integrity while the second relates to the spiritual dimension of life.

A person's integrity is shown by her actions and words having a solid base; a person of moral integrity is neither flimsy nor superficial. When Thoreau describes the mountains as moral structures because the foundations answer to the superstructure [1], we can interpret this as a metaphor for integrity. Thinking and acting like a mountain, in this sense, is far removed from thinking or acting like driftwood. Integrity as a virtue shows itself in knowing what one is talking about before talking, knowing what one is doing before acting, and yet neither being silent nor passive simply because one's knowledge is always imperfect. The superstructure, i.e. the behavior, answers to the foundation, the values and knowledge.

Like Leopold, Thoreau certainly saw the land as a community to be loved and respected, but in Thoreau's journals we see a spiritual dimension that Leopold does not venture to discuss.[8] Thoreau describes the mountains as stepping-stones to heaven [2]—they help us lift our spirits, not as a trivial diversion but as firmly grounded in the material earth to which we belong. That is why the gods might wander around Mount Wachusett.

Particulars and Idealized Images

In his book, *Una casa en Walden* (*A House by Walden*), Antonio Casado da Rocha reflects on the following passage from Thoreau's journals from October 3, 1859:

> Why does any distant prospect ever charm us—because we instantly & inevitably imagine a life to be lived there such as is not lived elsewhere or where we are—We presume that success is the rule. We forever carry a perfect sampler in our minds. Why are distant valleys—why lakes—why mts in the horizon, ever fair to us? Because we realize for a moment that they may be the home of man—& that man's life may be in harmony with them. Shall I say that we thus forever delude ourselves? We do not suspect that <u>that</u> farmer goes to the depot with his milk—<u>There</u> the milk is not watered. We are constrained to imagine a life in harmony with the scenery—& the hour. (OJT 30:30–31)

In this passage, Thoreau considers people's inclination to idealize what they see. A little later, he adds:

> Men go about sketching–painting landscapes, or writing verses which celebrate man's opportunities. To go into an actual farmer's family—at eve—see the tired laborers come in from their day's work—thinking of their wages—the sluttish help in the kitchen & sink-room—The indifferent stolidity and patient misery which only the spirits of the youngest children rise above—that suggests one train of thoughts—To look down on that roof from a distance in an October evening—when its smoke is ascending peacefully to join the kindred clouds above. That suggests a different train of thoughts. (OJT 30:32)

Casado da Rocha notes that this description is romantic in its recognition of beauty as something subjective and a source of moral inspiration, but he also says that Thoreau "at the same time deconstructs these sentiments of idealization, making them depend on the health and the objective circumstances of the subjects."[9]

The point Thoreau makes is important for our present times but something that is by and large lost, at least within the sciences. There is no shortage of studies on nature or the environment, but too often the knowledge sought is an abstract one, in the sense in which Friedrich's painting may be considered abstract. In a paper titled "Eco(il)logical knowledge," João Afonso Baptista recounts a meeting with a university professor and NGO consultant in forest management who worked from the Angolan city of Huambo.

> During our two-hour conversation he used geospatial images, graphs, and satellite maps to support his knowledge of a forest located in Gove, about one hundred kilometers from Huambo.…At one point, I asked him for photos from the forest. "I don't have [any]," he said, "because I was never there." He then continued: "The peasants living there cannot use the forest as theirs. Forests are a delicate matter." Alluding to the quality and usefulness of his work, Mateus concluded, "They have to be dealt with by experts who know them properly." He made it clear that he considered accurate forest knowledge to be possible when the knower is at some distance from the forest itself.[10]

What I find striking in this little episode is the utter disconnectedness of the professor from the land he is studying. Or perhaps "disconnection" is not the right word; "alienation" might be better. Contemporary science and education are preoccupied with abstract knowledge; the knowledge may be of concrete things, just as Friedrich's painting may be of concrete mountains and a particular person. The satellite maps of the forest in Gove are certainly maps of real things. But these representations lack all particularity. There is no physical connection—no smell of sweet-fern leaves, no blueberries for the milk, and no place for gods to dance. And for these reasons, the knowledge does not stir any emotions. Knowing as a way of relating becomes a mere cognitive activity, while Thoreau shows us how we can relate to nature with the whole body—the feet, the eyes, the nose, the ears, and, of course, also the intellect.

Thoreau is not satisfied with knowing nature at a remove; he wants to become a native, as Jane Bennett draws out in her essay "On Being a Native," stating "The ideal self lives in the presence of Nature, but must have the right presence toward it: the attitude of a 'native.'"[11] She then cites Thoreau where he looks for the individuality of nature around him: "O the evening robin…! If I could ever find the twig he sits upon! I mean *he*; I mean *the twig*" (*W* 312).[12] The person who does not see the individuality of nature, who does not get past general truths, never becomes a native.

The saying goes that we will only protect what we love, and we will only love what we know. My point here is that it is not enough to know the world in abstraction to love it. It matters *how* we know it. When Casado da Rocha reflects on the passage from Thoreau's journal where he moves from viewing the smoke rising from the chimney to imagining the harsh life below the roof, his point is that it is through placing ourselves, as human beings, within whatever situation we are facing that we get to know reality. In order to know, one must get a feeling for the subject.

Similar ideas about research and knowledge can be seen in the work of Barbara McClintock, who received the Nobel Prize in Medicine in 1983 for discoveries she made in the 1950s and '60s. In McClintock's biography, Evelyn Fox Keller raises the following question: "What enabled McClintock to see further and deeper into the mysteries of genetics than her colleagues?" The answer comes from McClintock herself.

> Her answer is simple. Over and over again, she tells us one must have the time to look, the patience to "hear what the material has to say to you," the openness to "let it come to you." Above all, one must have "a feeling for the organism."[13]

Over and over again, Thoreau tries to give the reader a feeling for what is before him, of what he is experiencing, of what he is a part. To get a feeling for what is before him when he overlooks the valley and sees the smoke rise from the chimney, he must consider what kind of life that house, that roof, that chimney and smoke, might indicate.

Mountains as Narrative Viewpoints

When we read Thoreau's journals and essays where he describes his hikes up various mountains—or walks up some hills, for some of these elevations in the landscape up which he hiked are almost too small to qualify as mountains—he sometimes describes the mountains themselves as what I would like to refer to as "narrative viewpoints." We see this in different ways, from the almost romantic view of the mountains in the horizon from May 1853, and the playful imagination of the gods dancing on top of Wachusett, to the harsh and challenging but at the same time sublime experience of being in the midst of the Maine woods on top of Mount Katahdin.

A narrative has a structure; it leads from somewhere to somewhere else. A storyline is not simply a sequence of events but a sequence that is organized in such a way that one thing leads to another; in the end, an overarching storyline emerges. Or at least that is typically the case. In New England today, it is rather difficult to see the land leading from one place to another; connections between different places are obscured by forests.

To get a feeling for context is difficult. A view of the landscape is usually obscured by trees; a river comes out of the woods and disappears again into the woods.

When Thoreau is on top of a mountain, after describing the vegetation that lies before his feet, he takes in the landscape—what had been hidden until he got to the clearing at the top. Only above the treeline can he read the land like a story that leads from where he is standing across the lower land, until his eyes finally rest on the mountains in the distance—some "terrene temples" as he calls them. And from there, he adds, "we gradually take our departure from earth…this bare actual earth, which has so little of the hue of heaven" and see how the entirety of the land is placed below a sky which at night is filled with stars.

Thoreau hiked up Wachusett with a companion in late July 1842 and wrote a short essay for *The Boston Miscellany* in January 1843 about the trip. Having spent the night on the mountain, Thoreau woke up early and describes the morning in question:

> At length we saw the sun rise up out of the sea, and shine on Massachusetts; and from this moment the atmosphere grew more and more transparent till the time of our departure, and we began to realize the extent of the view, and how the earth, in some degree, answered to the heavens in breadth, the white villages to the constellations in the sky. There was little of the sublimity and grandeur which belong to mountain scenery, but an immense landscape to ponder on a summer's day....
>
> We could at length realize the place mountains occupy on the land, and how they come into the general scheme of the universe. When first we climb their summits and observe their lesser irregularities, we do not give credit to the comprehensive intelligence which shaped them; but afterwards we behold their outlines in the horizon, we confess that the hand which moulded their opposite slopes, making one to balance the other, worked round a deep centre, and was privy to the plan of the universe. (*Exc* 41–42).

Earlier, I talked about how Thoreau showed us how to relate to the land by fitting together the abstract and the concrete ([1] to [4] and then "The sweet-fern leaves among odors now," the romantic scene of the smoke rising from the cottage chimney during the fading light and the harsh reality of the worn-out people inside) and how true objectivity is not grounded in generality—as is often the demand within the sciences—but in the locality of the subject.

This is the point made by Casado da Rocha to which I referred earlier, about the deconstruction of romantic idealization by considering the objective (even if imagined) circumstances of the subjects involved. But here, from the top of Wachusett, the scenery is different and so is the very idea of locality. In the example discussed by Casado da Rocha, the locality emerges when we imagine ourselves in the home of the people; when we get below the roof and realize that their life is harsh. From the top of Wachusett, the concept of locality is one of connectedness and spatial relations, a concept that Thoreau also saw as fundamental to the kind of science that he pursued.

> The great thoughts of a wise man seem to the vulgar who do not generalize to stand far apart like isolated mounts–but Science knows that the mountains which rise so solitary in our midst are parts of a great mountain chain-dividing the earth—And the eye that looks into the horizon–toward the blue sierra melting away in the distance may detect their flow of thought—(*PJ* 1:389)

Here we see Thoreau ascribe to the mountains—perhaps metaphorically—a flow of thought which the trained eye may detect.

From Massachusetts to Iceland

Icelandic mountains differ from those in New England. On a good day in Iceland, one can see many of them, no matter where one is located, and no forests obscure the view. Life in Iceland is conditioned by mountains, and although people may distance themselves from the mountains—such as in Reykjavik where Mount Esja rises on the other side of the bay—they are never far away, and their influence is impossible to escape. Mountains orchestrate how the winds blow, how the rain falls, where the snow accumulates, and how the rivers flow. And yet the mountains themselves are uninhabitable; in fact, Iceland is only a little more than mountains that have never been inhabited and never will, because it is practically impossible to survive the winters there. Thoreau describes an impression of inhospitality he felt on Mount Katahdin when he "felt the presence of a force not bound to be kind to man" (*MW* 70). Such inhospitality is inescapable on Icelandic mountains, except for a few good days in late summer. In Iceland, mountains have not only remained out of reach, but are also said to be the home of trolls and outlaws, a place of forces far from kind to the common person.

Geographically, Iceland is located in the most unstable part of the Earth—no place changes as much, whether through volcanic eruptions, glaciers retreating or advancing, rivers moving silt from higher ground to the lowlands, etc.[14] Because Icelandic mountains are constantly undergoing regeneration and destruction, they offer not only a spatial perspective like the ones Thoreau describes from the tops of Wachusett and Mount Katahdin, but also various temporal perspectives. Was the mountain formed before, during, or after the Ice Age? The shape and the constitution of a mountain will easily answer such questions, if one knows how to read them.

This temporal perspective is wonderfully—and humorously—captured by Thórbergur. He was born in 1888, twenty-six years after Thoreau passed away, in Southeast Iceland, where the rim of land separating the ocean and the large glacier is at its narrowest. In a book titled *The Stones Can Speak*, Thórbergur writes about growing up there under the steep cliffs.

> There were tremendously high crags at the top of the mountainside overlooking the farms to the south of Steinasandur plain. For the first few years of my life, they seemed just blank rock walls from the farmsteads and I never bothered to think more about them. But when I was gradually able to stagger upwards toward them, it was as if they became alive, and I was overwhelmed with an irresistible certainty that these crags were full of tremendous and magnificent life of their own. I didn't understand what kind of life it was, but I felt that it was life and a life so powerful that I grew weak when I looked up at them.[15]

For Thórbergur these old rocks, which had broken off the cliffs and made their ways towards the lowlands, stir up deep emotions. He does not use the language of the sublime but comes close to it. In that sense, Thórbergur's reaction to the crags is remarkably similar to Thoreau's strong reaction on his hike up Mount Katahdin.

The crags also opened up an imaginary world for Thórbergur, or were a source of reflection and a gateway into a different time. In much the same way as Thoreau, who was always acutely aware of the particularity and the materiality of the situation, Thórbergur also elaborates on the fact that although the falling of a large rock can be described in general terms, it must have taken place at a particular time, in particular circumstances, and having particular effects on its surroundings.

> I sometimes used to think: It'd be really nice to know when this rock had arrived, what year, what month and day of the month, what day of the week, whether during the day or at night, over which landmark was the sun or the Pleiades located then, from where in the crags did it come, if any great rumbling was heard when it was coming, whether there was much of a dust cloud to be seen in the crags when it came bouncing down, whether it made deep marks in the slopes, what was the weather like, what folk lived at Hali then, what were they doing, what was eaten that day at Hali, whether everybody had enough to eat, whether anyone at Hali said that day: 'There's a north-easterly over the Horn,' and many other things. But no one had recorded any of this, because rocks cannot end up as paupers supported by the parish.[16]

The Icelandic painter Kjarval, a contemporary of Thórbergur and the first artist to devote himself to painting Icelandic lava, describes sentiments evoked by the lava that resemble the ones Thórbergur experiences when confronted with the crags at Hali. Describing his relation to the motif, Kjarval likens the lava to a radio station.

> You don't know how terrifying it is to be alone in the lava, how fearful it is. When I have worked myself into the silence of the motif—then the discomfort comes through people's actions. This is what is terrible: when nature, which has elevated the people, created the individual, begins to reflect their influences.
>
> Imagine a volcanic crater with the stream of lava flowing into different directions. It is first and foremost a radio station. Lava streams harden and begin to receive from all over during thousands of years. Then they reflect. I have heard many different sounds in the lava. The whole of nature is one musical instrument; it is all music. One becomes so receptive to music in a lava field. (Kjarval 1954, translated by Ólafur Páll Jónsson)

Returning to Thórbergur and the crags, we also see how they evoke in him a sentiment of authenticity in nature.

> Of all "dead things," I felt the rocks and stones to be the most alive. This was because they were the most natural and definitely had the longest memories. No one had reshaped them and forced them to be anything other than nature had made them. The other "dead things" were deformed by man and were thus unnatural, and I felt that they had lost much of their souls and many of their memories by being made so. What was the life of a piece of iron, or a lad sinker, or a rake, in comparison to the life of stone?[17]

In this passage, Thórbergur describes a sentiment which is similar to what Thoreau experiences in the Maine woods, as Hoag remarks, saying that "wherever man leaves his mark on the wilderness, it almost always results in defilement."[18]

In the writings of both Thoreau and Thórbergur, we see a conception of perception that involves much more than a passive reception of sensory stimulus. For them, perception requires an interaction between the sensory organs and the mind; and it is a capacity which must be cultivated as any other capacity of the mind and the body.

> [S]ometimes I pressed my ear to them and listened to hear if they were telling me something. For me it was quite natural to think that you could hear voices from them and understand their thoughts if you just listened hard enough and were astute enough to understand. But you had to practice at it, and if you practiced long enough you'd be able to hear and understand. But I didn't know how to practice then.[19]

We can read this passage about Thórbergur's urge to learn to listen to the rocks as an urge to become a native in nature—to be able to listen to and understand the stories of those among whom one lives, whether people or rocks.

Closing Remarks

Thoreau and Thórbergur both offer us a way to think about mountains as moral structures, beings that may let us off and make it easier to die and easier to live. They offer no theory, neither of nature itself nor of how humans relate to nature or form part of it. Instead, they each describe in their own way attempts to become a native in the world. And they both see the world, not only the living world but also rocks and the mountains, as providing a language for describing human life, as Thoreau remarks earlier in the journal entry from May 10, 1853 with which I began this essay.

> He is the richest who has most use for nature as raw material of tropes & symbols with which to describe his life—If these gates of golden willows affect me they correspond to the beauty & promise of some experience on which I am entering. If I am overflowing with life—am rich in experience for which I lack expression—then nature will be my language full of poetry—all nature will fable & every natural phenomenon be a myth— (*PJ* 6:105)

As fellow human beings, we can take inspiration from the attempts of Thoreau and Thórbergur, although each person must look to their own horizon and find their own stones to listen to.

Acknowledgments

Several people have helped me to appreciate Thoreau. While reading Antonio Casado da Rocha's book, *Una casa en Walden*, I came to see Thoreau as contributing directly to contemporary philosophy of nature. The conference "Thoreau & the Nick of Time" held at The Snorrastofa Cultural and Medieval Centre, in Reykholt, Iceland, in May 2022, gave me both the opportunity to listen to many of the best Thoreau scholars, while also beginning to formulate my own ideas. In writing this chapter I have further been helped by critical and constructive comments by Kathryn C. Dolan, John Kucich, and Henrik Otterberg.

Works Cited

Baptista, João Afonso. "Eco(Il)Logical Knowledge: On Different Ways of Relating with the Known." *Environmental Humanities* 10 no. 2 (2018): 397–420. https://doi.org/10.1215/22011919-7156805.

Bennett, Jane. "On Being a Native: Thoreau's Hermeneutics of Self." *Polity* 22 no 4 (1990): 559–580. https://doi.org/10.2307/3234819.

Casado da Rocha, Antonio. *Una casa en Walden (y otros ensayos sobre Thoreau y cultura contemporánea)*. Logroño: Pepitas de calabaza, 2017. https://www.pepitas.net/libro/una-casa-en-walden.

Hoag, Ronald Wesley. "The Mark on the Wilderness: Thoreau's Contact with Ktaadn." *Texas Studies in Literature and Language* 24, No. 1 (Spring 1982): 23–46.

Kant, Immanuel. *Critique of Pure Reason.* Edited by Paul Guyer and Allen W. Wood. The Cambridge Edition of the Works of Immanuel Kant. Cambridge: Cambridge University Press, 1998. https://doi.org/10.1017/CBO9780511804649.

Keller, Evelyn Fox. *A Feeling for the Organism: The Life and Work of Barbara McClintock.* 10th anniversary edition. San Francisco: W. H. Freeman, 1984.

Kjarval, Jóhannes Sveinsson. "Kjarvalshús eða 'messa?'" *Þjóðviljinn*, 15 October 1954.

Leopold, Aldo. *A Sand County Almanac and Sketches Here and There.* Oxford University Press, 1987.

Matzke, J. P. Humans as "Part and Parcel of Nature": Thoreau's Contribution to Environmental Ethics. *Ethics in Progress*, 5 no. 2 (2014): 170–186. https://doi.org/10.14746/eip.2014.2.12

Thórdarson, Thórbergur. *The Stones Speak.* Translated by Júlían Meldon D'Arcy. Reykjavik: Mál og menning, 2012.

Thoreau, Henry David, *Elevating Ourselves: Thoreau on Mountains.* Edited by J. Parker Huber. Boston: Houghton Mifflin Harcourt, 1999.

Walls, Laura Dassow, *Material Faith: Thoreau on Science.* Boston: Houghton Mifflin Harcourt, 1999.

CHAPTER 12

"TAKING TIME BY THE FORELOCK": THOREAU'S TRANSCENDENTAL WRESTLINGS

François Specq

For the past two decades, academic studies of the relationships between American literature of the nineteenth century and issues of time and temporality have been a particularly vibrant field, constituting what is sometimes described as a "temporal turn" in literary studies.[1] This has been done in a very specific way, mostly centering on socio-historical perspectives. There has indeed prevailed an interest in the social and political dimensions of temporality, as linked to the construction and the crisis of the new nation. Thomas Allen thus focuses on the "social imagination" predicating "nationalist aspects of time," in other words the various ways time was incorporated into individual existences in the early Republic, constituting the "threads out of which the fabric of national belonging [were] woven"—therefore producing a temporal version of *E pluribus unum*.[2] In a study interweaving book history, theory of the novel, and postcolonial approaches, Lloyd Pratt takes the opposite view, arguing that the very multiplicity of temporalities, and the way "the expansion of print and transportation technologies magnified this pluralization," resulted in a "peculiar account of time," which was "deeply inhospitable to the consolidation of national and racial identity." While purporting to analyze divergences from the latter model, Pratt's analysis nevertheless entirely revolves around notions of "progress," "common time," "sense of national belonging," and "the nation's singular destiny."[3] As for Dana Luciano, in a book which is even more characteristic of the post-9/11 mood, she examines temporality from the perspective of what she describes as "our profound cultural faith in the productivity of mourning." The social significance of "this version of sacred time" is particularly explored in connection to the deep moment of grief caused by Lincoln's assassination, which was a very powerful tool of "national belonging"—itself associated with what Luciano calls a "sexual politics of time."[4] All these approaches thus intersect questions of temporality, literary culture, and democracy. More recently, Cindy Weinstein has focused on more formal aspects, i.e., the "temporal markers" (terms, dates, verb tenses, adverbs, etc.) which convey a "temporal grammar," more particularly the forms of "breakdown in temporal logic," or of "unhinged," "wobbly," temporality which she calls "tempo(e)rality"—thus turning time into an essentially linguistic construct.[5] However, here, also, the narrative—or even narratological—construction of time, is analyzed from a historicist perspective, reflecting the various ways the novels considered are as many interventions in contexts of political crisis (the debates on the Constitution, or the Civil War), or on questions of racial theory (linked to slavery).

While these are rich and stimulating studies, one cannot but be struck by the conspicuous absence of Transcendentalist authors (with the exception of a chapter on Emerson in Allen's *Republic in Time*)—for reasons that go unexplained, but which do not agree well with the wide-ranging interpretive models proposed.[6] Only very lately has Danielle Follett undertaken to re-examine the question of time in Emerson's writings per se, shedding light notably on a comparatively little-known text of 1870, "Works and Days," alongside the more classic essays and lectures of the 1830s and 1840s.[7] This precise, nuanced study, which stays away from the (post-)nationalist socio-cultural frameworks of the books centering on the "politics of time,"[8] nevertheless remains focused on a fundamentally discursive notion of temporality. That still leaves aside the individual's lived temporality, or existential time—i.e., aspects of time which pertain neither to socio-cultural and political structures, nor to philosophical discourse, but to individual existence and daily commitment. Of these Thoreau's œuvre is a striking example (while *also* having a cultural and philosophical dimension). It is thus particularly surprising that none of the main studies of temporal forms in nineteenth-century American literature considers him.[9]

Scholars may have deemed the topic to be exhausted. To be sure, questions of temporality have been the focus of a number of classic studies of Thoreau's œuvre, from Charles Anderson onwards.[10] Fundamentally, two models of temporality have prevailed in the scholarship on Thoreau. There has long been an emphasis on his desire to be in tune with time as it goes by, constituting it like a heightened, eternal present. Such is the perspective to be found in Charles Anderson's classic study, or in Alan Hodder's more recent book, in which that form of temporality is seen as the heart of what he regards as Thoreau's "religious life."[11] Alternatively, the notion of "deep time" (inspired by *longue durée* historians, and turned a major paradigm over the past two decades) has situated him, along with other American writers, within a broad cultural historical framework which tends to collapse the past and the future into one vast "temporal continuum."[12] That approach especially shapes one of the most substantial studies of the notion of time in Emerson's and Thoreau's writings, James R. Guthrie's *Above Time*, which is primarily devoted to the way their thinking relates to the major scientific developments of the nineteenth century.[13] Although both approaches do have some validity, and have resulted in a fascinating array of readings—including one, by Mark Luccarelli, boldly attempting and questioning their synthesis[14]—I would like to suggest they be supplemented by a different dimension of Thoreau's relation to temporality: indeed, his writings widely demonstrate how he envisioned the life of the fully committed individual as a hard-won battle against what Herman Melville hauntingly called "time's swamping sea."[15] The present essay will seek to bring to light this sense of time as personal wrestling, which has been largely overlooked as a result of the prevalent focus on overly abstract, or ethereal, forms of contemplation.

Thoreau's Retreat Outside Time?

"Time is but the stream I go a-fishing in." Approaches to Thoreau's writings have often seemed to assume that his practice of contemplation was merely a matter of uncovering some pre-existing harmony between the individual and the world. This turns the work of recovery into a comparatively simple one: it would suffice to get rid of the accumulated layers or strata of set notions and premises, which close one off from the world, to be treated to a grand, free serving of rapturous perception. For Hodder, "at all times Thoreau's religious life essentially revolved around—was predicated upon—experiences of inspiration and euphoria in the natural world, which he customarily referred to as ecstasy."[16] In a convergent manner, Guthrie emphasizes "revelatory moments" allowing one to "live, if only transiently, 'above time.'"[17]

To be sure, Thoreau's oft-recurrent phrasing has led him to misrepresent his own efforts, as it seems to suggest a celebratory, relaxed, even nonchalant approach, one in which it would suffice to allow oneself to be in a situation of alertness or receptivity, to be inherently granted the pleasure of welcoming the world as it presents itself to us. One of his more memorable phrasings, "Time is but the stream I go a-fishing in" (*W* 98), indeed suggests a form of transcendental homeliness. And so do, in the "Sounds" chapter of *Walden*, the passages where he states that he meant to enjoy "the bloom of the present moment" (*W* 111), and to be merely "reminded of the lapse of time. I grew in those seasons like corn in the night, and they were far better than any work of the hands would have been" (*W* 111). Such statements celebrate a natural process warranting an *otium* of the eye as much as an *otium* of the hand—thus echoing the age-old tradition of pastoral leisure liberally bestowing its gifts upon humans. From that perspective, Thoreau equates "contemplation" and "the forsaking of all works," the latter seemingly bound to result into the former (*W* 112). In his classic study of Thoreau's works, Charles Anderson could thus claim that Thoreau primarily devoted himself to "excursions out of his time scheme and out of time into the Eternal Now."[18] Because *Walden* narrates a retreat, Anderson, as well as a number of subsequent scholars, were misled into thinking that Thoreau merely advocates a retreat outside time, or at least away from the strife of time. My claim here will be that it is impossible to reduce Thoreau's writings to a single time scheme, and that an emphasis on a gift dubbed "the eternal present" provides too limited a focus to allow one to grasp Thoreau's stance.

Craving Reality, Craving Time. Thoreau's topic—or, rather, concern—was, unfailingly, the present, to be sure. But what does it mean, truly, to live fully in the present moment? Not some peaceful, appeased, taken-for-granted enjoyment of what passes by: the present is to be won—rather than conquered, since no subjugation is at stake—through a brave struggle, if not a frantic endeavor—evincing dedication and will. To that extent, I will suggest, Thoreau, while echoing it, departs from the model of ancient wisdom, which, as analyzed by Pierre Hadot, essentially revolved around self-abandonment, or the individual's effort to break free of the tyranny of the past, and, even more, of the future.[19]

In Thoreau's gentle fishing metaphor, we may indeed overlook the real nature of going a-fishing: Thoreau here refers to the popular image of a fisherman's "work" as one in which you just need to cast your line to catch fish, being patient, but he was obviously aware that things are not so simple. Taking time by the forelock—or seizing an opportunity—is certainly highly desirable, but opportunity is prone to slip away, so that one definitely needs to *take* time by the forelock, in the terms of a maxim Thoreau knew well.[20] There is no such thing as an easy continuity between oneself and the world: what is involved is a struggle—Thoreau made the nature of his thirsting for the world particularly clear, arguing that "be it life or death, we only crave reality" (*W* 98).[21]

Craving reality certainly implies a yearning to get rid of what obscures it. Readers of Thoreau are quick to recognize that this has to do with a rejection of set notions and prejudices, since that is a major theme of *Walden*—which explicitly urges us to this task: "Let us settle ourselves, and work and wedge our feet downward through the mud and slush of opinion, and prejudice, and tradition, and delusion, and appearance" (*W* 97). But, still more deeply, it has to do with the individual's liberation from their absorption within the flow of time—which amounts to a subjection to a mere external process.[22] In the course of ordinary life we are merely located within time: time is the milieu of our existence, rather than its very ground.[23] As a consequence, there is no reappropriating ourselves without reappropriating time. In other words, what is to be recovered is a sense of life as an event, rather than something that merely occurs: the seeking individual strives to create heterogeneity within the flow of time. The endeavor is not to wage a futile war on time, no more than to magically chime with it, but rather to carve a space out of it (albeit *not* away from it).

Let's dispel any ambiguity by underlining that this is not a question of emphasizing subjective time, but of resisting the blighting power of unredeemed temporality, i.e. one which is not humanized (such as that of "deep time"), or all-too-human (as that resulting from the demands of the economic and social world). Indeed, human beings are bound to be consumed by time, trapped ("walled-in," one is tempted to say, appropriating one of Thoreau's puns [*W* 183]) within the bland continuum of daily life. Thoreau definitely makes this theme central to *Walden*, which, in its most basic sense, narrates a break from the social world and its rhythms. *Walden* indeed gives pride of place to perceptual refocusing—as opposed to leading a distracted existence "in the midst of this chopping sea of civilized life" (*W* 91), "in this restless, nervous, bustling, trivial Nineteenth Century" (*W* 329). In other words, he celebrates the process of stripping away the unessential, paring life down to what feels essential, to a highly ethical commitment—to what can be called principled, disciplined living, and, to that extent, an ideal akin to ancient wisdom.[24] *Walden* undoubtedly does this—and that rarely fails to enthrall (or, occasionally, to put off) its readers—but barely addresses *how* that is to be achieved: the book does not propound any method beyond the gesture of retreat or withdrawal, so that we are left admiring the author but wondering whether, and how, *we too* could reach illumination.

Spacing Out Time: Thoreau's Journal

The relevant method, to a large degree, is to be found—or, rather, is exemplified—in the Journal, which Thoreau kept for twenty-five years, whose intensity should not be overlooked as a consequence of its shunning the alluring appeal of the personal diary. Indeed, its (almost) single object is the observation of nature.[25] Hodder regards Thoreau's Journal as "the chief vehicle and exhibit of his spiritual life"[26] —did he not set himself the task "to be always on the alert to find God in nature"? (*PJ* 4:53). But journalizing is liberating, above all, because of its distancing from daily time, its loosening the grip of time, thus allowing the writer to *space out* time. Spacing out time is a very different undertaking from turning it into space, which H. Daniel Peck has argued was Thoreau's primary endeavor, constituting the core of his "art of memory."[27] Turning time into space is a process of containment and (de)limitation, whereas spacing out time is a process of expansion. From that perspective, each act of perception, each observation, is an opening, a *punctum* which punctures the seamless web of ordinary routine (so do, in the first place, moments of leisure or idleness, which are the first steps on the way to self-recovery).[28]

Thoreau's most potent teaching here might be described as a two-tier approach. For sure, he lays emphasis on ridding oneself of what constitutes obstacles to enjoying the present moment: stripping oneself from worldly attachments. This indeed makes him heir to ancient wisdom. But self-surrender—the work of the negative, so to speak—is only a preliminary step: then come all the necessary efforts, the work of building. The Journal demonstrates what *Walden* tends to obscure: the bold, vigorous energy inherent in the process of contemplation and attunement to the world. The world is not a free gift. The Journal makes it clear that getting out of the grip of standard time is *a task*—as Danish philosopher Kierkegaard memorably put it, "time itself is the task."[29] Turning *chronos* into *kairos* is indeed a demanding task: it requires attentiveness, discipline, knowledge.

Thoreau amply demonstrates the first two throughout the Journal. As for the third, one of his deepest insights is that in order to *see* you need to *know*. No other writer has similarly emphasized, and demonstrated, how you need to know what to look at, how you need to have, not only the grammar, but the vocabulary of perception. Too often, insufficient attention is paid to the real import and significance of Thoreau's wide-ranging proficiency in the natural sciences, especially plants, birds, or fishes, which he was also able to turn to good account in pioneering works of ecological science.[30] In the same way that he regarded principled resistance as providing a most necessary "counter friction to stop the machine" (*RP* 103)—a political machine which ensured the continuing existence of slavery, and thus perpetuated the tragic failure of the national project of the U.S.—his Journalizing appears as a way of upsetting the machinery of time. Not the time that puts us to death by relentlessly wasting our bodies, but the one that silently, slyly, erases our agency through undifferentiation. The Journal makes this particularly clear, as it dramatizes Thoreau's efforts, not merely, or not primarily, to be in tune with time (as *Walden* propounds), but to *open up* time.

Fully adhering to the rhythms of the natural world is a hugely demanding task—and one that is characterized by an unfailing sense of urgency: "Nothing must be postponed—Take time by the forelock—Now or never. You must live in the present—launch yourself on every wave—find your eternity in each moment" (OJT 29: 51–2).[31] The coherence, or even the very existence, of the Journal relies upon the integrative effect of the poet's commitment or "discipline"—"All wisdom is the reward of a discipline conscious or unconscious" (*PJ* 4:47).[32] Thoreau conceived his journalizing not as a genteel practice but as a course of action which totally engaged the individual's mind and body—"My head is hands and feet" (*W* 98). Nature is what literally *grounds* Thoreau's desired inwardness—as it mediates consciousness to itself.[33]

Resisting Fate. For Thoreau, then, if Paradise is to be regained, that is through the individual's task, or commitment. So, in the end, it is essential to realize that Thoreau's purpose in reconnecting to the timelessness of nature—if that is indeed how things can be described—is *not* to escape into it, but, pointedly and emphatically, to prevent our existence's slipping into ideality as a result of its self-enclosed, and therefore diminished temporality. Indeed, we are bound to feel removed from time as a result of subjection to routine—which erases or cancels time as it mercilessly turns our existences into a forgetting. At the same time that delving into contemplation constitutes a counter-balance to the excessive linearity of our daily lives, it provides a useful reminder that we are, and will always remain, part and parcel of a wider world—"The universe is wider than our views of it" (*W* 320). This is where Thoreau's philosophical relation to time is also deeply ecocritical, as it propounds—and enacts—a resistance to the notion of environment: time is no more what environs us than the physical world is. In our striving for connection to the world, we simultaneously experience the fact that we are not a mere part of time, but also that time is not merely our own. Only by recovering a freer relationship with time, thus shaping a fully realized, intensified existence, do we experience what is not us, nor ours, and can we consequently relate to community—community being both the community of the living (i.e., man and nature, or physical milieu of mankind) and the community of enlightened citizens. Put in different, more traditional terms, Thoreau is intent on *resisting fate*, in all its guises—as that which seems destined to happen and to dictate itself to us. As he proudly muses in the "Sounds" chapter of *Walden*: "We have constructed a fate, an Atropos, that never turns aside.…Every path but your own is the path of fate. Keep on your own track, then" (*W* 118).

Thoreau meant time to become, through his dedicated pursuit, more than an external condition imposed on us—one that, in its relentless continuity, deprives us of any breathing space. No hubristic illusion of autonomy or self-mastery is implied here: Thoreau does not claim that one can abstract oneself from the constraints of time, nor of its corrupting power, but that it is nevertheless essential—and quintessentially human—to shape time, *our* time, through choosing daily to pay attention, not to our surroundings in a simple sense, but to *what lives along with us*—to that with which we are coeval.[34]

Conclusion

This discussion has foregrounded Thoreau's wrestling with time, one that points to a more literal reading of the phrase "take time by the forelock," thus seeking to recover all the energy and determination involved in laying hold of time, in getting time within one's compass, rather than being encompassed by it—carrying out not a struggle for dominance, but, literally, for survival. In so doing, it has meant to counter a blandness of tone that has prevailed in versions of Thoreau that celebrate unalloyed, ethereal contemplation. Thoreau's stance cannot be reduced to a mere enjoyment of unity or harmony, which would somewhat magically alight on us from heaven—grace-like—but requires striving for them—actively bringing them to life. Immanence is not contingency. The phrase "take time by the forelock" also appears at the very beginning of *Cape Cod*, in a broader metaphorical phrasing which sheds full light on what Thoreau meant: "Take Time by the forelock. It is also the safest part to take a serpent by" (*CC* 3). The image suggests less danger than the idea of a struggle which requires daring, keenness, resolution.

Indeed, Thoreau's Journal vividly calls upon each individual to make time *their* business—their task, in Kierkegaard's words. A task and *a responsibility*: "In existence, the individual is a concretion, time is concrete, and even while the individual deliberates he is ethically responsible for the use of time. Existence is not an abstract rush job but a striving and an unremitting 'in the meantime.'"[35] Time is not something which just flows or oscillates in a vacuum, but a living entity one must relate to *deliberately*. Thoreau just hated any idea of an inexorable necessity or fate that would prevail over us: taking time by the forelock, he strove for a path out of the prison of unexamined time, reflecting the primacy of human consciousness and purposes.

Works Cited

Allen, Thomas M. *A Republic in Time: Temporality and Social Imagination in Nineteenth Century America*. Chapel Hill: University of North Carolina Press, 2008.

———. ed., *Time and Literature*. Cambridge: Cambridge University Press, 2018.

Anderson, Charles. *The Magic Circle of Walden*. New York: Holt, Rinehart and Winston, 1968.

Berger, Michael. *Thoreau's Late Career and The Dispersion of Seeds: The Saunterer's Synoptic Vision*. Rochester: Camden House, 2000.

Cameron, Sharon. *Writing Nature: Henry Thoreau's Journal*. Oxford: Oxford University Press, 1985.

Case, Kristen. "Beyond Temporal Borders: The Music of Thoreau's Kalendar." In *Thoreau Beyond Borders: New International Essays on America's Most Famous Nature Writer*. Edited by François Specq, Laura Dassow Walls and Julien Nègre. Amherst/Boston: University of Massachusetts Press, 2020.

Constantinesco, Thomas. "The Dial and the Untimely 'Spirit of the Time,'" *American Periodicals* 28.1 (2018): 21–40.

Dimock, Wai Che. *Through Other Continents: American Literature across Deep Time.* Princeton: Princeton University Press, 2006.

Follett, Danielle. "Emerson's Temporalities: The Eternal Present vs. the Not Yet Present." *ESQ: A Journal of Nineteenth-Century American Literature and Culture* 67.3–4 (2021): 639–65.

Guthrie, James R. *Above Time: Emerson's and Thoreau's Temporal Revolutions.* Columbia: University of Missouri Press, 2011.

Haraway, Donna. *Staying with the Trouble: Making Kin in the Chthulucene.* Durham: Duke University Press, 2016.

Hodder, Alan D. *Thoreau's Ecstatic Witness.* New Haven: Yale University Press, 2001.

Luccarelli, Mark. "Thoreau and the Desynchronization of Time." In *Thoreau in an Age of Crisis: Uses and Abuses of an American Icon*, edited by Kristen Case, Rochelle L. Johnson, and Henrik Otterberg. Paderborn: Brill Fink, 2021, 91–106.

Luciano, Dana. *Arranging Grief: Sacred Time and the Body in Nineteenth-Century America*. New York: New York University Press, 2007.

Nelson, Daniel. "'That such things are': The Non-Teleological Poetics of Thoreau's Journal," *Arizona Quarterly: A Journal of American Literature, Culture, and Theory,* Vol. 78, N°3 (Fall 2022): 87–110.

Peck, H. Daniel. *Thoreau's Morning Work: Memory and Perception in A Week on the Concord and Merrimack Rivers, The Journal and Walden*. New Haven: Yale University Press, 1990.

Pratt, Lloyd. *Archives of American Time: Literature and Modernity in the Nineteenth Century*. Philadelphia: University of Pennsylvania Press, 2009.

Primack, Richard B. *Walden Warming: Climate Change Comes to Thoreau's Woods.* Chicago: The University of Chicago Press, 2014.

Thorson, Robert M. *Walden's Shore: Henry David Thoreau and Nineteenth-Century Science.* Cambridge: Harvard University Press, 2014.

Weinstein, Cindy. *Time, Tense, and American Literature: When Is Now?* Cambridge: Cambridge University Press, 2015.

CHAPTER 13

THE NICK OF TIME, IMPROVED

Paul Schacht and Elizabeth Witherell

"In any weather, at any hour of the day or night, I have been anxious to improve the nick of time, and notch it on my stick too; to stand on the meeting of two eternities, the past and future, which is precisely the present time."

These words from *Walden* are often quoted, and much has been written about what it might have meant to Thoreau, or what it should mean to us, his readers, to "improve the nick of time." Our essay explores different questions, however: what it might mean, if you are Thoreau, to improve what you have to say about improving the nick of time, and what it might mean, if you are Thoreau's reader, or any writer's reader, to stand on the meeting point of the words the writer wrote in the past and the words that will remain with that writer's readers into the future—the point, that is, of revision.[1]

The careful reader will have noticed that the words quoted from *Walden* above are not quite what we read in any published text of the book. What we do read is that the meeting of two eternities, the past and future, is "precisely the present *moment*" (*W* 17, emphasis added).[2] If we look at the manuscript leaf from the first of the seven extant draft versions of *Walden* that Thoreau composed between 1846 (while still at the pond) and 1854 (when the book was published by Ticknor and Fields), we see in Thoreau's racing cursive the word "time" struck out with a line, and the word "moment" inserted above it and to the right. In examining this point of revision, we may well have the sensation of witnessing, in real time, Thoreau's recognition that the precise and circumscribed word "moment" is a much better one for a meeting point than the generic word "time" (HM 924, 1:19).

As justly famous as the nick-of-time sentence is this one: "Time is but the stream I go a-fishing in. I drink at it; but while I drink I see the sandy bottom and detect how shallow it is. Its thin current slides away, but eternity remains" (*W* 98). Although studying one of Thoreau's manuscript pages may give us the feeling that we are with him in the moment, peering over his shoulder as his pen enacts a re-visioning of his intention in the replacement of one word by another, we are in fact gazing at the sandy bottom, or rather inky residue, long ago left behind by the stream of Thoreau's intentions. The moment of revision we imagine ourselves inhabiting is a reconstruction after the fact, and one in which we ourselves supply the intention behind the change, as a matter of interpretation. In its physical appearance, the leaf bearing Thoreau's first inditing of this passage (with additional revisions, the passage appears on two other leaves as well) is a perfect icon of its own siliceousness, its interlineation-laced hand overwritten with high-amplitude waves of ink serving to cancel the passage, the waves themselves overwritten with a large "X" (or was the "X" overwritten by the waves?), the whole accompanied by a conspicuous inkblot that coincidentally resembles nothing so much as a fish (HM 924, 1:86). Since Thoreau retained the passage, his wavy and crossing lines appear to reflect an intention not to cancel it altogether but rather to relocate it (as will be discussed below) within what would become the chapter "Where I Lived, and What I Lived For."

Or so it seems reasonable to suppose. But how can we know for sure? Perhaps by inscribing these lines he did intend to omit the passage from *Walden* but later changed his mind. Similarly, although the fish-like appearance of the inkblot is likely coincidental, can we rule out the possibility that while the ink was still wet he smudged and smeared it, idly or playfully, into something approaching piscine proportions?

A manuscript page of Thoreau—of any writer—is, like the earth the writer trod, a physical space bearing witness to a sequence of actions in time. But constructing from manuscript evidence what John Bryant calls a "revision narrative" is of course not at all the same as constructing a scientific narrative of geologic change, in which intentions have no place.[3] The fact that intentions are ultimately unknowable, and that most if not all authorial actions are overdetermined, makes it impossible to construct any but the simplest revision narrative with much confidence. In studying the manuscript of *Walden*, it might well seem safer to remain, as the tradition of documentary manuscript transcription does, on the firm ground of description, rather than step into the whirlpool of interpretation.

Yet arguably the necessarily tenuous and contestable nature of revision narratives is no more problematic than that of the stories we tell about the meaning of published poems, novels, and other texts. Those stories, too, translate space into time. We construct textual meaning in part by asking why we find *this* word in the text and not some hypothetical other, a question that implies a moment of choice, usually (though not always) authorial choice, conscious or unconscious. Meanwhile, in the case of revision narratives, we have the advantage that we often find ourselves asking why *this* word and not *that particular other word that is before our eyes on the page*, written and then canceled.

In what follows, we attempt to construct a partial revision narrative of "Where I Lived, and What I Lived For," looking in particular at changes Thoreau made in his own effort to think about the relationship between space and time. Before going further, however, let us first orient readers briefly to the complex history of the *Walden* manuscript.

The *Walden* Manuscript

Thoreau lived at Walden Pond between 1845 and 1847. While there, he delivered several lectures in Concord and elsewhere about his experience, using an initial draft of what would be published in 1854 as *Walden*.[4] After Thoreau's death in 1862, his manuscripts found their way into various hands. Roughly 600 manuscript leaves constituting the bulk of Thoreau's work on *Walden* were eventually obtained by Henry E. Huntington. At the Huntington Library in San Marino, California, they are cataloged as HM 924. (At least fifty additional extant leaves of *Walden* not in HM 924 reside in other libraries or with private collectors.)

In the 1950s, J. Lyndon Shanley, studying the 600 leaves—that is, 1200 pages—of HM 924, hypothesized that Thoreau put the work through seven distinct draft stages.[5] The first version, the one Thoreau used as a lecture text, which Shanley labeled "A," is the only complete one. The others ("B" through "G") are fragmentary and discontinuous. Shanley reasoned that Thoreau composed Version A between September 1846 and September 1847, B and C between mid-1848 and the summer of 1849, D between early 1852 and September of that year, E between September 1852 and sometime in 1853, F between late 1853 and early 1854, and G between February and March of 1854.[6] An eighth draft must have been provided to the printer, but that draft is lost. In place of the printer's copy, the best reflection we have of Thoreau's final version is the publisher's proof, bearing both the printer's and Thoreau's corrections, which is also at the Huntington and identified there as HM 925.

In 1967, building on Shanley's work, Ronald Earl Clapper filed a Ph.D. dissertation at UCLA titled "The Development of *Walden*: A Genetic Text." Clapper's dissertation collates Version A and the six other, fragmentary versions as witnesses, using Houghton Mifflin's 1906 edition of *Walden* as base text and registering the variant readings across the seven draft versions in footnotes. In 2014, the present authors, working with Clapper and a team of editors, published an XML-encoded web version of Clapper's dissertation as *Walden: A Fluid-Text Edition*. A project of Digital Thoreau, a collaborative initiative headquartered at the State University of New York at Geneseo, the fluid-text edition enables readers to compare the transcribed drafts of *Walden* side-by-side, in a browser window, with one another and the Princeton University Press edition of Thoreau's published text. A related Digital Thoreau undertaking, "The *Walden* Manuscript Project," provides a search tool for cross-referencing Clapper's transcription with the manuscript itself, which the Huntington digitized in 2019 with grant funding obtained through the State University of New

York. Our essay cites a given image of the manuscript (HM 924) by the volume and page number assigned to it on the website of the Huntington Digital Library.[7] It cites proof images (HM 925) by their assigned sheet numbers.

"Where I Lived, and What I Lived For": A Partial Revision Narrative

The first leaf containing "Where I Lived" (hereafter WIL) content in Version A (1846–1847) begins with language that would ultimately find its way into the chapter's eighth paragraph. The leaf does not contain a chapter title because at this stage Thoreau had not divided his text into chapters. In A, the opening words of WIL 8 are "When I first went to the pond to live…." (We consistently refer to paragraphs by their place in the published *Walden*. Again, in A these are the first words of the manuscript portion that would *ultimately* become WIL 8). In *Walden* as published in 1854, WIL 8 begins, "When first I took up my abode in the woods…." Between his first draft of this paragraph, then, and the published version, Thoreau decides to change how his words locate him in space, from "the pond" to "the woods"; as we shall see, paragraph 8 is not the only place in the chapter where he does this.

Thoreau's re-ordering of the first *three* words in the sentences above ("When first I…" in publication as opposed to the original "When I first…" in A), together with his introduction of the word "abode" to designate the location of his residence in the woods, may reflect the manuscript's overall trajectory from lecture text to literary work. The inverted word order in particular seems distinctly literary.

Notably absent from A is the published version's all-important reference to Independence Day 1845 as the location on the calendar—the moment in time, in other words—when Thoreau began living at Walden. What both versions of WIL 8 have in common, however, is that they focus largely on the details of Thoreau's house itself: the lack of plastering or chimney, the weather-stained boards, the white hewn studs and freshly planed doors.

In addition to WIL 8, the leaves of A contain what would become paragraphs 9, 10, and 13–23 of WIL in the published *Walden*. It is not until the fifth, or D version (1852), that the first three paragraphs of the published WIL appear, together with the fifth and seventh paragraphs. Paragraph 6 first appears in E (1852–1853), paragraphs 11 and 12 enter in F (1853–1854), and paragraph 4 makes its first appearance in G (1854).

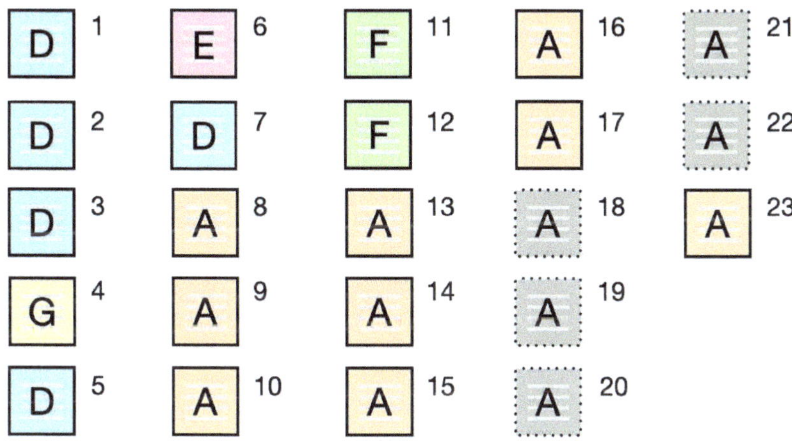

But the picture is a little more complicated still, for two reasons: first, some of the paragraphs in A that remained in the chapter were extensively rewritten in B; and second, paragraphs 18–22, while first written in A, originally followed what would become the second paragraph of the chapter "Sounds"; only later were they relocated to form the sequence we see in the published *Walden*.

Yet another wrinkle: in A the first part of WIL paragraph 23—the canceled version of the "Time is but the stream I go a-fishing in" passage we have already looked at—appears on the verso of the page containing paragraph 16. This is important because it means that in A, Thoreau's reflection on time follows immediately on the paragraph containing his most memorable explanation of why he went to Walden: "I went down to the pond," he writes in A, "because I wished to live deliberately." (The published *Walden*, in a shift parallel to one noted above, begins, "I went to the *woods*"—not "down to the *pond*" [emphasis added].)

In A, WIL paragraph 17 follows this sequence. It famously laments the superficial goals to which Thoreau feels too many of his fellow citizens are directing their lives, and advocates the value of simplicity. ("Simplicity–Simplicity–Simplicity" [HM 924, 1:87].)

To summarize, then: in its original shape, the stretch of A we have been discussing is not yet a chapter titled "Where I Lived, and What I Lived For." It begins with Thoreau describing where he lived, builds to what would become the published book's most memorable description of what he lived for, and ends shortly thereafter with a meditation on his relationship to time.

In fact, the title Thoreau would eventually choose for this chapter would in a sense flag the connection between time and space as the chapter's controlling idea. "Where I Lived" obviously invokes space, and "What I Lived For" less obviously, but just as certainly, invokes time. To live *for* something is to project oneself out into the future: to be oriented and in motion towards an objective. Thoreau's objective, as just noted, was to live deliberately: "I went down to the pond *because I wished to live deliberately*." Place and purpose, location and time.

Like many of the best narratives, our partial revision narrative of WIL contains more than one subplot. The first concerns a revision Thoreau makes to the "live deliberately" sentence within A itself—a revision internal to this version rather than a difference in wording between versions. Following "I went down to the pond because I wished to live deliberately," Thoreau in A originally wrote "and front only the essential facts of life...". He then, at some point, came back to this place in the sentence, changed the "a" of "and" to "o," added a "t" to the left of it to make the word "to," and scraped at the "nd" ending of "and" to cancel it (HM 924, 1:85). The revision alters the structure of the sentence in a crucial way. Before the change, the sentence seems to present Thoreau's purpose in going down to the pond as a list, its items joined by the coordinating conjunction "and":

I went down to the pond because I wished to live deliberately

| and

front only the essential facts of life

| and

see if I could not learn what it had to teach

| and

not . . . discover that I had not lived

After the change, the sentence describes his purpose by means of two grammatically parallel elements: two infinitive phrases, the second of which—"to front only the essential facts of life," and everything that goes with it structurally—may be read as an expansion or elaboration of the first: to live deliberately.

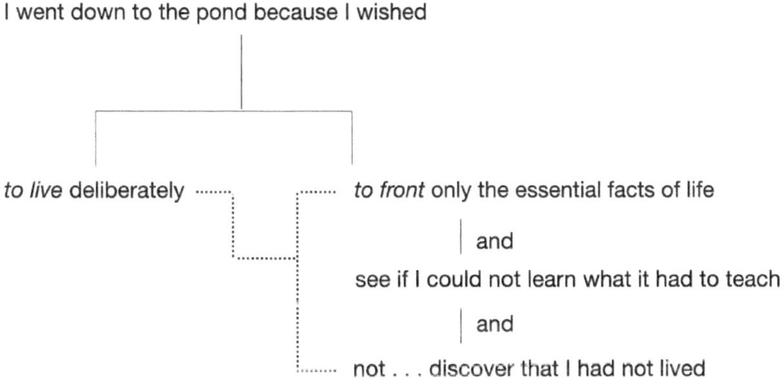

The sentence's revised grammatical structure clarifies that living deliberately was not one of a number of purposes for Thoreau, but the overall, organizing purpose, comprehending others related to it. It also paves the way for the elaborate parallelism of the next sentence but one. Here there are four phrases, each containing two parallel elements, the last containing two parallel sub-elements ("if" clauses joined by "or"), each one of those containing two parallel sub-elements joined by "and."

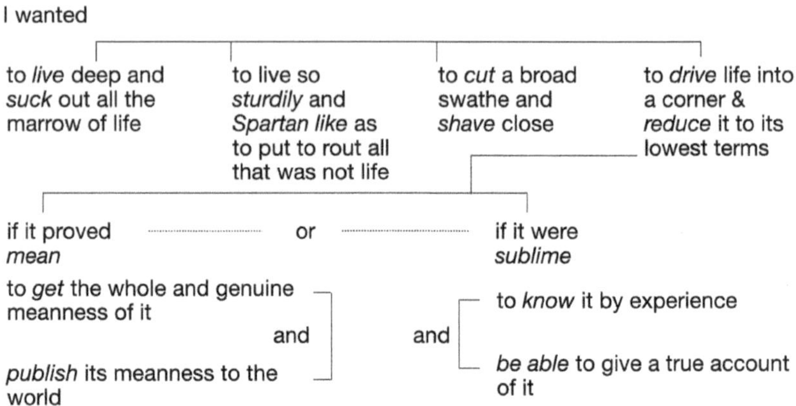

There is parallelism as well in the bit of verse Thoreau adds immediately following paragraph 23 in A:

> I seek the Present Time,
> No other clime,
> Life in to-day,
> Not to sail another way,
> To Paris or to Rome,
> Or farther still from home.
> That man, whoe'er he is,
> Lives but a moral death,
> Whose life is not coeval
> With his breath....

And so on, for a good many more lines. Here it is time and space that run parallel. Thoreau seeks "the Present *Time*, / No other *clime*," preferring "Life in *to-day*," at "*home*," to life in "*Paris*" or "*Rome*" (emphasis added).

Although he does not retain these lines in later drafts or the published *Walden* of 1854, he does retain their informing thought and structure. Indeed, his continued working out of the time-space parallel, as both idea and structural principle, explains much of his subsequent revision to WIL.

Space, Time, Structure

As we follow the evolution of WIL across multiple drafts, we see that it comes to assume a rough bipartite structure in which the first dozen paragraphs mainly emphasize *where he lived*, and the last ten mainly emphasize *what he lived for*, with correspondingly somewhat more emphasis on *space* in the first half, and somewhat more emphasis on *time* in the second. As the chapter takes on this shape, paragraph 13 becomes the pivot point between its two halves. One important bit of evidence that Thoreau himself sees a shift in emphasis after paragraph 13 is his note to the printer on the page proof for this chapter. As printed, the running heads for the three pages on this sheet alternate between "Where I Lived." and "Walden." But Thoreau marks the running head for the page that contains paragraph 14 to be revised from "Where I Lived." to "What I Lived For." and adds a note instructing the printer to continue the new running head "to the end of the chapter" (HM 925, 32).

Let us look at how Thoreau builds out the chapter on either side of paragraph 13. Then we can examine how paragraph 13 functions as a pivot.

Earlier, we noted that the first words of WIL in A end up in paragraph 8 of the published *Walden*. It is in D that Thoreau adds to the manuscript the words that would ultimately become the chapter's first paragraph. These words are all about the relationship of time and space in a person's life: "At a certain season of our life," he first writes in D, "we are accustomed to consider every spot as the possible site of a house" (HM 924, 4:65). The sentence picks out a particular time of life, a definite period, a "season." There comes a time in one's life, he is saying, when one sees the world in a particular way. And what one sees, interestingly, are "spots" and "sites"—spaces that, like this period of one's life, are definite or bounded, even if their boundaries are not precisely drawn.

The new opening paragraph represents a revision to Thoreau's plan for where and how to begin this part of his account. Instead of beginning by describing where he went to live and why he went to live there, Thoreau decides to put those details in a larger context, to place his own experience on a timeline common to human lives in general, or at least to the lives of his imagined readers. The "I" in A ("When I first went to the pond to live") becomes a "we" in D ("we are accustomed to consider"). This is another revision that seems consistent with the development of *Walden* from lecture to book. Thoreau framed his lecture expressly as an answer to his neighbors' questions about what he was doing in the woods. Even in the lecture, of course, he used his personal experience to draw larger conclusions with broad application to his fellow citizens of Concord and his fellow human beings, but the book uses that broader view as a frame more consistently, explicitly, and deliberately than the lecture.

The wider framing in D went through some revision itself before arriving at the wording we see in the published *Walden*. At first, Thoreau wrote, "At some seasons of our life we are accustomed to consider every spot..."; then he substituted "a certain" for "some" and made "seasons" singular. Before the change, the plural "seasons" seems to suggest that there might be multiple times in one's life, and not one particular time, when every spot might look like a possible site of a house. It is only after the change that we get that narrowing to a definite and particular phase of life, and the nice alignment of singularities in the sound and rhythm of the sentence: "At a certain *season* of our life we are accustomed to consider every *spot* as the possible *site* of a house" (emphasis added).

But there is still more to see here. Although one can barely make them out on the manuscript surface, there are two penciled words, one above and one below "accustomed." Above, Thoreau penciled "disposed," and below, he penciled "inclined." Neither word is explicitly canceled, but this is not the only place in the manuscript where Thoreau appears to use the space between the lines to brainstorm alternative wordings, as we shall shortly see. This brainstorming feels like a different process from writing words and then canceling them. It is not as if Thoreau wrote "disposed," changed his mind to "inclined," and finally settled on "accustomed." It seems most likely that he wrote "accustomed," questioned whether he should keep it, penciled in a couple of other words as possibilities, then decided to hold fast with "accustomed."

Why stick with "accustomed," especially since "inclined" and "disposed" both suggest a bit more agency, more of that sense of forward projection we spoke of earlier in connection with the phrase "What I Lived For"? By comparison, "accustomed" seems more passive, expressing habit more than intention. Yet it is also more consistent with the idea that looking out for possible home sites is usual—that is, customary—at the time of life he is describing, something we do without even really thinking about it. This consistency may explain Thoreau's decision.

The new first paragraph for WIL introduced in D goes on to explain that no matter what site Thoreau imagined himself occupying, "Wherever I sat, there I might live; and the landscape radiated from me accordingly." Thoreau then asks, "What is a house but a *sedes*–a seat?,–better if a country-seat" (HM 924, 4:66). The next eleven paragraphs of the chapter as published in 1854 mainly focus on one or another aspect of Thoreau's physical situation at the pond (*W* 82–87). Below, key words and phrases from these paragraphs are italicized to illustrate this emphasis on the physical:

2:…I even had the *refusal of several farms* …
3: I have frequently seen a poet withdraw, having enjoyed the *most valuable part of a farm*…
4: The real attractions of the *Hollowell farm*…
5: It makes but little difference whether you are committed to a *farm* or the *county jail.*
6: "When you think of getting a *farm*, turn it thus in your mind…"
8: When first I took up my *abode in the woods*…
9: The only *house* I had been the owner of before…
10: I was seated by the *shore of a small pond*…
11: This *small lake* was of most value as a neighbor…
12: Though the *view from my door* was still more contracted…

In this series of paragraphs, number 10 deserves just a moment's additional attention because of what happens to it between A, when it first appears in the manuscript, and Thoreau's re-writing of it in F. This is another subplot in the larger narrative of the chapter's revision history. That sentence about being seated by the shore is absent in A. In A, the paragraph begins with words that would be incorporated into the *second* sentence of paragraph 10 in the published *Walden*: "When I looked out on the face of the pond, it reminded me of a tarn…" (HM 924, 1:79). It is in F that we encounter the first iteration of what would become the initial sentence of the paragraph, which now begins, "I was seated by the shore of a beautiful pond, somewhat higher than the village of Concord, in the midst of an extensive wood between that town and Lincoln…" (HM 924, 6:13–14). What had changed between A and F that might have been a factor in Thoreau's decision to add this new first sentence? As we have seen, between A and F, in D, Thoreau had introduced that pun on a home as a seat. Now, in F, he seems to be building on the pun. Thoreau is not merely *sitting* by the shore of a beautiful pond but *seated* there: established, rooted in the location that it is fit for him to occupy at this season of his life. And from this seat, as he looks out on the face of the pond, the landscape does indeed radiate from him.

Let us skip paragraph 13 (the pivot point) for now and move ahead to paragraph 14.

Paragraph 14 is all about time: about morning and awakening. In it, time is joined to purpose: to what Thoreau is living for. "To be awake," he writes near the bottom of the paragraph, "is to be alive" (*W* 90). And as he will explain in paragraph 16, he came to the pond and the woods because "I did not wish to live what was not life."

From paragraph 14 onward, the emphasis of the entire chapter shifts from *where Thoreau lived* to *what he lived for*, to his own sense of purpose in life, often in contrast to how he sees others living (*W* 90–98). With this shift in emphasis comes, in many paragraphs, a concomitant shift in emphasis from space to time:

> **15:** We must learn to *reawaken* and keep ourselves awake, not by mechanical aids, but by an *infinite expectation of the dawn*...
> **16:** I went to the woods because I wished to live deliberately...and not, *when I came to die*, discover that I had not lived.
> **17:** The nation itself, with all its so called internal improvements...is just such an unwieldy and overgrown establishment.... *It lives too fast.*
> **18:** Why should we live with such *hurry* and waste of life?
> **19:** There was *such a rush*, as I hear, the other day at one of the offices to learn the foreign *news* by the last arrival...
> **20:** The preacher, instead of vexing the ears of drowsy farmers on their day of rest at the *end of the week*...should shout with thundering voice,—*"Pause! Avast! Why so seeming fast, but deadly slow?"*
> **21:** When we are *unhurried* and wise, we perceive that only great and worthy things have any *permanent and absolute* existence...
> **22:** Let us *spend one day* as deliberately as Nature...
> **23:** *Time* is but the stream I go a-fishing in.

This shift in emphasis is exactly that—it is not as though space drops out of the picture in the second half of the chapter. It would be odd if it did, if for no other reason than that it is difficult to talk about time without treating it metaphorically as space, as in the example of time as a stream, or the present moment as a point on a line, with eternity stretching out on either side of it. In fact, as the chapter's emphasis shifts from space to time in paragraph 14, we are offered a pointed contrast to linear metaphors of time. In the background of all the talk in 14 about morning, awakening, and renewal is the metaphor of time as a circle.

Paragraph 14 helps set the stage for the concluding words of *Walden*, not written until the final or G draft of the manuscript, with its assertion that there is "more day to dawn" (*W* 333). But 14 goes through extensive revisions in the B and F versions, and it is worth touching momentarily on one of these: the introduction in B, and revision in F, of Thoreau's sentence about the bathing tub of King Tching-thang: "They say that characters were engraven on the bathing tub of king Tching-thang to this effect: 'Renew thyself completely each day; do it again, and again, and forever again'" (*W* 88).

Thoreau inserts the sentence about the bathing tub of King Tching-thang between the third and fourth sentences of the paragraph, right after the description of his own ritual of bathing daily in the pond, a sentence that links time (he bathes "daily") and space (in the "pond").

In B, Thoreau adds the sentence vertically in the left margin of a leaf, in pencil, and the wording is not yet "again, and again, and forever again" but rather "anew, and anew, and forever anew" (HM 924, 2:91). In addition, he begins the sentence in B with the words "I have since read that," before canceling those words with a line. There is evidence that Thoreau had indeed recently read this anecdote about King Tching-thang at the time of the B draft of *Walden*; that is, 1849. A manuscript leaf not in HM 924 but from a commonplace book that Thoreau kept between 1841 and 1851, now in the Berg Collection at the New York Public Library, contains, at the top, his transcription and—as it turns out—translation of words about the bathing tub of Tching-thang. There the words are "do it anew, again anew, and always anew," and it is possible to see that he has penciled the word "regenerate" just above "do it anew" (Commonplace book 1841–1851, 129). Thoreau identifies as his source for the quotation an 1841 French translation by Guillaume Pauthier of the "Four Books," a collection of Confucian classics (Commonplace book 1841–1851, 127).[8] His "anew, again anew, and always anew" in the commonplace book is a faithful translation of Pauthier's "de *nouveau*, encore de *nouveau*, et toujours de *nouveau*"

(Pauthier 1841, 12). In F as in B, however, he adjusts his translation to make it more concise and arguably a little closer to idiomatic English: "anew, and anew, and forever anew" (HM 924, 6:20).

Close examination of the first "anew" in F reveals that Thoreau appears to start to write a "g" following the "a" rather than an "n," suggesting that "again"—the word he ultimately chooses, and which sounds still more idiomatic than "anew"—is already under consideration in his mind.

On the page proof this passage reads, "again, and again, and forever again" (HM 925, 32); presumably it also read that way in the final, fair copy of the manuscript provided to the printer, which, as mentioned earlier, has been lost.

To review, then: the original core, in A, of what would eventually become a chapter titled "Where I Lived, and What I Lived For," consisted of nine paragraphs, some of which would be expanded, or in other ways substantially revised, in subsequent drafts. Originally in A, paragraph 23, the "Time is but the stream" paragraph, followed immediately on 16, which began, "I went down to the pond because I wished to live deliberately." But then, as we have seen, Thoreau canceled 23, added 17, and recopied 23. Even in this initial phase, we have a few paragraphs—8, 9, and 10—emphasizing Thoreau's *location*, and another handful of paragraphs—14–17, plus 23—that seem to give more emphasis to Thoreau's *purpose* in going to the pond.

But then, across versions D through G, Thoreau builds out on either side of paragraph 13, retaining the placement of 23 as the final paragraph but pushing it away from 17 by bringing in 18–22 from the portion of the manuscript that would become the chapter "Sounds," where they were part of a general reflection on time and purpose. In the end, we have a dozen paragraphs very much focused on where Thoreau lived, with lots of language about place and space, and ten paragraphs very much focused on what Thoreau lived for, with lots of language about time.

We have said that the chapter pivots on paragraph 13. Let us go there now.

The Pivot

In the published *Walden*, paragraph 13 begins, "Both place and time were changed" (*W* 87). In A, the language is even more emphatic: "Both place and time had undergone a revolution" (HM 925, 1:80). Thoreau continues in A, "and I dwelt nearer to those eras in history which had attracted me, and as I had no clock nor watch, but the sun & moon, I also lived in primitive time."

Thus the paragraph that pivots us from place to time, from where Thoreau lived to what he lived for, begins by putting place and time together. A revolution of place and time makes Thoreau feel, at first, as though he dwelt in those eras in history that attracted him. But something is missing. History is time. What about place? Thoreau adds the phrase "to those parts of the globe &" ahead of "to those eras in history," keeping place and time in the same order as farther up in the sentence. The revised sentence reads, "Both place and time had undergone a revolution and I seemed to dwell nearer *to those parts of the globe &* to those eras in history which had attracted me, and as I had no clock nor watch, but the sun & moon, I also lived in a more primitive and absolute time" (emphasis added).

With neither clock nor watch, with only sun and moon to orient himself chronologically, it is as if Thoreau has been transported to a primitive time. Well, not *exactly* primitive: on the manuscript page, we can see that Thoreau has inserted both "a more" and "and absolute" as qualifiers, yielding "a more primitive and absolute time." "Absolute" is an interesting addition. It suggests that the revolution Thoreau is describing took him not simply back in time but onto some other temporal plane altogether, to a time that is no time and every time, a time outside of time.

Like Thoreau's sentences about living deliberately in paragraph 16, the first sentence of paragraph 13, in A, develops into a complex structure of parallelisms: a main clause connected by a coordinating conjunction to two further clauses, that, with their own internally coordinated rhythms (including a subordinate clause shown here off to the right) elaborate on the revolution in Thoreau's experience.

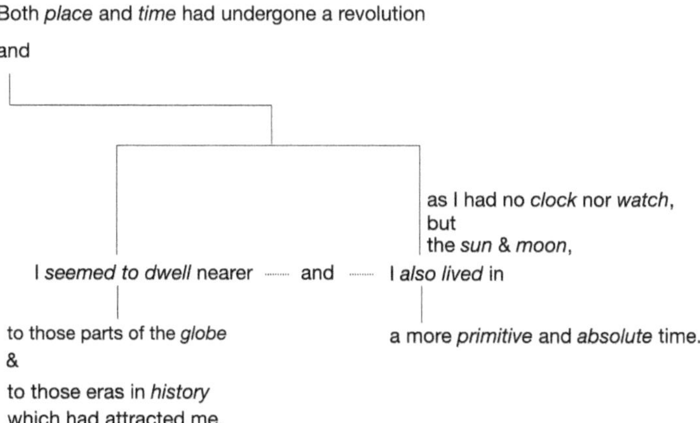

However, after all this tinkering in A, Thoreau scraps much of it in the published *Walden*. No more "revolution": place and time are simply "changed." No more sun, moon, clock, or watch; no more primitive and absolute time here or in "Sounds." Instead, we read, "Both place and time were changed, and I dwelt nearer to those parts of the universe and to those eras in history which had most attracted me" (*W* 87). Some interesting things get lost in the process, including the wonderful double meaning of the word "revolution," which can denote both a turning and a rupture. But perhaps the sentence as revised for the published version is stronger for being more compact and direct, its balanced structure more readily discerned.

The next sentence in A does not appear in *Walden* as published; after it, in A, a new paragraph goes on as follows:

> Where I lived was as far off as many a region viewed nightly by astronomers. We are apt to imagine rare and delectable places afar off whither astronomers look, in some remote and more celestial corner of the system, behind the constellation of Cassiopeia's Chair, far from noise & disturbance. I imagined that my house actually had its site in such a withdrawn, but forever new and unprophaned part of the universe. If it were worth the while to settle in those parts of the system near to the Pleiades or the Hyades, or Orion or Aldebaran, then I was really there, or at an equal remoteness from the life which I had left behind–as near to the immortal city–dwindled &

> twinkling with as fine a ray to my nearest neighbor and only to be seen in moonless nights by him. (HM 924, 1:80–81)

In view of all the talk here about constellations, systems, and stars, it is not hard to see why Thoreau would ultimately alter his reference to "parts of the globe" in the first sentence of the final version of the paragraph, so that it becomes, in the published *Walden*, "parts of the universe" (*W* 88).

The manuscript of A shows Thoreau giving a great deal of thought to the celestial references in this paragraph. Having begun by writing "to the Pleiades or the Hyades, or Orion or Aldebaran" he once again uses the space between the lines to brainstorm. Though impossible to reconstruct with any certainty, his sequence of revisions appears to be something like the following: he revises "Hyades, or" to "Hyades, to" by canceling "or" and interlining "to" in pencil; changes "Orion or Aldebaran" to "to Lyra or Orion or Aldebaran" by inserting "to Lyra or" in pencil; flirts, in pencil, with substituting "or Lyra or Andromeda" without canceling "Orion or Aldebaran"; pencils a series of other options—"Capella," "Procyon," "Sirius," "Altair," "Arcturus"—as candidates to pair either with "Orion" or "Aldebaran"; cancels the whole list, along with "Lyra or Orion" and "Lyra or Andromeda," using a single, wavy, penciled line; pencils "or Arcturus" after Aldebaran above the line, using a caret to position it before the comma, and "or Altair" below the line after the comma. By the time he re-copies this passage in F, if not before, he has resolved the final choice between "Arcturus" and "Altair" in favor of the latter, and he retains the choice in the published *Walden*: "to the Pleiades or the Hyades, to Aldebaran or Altair" (HM 924, 6:18–19; *W* 88).

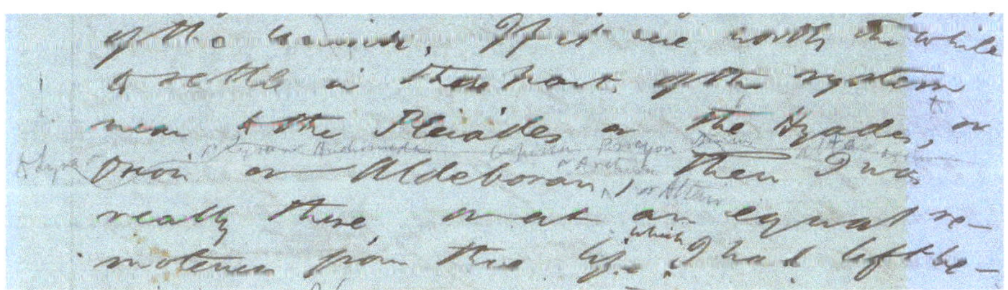
of the universe, If it were worth the while
to settle in those parts of the system
near to the Pleiades or the Hyades, or
Orion or Aldebaran then I was
really there or at an equal remoteness from the life which I had left be-

It is no more possible to reconstruct Thoreau's thinking as he worked through these options than it is to reconstruct the order in which he marked the page, but it seems plausible to suppose that he is interested, above all, in the poetry of his choices. "Cassiopeia's Chair" is a near alliteration. The "Pleiades or the Hyades" is not alliterative, but both words have three syllables and, depending on how one pronounces the first (Plee-a-deez, Ply-a-deez, or Play-a-deez—all three pronunciations are in the dictionary) they are either rhyming or assonant. Thoreau's original choice, in ink, of "Orion or Aldebaran" provided two subsequent words with similar vowel sounds and similar-sounding word-endings. But "to Orion or Aldebaran" sounds a bit flat-footed, and it is just another pair of assonant words containing three or more syllables. "To Aldebaran or Arcturus" is nicely alliterative, but it, too, pairs words of three or more syllables. "To Aldebaran or Altair," in addition to being alliterative, has the advantage that both words begin with the same syllable: "Al."" The two-syllable "Altair" introduces some rhythmic variation, and it also enables Thoreau to end the sentence with a stressed syllable, which makes for a more emphatic conclusion.

Finally, we might notice that the stresses in the "Aldebaran"/"Altair" pairing are nearly the inverse of those in the "Pleiades"/"Hyades" pairing: stress on the initial syllable in "Pleiades"/"Hyades," stress on the following syllable in "Aldebaran"/"Altair," making the two word-pairs lovely complements.

Should we imagine that Thoreau, pen or pencil in hand, deliberated internally about his choices in just the way we have described? Of course not. But is it reasonable to suppose that, in composing, he constantly weighed syllable and stress, with an eye, in particular, towards parallelism and balance? That conjecture seems to us supported by the myriad revisions throughout the *Walden* manuscript that show Thoreau adjusting word choices and sentence structures in just such a fashion. We have already looked at two similarly motivated revisions in WIL: the sentence about living deliberately in paragraph 16 and the one about time and place in paragraph 23.

Meanwhile, we should note another inversion that takes place in this paragraph. After a dozen paragraphs about where Thoreau lived that represent space largely through his own perspective—from his life-stage-appropriate perception of every spot as a potential site for a house, to the view from his door, to the horizon that radiates from him at his seat on the pond's shore—paragraph 13 suddenly and dramatically, at its conclusion, pivots to represent Thoreau as he presumably appears to his nearest neighbor: "dwindled & twinkling with as fine a ray to my nearest neighbor and only to be seen in moonless nights by him" (HM 924, 1:81).

The effect of this inversion or pivot or—to use the word Thoreau eventually rejected, "revolution"—is perhaps best described as analogous to the effect of the so-called iris transition in film, where the visible screen content becomes a gradually shrinking circle and finally disappears in blackness, ending one scene, and a gradually widening circle introduces the next scene. In A, at least, the scene begun in paragraph 1 closes in night and darkness at the end of paragraph 13, with Thoreau a distant, twinkling star. As a new scene opens in paragraph 14, it is morning, and we are with Thoreau in his remote corner of the universe, once again seeing the world through his eyes: "Every morning was a cheerful invitation to make my life of equal simplicity and purity with nature herself" (HM 924, 1:81).

Of course, Thoreau's remote corner of the universe is in actuality only a mile from any neighbor, and this is the whole point of the paragraph. It is interesting to see how Thoreau sharpened the point through revision. "We are *apt* to imagine rare and delectable places afar off," in A, becomes, in F, and remains in the published version, "we are *wont* to imagine" (emphasis added)—possibly because "wont" conveys a greater sense of passive habit (HM 924, 1:80, 6:18; *W* 88). Certainly its origin in Middle English *wunian*—"to dwell, inhabit, exist; be accustomed, be used to"—is a better fit with the theme of dwelling that lies at the heart of the passage, the chapter's focus on "Where I Lived," and the book as a whole.

At the same time, "I *imagined* that my house actually had its site in such a withdrawn, but forever new and unprophaned part of the universe," in A, becomes, in F, and remains in the published *Walden*, "I *discovered* that my house actually had its site..." (HM 924, 1:81, 6:18; *W* 88; emphasis added). Surely "discovered" is a better fit than "imagined" with the word "actually," a word whose significance to Thoreau in this sentence is made plain by his decision, in A, to relocate it from after "site" to after "house," where it gains in emphasis.

The change to "I discovered" sets up a direct contrast with "we are wont to imagine": we *imagine* that we have to travel to a distant corner of the universe to achieve solitude and space for meditation, but Thoreau *discovered* that in actuality he could achieve the requisite remoteness by moving a short distance away. What we mistakenly imagine to require a radical change in our physical circumstances, we can actually achieve through a small geographic change and a radical shift in perspective. The results can be revolutionary.

Summing Up

The contrast between imaginary wants and real needs is central to everything that follows paragraph 13 in WIL and is of course central to *Walden*. Where he lived, what Thoreau lived *for* was to discover that which is truly real. "Be it life or death we crave only reality," as he writes in the "Sounds" stretch of A that subsequently moved (presumably in B or C) to what became paragraph 22 of WIL (HM 924, 1:123). Unfortunately, too many people are looking for reality in all the wrong places: "I perceive that we inhabitants of Concord live this mean life, that we do," he writes in A, originally in that same "Sounds" stretch of the manuscript, "because our vision does not penetrate the surface of things–we think that that *is* which *appears* to be" (HM 924, 1:118).

"In eternity there is indeed something true and sublime," he writes near the bottom of the same page. "But all these times & places & occasions are now." And then, at some point, in pencil, he adds: "& here."

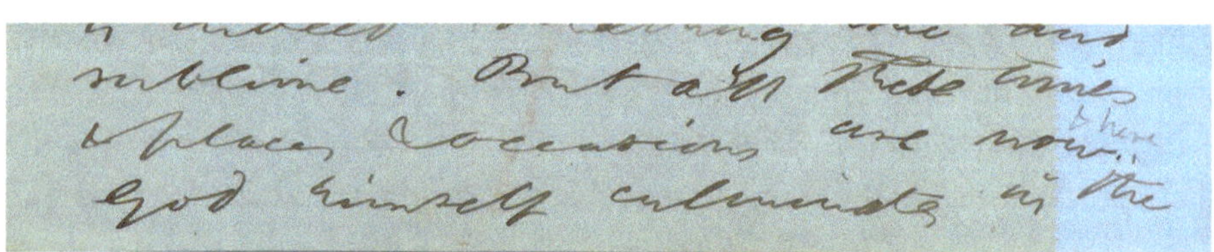
sublime. But all these times
& places & occasions are now. & here
God himself culminates in the

Once again, having begun by specifying a time, he emends to specify a place as well. "Now and here": time and place, purpose and location. Although we have seen that place gets more emphasis in the first half of WIL, while time and purpose get more emphasis in the second half, they are always, for Thoreau, inextricably linked. And in this sentence there is even a linking word: "occasions," that is, location-specific events in time. His use of the word here chimes with one that he retains in "Sounds," paragraph 2, the paragraph immediately preceding those he relocates to "Where I Lived": "A man must find his occasions in himself" (HM 924, 1:116; *W* 112).

"God himself culminates in the present moment," Thoreau goes on to say in "Where I Lived," version A, "and will never be more divine in the lapse of all the ages" (HM 924, 1:118, 122). The "present moment." That is the time and the space—the nick-shaped space in time—that Thoreau occupies, or at least seeks to occupy, at Walden. The present moment is both where he lives and what he lives for.

We have made a nice circle, one full revolution, one might say, and end where we began. As noted earlier, a large part of the attraction in studying Thoreau's revisions to *Walden* is the excitement of feeling that we are with Thoreau in the moment as he seeks the words that will best memorialize his quest for infinite renewal in a finite and densely material here and now.

We have noted that that feeling is an illusion, but it is important to recognize that it is no more an illusion than the feeling, when we read Thoreau's printed words, that he is here, now, speaking to us in the nick of time. It is no more an illusion than the sense that reading his printed words somehow makes his thought present to us as a continuous stream.

As readers, whether of printed texts or manuscripts, these illusions are, in some sense, where we live and what we live for. Meanwhile, the effort to understand a writer's revisions has this advantage, at least, over the effort to understand a text merely through its published words: it awakens us, again and again and forever again, to the reality that every publication belies the fluidity of thought that gave it life.

Works Cited

Bryant, John L. *The Fluid Text: A Theory of Revision and Editing for Book and Screen*. Ann Arbor: University of Michigan Press, 2002.

Clapper, Ronald E. "The Development of Walden: A Genetic Text." PhD diss., University of California, Los Angeles, 1967.

Dean, Bradley P. and Ronald Wesley Hoag, "Thoreau's Lectures before Walden: An Annotated Calendar." *Studies in the American Renaissance* (1995): 148–208 passim.

Pauthier, Jean-Pierre-Guillaume. *Confucius et Mencius: les quatre livres de philosophie morale et politique de la Chine*. Paris: Charpentier, 1841.

Sattelmeyer, Robert. "Thoreau's Projected Work on the English Poets." *Studies in the American Renaissance* (1980): 239–257.

Shanley, J. Lyndon. *The Making of "Walden," with the Text of the First Version*. University of Chicago Press, 1957.

Thoreau, Henry David. "[Commonplace Book]. Signed, undated," 1841–1851. The New York Public Library Digital Collections. https://digitalcollections.nypl.org/items/b80117a0-7e3a-0132-11ef-58d385a7bbd0.

CHAPTER 14

FORMS OF THE CHRONOTOPE IN THOREAU'S *CAPE COD*

Albena Bakratcheva

Cape Cod is Thoreau's fourth full-length book. Though he did not live long enough to see it in print, Thoreau kept on working on it until literally his final months, just as he tinkered with *Walden* to the last pending publication.[1] The work on the two books often overlapped[2] in the course of the extremely intense last decade of Thoreau's life, when the equation of Life with Art was not only the perfect mode of being for Thoreau, but when living had already been "simplified" to writing—and writing to living—to such an extent that the end of writing could only come—as it did—with the end of the writer's life. *Cape Cod* was published posthumously in 1865.

In the very end of his life Thoreau is known to have wished for *Walden* to be further published without the subtitle; perhaps the subtitle "or, Life in the Woods" already seemed limiting the limitless depths of his pure symbol; and perhaps his arranging for the posthumous publication of *Cape Cod*, which was never given a subtitle, also influenced this final wish. While *Walden* is Thoreau's limitless and timeless universe, *Cape Cod* is Thoreau's limitless *narration* which "extends" Time under the shadow of death, thus suggesting a particular manner of *carpe diem* writing, hitherto unexplored by Thoreau. *Cape Cod* turns out to be that travelogue of Thoreau's whose very narration equals life—conversely, the lack of narration would have equaled death, or the end of (life)Time.

Though *Walden* and *Cape Cod* were written and continuously revised in the years of Thoreau's shift towards what we now call ecocentrism, the relation between the two books is not of that kind. While living at Walden Thoreau became a writer, as Laura Dassow Walls so nicely emphasized in her recent biography of Thoreau;[3] after the two years at the pond, however, only the writing of *Walden* could bring Thoreau back to the lost harmony with nature. The experiment with life had been successful, but was over.

More and more, living "deliberately" was becoming possible only through and in writing—until writing began to literally retain living. *Cape Cod* is exactly that kind of book—a book retaining life. *Walden* celebrates the triumph of life; *Cape Cod* also asserts the triumph of life, but in the face of death. If *Walden* is a narrative about Thoreau's Homeric experiment,[4] *Cape Cod* is Thoreau's *Homeric narration*—his narration about human and nonhuman nature, his narration for the sake of narration itself which fully employs the classical epical, or Homeric life-asserting power.

Walden Pond was Thoreau's focus—the perfect place for a deliberate, "simplified" life, as well as the perfect symbol of that life. Thus, the writing about this life had to be perfect—crystal clean, ideally composed, symmetrical. *Walden* doubtlessly is Thoreau's masterful artistic harmony achieved. As most Thoreau scholars agree, there is something *heroic* in both the Walden experiment with life and the writing of it; quite naturally, during the two years at the pond the *Iliad* was Thoreau's constant companion.[5] But time had passed since those two years and though he had been "accustomed to make excursions to the ponds within ten miles of Concord," as Thoreau says in the beginning of *Cape Cod*, he had "latterly extended [his] excursions to the sea-shore" (*CC* 3). The ocean, however, cannot be a focus; it is all but the symbol of peaceful concentration. If Walden had been Thoreau's "own" pond, the ocean could not possibly be "his." This was as evident, as it was sought after. Thoreau had already stated in the end of *Walden* that he would not walk a trodden path, i.e. that he would not do again what he had already done. So he changed locus. Cape Cod was a very different place which also unlocked a very different sense of Time; and this was a somewhat changed and changing Thoreau, already declaring a preference for extended travels and employing a different narrational chronotope. If in the last decade of his life Thoreau's thinking was shifting towards ecocentrism, as Lawrence Buell has so convincingly shown,[6] Thoreau's travels to Cape Cod and the book they resulted in are rather the expression of *another shift* which has to do with accumulated life experience and thoughts of death.

In *Cape Cod*, however, there is no trace of desolation or Weltschmerz. Just like *Walden*, it is by no means an "ode to dejection;" just as in *Walden*, in *Cape Cod* Thoreau rejects such a Coleridgean state of mind again: but in different ways. One of these ways is *humor*. In *Cape Cod* Thoreau fully sets free his sense of humor—subdued in almost all his other work, in this book

Thoreau's humor flows freely, often tending towards irony and sarcasm, but never towards bitter misanthropy. If *Walden* counterpoints ecstasy to quiet desperation, *Cape Cod* is Thoreau's humorous anti-ode to dejection.

But Thoreau's major way to counterbalance dejection in *Cape Cod* is via *narration itself*. This book narrates with the immense passion and power of *the classical epic* to encompass virtually everything: its narrative flows into the realms of history, philology, geography, geology, botany, zoology, ichthyology, fishing and whaling, local and ethnic history, sailing and navigation, the history of New France and that of New England, the Vikings and North America, etc. Thoreau's vast competence in everything he narrates shows everywhere in the text. What also becomes apparent is Thoreau's exceptional philological training, his fluency in Greek, Latin, and at least four modern languages included. In *Cape Cod*, Thoreau's sense of language takes a direction as yet unexplored in his other work, a *classical epical* direction, inasmuch as his narration in this book often acquires the Homeric functionality of language not only to preserve and perpetuate the told, but also to make existent only the told, to truly make it appear to the audience.[7] In *Cape Cod* Thoreau revives this essential power of language and transforms it into a life-saving instrument. If while living at Walden Pond he had had the *Iliad* with him, in *Cape Cod* he would rather narrate like Homer—or in the most detailed manner, sticking to the very Homeric one-layer storytelling[8] where everything is equally significant—the oyster on the Atlantic shore as much as the Atlantic itself. In addition, not only would *Cape Cod* be filled with quotations from Homer in the original, but the ocean itself would be made to "speak" ancient Greek: "I put in a little Greek now and then, partly because it sounds so much like the ocean," Thoreau explains in order to add in a footnote: "We have no word in the English language to express the sound of many waves, dashing at once, whether gently or violently, πολυφλοίσβοιος to the ear, and, in the ocean's gentle moods, an ἀνάριθμον γέλασμα to the eye" (*CC* 51). It is this classical, or Homeric power of narration which is the enormous Time- and Life-preserving power of Thoreau's "oceanic" narrative—*Cape Cod*. In the essay "Walking," which he wrote in the early 1850s and revised through his last years of life, Thoreau declares that "in literature it is only *the wild* [italics mine] that attracts us;" and if "in wildness is the preservation of the world," then it is the classical "wildness" of *Cape Cod*'s *narration* that represents the preservation of Life (*Exc* 207, 202). As Ronald W. Hoag nicely puts it, "the wild is Thoreau's name for the boundlessness of nature in all its forms, including the *wild speech* [italics mine] that suggests nature's ultimate unfathomableness."[9] *Cape Cod*'s extensive narration is mature Thoreau's *writerly way* to "improve," as he puts it in *Walden*, "the Nick of Time" (*W* 17).

Amos Bronson Alcott, a close friend and fellow Concordian, thought of Thoreau as "belonging to the Homeric age"; Thoreau's prose Alcott found unsurpassable in "substance and pith," "dealing with objects as if they were shooting forth from his mind *mythologically*."[10] Although focused on Thoreau the natural philosopher, Alcott seems to have been among the very first to point to Thoreau's epic mode of expression. *Cape Cod* offers a very interesting case here: it records Thoreau's already more empirical or scientific thinking while still never losing its poetical or transcendental aura; at the same time, it unfolds as a narrative in a distinctively classical epical manner. As Lawrence Buell has noted, Thoreau often engaged a "strategy of substantialization,"[11] adding representational detail, particularly natural phenomena, to his excursion narratives. Thoreau pursues this strategy in *Cape Cod* in multiple registers, including the employment of typically epical modes and devices. In this book more than anywhere in his work Thoreau revives and explores the very essence and energy of classical narration, with all its verbal powers to eternalize and entertain. Like, for instance, this meticulously drawn image which fully exhausts the potentials of particularity without becoming exhausting at all, but rather provokes a desire for even more fresh and pleasing detail: "The great number of windows in the ends of the houses, and their irregularity in size and position, here and everywhere on the Cape, struck us agreeably,—as if each of the various occupants who had their *cunabula* behind had punched a hole where his necessities required it, and, according to his size and stature, without regard to outside effect. There were windows for the grown folks, and windows for the children,—three or four apiece; as a certain man had a large hole cut in his barn-door for the cat, and another smaller one for the kitten" (*CC* 62).

As Thoreau was considered Homeric, *Cape Cod* has been seen as Thoreau's epic,[12] but this categorization has been more figurative, not a recognition of Thoreau's debt to the epic tradition as such. Considering the text's literary contexts and in particular its classical epicality helps to make sense of the at times antagonistic critical judgement the book has received, having been labeled both Thoreau's sunniest and darkest book.[13] Moreover, classical epic mode in this case promises to be a key to mature Thoreau himself—Thoreau of the last decade of his life, finding his ways to cope with the passage of Time.

Thoreau begins *Cape Cod* with an elliptical allusion to Alcott: "I did not see why I might not make a book on Cape Cod, as well as my neighbor on 'Human Culture.' It is but another name for the same thing" (*CC* 3). In addition, Thoreau offers a definition of his book: it will be on "the same thing;" the titles will be made synonymous, their meaning "sandy" enough to incorporate, in effect, everything. Besides being an instance of Thoreau's typical metaphorical move to connect the specific with the abstract, this is also an advance notice of the large-scale scope of the book. *Cape Cod*, this is to say, will be an epic text.

Cape Cod opens with the author explicitly addressing his reader, a format that it will stick to throughout. The first thing Thoreau does in this book is turn to his readers and, thereby, outline his own figure as the author. The narrative therefore directly acquires the character of a something *told* by someone to another, its purely narrational, or epical capacities coming into focus. In fact, *Cape Cod* began with most successful lectures before the lyceums in Concord, Danvers, and Clinton in 1850 and 1851[14] and in this book, more than elsewhere in his work, Thoreau lays bare the orality of the book's prehistory and insists on the *oral* powers of the written text. Phrases like "we were told," "it is said," "we heard," etc., are abundant throughout Thoreau's book, as if to reinforce the impression that it is *a story told*, or a narrative that fully explores all the potentials of narration and, moreover, makes its own narration explicit. When such declarations of verbal sources persist, as Tzvetan Todorov astutely observes, there is "no need to scratch out the origin of narrative in time," as "it is time that originates in narrative;"[15] *Cape Cod*'s underscored orality produces exactly this effect.

In addition to evoking the age-old format of storytelling, Thoreau points to the "single companion" he had in his Cape Cod journey, which also contributes to the atmosphere of telling and listening, an ongoing process of conversing. But while William Ellery Channing accompanied Thoreau on two of the three Cape Cod visits described in the book, Thoreau also had another and, what's more, permanent companion to converse with in his travels: namely his reader.

In the course of his journey, Thoreau often reads and quotes from what he reads, making his reader read as if simultaneously along with him and, moreover, making the reader constantly aware that he, the writer, is a reader too: "The reader will imagine us, all the while, steadily traversing that extensive plain...and reading under our umbrellas" (*CC* 40). The *reading process* thus becomes both narrative device and part of the narrated story: that of the two travelers-readers exploring Cape Cod. Thoreau's "written epic situation"[16] not only presupposes/requires a reader who would constantly and explicitly be addressed in the (written) text, but also offers an author-reader-traveler (who is moreover accompanied by another reader-traveler). Therefore, the enormous amount of lengthy citations from histories, chronicles, "old accounts," geography books, etc. in *Cape Cod* is not merely set out in the format of vast reading done both during and before the period of travel, but also presented with a special emphasis on the reading process as a vital activity for both author-protagonist and his reader. *Cape Cod* shows Thoreau throughout this excursion always with a book in his hands, his reading and writing flowing into one another and forming a narrative which lays bare its readability and perpetually provokes its own reading.

If *Walden* has its chapter on "Reading," *Cape Cod* is very much a book about reading and writing which *tells* extensively and, at the same time, discusses extensive telling, thereby reviving *literary* traditions of genuinely epical nature such as those of the earliest times of the *novel*, when Henry Fielding, an epical writer of his own right who made explicit discourse with the reader an inherent trait of his books, dubbed the emerging genre nothing other than a "comic epic in prose."[17] There are moments when Thoreau, fully in Fielding's novelistic manner, focuses the reader's awareness on the reading process, as if to measure the sense of what is being told. For example, at the end of "The Plains of Nauset," following a series of excerpts from historical and liturgical sources, Thoreau says: "There was no better way to make the reader realize how wide and peculiar that plain was, and how long it took to traverse it, than by inserting these extracts in the midst of my narrative" (*CC* 43). While Walter Harding finds Thoreau here merely laughing "at the dullness of one of his chapters," the narrator's auto-commentary in this instance, very much in the tradition of Henry Fielding's, Tobias Smollett's, or Laurence Sterne's novels, is a clear case of a markedly present epic situation which goes along with the narrative about the Cape

Cod journey. Besides, the allusion to this very literary/epical context—even more interesting here as *Cape Cod* is a work of non-fiction—is reinforced by Thoreau's noting that his Cape Cod excursion was not intended "for a sentimental journey"[18] (*CC* 61).

Thoreau's mode of openly addressing the reader for the sake of providing a most vivid image is also apparent in his focus on sound. Thoreau's reader should ideally not only read, but hear too: "Though we might have indulged in some placid reflections of late, the reader must not forget that the dash and the roar of the waves were incessant. Indeed, it would be well if he were to read with a large conch-shell at his ear" (*CC* 100). As Philip F. Gura nicely puts it, "in that shell, as in *Cape Cod*, Thoreau wants us to hear nothing less than the sound of our own mortality."[19] Thoreau may even reach a fully onomatopoetic effect at the moment when he finds himself too focused on the desert and so turns to the sea: "All the while it was not so calm as the reader may suppose, but it was blow, blow, blow,—roar, roar, roar,—tramp, tramp, tramp,—without interruption" (*CC* 152). Such a passage expects as if to be *heard*, invites an *audience* in the strict meaning of the word, and thus calls to mind Homer and the oldest form of epical performance, that of singing and listening. When the inherent rhythm of Thoreau's writing – which, as American composer Charles Ives astutely observed, "were there nothing else, would determine his [Thoreau's] value as a composer"[20]—combines with the technique of directly involving the reader, one can even sometimes imagine Thoreau as the ancient rhapsode playing his harp and singing his story before his audience. The impression is so strong that it sounds very natural when Thoreau writes "Homer and the Ocean came in again with a rush," especially when this happens in Greek: "Ἐν δ᾿ ἔπεσ᾿ Ὠκεανῷ λαμπρόν φάος ἠελίοιο" (*CC* 117). Thoreau thus implies that the proper reading of his book should also include it "hearing," or the involvement of the ear along with that of the eye, and he finds the sound of Homer's language best for the purpose. For Thoreau the Transcendentalist, Homer's expression was "as if nature spoke," the pristine sound of nature's own language.

Cape Cod's many citations—predominantly in Greek, but in Latin too,—provoke and engage the reader's *knowledge* in the reading process and this happens not merely on a linguistic level. Thoreau presumes a reader quite knowledgeable in Greek and Latin in order to adequately read Thoreau's book, in fact, a reader as knowledgeable in the classics as the author, so as to share the same literary context and thus properly handle all the references to Homer, Ovid, Ossian, Rabelais, Chaucer, Boccaccio, and Shakespeare; to recognize who is "the blind bard of "Paradise Lost and Regained;" or catch the allusion to *A Sentimental Journey through France and Italy*. In addition, Thoreau's *Cape Cod* reader should have substantial knowledge in botany, zoology, history, geography, topography, etymology, philosophy, sailing, navigation, etc. Obviously, Thoreau's *Cape Cod* readers are supposed to be an inherent part of human culture themselves in order to be able to read and digest this polymathic book on human culture. And this comes into focus here more than anywhere else in Thoreau's work exactly because of the overall format of explicit discourse with the reader.

Thoreau invites, or rather requires his reader's *active participation* in the making of the meaning of his narrative, thus creating an image of a reader very "sagacious,"[21] and hence somewhat equal to the writer. This requirement is sometimes as intense as even to include the reader's own life experience: "The reader may remember this wreck, from the circumstance that a letter was found in the captain's valise…and from the trial which took place in consequence" (*CC* 56). In such cases author and reader share knowledge about realities of life as if independent of the processes of writing and reading, as if coming directly from their own daily experience. Having achieved such a degree of *closeness* to his reader, Thoreau can even ask him favors: "The reader will excuse my greenness,—though it is not sea-greenness, like his, perchance,—for I live by a river shore" (*CC* 53). Or he can safely play with his own name: "But whether Thor-finn saw the mirage here or not, Thor-eau, one of the same family, did" (*CC* 151). Along with so much more, *Cape Cod* is also, in fact, very much a book about names and naming. With the pristine energy of an American Adam Thoreau would seek back to the very origins of the names of places, or people, or plants, etc., and would retrace the history of the chosen name to the fullest extent. And, of course, he would need the constant partnership of his reader in his exploratory journey in etymology, which would unfold as a journey into the history of a place (Nauset, Cohasset, Truro, etc.), or into that of a botanical or zoological species, or yet again into the legendary or mythological past. All of these joint journeys with the reader are journeys in Time; but they are also journeys for the sake of Time—for the sake of the time "spent" with the reader; the more, the better—just as in the classical epic, just as in the classical epic mode of the early novel. But also—in

Thoreau's specific case—for the sake of the time grasped through writing—or *wording*.

In all possible ways Thoreau's *Cape Cod* reader is kept absorbed in an overall sense of journeying throughout the book. After all, Thoreau is telling the story of his own Cape Cod journey and is therefore both the narrator and the main character in his book, which duly qualifies as a travelogue too. Thoreau's Cape Code travelogue properly unfolds as the story of a journey in both Space and Time—the space of the Cape which the two companions "traverse" and the time of the journey(s); in other words, the chronotope of this story is that of a journey with its beginning, its course, and its ending in a specific space and time. However, the chronotope of the Cape Cod journey—Thoreau's "extended excursion" in space and time,—is one thing, while the Time of *Cape Cod*'s metanarrative—or the constantly tended discourse with the reader—is another. *By sticking to this metanarrative throughout the book Thoreau extends Time, or rather the configuration of Time in the book.* On the one hand, he does that in a distinctively traditional *literary* manner, by making his book deal *explicitly* with the processes of its own writing and reading; but on the other hand, in *Cape Cod*, Thoreau's only book preoccupied with death, such Time-extension acquires specific *existential*, or life-preserving significance.

Constantly implying[22] its reader, or rather the function of the reader, *Cape Cod* "gains" Time with that reader through extensive narration meant predominantly—in the classical epical tradition—to entertain. The many *Cape Cod* anecdotes certainly serve that purpose. However, they do not only bring in the fun of the story told, but also the fun of the *telling* of the story. They appear in the main narrative as inserted stories in the same manner the numerous lengthy citations from books come, but, unlike them, bring in the book the lively energy of the *spoken word*, thus contributing to the overall impression of a sustained *oral* epic. *Cape Cod* thus evokes the age-old format of *storytelling*. Thoreau's Wellfleet oysterman is the perfect storyteller: he is never done with his stories, his style of conversations is "coarse and plain" (*CC* 71), he talks "a steady stream" and is always ready to resume (77)—just like Homer, or Scheherezade, or Chaucer, or Boccaccio—or, of course, Henry Thoreau.

In fact, *Cape Cod* is very much a narrative consisting of stories told and listened to in the course of a journey and is thus very similar to Geoffrey Chaucer's *Canterbury Tales*, for instance. But above all it is a narrative that richly and panoramically unfolds as storytelling under the shadow of death very much in the manner of *The Arabian Nights*. *Cape Cod* opens with a most naturalistic picture of death, and death persists throughout the book in the form of shipwrecks, dead bodies, and the vast, black bottomlessness of the ocean. This picture of Chaos and Matter can only be grasped and neutralized by the grand power and energy of narration. Just as in *The Arabian Nights*, where "for Scheherazade narrative equals life and the lack of narrative equals death," as Tzvetan Todorov observes,[23] so too Thoreau's narrative equals life. And just as Scheherazade's model is applicable to Giovanni Boccaccio's *Decameron*, *Cape Cod* compares to *The Decameron* in being a narrative in the face of death. Boccaccio's book opens with a horrifying picture of the plague in Florence and points to the overall indifference at the sight of hundreds of dead bodies; Thoreau's book begins with the shocking picture of the shipwreck and the realization that "It is the individual and private that demands our sympathy. A man can attend but one funeral in the course of his life, can behold but one corpse" (*CC* 9). Both books then unfold as full-length narratives celebrating life.

So Thoreau did not see why he "might not make a book on Cape Cod"—and why not make this book be at once a book of America, a book of travel and adventure, of reading and writing, of nature and walking, on history and science, that is, in sum, a book on "human culture." The classical epic mode of *Cape Cod* is what makes it this all-encompassing book.

Usually Thoreau's first book, *A Week on the Concord and Merrimack Rivers*, is seen, in H. Daniel Peck's words, as his "most insistently and explicitly temporal work."[24] *Cape Cod* is also an insistently and explicitly temporal work; but its temporality is different. In this later book Thoreau does not explore the powers of memory; nostalgia is no longer his driving force; instead, in a masterfully classical literary manner *Cape Cod* textifies Time, thus keeping its nick wide open—the epically extended chronotope of the excursion of Life.

Works Cited

Alcott, Amos Bronson. "Thoreau," in *The American Transcendentalists: Their Prose and Poetry*. Edited by Perry Miller. New York: Doubleday Anchor Books, 1957.

Auerbach, Erich. *Mimesis: The Representation of Reality in Western Literature.* Princeton: Princeton University Press, 2013.

Buell, Lawrence. *The Environmental Imagination: Thoreau, Nature Writing, and the Formation of American Culture.* Cambridge: Harvard University Press, 1995.

———. *Henry David Thoreau: Thinking Disobediently*. New York: Oxford University Press, 2024.

Bridgman, Richard. *Dark Thoreau.* Lincoln: University of Nebraska Press, 1982.

Gura, Philip F. "A Wild, Rank Place: Thoreau's *Cape Cod.*" In *The Cambridge Companion to Henry David Thoreau*, edited by Joel Myerson. New York and London: Cambridge University Press, 1995.

Harding, Walter. *A Thoreau Handbook.* New York: New York University Press, 1959.

Hoag, Ronald W. "Thoreau's Later Natural History Writings." In *The Cambridge Companion to Henry David Thoreau*, edited by Joel Myerson. New York and London: Cambridge University Press, 1995.

Iser, Wolfgang. *The Implied Reader: Patterns of Communication in Prose Fiction from Bunyan to Beckett.* Baltimore: The Johns Hopkins University Press, 1978.

Ives, Charles. "Thoreau: Nature's Musician." In *Henry David Thoreau: A Profile*, edited by Walter Harding, New York: Hill and Wang, 1971.

McAleer, John J. "Thoreau's Epic *Cape Cod.*" In *Thought*, XLIII (Summer 1968), 227–246.

Peck, Daniel H. *Thoreau's Morning Work: Memory and Perception in "A Week on the Concord and Merrimack Rivers," the Journal, and "Walden."* New Haven/London: Yale University Press, 1990.

Romberg, Bertil. *Studies in the Narrative Technique of the First-Person Novel.* Stockholm: Norwood Editions, 1979.

Seybold, Ethel. *Thoreau: The Quest and the Classics.* New Haven: Yale University Press, 1951.

Todorov, Tzvetan. *The Poetics of Prose*. Oxford: Blackwell, 1977.

Laura Dassow Walls. *Henry David Thoreau: A Life*. Chicago and London: The University of Chicago Press, 2017.

CHAPTER 15

THE REMEDIATED WORLD OF THOREAU: A JOYFUL ACTIVE LEARNING PROJECT

Kathryn C. Dolan

This chapter begins with an observation. As universities increasingly emphasize practical and lucrative subjects, they have steadily moved focus—and funding—away from the humanities. This is a large part of the ongoing crisis in the humanities in U.S. universities. Meanwhile, there is a growing challenge to get students involved and interested in reading demanding texts, in making such works relevant to our current time. One way to bridge these competing forces is through the study of one of the most interdisciplinary authors in U.S. literature, Henry David Thoreau. He makes an interesting intervention in this moment, in the nick of time, as a literary figure who provides a useful guide for interdisciplinarity as well as foundational skills that the humanities emphasize, fostering informed, empathetic, and engaged citizens capable of addressing global challenges. For over twelve years, I have instituted an assignment in my U.S. literature classes that has resonated profoundly with students, even to the extent of being referenced by former students outside of class. This remediation assignment prompts students to reimagine a text from our class and transform it into a different medium. This process fosters a dynamic and joyful approach to engaging with classic American literature. In this chapter, I explore the efficacy of active learning within the realm of U.S. literature, specifically looking at the case of Thoreau's *Walden* (1854). I position myself within the discourse on theories of remediation as well as active and joyful learning, including Thoreau's own, and provide a detailed overview of the assignment's structure, accompanied by examples, project chart, and additional discussion and applications. As Thoreau did himself while teaching with his brother, John, I use an experiential approach in my remediation project. Ultimately, I hope to demonstrate how this approach breathes new life into work by esteemed U.S. authors like Thoreau, revitalizing students' connections to classic literature.

I have to date integrated the remediation assignment into fifteen of my seminar classes. Throughout, I have been amazed by the boundless creativity exhibited by students as they create projects across a wide variety of mediums including paintings, drawings, video games, music, digital media, board games, carpentry work, mixed-media art, needlework, and even baked goods. The process of transforming a story from one medium into another becomes a profound learning experience for students. In many respects, as Marshall McLuhan states, the medium truly is the message; as students reshape the form of a text, they gain valuable insights into the significance of both the original as well as the remediated forms. For example, as students reimagine Thoreau's *Walden*, they deepen their understanding of the language, themes, and style of this classic work in an immersive way. Thoreau is especially useful for an active learning assignment. He was himself a practical engineer, working as much with his hands as with his head, applying his critical thinking skills experientially. A project-based assignment that involves creativity, critical thinking, analysis, and communication teaches several skills that Thoreau encouraged in his own work. By closely engaging with a single text, students uncover new layers of meaning and explore fresh interpretations. The remediation assignment offers students a fun and fulfilling way to interact with the material, as well. They find joy in the creative process and discover that it enhances their overall delight in the original text. Thoreau encourages this kind of approach to learning in a Journal entry from June 23, 1840: "Not by constraint or severity shall you have access to true wisdom, but by abandonment and childlike mirthfulness" (*PJ* 1:140). Fundamentally, the remediation assignment uses an active and ideally joyful learning approach to enrich students' experience with classic literature, developing deeper engagement and understanding along the way.

Remediation

Media have always been in conversation with each other. I choose the term "remediation" advisedly. The concept of remediation, coined by Jay David Bolter and Richard Grusin in their much-cited work *Remediation* (1999), highlights the ongoing dialogue between different forms of media. Bolter and Grusin argue that all new technological advances in media essentially "present themselves as refashioned and improved versions of other media."[1] While they primarily focus on digital or new media, the concept extends to traditional forms as well. Intriguingly, I have observed that students often gravitate towards old rather than new media for their projects, demonstrating that remediation is not exclusive to topical digital platforms. For all the video games and computer graphic projects students create, there are perhaps twice as many embroidered wall hangings, clay models, and paintings produced. Bolter and Grusin allow for this as well, acknowledging that remediation has historical roots that transcend the digital age. "We can identify the same process throughout the last several hundred years of Western visual representation."[2] Media have continuously evolved by drawing inspiration from both past and present forms, emphasizing a dynamic interchange rather than a linear progression from old to new.

The term "remediation" is a flexible one, though, with similar projects often referred to as "adaptation," "transmediation," or "ekphrasis." Gabriele Rippl explores this plurality of theoretical terms within various fields, listing "theoretical concepts such as intermediality, multi- and plurimediality, intermedial reference, transmediality, intermedial methodology and related concepts such as visual culture, literary visuality, the musicalization of fiction and poetry, literary acoustics, remediation, adaptation, and multimodality etc."[3] Each form of media contributes to the communication, presentation, and experience of texts, adds Marie-Laure Ryan.[4] Henry Jenkins further explains this with his definition of transmedia storytelling, which involves narratives unfolding "across multiple media platforms...a more integrated approach to franchise development than models based on urtexts and ancillary products."[5] This approach, exemplified by franchises like Disney and Star Wars, emphasizes how transmedia works to expand a media constellation. In a conversation on transmedia engagement, Henry Jenkins and Richard Grusin theorize a hybrid and pleasurable way to materially engage with media.[6] In my course, projects embody the remediation concept, as students create original work not directly connected to media franchises. Students also explore the reasons behind their choices of medium and how those choices contribute to their deeper understanding of specific literary texts, as in the example of *Walden*. By sharing their work with the class, students create a collective experience that enriches their knowledge of both the original text and their chosen medium. This approach fosters creativity, experimentation, and meaningful student expression, enhancing their engagement with the course.[7]

Active and Joyful Learning

Since Jean Piaget's groundbreaking work on cognitive development of children and adolescents as well as constructivism in education during the early twentieth century, active and experiential learning has gained increasing popularity in academic settings. This approach encourages students to engage in their learning process through critical thinking, discussion, exploration, and creation. Charles Bonwell and James Eison emphasize the importance of engaging students in "higher order thinking tasks" for active learning to be truly effective, "in doing things and thinking about what they are doing."[8] This aligns with the core objectives of the remediation assignment, where students apply their understanding of literary texts and concepts. Discussing Thoreau's own active pedagogy, Martin Bickman observes, "Some progressive educators make the mistake of thinking it is enough for students to have experiences, but experiences are educative only if the students actively clarify, internalize, and reflect on them through their own language-making."[9] David Kolb's Learning Model, with its four components of active experimentation, concrete experience, reflective observation, and abstract conceptualization, offers a useful framework that underpins my chosen structure for the remediation assignment.[10] Students first imagine a remediated version of a story from the course (abstract), then bring it to life through the creation of a material artifact (active and concrete), and finally reflect on the process in an essay (reflective). Students thus create art, analyze their creation and its significance in the larger conversation about classic U.S. literature, and enjoy themselves. Moreover, they have the potential to cultivate empathy not only for the figures within the literary texts but also for the authors themselves, as well as for the broader world.[11]

In addition to its educational benefits, the process of remediation, where students recreate one form of media into another of their choosing, tends to offer a tangible sense of pleasure and accomplishment. These projects are not merely academic; they are also works of art in their own right. Discussing her pedagogy of engagement, bell hooks describes her style as "hopeful and exuberant," conveying "the pleasure and joy I experience teaching."[12] In this way, she mirrors Thoreau's own philosophy, stated in "Natural History of Massachusetts" (1842), that "surely joy is the condition of life" (*Exc* 5). hooks' emphasis on joy in pedagogy aligns with the broader movement in Black feminist activism, where joy is valued as an essential tool for addressing challenging topics. For example, U.S. literature courses often wrestle with critical issues such as racism, imperialism, misogyny, and the exploitation of the beyond-human world. Integrating joy into the curriculum serves as an important strategy to help students navigate these complex and difficult subjects. By participating in creative endeavor within a supportive environment, students are encouraged to explore their creative potential and tackle new challenges. Through this combination of joy and academic engagement as applied to authors such as Thoreau, students are better prepared to deal with complex issues and develop deeper understanding of the world around them.

The joyful aspect of this remediation assignment carries particular significance in a STEM-focused university environment where engineering students often undertake literature courses as part of their general education requirements. Jean J. Ryoo emphasizes the importance of joy in traditional STEM courses, noting that joy is needed "for supporting young people's critical thinking skills and communicative competence that sit at the heart of all fields of study."[13] Additionally, Richard Utz observes that the material nature of creative projects in a humanities course within a STEM-focused university adds a "joyfully communal, holistic, and applied dimension" to the educational experience.[14] As observed in my classes, the remediation assignment not only brings the students joy throughout the learning unit but also brings a sense of community as projects are shared among classmates through presentations. The hands-on, "maker" aspects of the assignment further demonstrate its applied nature, enriching the more analytical elements of literary analysis with a holistic perspective.[15]

My remediation assignment is part of a rich tradition of active learning initiatives in literature and composition courses. In the 1990s, for example, Carol S. Loranger devised a project that asked students to examine the cost of living in Dayton, Ohio, as depicted in Horatio Alger's novel, *Ragged Dick* (1868). Presenting their findings sparked "a lively and unpredictable discussion of Alger's novel and comparative class and economic politics in the United States from the Gilded Age to the era of diminished expectations," providing invaluable historical context for students reading the novel.[16] Similarly, in the 2010s, Heather Snyder introduced a creative assignment where students visually interpreted their chosen text through drawing. Students found the project to be "interesting and enjoyable," contributing positively to their learning experience.[17] Examples such as these demonstrate the increasing significance and popularity of innovative and enjoyable assignments in literature and writing classes over several decades. They not only complement objectives related to critical thinking, effective communication, and research skill development but also allow creativity, enthusiasm, innovation, and practical application of knowledge. Thoreau has been the subject of pedagogical study, as well, as seen in the 2017 issue of *The Concord Saunterer* on "Teaching Thoreau at 200: A Roundtable." The educators involved focused on a variety of topics to engage with Thoreau in the modern classroom, such as teaching his Journal and other texts, teaching his work in other cultures, and teaching him geared specifically toward twenty-first century students. A key theme throughout these essays was to bring students outside to study Thoreau, "stepping away from technology and the noise of day-to-day life in order to focus on surroundings and appreciate the landscape. This simple and effective activity is a favorite of students, and immerses them in the ideas of Transcendentalism," writes Luke Sundermeier and Heather Bise.[18]

Thoreau himself was a proponent of active education. In a letter to reformer Orestes Brownson on December 30, 1837, asking for a recommendation for a teaching position, Thoreau wrote, "Perhaps I should give some account of myself. I would make education a pleasant thing both to the teacher and the scholar. This discipline, which we allow to be the end of life, should not be one thing in the schoolroom, and another in the street. We should seek to be fellow students with the pupil, and we should learn of, as well as with him, if we would be most helpful to him" (*Cor* 1: 31). Thoreau spent a substantial amount of time teaching in his early career. In 1835 he worked with Brownson as a teacher in Canton, Massachusetts. He famously quit his teaching position in the Concord public school after three weeks, then started his own school in 1838 with his brother, John, and taking on the name Concord Academy shortly thereafter. Jonathan Kozol observes, "some of his most invigorating writing draws upon the hours that he spent outside the classroom with his pupils."[19] While the school was a moderate success, it was forced to close in 1841 due to John's ongoing battle with tuberculosis. Thoreau did not have a career as a teacher in the way we might consider one in the modern sense, yet he remained interested in pedagogy, writing of it in his Journal and in letters throughout his life. On March 21, 1856, while making sugar from red maple sap, Thoreau observed, "I noticed that my fingers were purpled evidently from the sap on my auger. Had a dispute with father about the *use* of my making this sugar when I knew it could be done—& might have bought sugar cheaper at Holden's. He said it took me from my studies. I said I made *it* my study. I felt as if I had been to a university" (OJT 20: 162). Throughout his life, Thoreau engaged with experiential learning in ways that resonate with modern theories of pedagogy.[20]

In my twelve years of teaching the remediation assignment, students have consistently expressed deep appreciation for the work. They particularly enjoy the hands-on nature of devising their projects, discovering that remediation embodies a combination of immediacy and hypermediacy. They value the level of creative control over the projects afforded to them, allowing for the cultivation of new skills or refinement of existing ones. However, along with their enthusiasm, students often find themselves surprised by the challenges presented in these projects, which are often more demanding than originally anticipated. They must perform repeated readings of the original work, which prompts them to scrutinize the author's choices, occasionally encountering frustration with elements such as vocabulary that may not align as well as desired with their chosen projects. Nevertheless, these same students usually develop a deeper admiration for the author's original decisions, recognizing the inherent "rightness" of those writing choices. Snyder notes that "some students appeared resistant to the project at the start of the semester."[21] I have also observed that students at times are resistant to the novel form of this assignment, at least at first. Other potential risks may include the corruption of quotes, propagation of clichés, and the role of AI software tools such as ChatGPT. Engaging with a single work of literature over an extended period, typically around five weeks, creates for students a profound connection with the text, leading to a greater appreciation for its complexities.

The Assignment

The remediation assignment constitutes 250 points, equivalent to 25% of the students' total semester grade based on a 1000-point grading system. It contains four distinct components: a) a rough-draft worth 25 points—graded checked or not-checked—primarily focused on the viability, process, and application of sources; b) the core remediation project itself, valued at 100 points; c) a presentation of the project, also worth 25 points and graded on a checked or not-checked basis; and d) an accompanying essay discussing the remediation process, including an external academic source that theorizes active learning, also valued at 100 points. While the assignment evaluates students' efforts and creativity, it does not demand perfection. Encouraging students to take on challenging projects allows them to explore their creativity and engage deeply with the material, even if their skills in a particular medium are not as developed as other students'. This approach can help students build confidence, resilience, and a fuller appreciation for literature and creative expression while fostering a supportive learning environment where the focus is on growth and exploration, rather than solely on polished outcomes.

Examples of remediation projects

I will now provide three examples of some of the most common kinds of remediation projects using Thoreau's *Walden* as a primary text: painting and drawing, 3D crafts, and audio or video works, with an additional example using alternative authors and demonstrating baked goods, as well. These categories engage all the senses: sight and sound as well as touch, smell, and taste. The examples presented are anonymized composites of the kinds of work students submit. *Walden* stands as a cornerstone text in my early American literature courses as well as American Romanticism. Thoreau's reverence for nature and his call to appreciate its wonders resonate with students, making *Walden* a perennial favorite for creative exploration and analysis in my courses.

[Figure 15.1]

Example One: Solitude in Nature

The first example of a remediated version of *Walden*, seen in figure 1, is a charcoal drawing based on the iconic title-page of *Walden*.[22] There are key differences in this example from the original drawing, however. For example, this version has a different quotation from *Walden* displayed. In the original, Thoreau's famous line reads, "I do not propose to write an ode to dejection, but to brag as lustily as chanticleer in the morning, standing on his roost, if only to wake my neighbors up" (*W* 84). In the student's project, the quotation reads, "I have never found a [the] companion that was so companionable as solitude" (*W* title-page). Intriguingly, making that change of quotation creates a near-opposite effect. In the first case, Thoreau is chanting and waking up his neighbors, people are mentioned and even emphasized—there is a sense of community and shared communication in the quote. In the remediated version, Thoreau is happily alone. Further, the student artist opted for fewer trees, more bushes, and an overall increase in white space, allowing for the quote to stand out at the forefront of the drawing. In addition, the path leading to the door changed between the two versions. While it previously extended off the page toward the viewer, it is now obscured behind a tree, redirecting focus towards the solitude within a natural setting. These changes encourage a dialogue between literature and visual art. Specifically, this charcoal print shifts focus to the element of solitude, emphasizing it as a positive and life-affirming component to the work. Viewers are invited to contemplate and appreciate the profound connection between humanity and the more-than-human world, as advocated by Thoreau. This remediation project invites a renewed sense reverence for nature and underlines the pursuit of a simpler, more meaningful existence—a central tenet of Thoreau's philosophy.[23]

[Figure 15.2]

Example Two: Table for Two for Friendship

In the second remediation project, as shown in figure 2, the student has 3D-printed a scene described in Thoreau's chapter, "Visitors," in which

Thoreau details the number of chairs he has in his cabin and their uses: "I had three chairs in my house; one for solitude, two for friendship, three for society" (*W* 140). In the project, the student added Thoreau's green desk in between two figures that represent friendship. In this way, the project looks different than Thoreau's scene where he describes two chairs set as far apart as possible to let his ideas have room to germinate, stated exaggeratedly when he writes, "I have found it a singular luxury to talk across the pond to a companion on the opposite side" (*W* 141). In this model, the student forces greater intimacy between the companions. The student includes hand gestures and facial expressions as well, adding more intensity to the transcendental conversation between two friends. The student had been particularly interested in Thoreau's materiality, his thick description of key objects in his world. A class discussion on Thoreau's famous green desk became one such foundational object. It led the student to contemplate the concept of friendship in *Walden*, placing two friends on either side of the desk where so much had been written. In a way, the two figures represent the mental work Thoreau describes. This project also pushes back against Thoreau's declaration in "Solitude" where he writes, "I find it wholesome to be alone the greater part of the time" (*W* 135). The student in question became intrigued by the idea that Thoreau was a more personable figure than he seems in the text, following class discussions about Thoreau's literary persona in *Walden* compared to his lived experience there. By designing a project that shows Thoreau sitting across from a friend having a meaningful conversation, the student communicates Thoreau's appreciation of transcendental friendship as much as solitude and a life of the mind.

Example Three: Thoreau's Words and Sounds

The third remediation example involves a student's recording of birds and other natural sounds—as well as human-connected sounds like traffic noise and yard equipment—while hiking the Audubon Trail near the university's campus. The school is fortunate to have a wilderness trail within walking distance for the students. During this hike and over these sounds, the student read chosen passages from *Walden*, including a section from "Conclusion": "As I stand over the insect crawling amid the pine needles on the forest floor, and endeavoring to conceal itself from my sight, and ask myself why it will cherish those humble thoughts, and hide its head from me who might perhaps be its benefactor, and impart to its race some cheering information, I am reminded of the greater Benefactor and Intelligence that stands over me the human insect" (*W* 332). Walking among the cedar trees native to this region, rather than Thoreau's home pines, the student is able to act out the scene described with a high degree of similarity. The student understood Thoreau's core message that getting outside was key. The audio recording was a timely and resonant artifact of this experience. The student observed that by remediating *Walden* into an audio recording, elements of the natural world are necessarily privileged. Thoreau's line from "Conclusion" is a call to pay close attention to what the more-than-human world can teach. The student's audio project demonstrates how Thoreau's experiment at Walden Pond remains relevant into the current moment, connecting students to the transcendental wisdom of the beyond-human world.

[Figure 15.3]

Other Examples

Examples of additional remediation projects from my various courses include a found-diary of Sarah Orne Jewett based on "A White Heron" (1886), an audio recording of Black Hawk from *Life of Ma-Ka-Tai-Me-She-Kia-Kiak or Black Hawk* (1833), and baked bread connected to Octavia Butler's *Parable of the Sower* (1993), seen in figure 3. The Butler example uses acorn flour and dried fruit and nuts, elements referenced in the novel. The main character, Lauren, describes how she "bit into a piece of acorn bread that was full of dried fruit and nuts. It's a favorite of mine."[24] Acorns are used in the post-apocalyptic setting, as cast-off foods not deemed truly edible to the mainstream world, but at the same time a significant source of protein. This links them historically to the region's Native peoples, for whom they had always been a significant food source. Thoreau also references bread and nuts throughout the "Economy" chapter, at one point citing John Evelyn's classic *Sylva* of 1664, where the English forestry writer tells of how "the wise Solomon prescribed ordinances for the very distances of trees; and the Roman prætors have decided how often you may go into your neighbor's land to gather the acorns which fall on it without trespass, and what share belongs to that neighbor" (*W* 9–10). In this remediation project, the bread was staged on a bread board, displaying quotes from the text as well as the recipe. While all projects change the medium of the original work, this project also transformed the senses used to engage with the text—from sight to touch, taste, and smell. The student notes that like bread, at its heart, remediation seems to work to create a transformative experience. Throughout, these projects demonstrate student creativity and critical thinking as seen in the earlier Thoreau examples.

Project Data

I was able to recover 90 of my roughly 180 projects submitted over 12 years, at an average of 15 per year over that period.

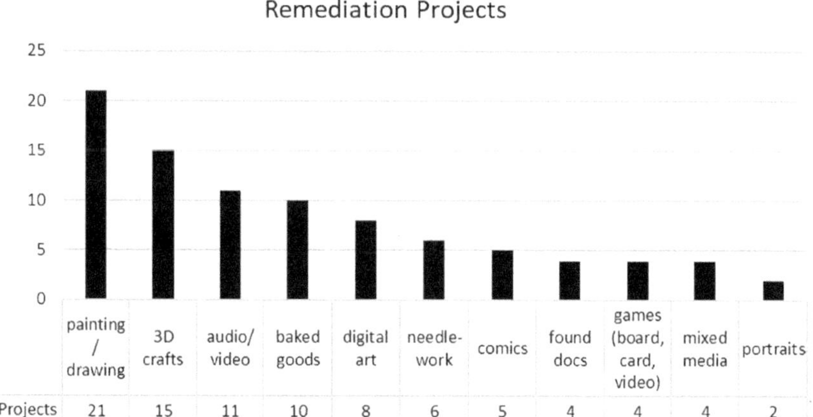

[Figure 15.4]

In figure 4, painting and drawing emerge as the most popular category, with more than 20% of the total number of projects. This category comprises a diverse array of artistic expression, including charcoal, pen and ink, pencil, oil, and acrylic works, some of which employ unconventional techniques such as glow-in-the-dark paints. Notably, two projects within this category used handwriting to create intricate ink lines, drawing inspiration directly from specific lines within the original text. There are also two portraits—depicting Edgar Allan Poe and Mark Twain—which stand out as distinct works and are placed in a separate category. The next most popular category, at 16.7%, are the 3D crafts. Within this category, students display their creativity through dioramas, ceramic and clay sculptures, 3D-printed or balsa wood constructions, and even sustainable terrariums. Audio and video projects are also regularly represented, constituting roughly 12% of the projects. These works encompass a variety of mediums, including spoken word translations and adaptations, filmed scenes, radio programs, and original musical compositions. Baking is also a consistently popular choice among students, with approximately 11% of projects falling into this category, or an average of two baking projects per course. Examples include muffins, cupcakes, cakes, sculpted chocolate, and the exemplar acorn bread. Other notable categories include comics, "found" style documents such as lost letters and diaries, various types of games (board, video, and card), mixed media wall art, and portraits, which might be considered a subset of the painting and drawing category.

Discussion and Applications

Based on my reflections over the strengths and weaknesses of the remediation assignment, I make the following suggestions for others attempting something similar:

Introduce the project to students early in the semester. Sometimes my official assignment drop does not occur until after the first assignment. (Currently, the remediation project is my second major assignment of the semester.) But I at least introduce the idea of the project during week one. I tell students to think about this as they are doing their reading homework. I ask them to consider hobbies they enjoy or skills they are interested in developing as they read. Then, when I present the assignment, explaining the paper element and the way I assess the projects, the students will have already developed some preliminary ideas and be better prepared to begin the production of the project itself.

Set aside class time for students to do some of the early research work, and possibly give them a "free" day to gather supplies or begin the drafting process. I regularly give students such exploratory time during the week after I have presented the assignment. In addition, I often take advantage of longer breaks such as spring break or the Thanksgiving holiday, making the projects due one or two weeks after that time. I do not want to assign too much work over breaks—students need that break time. But I also like giving them flexible time to use on projects if they want it.

Schedule frequent check-ins, and at least one rough draft assignment, to make sure students have properly thought their projects through, including giving serious thought to the time commitment involved. One of the most common caveats I give when checking drafts is to remind students of their current course loads, their other time commitments, and the need to make manageable goals.

Assign at least one background reading—I have been using the introduction to Bolter and Grusin's *Remediation* (1999), but newer sources would work here as well—to engage with theories of applied learning in this assignment. I find it useful to give students this theoretical backing. Sometimes they do not realize how a project like this helps them learn until they see it spelled out in print. The assignment is not just for fun—students are learning something, too!

Relatedly, the essay portion is critical. It promotes accountability by requiring students to reflect on their creative process, the choices they have made, and how those choices relate to the original text; it encourages students to think critically about their work; and it provides valuable insights for assessment. The essay serves as a necessary reflective tool for students and an assessment tool for instructors.

Do not be surprised if students often choose texts from the early readings of the semester. The majority of projects in my courses are chosen from early American literature texts. Usually by the time students choose their source materials, we will be in the early-to-mid portion of our syllabus. We often will not have read more recent texts yet. This is a common element of the assignment, though there are nearly always exceptions, and I am not sure how to encourage students to choose later texts if that is something to be desired.

When faced with the shift to online teaching in 2020, I was able to transition the remediation project to a digital format straightforwardly, allowing for continuity in the assignment. However, despite the ease of digital adaptation, students at my STEM-focused university still prefer the option of traditional creative forms. Approximately one-third of students create digital works, while two-thirds choose non-digital ones. The option to have both forms of expression works best in my courses.

Conclusion

The remediation assignment holds promise for adaptation to other forms of literature courses and can be easily transitioned onto online platforms, given its inherent connection to digital humanities fields. Alan Liu's interpretation of Bolter and Grusin's work emphasizes the interplay between old and new media, "the *déjà vu* haunting of new by old media," highlighting how the "content" of any new medium draws from older forms.[25] This perspective stresses the significance of McLuhan's theory on the medium being the message, while recognizing the malleability inherent in media. As online education is a growing trend at the university level, this assignment can be one addition to a variety of online curricula. Moreover, the remediation assignment would lend itself well to an U.S. environmental literature course. Its material nature aligns with the themes and theories inherent in such a course, which often explores questions like "what is the environment?" and "what does a material engagement with the more-than-human look like?" Framing the remediation assignment to specifically engage with the beyond-human world can further enhance students' understanding of the complex relationship between humans and the environment. For instance, Thoreau's emphasis on a materialist approach to life resonates with key themes in environmental literature. As Christopher Sellers observes, "This more inclusive and healing 'Nature' lay in neither the extra human world nor the human body alone but in their interrelations."[26] Thoreau's narrative intimately engages with the more-than-human, reflecting on the interactions between indigenous communities and the natural environment. This can be seen in the other examples, as well, as Butler spends much of her *Parable* series describing a world negotiating environmental degradation and climate change, highlighting the necessity of adapting to a new reality. The active learning approach can effectively engage students with various forms of literature, allowing them to explore broader issues addressed by digital humanities and environmental concerns. These two examples are just the start; the remediation assignment can be more broadly applied across a variety of curricula.

I have taught remediation assignments in a variety of U.S. Literature courses: Early American literature, American Short Story, American Romanticism, and American Gothic. The assignment has proven to be effective in encouraging enthusiasm and active student participation in the learning process throughout these courses. By fostering creative expression and critical engagement with the original material, the assignment not only reinforces key concepts but also creates a sense of ownership and agency among students. They generally appreciate the chance to express themselves creatively while deepening their understanding of the material and enjoying it at the same time. As Kozol observes, "In the long run, it is healthy to remind ourselves that Thoreau's most abiding legacy to educators...is the spirit of the man, the freshness and the merriment, the sheer delight he takes in mischievous self-contradiction, the defiant humor, and the ultimately irreducible morality of his existence that remain the gift of joy and courage he has left to us."[27] Students love this assignment, and they love Thoreau!

Works Cited

Bickman, Martin. "Introduction: Thoreau and the Tradition of the Active Mind." In *Uncommon Learning: Thoreau on Education.* Edited by Martin Bickman. New York: Houghton Mifflin, 1999.

Bonwell, Charles C. and James A. Eison. *Active Learning: Creating Excitement in the Classroom.* ASHE-ERIC Higher Education Report No. 1. Washington, D.C.: The George Washington University, School of Education and Human Development, 1991. https://archive.org/details/activelearningcr0000bonw/page/n3/mode/2up?view=theater

Butler, Octavia E. *Parable of the Sower.* New York: Grand Central Publishing, 2019.

Early, Jessica Singer. *Next Generation Genres: Teaching Writing for Civic and Academic Engagement.* New York: Norton, 2023.

Freeman, Scott et al. "Active Learning Narrows Achievement Gaps for Underrepresented Students in Undergraduate Science, Technology, Engineering, and Math." *Proceedings of the National Academy of Sciences*, 117.12 (March 2020), 6476-6483. https://doi.org/10.1073/pnas.1916903117

Grusin, Richard and Jay David Bolter. *Remediation: Understanding New Media.* Cambridge: MIT Press, 1999.

hooks, bell. *Teaching to Transgress: Education as the Practice of Freedom.* New York: Routledge, 1994.

Jenkins, Henry. *Convergence Culture: Where Old and New Media Collide.* New York: New York University Press, 2006.

———. "A Remediated, Premediated, and Transmediated Conversation with Richard Grusin (Part One)." http://henryjenkins.org/blog/2011/03/a_remediated_premediated_and_t.html

Kolb, David A. *Experiential Learning: Experience as the Source of Learning and Development.* 2nd edition. Upper Saddle River: Pearson Education, 2015.

Liu, Alan. "Imagining the New Media Encounter." In *A Companion to Digital Literary Studies.* Edited by Ray Siemens and Susan Schreibman. Malden: Wiley-Blackwell, 2013.

Loranger, Carol S. "*Ragged Dick* in the Nineties: An Active Student Learning Project." *Newsboy: The Horatio Alger Society Official Publication* 37.2 (March–April 1999): 9–10.

Rippl, Gabriele. "Introduction," in *Handbook of Intermediality: Literature, Image, Sound Music*. Edited by Gabriele Rippl. Berlin: De Gruyter, 2015.

Ryan, Marie-Laure. "Introduction." in *Narrative Across Media: The Languages of Storytelling*. Edited by Marie-Laure Ryan. Lincoln: University of Nebraska Press, 2004.

Ryoo, Jean J. "'Laughter Is the Best Medicine': Pedagogies of Humor and Joy That Support Critical Thinking and Communicative Competence." In *Deeper Learning, Dialogic Learning, and Critical Thinking: Research-Based Strategies for the Classroom*. Edited by Emmanuel Manalo. New York: Routledge, 2020.

Sellers, Christopher. "Thoreau's Body: Towards an Embodied Environmental History." *Environmental History* 4.4 (October 1999): 486–514. https://www.jstor.org/stable/3985398

Snyder, Heather T. "Designing Creative Assignments: Examples of Journal Assignments and a Creative Project." In *Teaching Creatively and Teaching Creativity*. Edited by Mary Banks Gregerson, Heather T. Snyder, and James C. Kaufman, 163–174. New York: Springer, 2013.

Straumann, Barbara. "Adaptation – Remediation – Transmediality." In *Handbook of Intermediality: Literature – Image – Sound – Music*. Edited by Gabriele Rippl. Berlin: De Gruyter, 2015.

Theobald, Elli et al. "Active Learning Narrows Achievement Gaps for Underrepresented Students in Undergraduate Science, Technology, Engineering, and Math." *Proceedings of the National Academy of Sciences*, 117.12 (March 2020), 6476-6483. https://doi.org/10.1073/pnas.1916903117

Utz, Richard. "Integrating STEM and the Humanities." *Inside Higher Ed* March 29, 2022. https://www.insidehighered.com/views/2022/03/30/humanities-thrive-stem-focused-universities-opinion#

CONTRIBUTORS

ALBENA BAKRATCHEVA is Professor of American Literature at New Bulgarian University, Sofia. She has written books and essays on nineteenth-century American literature and translated Thoreau's, Emerson's, and Fuller's major works into Bulgarian. In 2014 she received the Walter Harding Distinguished Service Award from the Thoreau Society. She was a Fulbright research scholar at Harvard (2023–2024).

KATHRYN C. DOLAN is a professor of English at Missouri University of Science and Technology, publishing on Thoreau in *Henry David Thoreau in Context* and *Rediscovering the Maine Woods*. She serves on the board of directors of the Thoreau Society.

KATHY FEDORKO's essay, "'Henry's brilliant sister': The Pivotal Role of Sophia Thoreau in Her Brother's Posthumous Publications," appeared in the June 2016 issue of *The New England Quarterly* and "Revisiting Henry's Last Words" in the Fall 2016 issue of the *Thoreau Society Bulletin*. She is writing a book about Henry Thoreau's friendships.

ROBERT A. GROSS, Draper Chair of Early American History Emeritus at the University of Connecticut, is author of two books about Thoreau's hometown, *The Minutemen and Their World* (originally published in 1976; reissued, 2022) and *The Transcendentalists and Their World* (2021).

RICHARD HIGGINS is writer, lecturer, and photographer. A former reporter and editor at *The Boston Globe*, his many publications include *Thoreau and the Language of Trees* (2017) and *Thoreau's God* (2024). He serves on the board of directors of the Thoreau Society.

ÓLAFUR PÁLL JÓNSSON is a professor of philosophy at the School of Education, University of Iceland. He studies philosophy in Iceland, Canada, and the US. He has published widely on philosophy of education, discussing issues such as democracy, creativity, and sustainability. He has also published on philosophy of nature and political philosophy.

DAVÍÐ GUÐMUNDUR KRISTINSSON is a lecturer at the University of Iceland, faculty of education and diversity. His article, "'How Much is a Mountain Worth?' Artistic Critique of the Icelandic State's Sellout of the 'Shitlandic Highlands' to a Foreign Multinational," Springer Verlag (coauthor Marteinn Sindri Jónsson) is due in 2024.

JOHN J. KUCICH is a professor of English at Bridgewater State University and president of the Thoreau Society. His most recent publication is *Unsettling Thoreau: Native Americans, Settler Colonialism, and the Power of Place.*

HENRIK OTTERBERG, a Swedish economist at Kagaku Analys AB, wrote his PhD on Thoreau's aesthetics, and serves as the Thoreau Society Bulletin bibliographer and review editor since 2017. He has organized international Thoreau conferences in Gothenburg, Sweden, and Reykholt, Iceland.

ROBERT SATTELMEYER is Regents' Professor Emeritus of American Literature from Georgia State University. His many publications include *Thoreau's Reading: A Study in Intellectual History* (1988) and volumes one and two of the *Writings of Henry David Thoreau.* He serves on the board of directors of the St. Simons Land Trust.

BEN SCHACHT, PhD, is a writer and editor working to fuse literature, history, and criticism speaking to present-day debates on politics and ideology. He is the digital editor for SAPIENS Anthropology Magazine. He has written on Thoreau as "An Anti-Work Manifesto for Our Times."

PAUL SCHACHT is Professor of English at the State University of New York at Geneseo. He is director of Digital Thoreau (https://digitalthoreau.org), a multi-project digital humanities initiative that includes Walden: A Fluid-Text Edition and The Walden Manuscript Project.

FRANÇOIS SPECQ is Professor of American Literature and Culture at Ecole Normale Supérieure de Lyon. He co-edited *Thoreauvian Modernities: Transatlantic Conversations on an American Icon* (2013) and *Thoreau Beyond Borders: New International Essays on America's Most Famous Nature Writer* (2020).

ROBERT THORSON is Professor of Earth Sciences at the University of Connecticut where he juggles teaching, writing, and community engagement. He's a Midwestern native, turned Northwestern geologist, turned Northeastern academic. He commutes to work along an off-trail woodland path.

LAURA DASSOW WALLS is Professor Emerita at the University of Notre Dame. She has written much on Thoreau, Emerson, and Humbolt, particularly her award-winning *Henry David Thoreau: A Life*, and *Passage to Cosmos: Alexander von Humboldt and the Shaping of America*.

ELIZABETH WITHERELL is Editor-in-Chief of *The Writings of Henry D. Thoreau*, based at the University of California, Santa Barbara, and published by Princeton University Press. She is also a member of the Digital Thoreau editorial team.

NOTES

Chapter 1 – Walls, Thoreau in the Nick of Time

[1] Charles A. Reich's bestselling book *The Greening of America* (1970) portrayed the nonviolent revolution of the Sixties generation as the arrival of "Consciousness III," which would end exploitation by the Corporate State and renew forever the relationship of people to each other and to nature. "The Age of Aquarius" was the ecstatic chorus that climaxed the wildly popular late-Sixties Broadway rock musical *Hair*, during which the full cast shed their clothes and presented themselves naked to the audience, Whitmanically proud of our beautiful human bodies. The Seattle production of "Hair" played at the Moore Theater for three months—a record—in spring 1970.

[2] Laura Dassow Walls, *Henry David Thoreau: A Life* (Chicago: University of Chicago Press, 2017), pp. 312, 332.

[3] See Laura Dassow Walls, *Passage to Cosmos: Alexander von Humboldt and the Shaping of America* (Chicago: University of Chicago Press, 2009), pp. 220–21. In this sense "Walden" becomes one of Bruno Latour's "beings of fiction"; see his *An Inquiry into Modes of Existence: An Anthropology of the Moderns* (Cambridge: Harvard University Press, 2013), pp. 233–57. As Latour writes, "No other type of being imposes such fragility, such responsibility," because beings of fiction can only exist so long as they are passed along "so they can prolong their existence" (249). In Latour's terms, Thoreau's innovation was to cross his beings of fiction with two other modes of existence, "beings of reproduction" which "enunciate themselves" without any assistance from human minds (as is true of Walden Pond), and "beings of reference" capable of bringing back a report from a remote place (as scientists do, and as Thoreau does in *Walden*). This three-way crossing, so characteristic of "nature writing," enables one to read Walden Pond (or any natural place) as if it were "set up for you," arranged for your aesthetic perception; see note 9.

[4] See John Dewey, *Art as Experience* (1934; New York: G. P. Putnam's Sons, 1958), p. 107: "there is self-expression in art because the self assimilates that material in a distinctive way to reissue it into the public world in a form that builds a new object."

[5] Ralph Waldo Emerson, *Essays and Lectures* (New York: Library of America, 1983), p. 59.

[6] Latour, *Modes of Existence*, 241.

[7] The concept of *Umwelt*, which has recently become enormously influential in animal studies and posthumanist philosophy, was popularized by Jakob von Uexküll in his 1934 book, translated into English as *A Foray into the Worlds of Animals and Humans* (Minneapolis: University of Minnesota Press, 2010).

[8] Dewey, *Art as Experience*, 89–90.

[9] Walls, *Henry David Thoreau*, 191–92.

[10] One could say that this is the work of nature writing, what Lawrence Buell calls "dual accountability" to both literary and natural-scientific truth (see note 3). It also adds risk, for a single false note—in either the author's subjectivity or their report of the objectively real—breaks the reader's faith. Yet the risk is necessary, for if it succeeds in merging the outer material world with our "aesthetic" engagement, on a deep level the planet itself becomes our responsibility: we realize that, like a work of fiction, without our continuing engagement and renewal, it will die—as, in fact, is happening today. Only if we take responsibility for the continued instauration of the trivalent "Walden," which is metonymically the Cosmos, will either "Walden" or "Cosmos" hold together so as to hold us together into futurity.

[11] Dewey, *Art as Experience*, 255.

[12] See Latour, *Modes of Existence*: If a work of art needs "a *subjective* interpretation, it is in a very special sense of the adjective: we are *subject* to it, or rather we *win* our SUBJECTIVITY through it. Someone who says 'I love Bach' becomes in part a *subject* capable of loving that music; he receives from Bach, we might almost say that he 'downloads' from Bach, the wherewithal to appreciate him" (241, emphasis in original). Note that the work of art constrains, but does not eliminate, interpretive freedom. (Bach's scores in their written abstraction at once constrain and demand their interpretation as live music.) While one is not free to do whatever one wants with it, there may certainly be many different interpretations—not because constraints of truth have been lifted but because "the work must possess many folds, engender many partial subjectivities," and the more we interpret it "the more we unfold the multiplicity of *those who love it* as well as the multiplicity of *what they love in it*. Someone who does not feel *held* and *engendered* by the requirements of the work will never be inhabited by it" (241, emphasis in original). This is one reason why meetings of the Thoreau Society continue to be so lively, year after year, as Thoreauvians unfold, in delighted conversation, the unending multiplicity of what we love in Thoreau.

[13] Cf. Bruno Latour, *Rejoicing, Or the Torments of Religious Speech* (Cambridge: Polity, 2013), 137: history does not descend from the past to the future, unfolding as it must, giving us no choice; rather, it "goes back from the present to the past, and everything depends on the capacity of the present event to replay the whole of history." This means that history "*can fail*"—and that, in "actual history, our history, the chips are not down. You have to choose" (emphasis in original). I have found Latour's work uniquely helpful for interpreting Thoreau's unusual capabilities and commitments—a connection that Latour himself, no fan of Thoreau, found mildly amusing (personal communication).

Chapter 2 – Kristensson, Time on Ice

[1] Andri Snær Magnason, *On Time and Water*, trans. Lytton Smith (London: Serpent's Tail, 2021). Henceforth abbreviated as *TW*. Magnason presented his book (virtually) at the University of New England in spring 2021.

[2] Magnason thematizes how James Watt's steam engine allowed humans to "stretch railroads across entire continents so that screaming locomotives could inspire poets who praised the new dawn of humans" (*TW* 191).

[3] Magnason's grandfather, a chief surgeon at New York hospital, operated on among others Robert Oppenheimer. Magnason quotes Oppenheimer quoting the *Bhagavad Gita*: "Oppenheimer himself realised the mythical context of his actions when he saw the bomb explode for the first time. He said in an interview: We knew the world would not be the same. […] I remembered a line from Hindu scripture, the Bhagavad Gita: *Now I am become Death, the destroyer of worlds*" (*TW* 125–126). Later on Magnason again uses Oppenheimer's paraphrase of the Bhagavad Gita and now paraphrases it himself, thereby moving from the fears of his youth to the current fears of the climate generation of his adulthood: "Oil is our life; it is also our death. When I was younger, the global arms race was at its ecstatic climax and my generation was feverish with terror at the idea of nuclear war. I thought I'd never make it past fifteen. Was my anxiety unnecessary or did a whole generation's worries ensure that the world survived? If we look at the effect burning oil has had, can we apply Oppenheimer's quote from the Bhagavad Gita to ourselves. Have we become Death, the destroyer of our world?" (*TW* 206).

In another chapter Magnason uses the Hindu goddess of time, change and destruction in his description of nature's development: "nature has no constant. Change is its essence. […] Nature is like the Hindu goddess Kali, who destroys as soon as she gives birth. She makes love as she kills, because creation and destruction take place simultaneously; in nature, there's no separation between them" (*TW* 254). Magnason furthermore uses the ancient Hindu writings to thematize the glaciers as a benevolent water source: "The Himalayan glaciers cumulate winter storms and monsoon rains and release them when people need water to persist through drought. The glaciers absorb seasonal fluctuations, but if they do not survive, exaggerated weather conditions will alternate between mass floods and droughts. In ancient Hindu writings, it is said that in the early days Ganges fell from the sky with enough force to destroy everything in his path. But Shiva saw this and caused Ganges to fall on his head so that the water seeped through his hair and flowed gently away to the people. The glaciers work this way: growing out from the mountains like Shiva's hair, they cling on to excessive, damaging waters and distribute them evenly throughout the year, for everyone's benefit" (*TW* 110).

[4] On the similarities between E. F. Schumacher's *Small is Beautiful* (1973) and Magnason's thinking see Reinhard Hennig, "Postcolonial Ecology: An Ecocritical

Reading of Andri Snær Magnason's *Dreamland.*" In *The Postcolonial North Atlantic*, ed., Lill-Ann Körber and Ebbe Volquardsen, Berlin: Nordeuropa-Institut der Humboldt Universität, 2014, 115.

[5] In his comparison of Aldo Leopold and Thoreau, Schneider comments on the same sentences in Thoreau's *Journal*: "There is, then, a crucial difference in urgency in the attitudes in Leopold and Thoreau. [...] Thoreau, too, is aware that the extermination of predators and other animals can significantly affect a place such as the Concord woods, but to him that effect is local and aesthetic only; he does not see it as part of a formula for more widespread ecological disaster, for if the larger animals no longer dwell in the Concord woods, they exist in abundance further west. [...] He feels the absence of these animals primarily in aesthetic terms [...]. Thoreau expresses his sense of loss only in artistic terms; the absence of these animals diminishes the number of artistic symbols available to him in the Concord woods, but it does not jeopardize the very existence of the woods. It is, of course, unfair to expect the same sense of urgency about ecological matters in Thoreau in the middle of the nineteenth century as one finds in Leopold in the middle of the twentieth" (Richard J. Schneider, *Thoreau's Sense of Place: Essays in American Environmental Writing*. Iowa City: University of Iowa Press, 2000, p. 6).

[6] Andri Snær Magnason. *Dreamland: A Self-help Manual for a Frightened Nation*, London: Citizen Press, 2008; directed by Andri Snær Magnason and Thorfinnur Gudnason, *Dreamland.* Documentary. Ground Control Productions, 2009. On Magnason's position in *Dreamland* see Marteinn Sindri Jónsson and David G. Kristinsson, "'How Much is a Mountain Worth?' Artistic Critique of the Icelandic State's Sellout of the 'Shitlandic Highlands' to a Foreign Multinational." In Marie Rosenkranz and Nina Tessa Zahner, *Plurale Verschränkungen. Zur Entdifferenzierung von Kunst, Politik, Wissenschaft und Wirtschaft*. Berlin: Springer Verlag (forthcoming).

[7] Marteinn Sindri Jónsson and David G. Kristinsson, "'How Much is a Mountain Worth?'"

[8] Andri Snær Magnason, *Dreamland*, 2008, p. 257.

[9] Magnason furthermore tells us: "I guide the interview in an environmental direction and ask him about the melting of the ice. 'I've been living at the foot of the Himalayas for the last fifty years and we have experienced great changes over the last forty to fifty years. In the early period, there was a lot of snow. Now, decade by decade, it gets less and less. Even where I live in Northern India, what will become of the water supply in a few decades? What will happen? Already we are worrying. The same thing is happening in Tibet'" (*TW* 97).

[10] The only mention of Iceland in *Walden* is the paragraph where Thoreau also talks about "the skin [...] of Walden Pond" (*W* 294)—this being one reason for the subtitle of our text.

[11] Since Iceland was a poor nation until the twentieth century the country lacks monumental historical buildings. That the Icelanders instead were proud of their middle age manuscripts (including the cosmogonal philosophy that the Poetic Edda contains) fits Thoreau's prioritizing well: "It should not be by their architecture, but why not even by their power of abstract thought, that nations should seek to commemorate themselves? How much more admirable the Bhagvat-Geeta than all the ruins of the East!" (*W* 57).

[12] *The* earliest written proof for this quotation is a letter written by the priest Karl Lotz in mid-October 1945 (Martin Schloeman, *Luthers Apfelbäumchen? Ein Kapitel deutscher Mentalitätsgeschichte,* Vandenhoeck & Ruprecht, 1994, pp. 55–56).

Chapter 3 – Otterberg, Victor IV's Dialogue with Thoreau

[1] Henry David Thoreau, *Walden and Other Writings*, ed. & with introduction by Brooks Atkinson (New York: The Modern Library, 1937). This oft-reprinted anthology contains all of *Walden*, significant portions of *A Week on the Concord and Merrimack Rivers*, *Cape Cod*, and *The Maine Woods*, as well as a handful of Thoreau's well-known essays, among them "Civil Disobedience," "Life Without Principle," and "Walking." Viktor's personal copy, as cited here, was a gift to the author by the artist's longtime companion Ina Munck (1935–2024), hereby gratefully acknowledged and much missed.

[2] Thoreau, *ibid.* (Viktor IV's copy), 51.

[3] Thoreau, *ibid.* (Viktor IV's copy), 226-229.

[4] Thoreau, *ibid.* (Viktor IV's copy), title page to *Walden* section.

[5] Reprinted in facsimile in Ad Petersen & Ina Munck's *Viktor IV* (Amsterdam: Meulenhoff/Landshoff & The Second Quality Construction Company, 1988), 16.

[6] Thoreau, *ibid.* (Viktor IV's copy), 83.

[7] Quoted in Ad Petersen & Ina Munck, *Viktor IV*, op. cit., 19.

[8] Ina Munck, *Viktor IV: An American in Paris* (Odder, Denmark: Narayana Press, 2013), 28.

[9] Cf. Ad Petersen & Ina Munck, *Viktor IV*, op. cit., 25. Petersen and Munck supply the date, while the intriguing speculation was first made by Iselin C. Hermann in her unpublished essay "The New Yorker in Amsterdam" (ca 2021), kindly made available to me in the context of the present work.

[10] Viktor 4, "Catalogue One: '4' Paintings" (Amsterdam: self-published, 1965), rear summary.

[11] For more on this topic, see my forthcoming "Liber Resartus: On Thoreau & the Book of Nature" in *The Oxford Handbook of Henry David Thoreau*, ed. Kristen Case and James Finley (Cambridge: Oxford University Press, ca 2026).

[12] Cf. Ina Munck, *Viktor IV: An American in Amsterdam*, op. cit., 33–52; and Ad Petersen & Ina Munck, *Viktor IV*, op. cit., 46.

[13] Quote from an unnumbered, unstamped (and hence abandoned?) Logbook sketch, including "The Story of the Onion & Turnip," dated June 16, 1974.

[14] Anton Heyboer (1924–2005) was a Dutch artist and printmaker based in Amsterdam, who received international recognition in the 1960s. His radical lifestyle, married to several women at once and periodically living on an Amsterdam barge, may have inspired Viktor beyond his art. In the mid-1980s Heyboer broke with the art market and various museums, finding his works overpriced and himself overly restricted regarding the creation of prints and variants. He wanted his art to be widely available and accessible. Accordingly Heyboer retreated to the village of Den Ilp just north of Amsterdam, where he lived and worked until his death. Upon his passing debates arose as to the provenance of a number of his works, with some labeled as forgeries made by others. Such posthumous quarrels among critics and curators would have delighted Heyboer, as a late interview with the artist makes clear.

[15] Personal interview with Ina Munck, Copenhagen, November 16, 2022.

[16] I am indebted to my friend and fellow Thoreauvian James Dawson for apprising me of this *TSB* profile.

[17] See e.g. Logbook #94 (January 1, 1972), with *TSB* cutout photo pasted in; #145 (June 2, 1976), containing portions of a letter from the Thoreau Society; #165 (December 17, 1978), showing Thoreau's house as per the *TSB* banner. While I have twice gone through the entire remaining Logbook inventory in the Viktor IV archive on Fredriksholms Kanal 26 in Copenhagen in the context of the present survey, the sheer wealth of materials makes oversights likely. Viktor's often compressed typing with small font, and what often appears as deliberately fuddled handwriting, probably harbors more meaningful mentions of Thoreau than I have discovered, while screening under some time constraints. I am however much indebted to the late Ina Munck and her daughter and fellow curator Sara Johansen for allowing me to spend several unforgettable days in the treasure trove that this unique archive presents. It is to be hoped that others will be able to mine the materials from other angles than my own, and in time also to present a fuller tally and *catalogue raisonné* of the Thoreau references to be found in Viktor's corpus.

[18] See Ina Munck, *Viktor IV: An American in Amsterdam*, op. cit, 88–89.

[19] For a comprehensive list of Viktor's exhibitions, solo as well as joint, see Ina Munck's *Viktor IV: An American in Amsterdam*, op. cit, 126.

[20] Many years later, Ina Munck's daughter Sara Johansen and her colleague Heidi Møller Christiansen would revive *Bulgartime* as an artistic company, whose signal achievement to date has been to commission Viktor's large, backwards-running wall clocks for commercial sale. Employing the factory responsible for Georg Jensen products, the results have been well received. Cf. www.bulgartime.com.

[21] See Ina Munck, *Viktor IV: An American in Amsterdam*, op. cit, 76.

[22] See Ad Petersen and Ina Munck, *Viktor IV*, op. cit, 7.

Chapter 4 – Sattelmeyer, Paradigms of Extinction

[1] Ralph L. Rusk, *Letters of Ralph Waldo Emerson*, vol 3. (New York: Columbia University Press, 1966), 3:384.

[2] See Linck Johnson, *Thoreau's Complex Weave: The Writing of* A Week on the Concord and Merrimack Rivers *With the Text of the First Draft* (Charlottesville: University Press of Virginia, 1986), esp. Ch. 4, "The Uses of the Past."

[3]See, for example, his acknowledgment at the end of his account of Lovewell's Fight that it was the victors who got to write the history. *A Week,* p. 122.

[4] This term originated in 1972, in Alfred Wallace's groundbreaking work of the same title; about a decade later, William Cronon would undertake the first detailed study of these phenomena in New England in *Changes in the Land: Indians, Colonists, and the Ecology of New England* (New York: Hill and Wang, 1983). A recent popular exploration of the topic is Charles C. Mann's *1493: Exploring the New World Columbus Created* (New York: Alfred A. Knopf, 2011)

[5] An illuminating recent study on this process is Nell Irvin Painter's *The History of White People* (New York: W. W. Norton), 2010. She singles Emerson out for particular blame in institutionalizing and authorizing this privileging of Anglo-Saxon white people.

[6] Though not without its own controversies, Stephen Jay Gould's *The Mismeasure of Man* (1981) is still the best account of these early anthropological movements .

[7] Quoted in Christopher Hanlon, "The Old Races Are All Gone": Transatlantic Bloodlines and "English Traits," *American Literary History,* 19, No. 4 (Winter, 2007), pp. 800–823.

[8] Turner's influential study, published in the first decade of the nineteenth century, helped inaugurate Anglos-Saxon studies, but its nationalist fervor during the era of the Napoleonic Wars also boosted racist and colonial ideologies in the Britain and the U.S.: See Donna Beth Ellard, "Ella's bloody eagle: Sharon Turner's History of the Anglo-Saxons and Anglo-Saxon history", *Postmedieval: A Journal of Medieval Cultural Studies*, 5 (2014), 215–34.

[9] Ralph Waldo Emerson, "Thoreau," *Atlantic Monthly* vol. 10, (August 1862), p. 239

[10] See *Faith in a Seed: The Dispersion of Seeds and Other Late Natural History Writings*, ed. Bradley P. Dean (Washington, D.C.: Island Press, 1993)

[11] See Cronon, *Changes in the Land,* pp. 108–26, and Dan Flores, *Wild New World* (New York: W. W. Norton, 2022), pp. 168–70 and passim.

[12] Walls, 186; He had begun to draft this lecture late the previous summer. See PEJ, 2:103–12

[13] Walls, p. 229.

[14] The actual state of the New England landscape at first contact—especially in areas like Concord where agriculture prevailed—is summarized by William M.

Denevan in the abstract to "The Pristine Myth: The Landscape of the Americas in 1492," *Annals of the Association of American Geographers,* Vol. 82, No. 3, (Fall 1992), p. 369: "The Native American landscape of the early sixteenth century was a humanized landscape almost everywhere. Populations were large. Forest composition had been modified, grasslands had been created, wildlife disrupted, and erosion was severe in places. Earthworks, roads, fields, and settlements were ubiquitous."

[15] In other portions of *A Week* Thoreau notices habitat alteration along the Merrimack and speculates about its cause and effect. He describes a fifteen-acre "desert" near Tyngsboro caused by fishermen destroying the vegetation along the bank to make a landing place, inadvertently revealing the remains of a Native American dwelling place (146-47).

[16] The second part of Robert M. Thorson's *The Boatman: Henry David Thoreau's River Years* (Cambridge, MA: Harvard University Press, 2017), tells this story in great detail.

[17] This dam's effect on migratory fish was a local and small-scale instance of a much larger environmental problem that we are still wrestling with, and just as mitigating the effects of the Billerica dam is still under discussion, so too throughout the continent environmental and economic interests still compete over the long-term consequences of dam construction.

[18] See John McPhee's *The Founding Fish* (New York: Farrar, Straus, and Giroux, 2002), pp. 148-91, for a condensed history of the American Shad.

[19] E.O. Wilson, *Biophilia* (Cambridge: Harvard UP) 1984, p. 1.

[20] See, for example, Ed Yong, *An Immense World* (New York: Random House, 2023), as well as a host of other recent works that explore complex animal perception and cognition from corvids to octopuses.

[21] The role of David Brower and a growing militancy in the environmental movement against such vast dam projects is told in John McPhee's *Encounters with the Archdruid* (New York: Farrar, Straus and Giroux, 1971)

[22] U.S. Fish and Wildlife Service, "Talbot Mills Dam Removal on the Concord River." (https://www.fws.gov/project/talbot-mills-dam-concord-river-removal)

Chapter 5 – Gross, Representative Men

[1] Robert A. Gross, *The Transcendentalists and Their World* (New York: Farrar, Straus and Giroux, 2021), 310–15; George Ripley, "Jesus Christ, the Same Yesterday, Today, and Tomorrow," in Perry Miller, ed., *The Transcendentalists* (Cambridge: Harvard University Press, 1950), 290.

[2] Ralph Waldo Emerson, "The American Scholar" (1837), in Ronald A. Bosco and Joel Myerson, eds., *Ralph Waldo Emerson: The Major Prose* (Cambridge: Harvard University Press, 2015), 105.

[3] J. Lyndon Shanley, *The Making of Walden with the Text of the First Edition* (Chicago University Press, 1957), 108–09.

[4] Gross, *Transcendentalists and Their World,* Part One, passim.

[5] Gross, *Transcendentalists and Their World,* 393–94; Ralph Waldo Emerson, "Introductory" lecture to series on "Human Culture," *The Early Lectures of Ralph Waldo Emerson,* ed. Stephen E. Whicher, Robert E. Spiller, and Wallace E. Williams. Volume II: 1836–1838 (Cambridge, 1964), 213–214; Emerson, "Historic Notes on Life and Letters in New England," *Atlantic Monthly* 52 (October 1883): 529.

[6] Gross, *Transcendentalists and Their World,* 395, 505, 575, 728, n. 34. Thoreau was far more interested in the cyclical rhythms of nature, its enduring "revolutions," than in the temporary upheavals that periodically unsettled politics and society. "The sudden revolutions of these times and this generation, have acquired a very exaggerated importance–," he wrote on January 7, 1842. "They do not interest me much– for they are not in harmony with the longer periods of nature." The following October he reaffirmed this outlook, characteristic of naturalists in his day. "All things are in revolution it is the one law of nature by which order is preserved, and time itself lapses and is measured." When Thoreau did refer to "the Revolution" in the history of Concord and the United States, he meant the War of Independence. *PJ* 1:244, 360, 2:102.

[7] Robert D. Richardson, *Henry Thoreau: A Life of the Mind* (Berkeley: University of California Press, 1986).

[8] Gross, *Transcendentalists and Their World*, 505–07.

[9] This portrait of Ezra Ripley draws from Gross, *Transcendentalists and Their World*, 44–53, 59, 82.

[10] Gross, *Transcendentalists and Their World,* 46–47, 311.

[11] William H. Gilman et al., eds., *The Journals and Miscellaneous Notebooks of Ralph Waldo Emerson* (16 vols.; Cambridge, Mass.: Harvard University Press, 1960–82), 4: 338–39, 5: 326, 7:22.

[12] Ralph Waldo Emerson to Mary Moody Emerson and to William Emerson, both on September 21, 1841, in Rusk, *Letters of Ralph Waldo Emerson*, 2:450–53; E., "The Late Rev. Dr. Ripley," *The Republican*, October 1, 1841. Emerson's memorial of Ripley was appended to "Two Sermons on the Death of Rev. Ezra Ripley, D.D." (Boston: James Munroe & Co. 1841), 41– 43.

[13] "Rev. Dr. Ripley," *Christian Register and Boston Observer* 20 (October 9, 1841): 163; Robert A. Gross, "Doctor Ripley's Church: Congregational Life in Concord, Massachusetts, 1778–1841," *Journal of Unitarian Universalist History* 33 (2009–10): 1–3.

[14] Robert A. Gross, "'The Nick of Time': Coming of Age in Thoreau's Concord," in Kristen Case and K. P. Van Anglen, eds., *Thoreau at 200: Essays and Reassessments* (New York: Cambridge University Press, 2016), 102–17.

[15] For Thoreau's frequent references to "revolution of the seasons," see *PJ* 1: 87; 5: 49, 96, 113; 6: 12, 182; 8: 144, 155.

[16] John Hildebidle, *Thoreau: A Naturalist's Liberty* (Cambridge, Mass.: Harvard University Press, 1983), 122; Gross, *Transcendentalists and Their World,* 352–58.

[17] Gross, *Transcendentalists and Their World*, 4–5, 761, n. 13; Robert A. Gross, *The Minutemen and Their World* (rev. and expanded ed.; New York: Picador Books, 2022), 170–71.

[18] Philip F. Gura, "Thoreau's Maine Woods Indians: More Representative Men," *American Literature* 49, no. 3 (Nov. 1977): 366–84. For another interlocutor with Thoreau, the star-gazing farmer Perez Blood, an aged bachelor from a once-wealthy family in the Estabrook Woods on the edge of Concord, see John Kaag, *American Bloods: The Untamed Dynasty That Shaped a Nation* (New York: Farrar, Straus and Giroux, 2024), 108–34.

[19] Gross, *Transcendentalists and Their World,* 177–83.

[20] Walter Harding, ed., *Thoreau as Seen by His Contemporaries* (New York: Dover, 1989), 82–83.

[21] George Melvin was the first-born son of Samuel Melvin, Jr., and Rebecca Farwell. Born in November 1813, seven months after the parents' marriage, he was another of Thoreau's bachelor friends. In 1860 George lived with his mother, earning his living as a laborer. Widow Rebecca Farwell died on 14 May 1864; George died on 30 March 1868 of "accidental drowning." See *Concord, Massachusetts, Births, Marriages, and Deaths, 1635-1860* (Boston, 1891), 298; Concord, Massachusetts, Death Records, 1841-1915, and U.S. Census for 1860, both accessed on Ancestry.com.

Chapter 6 – Schacht, The Condition-of-(New)-England Question

[1] For a brief and accessible overview of Carlyle's contribution to the development of the "Condition-of-England Question," see Andrzej Diniejko, "Thomas Carlyle and the Origin of the 'Condition of England Question,'" https://www.victorianweb.org/authors/carlyle/diniejko1.html, accessed September 13, 2012.

[2] Of course, I am not the first to emphasize the importance of the Transcendentalists' social context. Two studies that in some respects overlap with the concerns of the present chapter are Anne C. Rose, *Transcendentalism as a Social Movement, 1830–1850* (New Haven, Yale University Press, 1981) and Lance Newman, *Our Common Dwelling: Henry Thoreau, Transcendentalism, and the Class Politics of Nature* (New York: Palgrave Macmillan, 2005).

[3] With the term "libertarian," I denote the tradition of political philosophy that defines freedom primarily in terms of private property and free markets. Libertarianism can also be defined more broadly to include left-wing anarchism and anarcho-syndicalism. Though I argue here that Thoreau does not belong to the former tradition, he does belong to the latter. Indeed, he was embraced by Emma Goldman,

Rudolf Rocker, and the Jewish anarchists of the early 20th century, who translated Thoreau's essay "Civil Disobedience" into Yiddish.

[4] In her 2015 *New Yorker* essay on Thoreau, which appeared in print under the headline "Pond Scum," Kathryn Schulz writes: "Although Thoreau is often regarded as a kind of cross between Emerson, John Muir, and William Lloyd Garrison, the man who emerges in 'Walden' is far closer in spirit to Ayn Rand: suspicious of government, fanatical about individualism, egotistical, élitist, convinced that other people lead pathetic lives yet categorically opposed to helping them. It is not despite but because of these qualities that Thoreau makes such a convenient national hero." In his review of Laura Dassow Walls' 2017 biography of Thoreau in *The Nation,* Jedediah Britton-Purdy offers a persuasive reply to Schulz which broadly informs my discussion here. Kathryn Schulz, "The Moral Judgements of Henry David Thoreau," *The New Yorker*, October 2015; Jedediah Purdy, "A Radical for All Seasons," *The Nation*, June 2017.

[5] William Wordsworth, "Steamboats, Viaducts, and Railways," in *The Norton Anthology of English Literature, vol. 24, seventh edition: The Romantic Period*, ed. M. H. Abrams (New York: Norton, 2000), 299.

[6] William Blake, "And did those feet in ancient time," in *The Complete Poetry and Prose of William Blake* (New York: Anchor Books, 1988), 95.

[7] For a discussion of social time in terms of everyday, biographical, and historical "levels," see Hartmut Rosa, *Social Acceleration: A New Theory of Modernity*, trans. Jonathan Trejo-Mathys (New York: Columbia University Press, 2013), 8.

[8] Eric Hobsbawm, *Industry and Empire: The Birth of the Industrial Revolution* (New York: The New Press, 1999), 70–4.

[9] David Montgomery, "Social Attitudes of American Workers in the 1840s," in *A David Montgomery Reader: Essays on Capitalism and Worker Resistance*, ed. Shelton Stromquist and James R. Barrett (Chicago: University of Illinois Press, 2024), Ch 3. E-book.

[10] Robert Sattelmeyer, *Thoreau's Reading: A Study in Intellectual History* (Princeton University Press, 1988), 38–39.

[11] David Herreshoff, *Labor into Art: The Theme of Work in Nineteenth-Century American Literature* (Detroit: Wayne State University Press, 1991), 15.

[12] Sattelmeyer, 39.

[13] Herreshoff, *Labor into Art*, 11.

[14] Herreshoff, *Labor into* Art, 16.

[15] William Morris, "How I Became a Socialist," in *How I Became a Socialist*, ed. Owen Holland, with an introduction by Owen Hatherley (New York: Verso, 2020), 168. Along with John Ruskin and Karl Marx, Morris cites Carlyle as of one of three major intellectual influences that led him to become a socialist.

[16] Sven Beckert, *Empire of Cotton: A Global History* (New York: Vintage Books, 2014), 145–146. Jonathan Prude, *The Coming of Industrial Order: Town and Factory Life in Rural Massachusetts, 1810–1860* (Amherst: Massachusetts University Press, 1999), 35.

[17] On conflicts over water rights, see Gary Kulik, "Pawtucket Village and the Strike of 1824: The Origins of Class Conflict in Rhode Island," in *Material Life in America, 1600–1860*, ed. Robert Blair St. George (Boston: Northeastern University Press, 1988), 394. On the more general spread of cotton mills in the region and industrial discipline, see Kulik, 385–406, and *Who Built America? Vol. 1*, ed. Herbert Gutman et al. (New York: Pantheon Books), 251–6.

[18] The most comprehensive scholarly discussion of the strike is Kulik. A shorter and more accessible discussion on which I have also drawn can be found in Joey La Neve DeFrancesco, "Pawtucket, America's First Factory Strike," *Jacobin*, June 2018. Finally, my discussion here is influenced by this informative interview with DeFrancesco: "The Pawtucket Mill Strike," *Working Class History*, episode 32, https://workingclasshistory.com/podcast/e28-the-pawtucket-mill-strike/.

[19] Kulik, 395. As Kulik and DeFrancesco explain, women were increasingly employed in factories instead of children because they were better at tending the more advanced power-loom machinery that was then being introduced. As adults, however, they were less compliant with their employers' demands.

[20] Kulik, 398; DeFrancesco, "The Pawtucket Mill Strike."

[21] *The Manufacturers' and Farmers' Journal*, May 31, 1824; quoted in Kulik, 397.

[22] Kulik, 398–99.

[23] Louis Hartz, "Seth Luther: The Story of a Working-Class Rebel," in *Peaceably If We Can, Forcibly If We Must: Writings by and about Seth Luther*, ed. Scott Molloy, Carl Gersuny, and Robert Macieski (Providence: Rhode Island Labor History Society, 1998), 52–7.

[24] The quotations cited here come from the third edition, which appeared in 1836.

[25] Seth Luther, *An address to the working men of New England, on the state of education, and on the condition of the producing classes in Europe and America*, third edition (Philadelphia, 1836), 8.

[26] For a discussion of how early nineteenth-century advocates of shorter working time used the rhetoric of the American Revolution, see Benjamin Hunnicutt, *Free Time: The Forgotten American Dream* (Philadelphia: Temple University Press, 2013), 35–40.

[27] Luther, *Address*, 9.

[28] Luther, *Address*, 14.

[29] Hartz, 59; 71.

[30] On Carlyle's influence on Marx and Engels, see Stephen Marcus, *Engels, Manchester, and the Working Class* (New York: W. W. Norton, 1974), 102–12.

[31] For an overview of Brownson's life and thought, especially his complex and questionable views on slavery and abolition, see David Herreshoff, *The Origins of American Marxism: From the Transcendentalists to DeLeon* (Detroit: Wayne State University Press, 1967), 31–48.

[32] In a letter to Brownson, Thoreau writes that he has read the journal's first issue. Sattelmeyer, 136.

[33] Sattelmeyer, 19.

[34] Orestes Brownson, "The Laboring Classes" (Boston: Benjamin H. Greene, 1840), 5.

[35] On the currency of education as a means of addressing poverty among Transcendentalists, see Tess Lloyd, "A Transcendentalist Scoops Marx and Engels: Orestes Brownson's 'The Laboring Classes,'" https://teslloyd.com/blog/a-transcendentalist-scoops-marx-and-engels-orestes-augustus-brownsons-the-laboring-classes, accessed September 13, 2024.

[36] Brownson, 9.

[37] Brownson, 9.

[38] Barbara Adam, *Time* (Polity Press, 2004), 117.

[39] Wolfgang Schivelbusch, *Railway Journey: The Industrialization of Time and Space in the Nineteenth Century* (Oakland: University of California Press, 1977), 129.

[40] Thomas Carlyle, *Sartor Resartus* (Oxford: Oxford University Press, 1987), 127.

[41] Indeed, Dickens dedicated his 1854 novel *Hard Times*, a satire on industrial England, to Carlyle.

[42] On the theme of change in Dickens's novel and its ambiguous status, see Stephen Marcus, *Dickens: From Pickwick to Dombey* (New York: Basic Books, 1965), 293–357.

[43] Charles Dickens, *Dombey and Son* (New York: Penguin, 2002), 311.

[44] Aspects of the following discussion are influenced by Herreshoff, *Labor into Art*. See especially pages 10–11

[45] Engels, *The Condition of the Working Class in England* (Oxford: Oxford University Press, 1993), 101; 104.

[46] Thoreau's library contained a volume of Shelley's works that included both poems, and Shelley was reviewed in leading Transcendentalist publications, including *The Dial*, *The Harbinger*, and *The Boston Quarterly Review*. See Sattelmeyer, 155; Jen Morgan "The Reception of P. B. Shelley in Owenite and Chartist Newspapers and Periodicals, PhD Thesis (University of Salford, UK, 2014), 71.

[47] For a thorough and meticulously documented discussion of Shelley's influence on Chartism, see Morgan.

[48] Bertolt Brecht, *Selected Poems* (New York: Grove Press, 1959), 108–9 (translation modified).

[49] It would be interesting to compare Benjamin's remark with Thoreau's comment about the "supernumerary" sleepers which get out of alignment and force the train to stop. Herreshoff reads this passage suggestively as an intimation of revolution. See *Labor into Art*, 27.

[50] Walter Benjamin, "On the Concept of History," *Selected Writings Vol. 4* (Cambridge: Harvard University Press, 2003), 392.

[51] Regrettably, space does not permit a full discussion of this pregnant (and dubious) remark, but I submit that it should be read as an expression of what political theorists call "labor republicanism," a tradition which defines liberty in terms of freedom from dependence and domination. Wage labor, labor republicans argued, failed to meet such a standard because workers were dependent on and subject to their employers. Examples of this ideology in the context of Transcendentalism can be seen in the publications associated with the Brook Farm community, especially the writings of Charles A. Dana in the community's journal, *The Harbinger*.

[52] Karl Marx, *Dispatches from the New York Tribune: Selected Journalism of Karl Marx*, ed. James Ledbetter (New York: Penguin, 2007), 280.

[53] Mark M. Smith, *Mastered by the Clock: Time, Slavery, and Freedom in the American South* (Chapel Hill: University of North Carolina Press, 1997), 16.

[54] Note by Jeffrey S. Cramer in Henry D. Thoreau, *Essays: A Fully Annotated Edition*, ed. Jeffrey S. Cramer (New Haven: Yale University Press, 2013), 347, note 9.

[55] Charles Dickens, *Hard Times* (New York: Penguin, 2003), 28.

Chapter 7 – Kucich, Thoreau's Indian Notebooks

This essay is adapted from a chapter in *Unsettling Thoreau: Native Americans, Settler Colonialism, and the Politics of Place* (Amherst: University of Massachusetts Press, 2024).

[1] Robert F. Sayre, *Thoreau and the American Indian* (Princeton University Press, 1977), 118. The Indian Notebooks are housed at the Morgan Library in New York City, and I am grateful to the Morgan for making available digitized copies of some of the notebooks, as well as the existing transcriptions made in the 1930s by graduate students at Columbia University under the supervision of Arthur Christie. Final versions of most of the transcripts exist as MA theses; two others are in the Arthur Christie Papers held at Columbia, including one for Notebook 11 (MA 605/Thoreau 53), which is not available at the Morgan. I follow the work of Sayre in ordering and dating the Notebooks.

[2] Suzanne Rose argues that the labels on the Indian Notebooks were written by Thoreau himself, and not by H. G. O. Blake, who was given the manuscripts by

Sophia Thoreau, nor by Henry Russell, who bought them from Blake. "Tracking the Moccasin Print: A Descriptive Index to Thoreau's Indian Notebooks and a Study of the Relationships of the Indian Notebooks to Walden." Ph.D. diss, University of Oklahoma, 1994, 54–5.

[3] Richard F. Fleck published *The Indians of Thoreau: Selections from the Indian Notebooks* (Albuquerque: Hummingbird Press) in 1974, and Suzanne Rose included detailed summaries of first five of them in her dissertation in 1994, but the bulk them are not in print.

[4] For a more detailed account of Thoreau's use of Copway's book, including a transcription of Thoreau's marginal notations in Traditional History, see my "Thoreau's Reading of George Copway: An Additional Indian Notebook" in the *Thoreau Society Bulletin*, no. 302, Summer 2018, 1–5.

[5] Franklin Sanborn, *Henry D. Thoreau* (Boston: Houghton Mifflin, 1882), 248.

[6] Joshua Bellin, "In the Company of Savagists: Thoreau's Indian Books and Antebellum Ethnology," *The Concord Saunterer* 16 (January 2008): 1–32; Richard J. Schneider, *Civilizing Thoreau: Human Ecology and the Social Sciences in the Major Works* (Rochester: Camden House, 2016).

[7] Jean O'Brien, *Firsting and Lasting: Writing Indians Out of Existence in New England* (Minneapolis: University of Minnesota Press, 2010). Thoreau assumed the Musketaquid tribe of the Massachusetts nation had vanished by the nineteenth century after relocating to nearby Nashobah. Some may have joined Abenaki communities on the New England frontier in the wake of Metacom's Rebellion, but others joined relatives in Natick and other Massachusetts communities. Though they kept a low profile in the nineteenth century, the Natick Praying Indian Tribe remains a vibrant community today. For a history of the tribe in the seventeenth and eighteenth centuries, see Jean O'Brien, *Dispossession by Degrees: Indian Land and Identity in Natick, Massachusetts* (Lincoln: University of Nebraska Press, 2003). For a history of the Nashobah Indian Tribe and its connections to Natick, see Daniel V. Boudillion, *History of the Nashobah Praying Indians: Doings, Sufferings, Survival, and Triumph* (Norris: Raven Publishing, 2023).

[8] Kevin Bruyneel, *Settler Memory: The Disavowal of Indigeneity and the Politics of Race in the United States* (Chapel Hill: University of North Carolina Press, 2021), xiii.

[9] Sanborn, *Henry D. Thoreau*; Henry Salt, *Life of Henry Thoreau* (London: Richard Brentley and Son, 1890), 128; Albert Keiser uses the phrase for his chapter on Thoreau in *The Indian in American Literature* (New York: Oxford University Press, 1932), 209–32. In Keiser's summary of the Indian Notebooks, "Thoreau's Manuscripts on the Indians," *The Journal of English and German Philology* 27:2 (Spring 1928), 183–99, he offers a cogent summary of the notebooks and argues that Thoreau clearly intended to write a book.

[10] Bellin, "In the Company of Savagists," 8, 13.

[11] Paul Giles, *The Global Remapping of American Literature* (Princeton: Princeton University Press, 2011), 70–96.

[12] Henry Aupaumut, "History of the Muh-he-con-nuk Indians," *Collections of the Massachusetts Historical Society*, Volume 9, Series 1 (Boston: Munroe, Francis and Parker,1804), 99–102; Samson Occom, "Account of the Montauk Indians," *Collections of the Massachusetts Historical Society*, Volume 10, Series 1 (Boston: Munroe, Francis and Parker, 1809), 105–111.

[13] Branka Arsič, *Bird Relics: Grief and Vitalism in Thoreau* (Cambridge: Harvard University Press, 2016), 129. Mark Rifkin, *Beyond Settler Time: Temporal Sovereignty and Indigenous Self-Representation* Durham, NC: Duke Univeristy Press, 2017), ix.

[14] Sayre, 128.

[15] Suzanne Rose, in "Following the Trail of Footsteps: From the Indian Notebooks to *Walden*." *New England Quarterly* 67:1 (March 1994) 77–91, argues that the Earth-Diver myth informs the loon episode in "Brute Neighbors, yet none of the half-dozen Earth Diver stories Thoreau copies into the Notebooks feature a loon as the diver, and the key element—the creation of a world from a bit of mud brought from the bottom of a boundless sea—is absent in the loon episode.

[16] Sayre argues that *Walden* is a vision quest, a framework that certainly matches the broad outlines of retreat to the marginal edges of his community, his spiritual insight, and his return, though there is little evidence that Thoreau himself framed his experience in terms of this widely shared, though highly variable, Native ritual. Thoreau took notes on John Tanner's account, in his captivity narrative, of the Ojibwe story "Origin of the Robin," which centers on a vision quest, in IN 8:353, near the end of his drafting of *Walden*.

[17] Robert Bringhurst calls these stories "the old growth forest of the mind," and translates and comments on traditional Haida literature in *A Story as Sharp as a Knife: The Classic Haida Mythtellers and Their World* (Vancouver: Douglas and MacIntyre, 1999). Accounts of the ceremonial nature of Native mythology are numerous, including many by Native writers from Charles Eastman to Vine Deloria, Jr. to Paula Gunn Allen to Winona Laduke. This view was not a feature of the nineteenth-century accounts available to Thoreau, though it certainly aligned with Transcendental approaches to classical mythology.

[18] Basso draws on Clifford Geertz's term "local knowledge" in framing the cultural landscape he learns to see from his Apache mentors in *Wisdom Sits in Places* (Albuquerque: University of New Mexico Press, 1996). Brooks draws on her Abenaki heritage in applying the concept of a place-world to early Native history in New England in *The Common Pot* (Minneapolis: University of Minnesota Press, 2008).

[19] Jace Weaver, "Indigenousness and Indigeneity," *Companion to Postcolonialism*, eds. Henry Schwartz and Sangeeta Ray (Hoboken, NJ: Wiley, 2003), 228.

[20] Sayre, 25; Patrick Wolfe, "Settler Colonialism and the Elimination of the Native." *Journal of Genocide Research* 8:4 (December 2006), 388.

Chapter 8 – Fedorko, Thoreau's Spiritual Time

[1]In the translation that Thoreau read, Charles Wilkins uses the title *The Bhagvat-Geeta*. In a Journal entry Thoreau refers to it as the *Bhag vat-Geeta* (*PJ* 2:253). The work has also has been referred to as *The Bhagvat* and the *Bhagavat Geta*. *The Bhagvat-Geeta*. Trans. Sir Charles Wilkins, intro. George Hendrick (New York: Scholars' Facsilimiles & Reprints, Inc., 1971), vi.

[2] Mary Hosmer Brown, *Memories of Concord* (Boston: The Four Seas Company, 1926), 103.

[3] Laura Dassow Walls, *Henry David Thoreau: A Life* (Chicago: The University of Chicago Press, 2017), 165.

[4] Brown, *Memories of Concord,* 91.

[5] *The Bhagvat-Geeta,* 46.

[6] Ralph Waldo Emerson, "Thoreau," *Atlantic Monthly,* August 1862, 245.

[7] John Weiss, "Thoreau," *Christian Examiner* 79 (July 1865), 102.

[8] Annie Russell Marble, *Thoreau: His Home, Friends and Books* (New York: Thomas Y. Crowell & Co., 1902), 23, 183.

[9] Joseph Hosmer, "[Reminiscences of Thoreau] (1878, 1881, and 1882)," *Thoreau in His Own Time,* ed. Sandra Harbert Petrulionis (Iowa City: University of Iowa Press, 2012),102, 104.

[10]Anna and Walton Ricketson, eds. *Daniel Ricketson and His Friends: Letters, Poems, Sketches, Etc.* (Boston: Houghton, Mifflin and Company, 1902; rpt. 2009), 142.

[11] My discussion of Thoreau's spiritual practices aligns with Barry Andrews' discussion of the spiritual practice of "self-culture," which, he argues, was key to Transcendentalism. He calls Thoreau "a perfect example of self-culture." Indeed, Thoreau knew the philosophy well. He walked nineteen miles to Boston to hear Emerson lecture on "Human Culture" and became his apprentice and friend. He attended discussions with other Transcendentalists at Emerson's home that centered on self culture. With that said, Thoreau's college essays and early journal entries reveal that he came to these experiences predisposed to many of the values Emerson taught. I believe Thoreau honed his individual spiritual practices not only from Transcendentalist influences but also from his boyhood encounters with nature and his early recognition of his "difference," the latter requiring that he practice a way of being in the world that nurtured his sense of self. See Barry M. Andrews. *Transcendentalism and the Cultivation of the Soul* (Amherst: University of Massachusetts Press, 2017), 44.

[12] Andrews, *Transcendentalism*, 103.

[13] Alan D. Hodder, *Thoreau's Ecstatic Witness* (New Haven: Yale University Press, 2001), 171.

[14] Hodder, *Thoreau's Ecstatic Witness*, 77, 78.

[15] Thich Nhat Hanh, *The Heart of the Buddha's Teaching* (New York: Harmony Book, 2015), 152-3.

[16] Robert Richardson comments that "The awakening Thoreau calls for is a spiritual, perhaps even a mystical awakening, no doubt… .The awakening is a religious experience in the broad sense of the word, and the language turns to Hindu, Chinese, and above all Greek religion to the pointed exclusion of Christianity," in that it doesn't relate to "eternal redemption" (Robert D. Richardson, *Thoreau: A Life of the Mind* [Berkeley: University of California Press, 1986], 174). Concerning Christianity, however, Hodder observes that, "the figure of Jesus served Thoreau as guarantor and symbol for a mode of spiritual awakening possible to anyone, at anytime, anywhere" (148).

[17] Walls notes that "Thoreau's walks became a form of meditation, a spiritual as well as physical discipline" (305). Hodder points out that "The peripatetic philosophers of the ancient world, East and West, were so named for their habit of teaching in the act of walking" (287). Thoreau notes this too when he writes in "Walking" that, "I walk out into a nature such as the old prophets and poets Menu, Moses, Homer, Chaucer, walked in" (*Exc* 192).

[18] Online Journal Transcripts, https://thoreau.library.ucsb.edu/writings_journals.html. Journal Manuscript 22, September 7, 1856 – April 1, 1857, Jan 7th '5[6]. [Editor's note: "brackets are 'T's' "] The previous time the year is mentioned, however, is Jan 2 '57, suggesting that this Jan 7th entry should be '57, not '55 or '56.

[19] Although not from *Walden*, Thoreau's description of his mystical experience with a higher power resembles the description of what Paul Friedrich, in *The Gita Within Walden,* refers to as "God." Friedrich writes that *Walden* and *The Gita* share a focus on a "divine power" that is "suffused with mystery" and "immanent and transcendent." When absorbed in it, a person experiences a "total loss of self," or, as Thoreau puts it in the description above, becoming "a restful kernel in the magazine of the universe." Paul Friedrich. *The Gita Within Walden.* Albany, NY: State University of New York Press, 2008, 11, 14, 13.

Chapter 9 – Higgins, Thoreau's Eternal Return

[1] Paula Gunn Allen discusses the Native American concept of ceremonial time and ritual in contrast to the Western chronological time and linear order in "The Ceremonial Motion of Indian Time: Long Ago, So Far," *The Sacred Hoop* (Boston: Beacon Press, 1986). See also John Hanson Mitchell, *Ceremonial Time: Fifteen Thousand Years in One Square Mile* (Hanover, NH: University Press of New England, 1984 and 2013) and Bruce Charlton, "Ceremonial Time Versus Technological Time,"

Abraxis (2001, 18: 19-23), (https://www.hedweb.com/bgcharlton/ceremonial-time.html).

[2] Mircea Eliade, *Myths, Dreams and Mysteries* (New York: Harper Bros., 1961), 23.

[3] See Candace Osmond, "In the Nick of Time—Idiom, Origin & Meaning" (https://grammarist.com/idiom/in-the-nick-of-time/). "Pudding time" is first referred to in John Heywood's glossary *A Dialogue conteinyng the nomber in effect of all the Prouerbes in the Englishe tongue* (1546). See "In the Nick of Time," (https://www.phrases.org.uk/meanings/in-the-nick-of-time.html).

[4] "Inspiration," Collected Essays and Poems, ed. Elizabeth Witherell (Library of America, 2001), 566.

[5] Edward Craig, *The Shorter Routledge Encyclopedia of Philosophy* (New York: Routledge: 2005), 1076.

[6] Nietzsche presents his idea of the Eternal Recurrence as a thought experiment in Aphorism 341 of *The Gay Science* (New York: Cambridge University Press, 2001), 194.

[7] "neither future nor past," Augustine, *Confessions: Books 9–13*, ed. Carolyn Hammond, Loeb Classical Library (Cambridge, MA: Harvard University Press, 2016), 231.

[8] "The foundation of reverence," Alfred North Whitehead, *The Aims of Education* (New York: Simon & Schuster, 1967), 14; "Eternity is at our hearts," Thomas Kelly, *A Testament of Devotion* (Harper & Row, 1941), 29.

[9] "The Eye and the Ear" (lecture, December 27, 1837), in *The Early Lectures of Ralph Waldo Emerson*, ed. Stephen Whicher, Robert Spiller, and Wallace Williams (Harvard University Press, 1966–72), 2:274.

[10] "Literary Ethics," Ralph Waldo Emerson, *Nature, Addresses and Lectures* (Honolulu, HI: University Press of the Pacific, 2001) 158.

[11] John Hanson Mitchell, *Ceremonial Time.*

[12] "Address by William James," *The Centenary of the Birth of Ralph Waldo Emerson: As Observed in Concord, May 25, 1903* (Riverside Press, 1903) 72.

Chapter 10 – Thorson, *Walden*'s Core Idea

[1] Though not all specific choices made by individuals become fossilized, they do influence the local physical environment which may be recorded (as with footprints). Such choices also aggregate into individual lives, which aggregate into species, which aggregate into ecosystems, which are preserved in various geological archives.

[2] Robert Sattelmeyer, *Thoreau's Reading* (Princeton: Princeton University Press, 1988), 88.

[3] In sequence he called it "architectural foliage...this kind of foliage... luxuriant foliage" (*W* 305–306).

[4] As of this writing, no other planet has shown evidence of life, present or past. This is surprising, given the abundance of organic compounds in meteorites. Mars once had conditions suitable for earth-like microbial life.

[5] Here, Thoreau was quite wrong, given that these taxa emerged late in the history of plants.

[6] For background on the social/religious culture of Concord, consult Robert Gross, *The Transcendentalists and their World* (New York: Farrar, Strauss, and Giroux, 2021).

[7] Charles Lyell, *Principles of Geology, First Edition, Volume 1, edited by Martin J. S. Rudwick* (Chicago: University of Chicago Press, 1960, originally London: 1830).

[8] Robert D. Richardson, Jr, *Henry Thoreau: A Life of the Mind* (Berkeley: University of California Press, 1986), 82.

[9] On the one hand, this "tea party" connotes ageism and sexism. On the other hand, it connotes the wisdom and longevity of women.

[10] For sources and an expanded discussion, see Robert Thorson, *Walden's Shore: Henry David Thoreau and Nineteenth Century Science* (Cambridge: Harvard University Press, 2014), 289–293.

[11]Physical science in general, and geology in particular, is only a small portion of Laura Dassow Walls's comprehensive biography *Henry David Thoreau: A Life* (Chicago: University of Chicago Press, 2017), In her previous *Seeing New Worlds: Henry David Thoreau and Nineteenth-Century Science* (Madison, WI: Univ. Wisconsin Press, 1995), she brought attention to Thoreau's geology in the context of natural history. Robert Sattelmeyer's *Thoreau's Reading* and William Rossi's "Thoreau's Transcendental Ecocentrism" in Richard J. Schneider, ed., *Thoreau's Sense of Place* (Iowa City: University of Iowa Press, 2000), 28–43, brought special attention to evolution.

[12] In particular, pages 46–48 of Thorson, *Walden Shore,* highlight his rock and mineral collection, geological sketches, and key descriptions.

[13] Arnold Henry Guyot's *The Earth and Man,* translated by Cornelius. C. Felton, 3rd edition (Boston: Gould & Lincoln, 1851). Sadly, one of Guyot's most significant conclusions involved fallacious regional-racial human differences and overstated American exceptionalism.

[14] Charles R. Darwin, *Journal of Researches,* reprinted as Charles Darwin, *The Voyage of the Beagle* (New York: Doubleday, 1962). Thoreau's engagement with Darwin is detailed in *Walden's Shore,* 119–123.

[15] Charles Darwin, *Voyage of the Beagle* (New York: Doubleday, 1962), 174–176.

[16] Darwin, *Voyage of the Beagle*, 174, 175, 84.

[17] Edward Hitchcock, sourced as Massachusetts Geological Survey, *Final Report on the Geology of Massachusetts*, 2 volumes and foldout map (Northhampton: J. H. Butler, 1841).

[18] Robert Chambers, *Vestiges of the Natural History of Creation with a Sequel* (New York: Harper & Brothers, 1857), 106, 105, 19, 76. See also Thomas Peyser, "Walden's Sandbank and the *Vestiges* Controversy," *ANQ: A Quarterly Journal of Short Articles, Notes and Reviews* 30:1 (2017), 38–41, who argues that, following Thoreau scholars Richardson, Rossi, Sattelmeyer, Tauber, and Walls, Chambers was very influential to Thoreau.

[19] Chambers, *Vestiges of the Natural History of Creation*, 26, 83, 70.

[20] Sattelmeyer, *Thoreau's Reading*, 86–87.

[21] Henry David Thoreau, *Walden: A Fluid-Text Edition* (Digital Thoreau. https://digitalthoreau.org/fluid-tet-toc), version A, paragraph 5, sentence 2 of 2. Accessed May, 2024.

[22] Gross, *The Transcendentalists and Their World*, 596.

[23] William Rossi, "Making *Walden* and its Sandbank," showed that Thoreau's thinking about the sandbank became more refined even as he made no changes in *Walden* versions A, B, C, D, and E. Version F is the main change and only in version G do we get the final insights that there is nothing inorganic and that Earth, going full blast within, experiences continuous creation.

[24] This linkage is told in much greater detail in Robert Thorson's *Walden's Shore*, 333–334.

[25] Richardson, *A Life of the Mind*, 311.

[26] Thorson, *Walden's Shore*, 284.

[27] That this is the climax of *Walden* has held steady for more than a generation across a broad swath of writers.

[28] Toby Tyrrell, *On Gaia: A Critical Investigation of the Relationship between Life and Earth* (Princeton: Princeton University Press, 2013).

[29] The inset quote is attributed to "Hunt" unspecified.

[30] James Hutton, *Theory of the Earth with Proofs and Illustrations: In Four Parts Volume 1* (Edinburg: Royal Society of Edinburg, 1795), unpaginated http://www.gutenberg.org/files/12861/12861-h/12861-h.htm. Accessed July 21, 2024.

Chapter 11 – Olafur, Thoreau and Mountains

[1] In Icelandic people are always referred to by their first name and Thórbergur is such a cultural icon that I find it awkward to refer to him by his patrionymic, even if that is the "academic" convention.

[2] See e.g. Ronald Wesley Hoag's interpretation of the Ktaadn passage in "The Mark on the Wilderness: Thoreau's Contact with Ktaadn," *Texas Studies in Literature and Language* 24, No. 1 (Spring 1982), https://www.jstor.org/stable/40754670

[3] Hoag, "The Mark on the Wilderness," 33.

[4] Laura Dassow Walls, *Material Faith. Thoreau on Science*, (Boston: Houghton Mifflin Harcourt, 1999), xiii.

[5] Aldo Leopold, *A Sand County Almanac and Scketches Here and There*, (Oxford: Oxford University Press, 1949).

[6] Leopold, *A Sand County Almanac*, viii–ix.

[7] Walls, *Material Faith*, xvii.

[8] See also Jason P. Matzke, "Humans as "Part and Parcel of Nature": Thoreau's Contribution to Environmental Ethics," 5 no. 2 (2014).

[9] Antonio Casado da Rocha, *Una casa en Walden (y otros ensayos sobre Thoreau y cultura contemporánea)*, (Logroño: Pepitas, 2017), 78, (translated from the Spanish by Ólafur Páll Jónsson).

[10] João Afonso Babtista, "Eco(Il)Logical Knowledge: On Different Ways of Relating with the Known," *Environmental Humanities* 10 no. 2 (2018): 398.

[11] Jane Bennett, "On Being a Native: Thoreau's Hermeneutics of Self," *Polity* 22, No. 4 (1990), 565.

[12] Bennett, "On Being a Native," 565.

[13] Evelyn Fox Keller, *A Feeling for the Organism: The Life and Work of Barbara McClintock*, (San Francisco: W. H. Freeman,1984), 197.

[14] Iceland may perhaps lose this place now that we have moved into the Anthropocene, where the forces acting upon and shaping the crust of the Earth are not the same as before.

[15] Thórdarson, *The Stones Speak*, 201.

[16] Thórdarson, *The Stones Speak*, 235.

[17] Thórdarson, *The Stones Speak*, 238–239.

[18] Hoag, "The Mark on the Wilderness," 25.

[19] Thórdarson, *The Stones Speak*, 239.

Chapter 12: Specq, Thoreau's Transcendental Wrestlings

[1] For an overview of the development and importance of this notion, see Thomas M. Allen, ed., *Time and Literature* (Cambridge: Cambridge University Press, 2018), especially Allen's "Introduction," 1–14.

[2] Thomas M. Allen, *A Republic in Time: Temporality and Social Imagination in Nineteenth-Century America*. (Chapel Hill: University of North Carolina Press, 2008), 11.

[3] Lloyd Pratt, *Archives of American Time: Literature and Modernity in the Nineteenth Century*. (Philadelphia, University of Pennsylvania Press), 2009, 3–5.

[4] Dana Luciano, *Arranging Grief: Sacred Time and the Body in Nineteenth-Century America*. New York: New York University Press, 2007, 23, 7, 62.

[5] Cindy Weinstein, *Time, Tense, and American Literature: When Is Now?* Cambridge: Cambridge University Press, 2015, 2–5.

[6] We can only guess at one reason for the absence of the Transcendentalists, when one comes across Lloyd Pratt's assertion that they were "indebted...to an

ideology of linear progress" (*Archives* 5): they would thus fail to agree with the book's argument, i.e. "a pluralization of time—a splitting of time into temporalities—characteristic of modernity" (6). This notion of Transcendentalism as aligned with the ideology of progress, however, is anything but self-evident, and would require demonstration.

[7] Danielle Follett, "Emerson's Temporalities: The Eternal Present vs. the Not Yet Present," *ESQ: A Journal of Nineteenth-Century American Literature and Culture* 67.3–4 (2021): 639–65.

[8] "cultural politics of time" (Luciano, *Arranging* 17); "sexual politics of time," "gendered politics of time" (Luciano, *Arranging* 62, 119, 269); "politics of time" (Pratt, *Archives* 168). Luciano and Pratt both refer to Peter Osborne, *The Politics of Time: Modernity and Avant-Garde* (London: Verso, 1995).

[9] Thoreau's name appears neither in Dana Luciano's book, nor in Lloyd Pratt's, nor Cindy Weinstein's. Thoreau is only indirectly present in Thomas Allen's study, in the course of a brief comparison with Catharine Beecher.

[10] Charles Anderson, *The Magic Circle of Walden* (New York: Holt, Rinehart and Winston, 1968).

[11] Alan D. Hodder, *Thoreau's Ecstatic Witness* (New Haven: Yale University Press, 2001), 21.

[12] Wai-Chee Dimock defines "deep time" as "a set of longitudinal frames, at once projective and recessional...binding continents and millennia into many loops of relations" (*Through Other Continents: American Literature across Deep Time* [Princeton: Princeton University Press, 2006], 3). "This *longue durée* is not just a matter of time past; it is also a matter of time present...[a] temporal continuum" (31). Dimock links the notion of *deep time* to Thoreau's interest in Asian texts, which she frames as "the threads of deep time that string [each of Thoreau's sentences] together, giving us a civil society woven of continents and millennia" (22). To be sure, Thoreau's wide-ranging culture allowed him to think beyond narrow national borders, but connecting him to "deep time" merely describes his grounding in a rich cultural soil, while failing to address his own relation to time in a specific way. Among the vast bibliography on deep time and the complexity of the issues and criticisms the notion raises, see especially Cécile Roudeau, ed., "Hidden in Plain Sight: Deep Time and American Literature," *Transatlantica* 2015/1 (https://journals.openedition.org/transatlantica/7257).

[13] James R. Guthrie, *Above Time: Emerson's and Thoreau's Temporal Revolutions* (Columbia: University of Missouri Press, 2011).

[14] Mark Luccarelli, "Thoreau and the Desynchronization of Time," in Kristen Case, Rochelle L. Johnson, and Henrik Otterberg, ed., *Thoreau in an Age of Crisis: Uses and Abuses of an American Icon* (Paderborn: Brill Fink, 2021), 91–106. Focusing on *A Week on the Concord and Merrimack Rivers* and *The Maine Woods*, Luccarelli sees Thoreau as "caught among colliding time scales: the crushing inevitability of

modernization, the longing for a past vivid in memory, and the hope for a future in correspondence to the organic principle of earthly renewal, with very little to suggest how these measures of time could be mediated" (105–106). While this is arguably an accurate description of Thoreau's complex ties to socio-historical temporalities, my own perspective, which centers on the *Walden*/Journal pair, is less oriented toward Thoreau's thinking about different, even divergent, temporal modes, than about his life-defining time consciousness and related questions of pacing and spacing.

[15] Herman Melville, *Clarel*, ed. Harrison Hayford *et al.* (Evanston/Chicago: Northwestern University Press & The Newberry Library, 1991), 9 [I.ii. 49].

[16] Hodder, *Ecstatic Witness*, 21.

[17] Guthrie, *Above Time*, 64.

[18] Anderson, *Magic Circle*, 39.

[19] Pierre Hadot, *What is Ancient Philosophy?* (Cambridge, MA: The Belknap Press of Harvard University Press), 2002.

[20] This maxim, which Thoreau quotes a number of times in his writings, refers to an age-old tradition of allegorical representation of time as a bald figure, apart from a large forelock, to be grasped by those eager to make the most of life. It goes back at least to a statue by Lysippos, Alexander the Great's favorite sculptor, who gave shape to a maxim (Καιρὸν γνῶθι [Know the occasion]) ascribed to Thales of Miletus or Pittacus of Mytilene, which was inscribed in Apollo's temple in Delphi. Lysippos's sculpture, which is only known through an *ekphrasis* to be found in a book which was hugely popular during the Renaissance, Maximus Planudes's *Greek Anthology* (1301, first printed version in 1494) was subsequently taken up in emblem books (especially Andrea Alciati's *Emblematum liber*, 1531) and many literary works (Spenser, Marlowe, Shakespeare, etc.), establishing a foundational continuity between the Greek *Kairos*, the Roman *Occasio*, and the Medieval and Renaissance Fortune. Thoreau was not only familiar with Spenser's *The Faerie Queene* (1590–1596) and Shakespeare's plays, but with the *Greek Anthology* itself, to which he refers in *A Week on the Concord and Merrimack Rivers* (1849).

[21] Thoreau's phrasing echoes Emerson's in his essay "New England Reformers" (included in *Essays: Second Series*, 1844): "We are weary of gliding ghostlike through the world, which is itself so slight and unreal. We crave a sense of reality, though it come in strokes of pain" (Ralph Waldo Emerson, *Essays and Lectures*, ed. Joel Porte, [New York: The Library of America, 1983], 603). Significantly, Thoreau's words about his desire for the real immediately come before the passage in which he describes himself as fishing in the river of time, thus indissolubly connecting the two aspects.

[22] Thoreau himself emphasizes how the individual is threatened with "absorption": "the life of a civilized people [is made] an *institution*, in which the life of the individual is to a great extent absorbed" (*W* 31–32).

[23] That distinction tends to relate Thoreau to Aristotle's notion of time. Indeed, for Aristotle (in *Physics*, Book IV, section 12, 221a26–221b3), "everything in time is bound to be contained by time," while "anything eternal...is not contained by time, nor is its existence measured by time" (*Physics*, ed. and trans. Robin Waterfield and David Bostock, [Oxford: Oxford World's Classics, 2008], 111). For Kant, conversely, "Time is not an empirical concept that is somehow drawn from an experience. For simultaneity or succession would not themselves come into perception if the representation of time did not ground them *a priori*.... Time is a necessary representation that grounds all intuitions" (Immanuel Kant, *Critique of Pure Reason*, ed. and trans. by Paul Guyer and Allen W. Wood [Cambridge: Cambridge University Press, 1998], 178 ["Transcendental Aesthetics" § 4]). Whereas Kant sees time as one of the necessary foundations of experience, Aristotle is somehow on the side of an original experience of temporality. Although the Transcendentalists are traditionally regarded as heirs to Kant's "transcendental" (primarily by way of Coleridge), because of their opposition to Locke's philosophy of knowledge (according to which all knowledge comes from the senses), this does not prejudge their experience of lived time: actually, the individual's experience of time (included Kant's perhaps!) is not primarily as *a priori* form of understanding. On the Transcendentalist critique of Locke, see Barbara L. Packer, "The Transcendentalists." *Cambridge History of American Literature, 1820–1865*, ed. Sacvan Bercovitch (Cambridge: Cambridge University Press, 1995), 350–61.

[24] This has been particularly emphasized by Pierre Hadot, who gives pride of place to the notion of "spiritual exercises," aimed at freeing oneself of any concern over the future, as much as of the shadows of the past. See especially *What is Ancient Philosophy?* 190–98, and "There Are Nowadays Professors of Philosophy, but not Philosophers," *Journal of Speculative Philosophy: A Quarterly Journal of History, Criticism, and Imagination*, Vol. 19, No. 3 (2005): 229–37. The present essay, however, as pointed out above, intends to show that, if the aim was similar, the means were significantly different.

[25] Thoreau's Journal, long dismissed as ancillary to his published writings, has been the focus of intense scrutiny since the publication of Sharon Cameron's *Writing Nature: Henry Thoreau's Journal* (Oxford: Oxford University Press, 1985). For a perspective congruent with the one pursued in this essay, see especially François Specq, "Thoreau's Journal or the Workshop of Being," *Criticism* 58.3 (Summer 2016): 375–408), and Daniel Nelson, "'That such things are': The Non-Teleological Poetics of Thoreau's Journal," *Arizona Quarterly: A Journal of American Literature, Culture, and Theory*, Vol. 78, N°3 (Fall 2022): 87–110. In Thoreau studies, usage is not to italicize the word Journal, when the term refers to Thoreau's Journal as a project and a practice, in so far as it was not published in his lifetime.

[26] Hodder, 262.

[27] H. Daniel Peck, *Thoreau's Morning Work: Memory and Perception in* A Week on the Concord and Merrimack Rivers, *The* Journal *and* Walden (New Haven: Yale University Press, 1990), 43. Pursuing Peck's approach, Kristen Case has analyzed the manuscript charts constituting the "Kalendar"—in which Thoreau, during the final years of his life, synthetized the core seasonal phenomena, month per month—as "a strategy for counteracting the barrenness associated with linear time, with death, and with the loss of human friends" ("Beyond Temporal Borders: The Music of Thoreau's Kalendar," *Thoreau Beyond Borders: New International Essays on America's Most Famous Nature Writer*, ed. François Specq, Laura Dassow Walls et Julien Nègre [Amherst/Boston: University of Massachusetts Press, 2020], 161). Although the "Kalendar" seems to me to be less important an undertaking than the Journal, Case's fine analysis puts in sharp relief the psychological dimension of the Thoreauvian *agon*—whose dynamics, in my view, is primarily ontological.

[28] My analysis does in no way seek to echo Agamben's notion of the "contemporary." For Agamben the "contemporary" is that which, by virtue of its being out of step with the present world, reveals the truth of the latter. The two approaches are not irreconcilable, but they are situated on different planes (individual-existential / social-collective). For an analysis of Transcendentalism in the light of Agamben's notion of the contemporary, see Thomas Constantinesco, "The *Dial* and the Untimely 'Spirit of the Time,'" *American Periodicals* 28.1 (2018): 21–40. My analysis here converges with Danielle Follett's understanding of time in Emerson's thinking, in so far as Emerson celebrated the possibility of "extracting [the present moment] from linear time"; but it differs from it because of the far more theological character of Emerson's thought, in which the creation of "a highly charged eternal present" explicitly follows from the "underlying and omnipresent...divine energy" ("Emerson's Temporalities," 639–40). Emerson is thus clearly on the side of a merely contemplative grace, granted without any particular effort.

[29] Søren Kierkegaard, *Concluding Unscientific Postscript*, ed. Howard V. Hong et Edna H. Hong (Princeton: Princeton University Press, 1992), Vol. I, 164.

[30] See Henry D. Thoreau, *Faith in a Seed: The Dispersion of Seeds and Other Late Natural History Essays*, ed. Bradley P. Dean (Washington, D.C.: Island Press, 1993), and Michael Berger, *Thoreau's Late Career and The Dispersion of Seeds: The Saunterer's Synoptic Vision* (Rochester, N.Y.: Camden House, 2000). The most detailed account of Thoreau's engagement with contemporary science is Laura Dassow Walls, *Seeing New Worlds: Henry Thoreau and Nineteenth-Century Natural Science* (Madison: University of Wisconsin Press, 1995). Contemporary scientists have drawn upon Thoreau for their own research: see especially Richard B. Primack, *Walden Warming: Climate Change Comes to Thoreau's Woods* (Chicago: The University of Chicago Press, 2014), and Robert M. Thorson, *Walden's Shore: Henry David Thoreau and Nineteenth-Century Science* (Cambridge, MA: Harvard University Press), 2014.

[31] The phrasing in this journal entry (from April 24, 1859) emphasizes two essential aspects: first, it brings forward "your eternity," not "eternity," thus relocating the stakes at an individual level; second, the eternalness of each instant is not a stationary wave, but an ever-renewed absolute.

[32] Written on September 5, 1851.

[33] Painter Paul Cézanne beautifully voiced a convergent sense of the interweaving of nature and consciousness by stating that "The landscape thinks itself in me... and I am its consciousness," as reported by philosopher Maurice Merleau-Ponty in "Cézanne's Doubt" (*Sense and Non-Sense*, Evanston: Northwestern University Press, 1964), 17.

[34] To that extent Thoreau's thinking vividly anticipates a central ecocritical concern, which Donna J. Haraway has called "thick copresence" in *Staying with the Trouble: Making Kin in the Chthulucene* (Durham: Duke University Press, 2016), 4.

[35] Kierkegaard, *Concluding Unscientific Postscript*, Vol. I, 526.

Chapter 13: Schacht and Witherell, The Nick of Time, Improved

[1] A digital version of this essay containing additional graphics may be found at https://digitalthoreau.org/the-nick-of-time-improved/.

[2] This essay makes parenthetical reference to three different instantiations of Thoreau's *Walden*: the Princeton University Press edition, edited by J. Lyndon Shanley (1971), cited parenthetically as *W*; the digitized collection of *Walden* manuscript leaves at the Huntington Library, cited parenthetically as HM 924; and the digitized proof sheets of *Walden* at the Huntington, cited parenthetically as HM 925.

[3] Bryant, *Fluid Text*, 144.

[4] See Bradley P. Dean and Ronald Wesley Hoag, "Thoreau's Lectures before *Walden*," 148–208 passim.

[5] Shanley, *Making of Walden*, 4.

[6] Shanley, *Making of Walden*, 18–33.

[7] The landing page on the Huntington website identifies each draft both by letter and by the number of the physical volume containing that draft. (For example, draft A is in Volume 1.) Each volume is individually paginated beginning with the first manuscript page in the volume. Pages can be accessed via thumbnails in the sidebar.

[8] It is not known for sure where or when Thoreau encountered Pauthier's book. However, evidence from Harvard Library's charging records and from quotations of material in Thoreau's Journal provides reliable dates for his use of some of the other sources excerpted in the commonplace book and supports the assumption that he read Pauthier in 1849. The first eighty-nine pages of the commonplace book contain transcriptions of poetry probably made in November and December 1841, when Thoreau spent several weeks in the Harvard Library making selections for an anthology of

English poetry (Sattelmeyer 1980, 241–242, 245). Pages 91–122 contain passages from *The Genuine Remains of Ossian* (now attributed to James MacPherson); some of these are quoted in November 1843 entries in Thoreau's Journal (*Journal* 1981, 483–493). Page 123 lists works containing Gaelic poetry, and pages 124–126 are blank. The Pauthier translations, on pp. 127–149, are followed by passages from a work identified by Thoreau as "Harivansa ou Histoire de la Famille de Hari, ouvrage formant un appendice du Mahabharata, et traduit sur l'original Sanscrit par M. A. Langlois. Oriental Trans. Fund. 2 vols large 4to Paris & London. 1834." According to the Harvard Library charging records, Thoreau charged out both volumes of the *Harivansa* on September 11, 1849.

Chapter 14 – Bakratcheva, Chronotopes of Cape Cod

[1] Laura Dassow Walls, *Henry David Thoreau: A Life* (Chicago and London: The University of Chicago Press, 2017), 278.

[2] Lawrence Buell, *Henry David Thoreau: Thinking Disobediently* (New York: Oxford University Press, 2024), 64.

[3] Laura Dassow Walls, *Henry David Thoreau: A Life*, 190–191.

[4] Ethel Seybold, *Thoreau: The Quest and the Classics* (New Haven: Yale University Press, 1951), 48–61.

[5] See Thoreau, *Walden*, 402.

[6] Lawrence Buell, *The Environmental Imagination: Thoreau, Nature Writing, and the Formation of American Culture* (Cambridge, MA: Harvard University Press, 1995), 117–139.

[7] As in the *Odyssey*: only when Odysseus *hears* a rhapsode singing and telling the story of the Trojan war, the events of the war acquire such a "reality" in his eyes, that he is moved to tears and reveals his identity before the Phaeacians.

[8] Erich Auerbach, *Mimesis: The Representation of Reality in Western Literature* (Princeton, NJ: Princeton University Press, 2013), 3–23.

[9] Ronald W. Hoag, "Thoreau's Later Natural History Writings," in *The Cambridge Companion to Henry David Thoreau*, ed. Joel Myerson (New York and London: Cambridge University Press, 1995), 154.

[10] Amos Bronson Alcott, "Thoreau," in *The American Transcendentalists: Their Prose and Poetry*, ed. P. Miller (New York: Doubleday Anchor Books, 1957), 94–5.

[11] Lawrence Buell, *The Environmental Imagination*, 116.

[12] John J. McAleer, "Thoreau's Epic *Cape Cod*," in *Thought*, XLIII (Summer 1968), 227–246.

[13] Walter Harding, *A Thoreau Handbook* (New York: New York University Press, 1959), 76; Richard Bridgman, *Dark Thoreau* (Lincoln: University of Nebraska Press, 1982), 161.

[14] Harding, *A Thoreau Handbook*, 76.

[15] Tzvetan Todorov, *The Poetics of Prose* (Oxford: Blackwell, 1977), 238.

[16] Bertil Romberg, *Studies in the Narrative Technique of the First-Person Novel* (Stockholm: Norwood Editions, 1979), 33–5.

[17] Henry Fielding. Preface to *Joseph Andrews* (London: Penguin Books, 1984).

[18] Harding, *A Thoreau Handbook*, 78; Bertil Romberg, see note 12; I take that as a clear reference to Laurence Sterne's *A Sentimental Journey through France and Italy* (first published 1768), another earliest representative work of the genre of the novel.

[19] Philip F. Gura, "A Wild, Rank Place: Thoreau's *Cape Cod*," in *The Cambridge Companion to Henry David Thoreau*, 149.

[20] Charles Ives, "Thoreau: Nature's Musician," in *Henry David Thoreau: A Profile*, ed. Walter Harding (New York: Hill and Wang, 1971), 105.

[21] Henry Fielding's favorite attribute for his reader.

[22] Wolfgang Iser, *The Implied Reader: Patterns of Communication in Prose Fiction from Bunyan to Beckett* (Baltimore: The Johns Hopkins University Press, 1978).

[23] Tzvetan Todorov, *The Poetics of Prose*, 74.

[24] H. Daniel Peck, *Thoreau's Morning Work: Memory and Perception in 'A Week on the Concord and Merrimack Rivers,'* the Journal, *and 'Walden.'* (New Haven/London: Yale University Press, 1990), 9.

Chapter 15 – Dolan, Remediated Thoreau

[1] Richard Grusin and Jay David Bolter, *Remediation: Understanding New Media* (Cambridge: MIT Press, 1999), 14.

[2] Grusin and Bolter, *Remediation*, 11.

[3] Gabriele Rippl, "Introduction," *Handbook of Intermediality: Literature, Image, Sound Music*. Ed. Gabriele Rippl (Berlin: De Gruyter, 2015), 2.

[4] Marie-Laure Ryan, "Introduction," *Narrative Across Media: The Languages of Storytelling*. Ed. Marie-Laure Ryan (Lincoln: University of Nebraska Press, 2004), 18.

[5] Henry Jenkins, *Convergence Culture: Where Old and New Media Collide* (New York: New York University Press, 2006), 293.

[6] Henry Jenkins, "A Remediated, Premediated, and Transmediated Conversation with Richard Grusin (Part One)." March 7, 2011. Accessed June 6, 2023. http://henryjenkins.org/blog/2011/03/a_remediated_premediated_and_t.html

[7] Barbara Straumann, "Adaptation – Remediation – Transmediality." In *Handbook of Intermediality: Literature – Image – Sound – Music*. Ed. Gabriele Rippl (Berlin: De Gruyter, 2015): 249–267, 255, 261. I appreciate Straumann's analysis of the three terms "adaptation," "remediation," and "transmediation" as applied to a text like Baz Luhrmann's *Romeo + Juliet* (1996). Her definitions are useful when considering the remediation assignment through various media choices. Students in my courses in corporate painting and drawing, baking, audio and visual media.

[8] Charles C. Bonwell and James A. Eison, *Active Learning: Creating Excitement in the Classroom* ASHE-ERIC Higher Education Report No. 1. (Washington, D.C.: The George Washington University, School of Education and Human Development. 1991), iii. https://archive.org/details/activelearningcr0000bonw/page/n3/mode/2up?view=theater.

[9] Martin Bickman, "Introduction: Thoreau and the Tradition of the Active Mind," *Uncommon Learning: Thoreau on Education*. Martin Bickman, ed. (New York: Houghton Mifflin, 1999), xxxi.

[10] David A. Kolb, *Experiential Learning: Experience as the Source of Learning and Development*. 2nd edition. (Upper Saddle River: Pearson Education, 2015), xxii–xxiii.

[11] In the 2020s, Jessica Singer Early advocated for using genres to actively teach writing, letting students express their ideas authentically while engaging new information and audiences, "defining what they care about and why" (*Next Generation Genres: Teaching Writing for Civic and Academic Engagement* [New York: Norton, 2023], xx).

[12] bell hooks, *Teaching to Transgress: Education as the Practice of Freedom* (New York: Routledge, 1994), 150.

[13] Jean J. Ryoo, "'Laughter Is the Best Medicine': Pedagogies of Humor and Joy That Support Critical Thinking and Communicative Competence." In *Deeper Learning, Dialogic Learning, and Critical Thinking: Research-Based Strategies for the Classroom*. Emmanuel Manalo, ed. (New York: Routledge, 2020), 178.

[14] Richard Utz, "Integrating STEM and the Humanities." *Inside Higher Ed* March 29, 2022. Accessed June 21, 2023. https://www.insidehighered.com/views/2022/03/30/humanities-thrive-stem-focused-universities-opinion#

[15] In one notable study, Scott Freeman et al. observed a remarkable improvement of over 50% in STEM-focused areas when active learning strategies were implemented ("Active Learning Narrows Achievement Gaps for Underrepresented Students in Undergraduate Science, Technology, Engineering, and Math." *Proceedings of the National Academy of Sciences*, 117.12 (March 2020), 6476-6483. https://doi.org/10.1073/pnas.1916903117). In addition, Elli Theobald et al. observed a similar improvement, particularly among underrepresented student groups ("Active Learning Narrows Achievement Gaps for Underrepresented Students in Undergraduate Science, Technology, Engineering, and Math." *Proceedings of the National Academy of Sciences*, 117.12 (March 2020), 6476-6483. https://doi.org/10.1073/pnas.191690 3117). These statistics are impressive at a science and technology university where roughly 75% of the student body, including those in my classes, pursue engineering majors.

[16] Carol S. Loranger, "*Ragged Dick* in the Nineties: An active student learning project." *Newsboy: The Horatio Alger Society Official Publication* 37.2 (March–April 1999): 9–10, 10.

[17] Heather T. Snyder, "Designing Creative Assignments: Examples of Journal Assignments and a Creative Project." *Teaching Creatively and Teaching Creativity*. Ed. Mary Banks Gregerson, Heather T. Snyder, and James C. Kaufman (New York: Springer, 2013. 163–174), 170.

[18] Luke Sundermeier and Heather Bise, "Tweeting Thoreau, and other 21st Century Strategies," *The Concord Saunterer*. New Series, Vol. 25 (2017): 135–137, 136.

[19] Jonathan Kozol, "Foreword," *Uncommon Learning: Thoreau on Education*. Ed. Martin Bickman (New York: Houghton Mifflin, 1999), ix.

[20] Bickman, "Introduction," xix–xxi.

[21] Snyder, "Designing Creative Assignments," 170.

[22] The origins of the original engraving have been attributed to Sophia Thoreau, though the original is unfortunately lost. An alternate source is Susanna Moodie's *Roughing It; or, Life in Canada* of 1852. Thoreau himself copied from this work in one of his Indian Notebooks for 1853.

[23] The student might have learned of the fact that the Concord Pond area, and thus Thoreau's house surroundings, were much less wooded in his time than today. Seeing the Herbert W. Gleason photographs from Fair Haven and comparing to today, the difference is striking,

[24] Octavia E. Butler, *Parable of the Sower* (New York: Grand Central Publishing, 2019), 55.

[25] Alan Liu, "Imagining the New Media Encounter." *A Companion to Digital Literary Studies*. Ed. Ray Siemens and Susan Schreibman (Malden, MA: Wiley-Blackwell, 2013) 36–37.

[26] Christopher Sellers, "Thoreau's Body: Towards an Embodied Environmental History." *Environmental History* 4.4 (October 1999): 486–514, 486. https://www.jstor.org/stable/3985398

[27] Kozol, "Foreword," x.

INDEX